50

 W9-DCW-808

Exploring Paths

HBJ BOOKMARK READING PROGRAM

MARGARET EARLY
DONALD GALLO
GWENDOLYN KERR

Exploring Paths

HBJ HARCOURT BRACE JOVANOVICH

New York   Chicago   San Francisco   Atlanta   Dallas **and** *London*

Copyright © 1979 by Harcourt Brace Jovanovich, Inc.

All rights reserved. No part of this publication may
be reproduced or transmitted in any form or by any means,
electronic or mechanical, including photocopy, recording,
or any information storage and retrieval system, without
permission in writing from the publisher.

Requests for permission to make copies of any part of the
work should be mailed to:
Permissions, Harcourt Brace Jovanovich, Inc.,
757 Third Avenue, New York, New York 10017.

PRINTED IN THE UNITED STATES OF AMERICA

ISBN 0-15-331792-2

ACKNOWLEDGMENTS: For permission to reprint copyrighted material, grateful ac-
knowledgment is made to the following sources:

ADDISON-WESLEY PUBLISHING COMPANY: Text and art on p. 360 from *The Human Adventure* by Mariah Marvin,
Stephen Marvin, and Frank J. Cappelluti. Copyright © 1976 by Addison-Wesley Publishing Company, Inc.
ALLYN AND BACON, INC.: On p. 346 from *The Western Hemisphere* (Our World Today Series) by Harold D. Drum-
mond. © Copyright 1970 by Allyn and Bacon, Inc. Selections on pp. 8, 146, 380, and text and art on p. 446 from
Exploring Life Science by Walter A. Thurber, Robert E. Kilburn, and Peter S. Howell. © Copyright 1975 by
Allyn and Bacon, Inc.
AMERICAN BOOK COMPANY: On pp. 254 and 492 from *Patterns of Language* by Martin and Olson. © 1977 American
Book Company.
THE AMERICAN MUSEUM OF NATURAL HISTORY: Adaptation of "To the Singing, to the Drums" by N. Scott Momaday
from *Natural History* Magazine, February 1975. Copyright © The American Museum of Natural History, 1975.
ASTRONOMY MAGAZINE: Adaptation of "The Constellations' Changing Faces" by Henry J. Phillips from *Astronomy*
Magazine, April 1976. Copyright © 1976 by AstroMedia Corp. All rights reserved.
BOYS' LIFE AND CURTIS BROWN, LTD.: Adaptation of "A Creature Called Bigfoot" by William Wise from *Boys' Life*,
published by The Boy Scouts of America, November 1974. Copyright © 1974 by The Boy Scouts of America.
BOYS' LIFE AND MARY FIORE: Adaptation of "Searching for the Loch Ness Monster" by Mary Fiore from *Boys' Life*,
published by The Boy Scouts of America, July 1972.
BOYS' LIFE AND GLENN WAGNER: Adaptation on p. 152 from "Egg on a Raft" by Glenn Wagner from *Boys' Life*, pub-
lished by The Boy Scouts of America, April 1974.
BROWNSTONE REVIVAL COMMITTEE OF NEW YORK CITY: Adaptation of "The Magnolia Tree Lady" by Benita Korn
from *The Brownstoner*, a copyright publication of The Brownstone Revival Committee of New York.
CHILTON BOOK COMPANY, RADNOR, PENNSYLVANIA: Adaptation of "Mary Cassatt" from *Seven Women: Great Painters*
by Winthrop and Frances Neilson. Copyright © 1968, 1969 by the authors.
THOMAS Y. CROWELL COMPANY: Adapted from "Victoria" from *A Book of Famous Queens* by Lydia Farmer, revised
by Willard A. Heaps. Copyright © 1964 by the Thomas Y. Crowell Company.
THOMAS Y. CROWELL AND DAVID K. BOYNICK: Adapted from "Alice Hamilton, Doctor in Industry" from *Women Who
Led the Way: Eight Pioneers for Equal Rights* by David K. Boynick. (Original title: *Pioneers in Petticoats*). Copy-
right © 1959 by David K. Boynick.
DODD, MEAD & COMPANY: Adaptation of "Annie Dodge Wauneka" from *Contemporary American Indian Leaders* by
Marion E. Gridley. Copyright © 1972 by Marion E. Gridley. (HBJ title: "Annie Dodge Wauneka, Navajo Cru-
sader").
DOUBLEDAY & CO., INC.: Adaptation of "The Giants of Easter Island" from *Mysteries of the Past* edited by Tom
Aylesworth. Copyright © 1964, 1965, 1966, 1967, 1968 by The American Museum of Natural History. Adapta-
tion of "The Case of the UFO's" by Andrea Balchan from *Nature and Science*, October 2, 1967. Copyright ©
1967 by The American Museum of Natural History. Adaptation from *Shirley Chisholm: A Biography* by Susan
Brownmiller. Copyright © 1970, 1971 by Doubleday & Company, Inc. Adapted from *Man the Measurer* by Roy
A. Gallant. Copyright © 1972 by Roy A. Gallant.
DOUBLEDAY & CO., INC., AND WILLIAM MORRIS AGENCY, INC., ON BEHALF OF THE AUTHORS: Adaptation of "Horace Pip-
pin" from *Six Black Masters of the American Art*. Copyright © 1972 by Romare Bearden and Harry Henderson.
Adapted from "El Viejo's Grandson" from *Great Latin Sports Figures* by Jerry Izenberg. Copyright © 1976 by
Jerry Izenberg.
E. P. DUTTON AND JOHN SCHAFFNER LITERARY AGENT: Adaptation from *Ahdoolo! The Biography of Matthew A. Hen-
son* by Floyd Miller. Copyright © 1963 by Floyd Miller.
DUTTON-SUNRISE, INC., A SUBSIDIARY OF E. P. DUTTON: Adaptation of "A Lover of Nature" from *Touch the Earth* com-
piled by T. C. McLuhan. Copyright © 1971 by T. C. McLuhan.
FIRESTONE FOUNDATION: Adapted from *Man on the Move* by Harvey S. Firestone, Jr. Copyright © 1967 by the Fire-
stone Foundation.

GROSSET & DUNLAP, INC.: Adaptation of "A World in a Jar" from *A Guide to Nature Projects* by Ted S. Pettit. Copyright © 1966 by Ted S. Pettit.

HARCOURT BRACE JOVANOVICH, INC.: On p. 390 from "Musicians and Composers" in *A Probe into Leadership* by Lee Williams. On p. 242 from *A History of Black Americans* by Katz and Halliburton. Selections on pp. 126, 214, 234, 422, and 493 from *Life: A Biological Science*, Newton Edition, by Paul F. Brandwein et al. Copyright © 1975 by Harcourt Brace Jovanovich, Inc. Selections on pp. 6, 239, 278, and 262 from *Language for Daily Use*, Explorer Edition (Silver) by Mildred A. Dawson et al. Copyright © 1978 by Harcourt Brace Jovanovich, Inc. Excerpt and art on p. 148 from *Growth in Mathematics* (Silver) by David Wells et al. Selections on pp. 44, 85, 105, 238, 444, 468, and 510 from *Sources of Identity: The Social Sciences, Concepts and Values*, Second Edition by Paul F. Brandwein et al. Copyright © 1977 by Harcourt Brace Jovanovich, Inc. Entries taken from (or adapted from) *The HBJ School Dictionary.* Copyright © 1977, 1972, 1968 by Harcourt Brace Jovanovich, Inc.

HASTINGS HOUSE, PUBLISHERS: Adaptation of "The Cave People of the Philippines" from *Survivors of the Stone Age.* © Copyright 1975 by Rebecca B. Marcus.

D. C. HEATH AND COMPANY: On p. 104 from *Heath Mathematics* by Dilley and Rucker. © 1975 by D. C. Heath and Company, Lexington, Massachusetts.

HOLT, RINEHART AND WINSTON, PUBLISHERS: On p. 186 from *People, Places and Change* by Berry et al. Copyright © 1977 by Holt, Rinehart and Winston, Publishers. Text and art on pp. 46 and 300 from *Modern Life Science* by Fitzpatrick and Hole. Copyright © 1974 by Holt, Rinehart and Winston, Inc. Selections on pp. 28, 403, 509, and text and art on p. 340 from *World Geography Today* by Israel et al.

ALFRED A. KNOPF, INC., AND MCINTOSH AND OTIS, INC.: Adaptation of "Taking Action—The Story of Mount Trashmore" from *Save the Earth! An Ecology Handbook for Kids* by Betty Miles. Copyright © 1974 by Betty Miles.

LAIDLAW BROTHERS, A DIVISION OF DOUBLEDAY & COMPANY, INC.: Selections on pp. 212, 382, and 402 from *Growth in English* by Hand et al.

J. B. LIPPINCOTT COMPANY: Adapted from *My Orphans of the Wild: Rescue and Home Care of Native Wildlife* by Rosemary K. Collett with Charlie Briggs. Copyright © 1974 by Rosemary K. Collett and Charlie Briggs.

LOTHROP, LEE & SHEPARD CO.: Adaptation of "How Words Change" from *Our Language* by Eloise Lambert. Copyright © 1955 by Lothrop, Lee & Shepard Co.

MACMILLAN PUBLISHING CO., INC.: Adapted from *Estuaries: Where Rivers Meet the Sea* by Laurence Pringle. Copyright © 1973 by Laurence Pringle.

CHARLES E. MERRILL PUBLISHING COMPANY, COLUMBUS, OHIO: Adaptations on pp. 84 and 168 from *Focus on Life Science* by Heimler and Lockard.

JULIAN MESSNER, A DIVISION OF SIMON & SCHUSTER, INC.: Adaptation on p. 189 from *How Did Life Get There?* by Daniel Cohen. Copyright © 1973 by Daniel Cohen. Adapted from *Dr. George Washington Carver, Scientist* by Shirley Graham and George D. Lipscomb. Copyright © 1944, 1971 by Shirley Graham and George D. Lipscomb.

NATIONAL GEOGRAPHIC MAGAZINE: Adapted from "Into the Lairs of 'Sleeping' Sharks" by Eugenie Clark, Ph.D. from *National Geographic* Magazine, April 1975. Adapted from "Mystery of the Ancient Nazca Lines" by Loren McIntyre from *National Geographic* Magazine, May 1975. Adapted from "More Years with Mountain Gorillas" by Dian Fossey from *National Geographic* Magazine, January 1970.

NATIONAL PARKS & CONSERVATION MAGAZINE: Adapted from "Saguaro" by Leslie Payne from *National Parks & Conservation* Magazine, April 1971. Copyright © 1971 by National Parks & Conservation Association. Adaptation on p. 134 from "New River Country: Wild and Scenic" by Elizabeth Watson from *National Parks & Conservation* Magazine, February 1975. Copyright © 1975 by National Parks & Conservation Association.

NATIONAL WILDLIFE: Adapted from "And Then There Were None" by Mark Wexler from *National Wildlife* Magazine, April–May 1974. Copyright 1974 by the National Wildlife Federation.

NEW YORK MAGAZINE: On p. 243 from "What Are Your Chances of Surviving a High-Rise Fire?" by Bryna Taubman from *New York* Magazine, May 27, 1974. Copyright © 1974 by the NYM Corp.

POPULAR SCIENCE: Adaptation on p. 191 from "The Parachute That Glides Like a Plane" by Douglas Garr from *Popular Science*, August 1971. © 1971 Popular Science Publishing Co.

G. P. PUTNAM'S SONS AND ART BUCHWALD: Adapted from *Have I Ever Lied to You?* by Art Buchwald. Copyright © 1966, 1967, 1968 by Art Buchwald

G. P. PUTNAM'S SONS AND HAROLD MATSON CO., INC.: Adapted from *Tales of the Warrior Ants* by Dee Brown. Copyright © 1973 by Dee Brown.

THE SATURDAY EVENING POST: Adaptation of "Rowing the Atlantic" by Captain John Ridgway with James Atwater from *The Saturday Evening Post*, November 5, 1966. © 1966 The Curtis Publishing Company.

SCHOLASTIC MAGAZINES, INC.: On p. 331 from "Your Home Room Is in the Factory" by Peter Jones from *Senior Scholastic*, March 6, 1975. © 1975 by Scholastic Magazines, Inc.

SCHOLASTIC MAGAZINES, INC., AND PAUL R. REYNOLDS, INC., 12 EAST 41ST STREET, NEW YORK, NY 10017: Adaptation of "Key to the Unknown: Decoding the Rosetta Stone" from *Ancestral Voices* by James Norman. Copyright © 1975 by James Norman Schmidt.

SCOTT, FORESMAN AND COMPANY: On p. 298 from *America! America!* by L. Joanne Buggey et al. Copyright © 1977 by Scott, Foresman and Company.

CHARLES SCRIBNER'S SONS: Adapted from *Animals That Hide, Imitate and Bluff* by Lilo Hess. Copyright © 1970 by Lilo Hess.

SEVENTEEN MAGAZINE: Adaptation of "Courage on Crutches" by Celeste Callahan from *Seventeen* Magazine, April 1976. Copyright © 1976 by Triangle Communications, Inc. All rights reserved.

SILVER BURDETT COMPANY: Text and art on p. 184 from *The Natural World/1* (pp. 35 and 38). © 1975 General Learning Corporation.

SIMON & SCHUSTER, INC.: Adapted from *A Special Kind of Courage* by Geraldo Rivera. Copyright © 1976 by Geraldo Rivera.

TIME, THE WEEKLY NEWSMAGAZINE: Adaptation on p. 190 from "A Ghost Town of Gantries" from *Time*, April 15, 1974. Copyright Time, Inc.

THE VIKING PRESS: Adaptation of "A Park of Life" from *Everglades Country* by Patricia Lauber. Copyright © 1973 by Patricia Lauber.

FRANKLIN WATTS, INC.: On p. 329 from *Recycling (A First Book)* by James and Lynn Hahn. Copyright 1973 by Franklin Watts, Inc.

ART CREDITS

The artists in this book and the pages on which their work appears are as follows:

Howard Berelson: 38–39, 40, 42, 80 (t), 158, 161, 162, 163, 164, 166; Walter Brooks: 94–95, 96, 97, 98–99, 100, 101, 102; Naiad Einsel: 476–477, 478–479, 480–481, 482–483, 502, 504, 506; Doris Ettlinger: 438; Betty Fraser: 138, 139, 140, 141, 312, 314, 315, 316; Ethel Gold: 177, 179, 181; Joan Goodman: 370, 372; John Hamberger; 334; Gordon Kibbee: 1, 2–3, 129, 130–131, 257, 258–259, 385, 386–387; Robert Lapsley: 14, 15, 17, 18–19, 194–195, 196–197, 198–199, 200–201, 202–203, 204, 230, 394, 395, 397, 398, 400; Sal Murdocca: 4, 5, 7, 30, 32, 34, 36, 48, 53, 68, 69, 70, 71, 72, 87, 89, 91, 107, 111, 132, 134, 152, 154, 170, 173, 174, 188, 191, 216, 241, 260, 261, 264, 281, 283, 304, 305, 307, 309, 328, 332, 343, 364, 365, 366, 367, 388, 391, 392, 405, 406, 410–411, 412, 424, 425, 426, 448, 449, 450, 451, 470, 471, 472, 495, 496, 499; Marty Norman: 10–11, 37, 54–55, 74–75, 92–93, 112–113, 136–137, 155, 175, 192–193, 220–221, 245, 267, 288–289, 310–311, 333, 349, 368–369, 393, 408–409, 428–429, 452–453, 474–475, 500–501; Oni: 336, 337, 338; Michael Sullivan: 114–115, 356–357, 464, 465, 466; Richard Tate: 354; Julia Van Nutt: 246–253; Robert Van Nutt: 56–65; 290–295, 463.

HBJ maps: 31, 35, 41, 244, 319.

Vocabulary Study pages were designed by Kaeser & Wilson Design, Ltd.

PHOTO CREDITS

Cover photo, N. de Vore III/Bruce Coleman; pages 5, 33, HBJ Photos; 12–13, 20, George Holton/Photo Researchers; 23, 24, 25 (t), 26, 272, 303, Dr. Georg Gerster/Photo Researchers; 25 (b), Loren McIntyre; 45, Brian Enting/Photo Researchers; 76–77, 120, 123, 125, 324, Russ Kinne/Photo Researchers; 79, American Museum of Natural History; 80 (b), Academy of Applied Science/Photo Trends; 82, Photo Researchers; 90, New York Public Library; 60, 108, 168, 242, 285, 298, 354, 390, 414, 417, 418–419, 420, 421, 441, 442 (t), Bettmann Archives; 109, 118, 286, United Press International; 117, United States Air Force; 126, A. W. Ambler/Photo Researchers; 133 (lt), Jacana/The Image Bank; 133 (rt), C. C. Lockwood/Animals, Animals; 135, 153, 218, 287, Culver Pictures; 142, Dan Ferlic/Seventeen: 147, United States Forest Service; 150 (lt), Robert Houser; 150 (c), Hanson Carroll/Peter Arnold; 150 (rt), Andy Bernhaut/Photo Researchers; 159, 165, Monkmeyer; 156–157, Ted Spiegel/Black Star; 171, Wide World Photos; 206, 208, 209, 210, Martha Swope; 214, 215, Arthur Swoger; 222–223, Lawrence Fried/Magnum; 224, 226, 228, Dennis Brack/Black Star; 227, Paul Fusco/Magnum; 229, Shirley Chisholm; 233 (inset), 330, Dennis Stock/Magnum; 236 (inset), Paul Conklin/Monkmeyer; 233 (b), 234, 236 (b), Michal Heron; 246, Albright-Knox Art Gallery; 250, William Penn Memorial Museum; 251, Pennsylvania Academy of Fine Arts; 253, Private collection courtesy of the Brandywine River Museum; 263, Tom McHugh/Photo Researchers; 266, Grant Heilman; 268, B. C. Hermes/Photo Researchers; 270 (t, lt), Tim Loose/Photo Researchers; 270 ,t, rt), David Hughes/Bruce Coleman; 270 (b), Dan Sudia/Photo Researchers; 274, Alexander Lowry/Photo Researchers; 275, Richard Jepperson/Photo Researchers; 276, Murl Duesing/Photo Researchers; 318–319, Jim Foott/Bruce Coleman; 320, J. Dermid/Bruce Coleman; 320 (rt), J. A. L. Cooke/Bruce Coleman; 321 (lt), Tom Brakefield/Bruce Coleman; 321 (rt), 432, Leonard Lee Rue III/Bruce Coleman; 322, C. Haagner/Bruce Coleman; 326, Felix Saunders/Photo Researchers; 345, NASA; 346, Neil Newton/Magnum; 350–351, 352, Virginia Department of Parks and Recreation; 370, Magnolia Tree Hearth; 372, Paul Hosefros/The New York Times; 374, Art Seitz/F.O.S.; 375, 377, 378, Kevin Galvin/F.O.S.; 376, Tom Sic/F.O.S.; 379, F.O.S.; 381, Runk/Schoenberger/Grant Heilman; 388, 498, Library of Congress; 415, 416, Brown Brothers; 422, Charles R. Knight (artist)/Field Museum of Natural History; 430–431, Norman Myers/Bruce Coleman; 433 (t), Bill Ruth/Bruce Coleman; 433 (inset) Stouffer Products Ltd./Bruce Coleman; 434 (t), 436, Jane Burton/Bruce Coleman; 434 (b), G. B. Schaller/Bruce Coleman; 435 (b), P. Ward/Bruce Coleman; 435 (inset), Alan Blank/Bruce Coleman; 442 (b), Granger Collection; 454, 456, The National Gallery of Art; 455, National Collection of Fine Arts, Smithsonian Institute; 456 (b), Brooklyn Museum, New York; 457, Metropolitan Museum of Art, Bequest of Mrs. H. O. Havemeyer, The H. O. Havemeyer Collection; 458, Museum of Fine Arts, Boston; 459, Museum of Fine Arts, Boston, Hayden Collection; 460 (t, rt), National Gallery of Art, Washington D.C.; 460 (t, lt), The Brooklyn Museum, New York; 460 (b, lt), The Metropolitan Museum of Art, New York, Samuel Isham Gift; 462, California Institute of Technology; 485, 487, 489, 490, John Nance/Magnum.

Contents

The Unknown
1

SKILLS LESSON / *What's It All About? . . .* Using Textbooks _____ 4

VOCABULARY STUDY / *The Reverse Machine . . .* Antonyms _____ 10

The Giants of Easter Island *by* CARROL ALICE STOUT _____ 12

The Mystery of the Ancient Nazca Lines *by* LOREN MCINTYRE _____ 22

TEXTBOOK STUDY / Using the Index in Social Studies _____ 28

SKILLS LESSON / *One Picture Is Worth a Thousand Words . . .*
Using Graphic Aids _____ 30

VOCABULARY STUDY / *The Letter from Lester . . .* Synonyms _____ 37

Into the Lairs of "Sleeping" Sharks *by* DR. EUGENIE CLARK _____ 38

TEXTBOOK STUDY / Using Graphic Aids in Social Studies _____ 44
Using Graphic Aids in Science _____ 46

SKILLS LESSON / *The Most Useful Tool of All . . .*
Using the Dictionary _____ 48

VOCABULARY STUDY / *The Parasite and the Maze . . .*
Meanings from Context _____ 54

Key to the Unknown: The Rosetta Stone *by* JAMES NORMAN _____ 56

TEXTBOOK STUDY / Using the Dictionary _____ 66

SKILLS LESSON / *The Heart of the Matter . . .*
Finding Topics and Stated Main Ideas _____ 68

VOCABULARY STUDY / *The What-Do-You-Mean-by-That? Game . . .*
Multiple Meanings _____ 74

The Search for Nessie *by* MARY FIORE _____ 76

TEXTBOOK STUDY / Finding Topics in Science _____ 84
Finding Stated Main Ideas in Social Studies _____ 85

SKILLS LESSON / *Figure It Out . . .*
Finding Unstated Main Ideas and Recognizing Details _____ 87

VOCABULARY STUDY / *The Contest . . .* Prefixes and Suffixes _____ 92

The Warrior Ants *by* DEE BROWN _____ 94

TEXTBOOK STUDY / Recognizing Important and Unimportant
Details in Mathematics _____ 104
Recognizing Main Ideas and Details in Social Studies _____ 105

SKILLS LESSON / *Beginnings, Middles, Ends . . .*
Recognizing Different Kinds of Paragraphs _____ 107

VOCABULARY STUDY / *Say Something in Scientific . . .*
Greek and Latin Roots _____ 112

The Case of the UFO's *by* ANDREA BALCHAN _____ 114

The Creature Called Bigfoot *by* WILLIAM WISE _____ 120

TEXTBOOK STUDY / Recognizing Different Kinds of Paragraphs
in Science _____ 126

BIBLIOGRAPHY / *Books About the Unknown* _____ 128

Meeting the Challenge
129

SKILLS LESSON / *For Example . . .* Organization by Example _____ 132

VOCABULARY STUDY / *The Right Person for the Job . . .*
Greek and Latin Roots _____ 136

Making Friends with Mountain Gorillas *by* DIAN FOSSEY _____ 138

A Champion's Spirit *by* CELESTE CALLAHAN _____ 142

TEXTBOOK STUDY / Organization by Example in Science _____ 146
Organization by Example in Mathematics _____ 148

SKILLS LESSON / *Just Like Clockwork! . . .*
Recognizing Time Clues _____ 150

VOCABULARY STUDY / *The Letter from Big Burst* . . . Synonyms ... 155

At the Pole *by* FLOYD MILLER ... 156

TEXTBOOK STUDY / Recognizing Time Clues in Science ... 168

SKILLS LESSON / *Time and Time Again* . . .
Recognizing Time Relationships ... 170

VOCABULARY STUDY / *Alfonso* . . . Meanings from Context ... 175

A Special Kind of Courage *by* GERALDO RIVERA ... 176

TEXTBOOK STUDY / Recognizing Time Relationships in Science ... 184
Recognizing Time Relationships in Social Studies ... 186

SKILLS LESSON / *Like It or Not* . . .
Organization by Comparison and Contrast ... 188

VOCABULARY STUDY / *The Wonder Word Jackpot* . . .
Multiple Meanings ... 192

Rowing the Atlantic
by CAPTAIN JOHN RIDGWAY *with* JAMES ATWATER ... 194

Arthur Mitchell, Dancer *by* NICHOLAS PEASE ... 206

TEXTBOOK STUDY / Organization by Comparison and Contrast in
Language Arts ... 212
Organization by Comparison and Contrast in Science ... 214

SKILLS LESSON / *Tell Me Why* . . .
Organization by Cause and Effect ... 216

VOCABULARY STUDY / *Maxwell's Words* . . . Prefixes ... 220

The Congresswoman from Brooklyn *by* SUSAN BROWNMILLER ... 222

Annie Dodge Wauneka, Navajo Crusader *by* MARION E. GRIDLEY ... 230

TEXTBOOK STUDY / Organization by Cause and Effect
in Social Studies ... 238
Organization by Cause and Effect in Language Arts ... 239

SKILLS LESSON / *Sort It Out* . . . Mixed Patterns of Organization ... 241

VOCABULARY STUDY / *Grandma, What's a Concoction?* . . . Suffixes ... 245

Horace Pippin's Struggle to Create
by ROMARE BEARDEN and HARRY HENDERSON _____ 246

TEXTBOOK STUDY / Mixed Patterns of Organization
in Language Arts _____ 254

BIBLIOGRAPHY / *Books About Meeting Challenges* _____ 256

The Great Outdoors

257

SKILLS LESSON / *The Big Picture . . .* Writing Topical Outlines _____ 260

VOCABULARY STUDY / *The Case of the Missing Words . . .*
Suffixes _____ 267

A Park of Life *by* PATRICIA LAUBER _____ 268

Saguaro, Forest of Unreality *by* LESLIE PAYNE _____ 274

TEXTBOOK STUDY / Writing Topical Outlines in Language Arts _____ 278

SKILLS LESSON / *Do You Have the Time? . . .*
Writing Chronological Outlines _____ 281

VOCABULARY STUDY / *Aesop's Jokes . . .* Multiple Meanings _____ 288

George Washington Carver, Pioneer Ecologist
by SHIRLEY GRAHAM and GEORGE D. LIPSCOMB _____ 290

TEXTBOOK STUDY / Writing Chronological Outlines in Social Studies _____ 298
Writing Chronological Outlines in Science _____ 300

SKILLS LESSON / *The Same and Yet Different . . .*
Another Look at Topical Outlines _____ 303

VOCABULARY STUDY / *Interview with Zim Three . . .* Antonyms _____ 310

An Orphan of the Wild
by ROSEMARY K. COLLETT *with* CHARLIE BRIGGS _____ 312

Where Rivers Meet the Sea *by* LAURENCE PRINGLE _____ 318

TEXTBOOK STUDY / Writing Topical Outlines in Science _____ 324

SKILLS LESSON / *Once Over Lightly* . . . Skimming and Scanning   328

VOCABULARY STUDY / *Aesop's Jokes, Act II* . . . Multiple Meanings   333

And Then There Were None *by* MARK WEXLER   334

A World in a Jar *by* TED S. PETTIT   336

TEXTBOOK STUDY / Skimming and Scanning in Social Studies   340

SKILLS LESSON / *Short and Sweet* . . . Summarizing   343

VOCABULARY STUDY / *Lester's Reply to Big Burst* . . . Synonyms   349

Taking Action: The Story of Mount Trashmore *by* BETTY MILES   350

A Lover of Nature *by* CHIEF LUTHER STANDING BEAR   354

Fresh Air Will Kill You *by* ART BUCHWALD   356

TEXTBOOK STUDY / Summarizing in Social Studies   360
Summarizing in Language Arts   362

SKILLS LESSON / *Who? What? When? Where? Why?* . . .
Taking Notes   364

VOCABULARY STUDY / *The Tomb of the Latin Magician Dentist* . . .
Etymologies   368

The Tree Lady *by* BENITA KORN   370

El Viejo's Grandson *by* JERRY IZENBERG   374

TEXTBOOK STUDY / Taking Notes in Science   380
Taking Notes in Language Arts   382

BIBLIOGRAPHY / *Books About the Great Outdoors*   384

Changes

385

SKILLS LESSON / *Prove It!* . . . Separating Fact from Opinion   388

VOCABULARY STUDY / *Big Burst's Reply to Lester* . . . Synonyms   393

To the Singing, to the Drums *by* N. SCOTT MOMADAY   394

TEXTBOOK STUDY / Separating Fact from Opinion in Language Arts___402
    Separating Fact from Opinion in Social Studies___403

SKILLS LESSON / *Is That a Fact? . . .*
    Separating Facts from Fictional Details___405

VOCABULARY STUDY / *Quick Change, Inc. . . .* Suffixes___408

How Words Change *by* ELOISE LAMBERT___410

Alice Hamilton: Doctor in Industry *by* DAVID K. BOYNICK___414

TEXTBOOK STUDY / Separating Facts from Fictional Details
    in Science___422

SKILLS LESSON / *More Than Meets the Eye . . .* Drawing Conclusions___424

VOCABULARY STUDY / *The First Wooden Cave . . .*
    Meanings from Context___428

Animals That Hide, Imitate, and Bluff *by* LILO HESS___430

Victoria *by* LYDIA FARMER___438

TEXTBOOK STUDY / Drawing Conclusions in Social Studies___444
    Drawing Conclusions in Science___445

SKILLS LESSON / *Use Your Judgment . . .*
    Finding and Judging the Author's Conclusions___448

VOCABULARY STUDY / *The 16-Kilometer Journey . . .*
    Prefixes and Suffixes___452

Mary Cassatt *by* WINTHROP NEILSON *and* FRANCES NEILSON___454

The Constellations' Changing Faces *by* HENRY J. PHILLIPS___462

TEXTBOOK STUDY / Finding and Judging the Author's Conclusions
    in Social Studies___468

SKILLS LESSON / *All Things Considered . . .* Generalizing___470

VOCABULARY STUDY / *The Wanted Poster . . .* Antonyms___474

Measure for Measure *by* ROY A. GALLANT___476

The Tasaday: Cave People of the Philippines
    by REBECCA B. MARCUS___484

TEXTBOOK STUDY / Generalizing in Language Arts 492
Generalizing in Science 493

SKILLS LESSON / *A Different Way to Look at It . . .*
Recognizing Slanted Writing 495

VOCABULARY STUDY / *The Problem . . . Multiple Meanings* 500

If I Had Wings *by* HARVEY S. FIRESTONE, JR. 502

TEXTBOOK STUDY / Recognizing Positive Slanted Writing
in Social Studies 509
Recognizing Negative Slanted Writing in Social Studies 510

BIBLIOGRAPHY / *Books About Changes* 512

Glossary 513
Index of Titles and Authors 530

xiii

To the Reader

Put on your walking shoes and pack your imagination in a knapsack. You are about to go exploring.

Along the way you will encounter mysteries to make you tingle with curiosity. You will meet people who dared to face a challenge, armed with the knowledge that success was within their grasp. You will see and touch the beauty of the great outdoors, and you will feel the excitement of sweeping changes.

This book is divided into four parts, and each has its own special personality. The parts contain *Skills Lessons, Vocabulary Studies, Textbook Studies,* and, of course, the reading selections themselves. You will *learn* ways to improve your reading with the *Skills Lessons.* The *Vocabulary Studies* will make you *laugh* and help you build a strong vocabulary at the same time. The *Textbook Studies* will show you how to *apply* your reading skills so you can get the most out of your textbooks. The reading selections will give you a chance to *practice* these important skills. But mostly, this book is yours to *enjoy* while you discover new and interesting people, places, and things.

A fascinating world lies stretched out before you. Now is the time for *Exploring Paths.*

THE UNKNOWN

SKILLS LESSON

What's It All About? . . . Using Textbooks

You're aboard an ocean liner for the first time. The ship impresses you with its size, dozens of passageways, and many decks. How do you get from your cabin to the dining room? Where's the sundeck? Is there a swimming pool? Which lifeboat station do you go to in case of emergency?

In many ways, a textbook is like a ship. Once you understand the general layout, you can easily make use of all the things it has to offer.

The Table of Contents

When you see a new textbook, your first question is likely to be, "What is it about?" The title will give you some information, but it won't always be specific. For example, look at these textbook titles:

One of the books is a mathematics text. But does it deal with geometry, algebra, or what? What does the first book say about biology? What does the third book tell you about language? The titles don't tell you the specific topics treated in these books.

To find out the topics you have to turn to the **table of contents** in the front of the book. Look at the sample table of contents on the next page. What does the table of contents tell you about the organization and topics covered in the book?

INTRODUCTION   *YOUR ENGLISH LANGUAGE*   **1**

PART I
SPEAKING AND WRITING YOUR LANGUAGE

CHAPTER 1   *HOW LANGUAGE WORKS: NOUNS,*
             PRONOUNS, AND VERBS   **16**
CHAPTER 2   *SPEAKING EFFECTIVELY*   **47**
CHAPTER 3   *USING MODIFIERS*   **75**
CHAPTER 4   *BUILDING GOOD PARAGRAPHS*   **107**
CHAPTER 5   *HOW SENTENCES WORK*   **127**
CHAPTER 6   *ENRICHING YOUR VOCABULARY*   **157**
CHAPTER 7   *PATTERNS OF SENTENCES*   **181**
CHAPTER 8   *WRITING STORIES AND REPORTS*   **213**
CHAPTER 9   *PRONOUN AND VERB USAGE*   **234**
CHAPTER 10   *WRITING A GOOD LETTER*   **265**
CHAPTER 11   *VERBALS*   **288**

PART II
LANGUAGE STUDY AND APPRECIATION

CHAPTER 12   *HELPFUL STUDY SKILLS*   **303**
CHAPTER 13   *USING YOUR DICTIONARY*   **321**
CHAPTER 14   *POETRY*   **339**
CHAPTER 15   *GETTING THE MOST FROM YOUR*
             READING   **357**
CHAPTER 16   *MAKING SENTENCE DIAGRAMS*   **380**

PART III
REVIEW HANDBOOK

Composition   **406**
The Parts of Speech   **412**
Mechanics   **420**
Usage   **437**

MAKING SURE   **458**
INDEX   **489**

The table of contents in a textbook is usually organized by major divisions called **units, parts,** or **sections.** These major divisions cover very large topics. What large topic is treated in Part I of the sample table of contents on page 6?

Each part is broken down into smaller subtopics called **chapters.** The chapters give you specific information about the part. What subtopic is discussed in Chapter 10? What kind of information can you find in Chapter 12? What pages would you turn to for information about the following?

a. how to write a good paragraph
b. letter writing
c. how to use the dictionary

The Index

Suppose you are interested in a topic that is not listed in the table of contents. It's possible, of course, that the textbook doesn't treat that topic. But before you give up your search, you can check the most detailed listing in the textbook: the **index.** The index is found in the back of the book. It is an alphabetical list of all the topics covered in the book. Look at the following sample index.

Independent variable, **64, 160, 383–** 384

Infections, **78,** 83

Influenza, 82

Insects: ants, 238–239, 338; behavior of, 234–239, 282–283, 309; diapause in, 312–313; hearing, 258; at low temperatures, 309; navigation, 319; parasites, 337; smell, 263; vision, 252–253

Instincts, **237**

Insulin, **125;** amino acid units in, 121

Interferon, **81**

Internal parasites, **336**

Intestines, small, 124, 153

Involuntary muscles, **140**

Ions, **146**

Iris, **244**

Isle Royale study, 338–393

Liver, 124–125, 150

Living space, changes in, 395, 397

Long-range economic value, **400**

Lorenz, Konrad, 277

Lungs, 150; in breathing, 112–114; capacity, 114; smoking and, 182–183

Maltase, **120**

Maltose, 14, 44, 45; digestion of, **120**

Marrow, 134; composition of, 135

Mastax, **9**

Maumee River, 406

Maxim, Hiram, 258

Medulla, **148**

Meiosis, **211,** 217

Membranes: diffusion through, 28, 375; embryos, 156

Microclimates, **306**–308, 343; in soil, 307; in water, 307–308

Why do you think some of the page numbers are printed in boldface type? Boldface type is used to catch your attention. It tells you that important information, such as a definition or an explanation, is found on that page. On what page might you find a definition of *microclimates*? Notice that the listing for *insects* is fairly long. Why do you think that the general topic *insects* has been broken down into several subtopics? What are these subtopics? What pages would you turn to if you wanted information only on insect sight?

The Glossary

A **glossary** is a special kind of dictionary. It usually is found in the back of textbooks or other specialized books. Look at the sample glossary at the top of the next page.

Generally, a glossary provides short definitions of unfamiliar words found in the textbook. The glossary is the first place to look if you come across a word whose meaning you don't know. What should you do if the word you are looking for is not in the glossary?

a·bid·ing [ə·bī′dǐng] *adj.* Continuing without changing or growing less; lasting.

a·bol·ish [ə·bol′ish] *v.* To do away with; put an end to.

a·bom·in·a·ble [ə·bom′in·ə·bəl] *adj.* Horrible.

a·bun·dance [ə·bun′dəns] *n.* A full or plentiful supply.

ac·com·plished [ə·kom′plisht] *adj.* Skillful, as in an art or in social graces; well-trained.

ac·quaint [ə·kwānt′] *v.* To introduce; make known to: *acquaint* someone with the law.

a·cre·age [ā′kər·ij] *n.* The number of acres in an area.

bal·loon·ist [bə·loon′ist] *n.* A person who rides in or operates a balloon.

ban·do·leer [ban′də·lir′] *n.* A broad belt worn over one shoulder and across the chest. Often a bandoleer has pockets for carrying ammunition or is worn as part of an official or ceremonial costume.

bank·ing [bang′king] *v.* **1** Hitting (a ball) in such a way that it bounces off the rim or edge; a term in billiards. **2** Heaping dirt or snow into a pile.

ban·ter [ban′tər] **1** *v.* To tease or joke playfully. **2** *n.* Playful teasing; joking.

Other Parts of Textbooks

In addition to the table of contents, index, and glossary, textbooks may contain an **introduction,** or a section addressed to the reader. The introduction may give you an overview of the book or point out special features.

Some textbooks have separate sections with maps, charts, tables, and diagrams for easy reference.

A **bibliography** is sometimes found in the back of a textbook or following each unit or part. The bibliography is an alphabetical listing of books and other writings that the author refers to in the book. It may list other books that contain related information. You may want to refer to these sources for more information about the topics covered in the textbook.

Once you become familiar with the way your textbooks are organized, you will be able to use them more efficiently.

Try This

1. Survey this textbook. What are the different parts it contains? Compare it to your science or mathematics textbook. What are the similarities and differences?
2. Compare the glossary of this book to a dictionary. How are they different? How are they similar?

9

The Reverse Machine . . . Antonyms

"What did you say that thing is?" asked the Skeptic.

The Inventor smiled proudly. "It's a Reverse Machine. It makes antonyms."

"Sounds complicated," the Skeptic replied.

All at once a door opened and a card slipped out. The Inventor read it: " 'I am not *complicated;* I'm really very *simple.'* Wow!" cried the Inventor. "Isn't that terrific!"

"Phooey!" said the Skeptic. "That gizmo of yours just got lucky. Besides, the whole idea of a machine that makes antonyms is something I have to reject."

"Reject!" echoed the machine, and the gears and dials sprang into action. Seconds later another card appeared.

"The machine is right again!" cried the Inventor. "Listen: 'Do not *reject* me just because I am unusual. Try to *accept* me for what I am.' "

"Fake!" screamed the Skeptic, stamping his feet.

"Steady," said the Inventor. "Don't be such a skeptic."

"Skeptic!" clicked the machine. "The opposite of a *skeptic* is a *believer.*"

"Now, Skeptic," said the Inventor. "What do you say to that?"

The Skeptic burst out laughing. "I guess I have to say the Reverse Machine really works. After all," he snickered, "it made a believer out of me!"

Word Play

If you were writing a dictionary, how would you define *complicated, reject,* and *skeptic?*

Use the glossary in the back of this textbook when you come across an unfamiliar word. If the word is not in the glossary, look it up in your dictionary.

Huge stone statues stand on a lonely island in the Pacific Ocean. Where did they come from? For archaeologists, one of the greatest puzzles of history has been . . .

The Giants of Easter Island

by Carrol Alice Stout

The stone carvers "released" the giant moai, *or statue, from the rock on top of the dead volcano. The workers laid down their stone picks and returned to their village. Then the twelve-foot-high moai "came to life." It walked across the island and then climbed onto a stone platform that had been built for it near the village.*

This was the story the people of Easter Island told Norwegian archaeologist Thor Heyerdahl. In the 1950's, Heyerdahl led a group to investigate the strange stone statues found on the lonely island in the South Pacific. For over 200 years, scientists have wondered how the huge statues—some weighing as much as twenty-five tons—had been carved with simple tools and moved across the island.

But the story told by the Easter Islanders didn't make sense. Statues just don't "come to life." Besides, these long-nosed, long-eared, blank-eyed statues with long-fingered hands clasped under their stomachs had no legs!

The Dutch admiral Jacob Roggeveen "discovered" the island on Easter Sunday in 1722. He saw many of these statues standing on stone platforms. Fifty-two years later, the English captain James Cook visited Easter Island. Most of the statues lay face down at the base of their platforms.

When Heyerdahl's group got there, no statues were standing. For months, the scientist and helpers in his group checked the statues, looking for signs of the past. They found that people had been living on the island much earlier than scientists had believed. Tests showed that the platforms had been built sometime between 900 and 1,300 years ago.

According to legends, two groups of people once lived on the island. A war took place and one of the two groups was nearly wiped out. Only one man remained. This group was known as the "long ears," whose custom was to stretch their earlobes by making holes in them and putting in weights.

Heyerdahl made friends with the island's mayor, Pedro Atan. Atan said that he was descended from the only long ear to live through the war. Heyerdahl asked Atan if he knew how the statues were carved.

"Yes," he said. "I will carve you a statue. My family and I. Only a real long ear can carve a statue."

Many people in the camp didn't think that Atan could keep his promise. Heyerdahl believed him, however. The following night, Heyerdahl sat in his tent with two friends, talking about their work. All of a sudden they heard a strange kind of singing. The sound grew louder. Through the tent opening they could see men wearing feather crowns. They were crowded in a circle in the middle of the camp. Each man was hitting the ground with either a war club, a paddle, or a stone pick.

Soon two people wearing bird masks began to dance. They moved to the low-pitched song of a man and the shrill voice of an old woman. After the dance, Heyerdahl told Atan how much he had enjoyed it. Atan said that it was not meant to entertain Heyerdahl's group. The song was for the blessing of their god, Atua.

Next day Atan and five of his family took a few members of the group to the quarry. It was on top of the crater of a dead volcano called Rano Raraku. There they found hundreds of partly finished statues. The statues had stood there for centuries, since the day when the stonecutters laid down their picks never to return.

The long ears began gathering some of the stone picks dropped around the quarry. The picks looked like the flat front teeth of some giant animal. The men went right to work. They spread out their picks along the base of the rocky wall. Each man set a gourd of water near him. Atan measured a wall of rock using his stretched-out arms and spread-out fingers as a ruler. With a pick he marked the stone.

The mayor gave a signal and the men lined up in front of the wall. Suddenly they began singing, while they hit the wall to the rhythm of the song. It was the first time in centuries that the sound of stonecutting had been heard at Rano Raraku. One man became so excited that he danced as he sang and hit the rock. Little by little the marks grew deeper under the men's picks. Without breaking the timing, a worker would grab his gourd and splash water on the rock to soften it and prevent rock chips from flying into his eyes. Whenever one of the men threw aside a dull pick, the mayor grabbed it and struck it against another pick on the ground to sharpen it.

After three days, faint outlines of the statue could be seen. The stonecutters stopped their work. They were actually wood carvers and not trained to work with stone for long periods of time. Atan said that it might have taken twelve months, with two teams working all day, to finish a statue. An archaeologist with the group agreed. But Atan had shown how a huge statue could be carved from hard stone with only the tools people had used centuries ago.

Heyerdahl asked the mayor if he also knew how the statues were lifted onto the platforms.

"Of course," said Atan.

Heyerdahl offered to pay Atan $100 on the day the largest statue lying on its face once again stood on its platform. The mayor accepted the challenge.

To raise a statue, Atan needed twelve men, three poles, and a huge pile of both large and small rocks. To begin, three men put the ends of their poles under the statue and pushed down on the other ends. The figure did not move. They kept pushing. Finally, a tiny space opened between the ground and the statue. Lying beside the statue, Atan quickly shoved tiny rocks under it. The process was repeated. Lift, push stones under the statue, rest, and lift again. Now all the men except the lifters were gathering rocks. Larger and larger rocks were needed as the huge figure slowly rose.

When the men could no longer reach the ends of the poles, they pulled on ropes fastened to them. They had to climb up the rock pile to place new rocks under the statue. One false move and the statue and rocks would fall.

Atan passed ropes around the stone head and fastened them to stakes driven into the ground. The ropes would hold the statue on the platform. After eighteen days of work, the statue was finally pushed to a standing position. The pile of rocks was removed.

Atan had kept his promise. A statue had been lifted onto a platform in much the same way the Easter Islanders of long ago might have done it.

Heyerdahl asked Atan how the statues were moved from Rano Raraku crater, where they were carved, to different places around the island.

"They walked," said the mayor.

Heyerdahl kept asking. Finally the mayor told him that a sledge made out of a forked tree trunk had been used. He knew such sleds were used to move heavy stones to the top of the platforms. He also knew how to make one. But he did not have enough people in his family to move a statue. None of the other Easter Islanders was interested in helping.

Heyerdahl wouldn't give up so easily. At the camp two large oxen were killed and cooked. Everyone on the island was invited. Once the people had enjoyed a good picnic, it was not hard to get nearly 200 of them to help move the statue.

They put the sledge under a twelve-foot statue that long ago had been left on a road. Carefully they tied the statue to the sledge with strong ropes and pulled the giant over the ground.

In this way, scientists got an idea of how the giant statues may have been carved, carried across the island, and raised onto their platforms. Why the statues were made is another question. Present-day islanders believe that the statues look like ancestors of the people who made them. Those people may have thought the statues had "magic" powers.

The statues are not the only remains found on the island. There are many above-ground tombs and hundreds of stone towers that must have marked land boundaries. There are caves lined with stones fitted together, rocks carved with pictures, and the remains of farmyards and stone houses. There are also wooden tablets carved with a writing like no other writing known today.

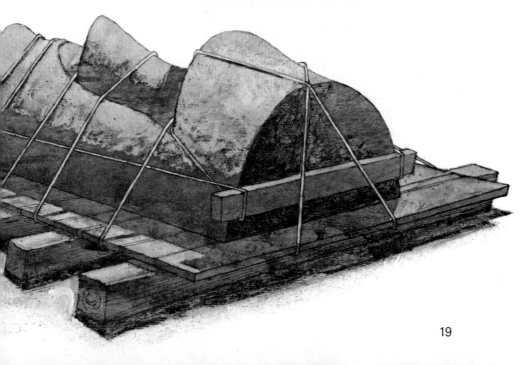

These remains seemed very important to Dr. William Mulloy, an anthropologist. Dr. Mulloy studied the remains on Easter Island and directed the workers to put the giant statues back onto their platforms. He believes that the small island could never have had more than three or four thousand people living on it. He doesn't think many visitors could have reached the far-off island bringing new ideas with them. Yet the island people must have had a fairly complicated way of living to make the things they did before war almost wiped them out.

Scientists are still studying the remains left by these people. They hope to learn more about how the people lived, worked, played, and worshiped. They hope someone finds the key to the writing on the tablets and learns to read the messages. Then the mystery of Easter Island may be solved.

Workers restore a statue's base.

Understanding What You've Read

1. What story did the people of Easter Island tell to explain how the stone statues moved across the island?
2. How did the present-day people of Easter Island carve the statue?
3. How did the present-day Easter Islanders raise the statue? How did they move it across the island?
4. How did the Easter Islanders treat Heyerdahl and his group? Explain your answer with examples from the selection.

Applying the Skills Lesson

1. What is the meaning of the following words as used in this selection? Use the glossary if you need help.
   a. quarry
   b. gourd
   c. archaeologist
   d. sledge
   e. anthropologist
2. Suppose you took a book about Easter Island out of the library. Tell whether you would use the index, the table of contents, or the glossary to answer each of these questions about the book.
   a. Does the book provide an explanation for how Easter Island got its name?
   b. Does the book have a chapter on the history of Easter Island?
   c. Does the book give a description of the individual statues?
   d. What are the major topics covered in the book?
   e. Does the book have a special section devoted to maps of the islands in the South Pacific?

After you read this selection, you may want to learn more about the Nazca lines. Remember that the indexes of textbooks can direct you to this information.

Why did a group of people create something they were never able to see? Who were these people? And what is the key to . . .

THE MYSTERY OF THE ANCIENT NAZCA LINES

by Loren McIntyre

Ruler-straight, a curious marking more than a mile long cuts through the desert in southern Peru. Mule paths that cross it point out how exact its design is. Other markings cover hundreds of square miles of dry plateau between the towns of Nazca and Palpa. These are the Nazca lines. They form triangles, spirals, flowers, and a desert zoo of giant birds, reptiles, and whales, a monkey and a spider.

Some of the figures look like those decorating Nazca pottery. Archaeologists attribute the lines to the Nazcas, a coastal people who lived between — roughly speaking — 100 B.C. and A.D. 700.

Making the marks must have taken a great deal of time. A few million rocks had to be removed to expose the lighter ground beneath. Then the rocks had to be piled in rows to form designs. In the desert, these designs can last thousands of years.

But why did the Nazcas make them? Nobody really knows. There have been many guesses. Some say they were prehistoric roads or farms. Others say they carry some kind of message.

Dr. Paul Kosok studied the markings after they were first seen from the air in the late 1920's. He believes they were part of a giant calendar, an almanac for farmers.

A 1968 study found that some of the lines do indeed point to positions of the sun and moon in ancient times. They also show the rising and setting points on the horizon of some of the brighter stars. But, the study says, this could be due to chance.

And so the mystery remains, including the most tantalizing question of all: Why did the Nazcas make huge designs that they themselves could never see, designs that can be seen only from the air?

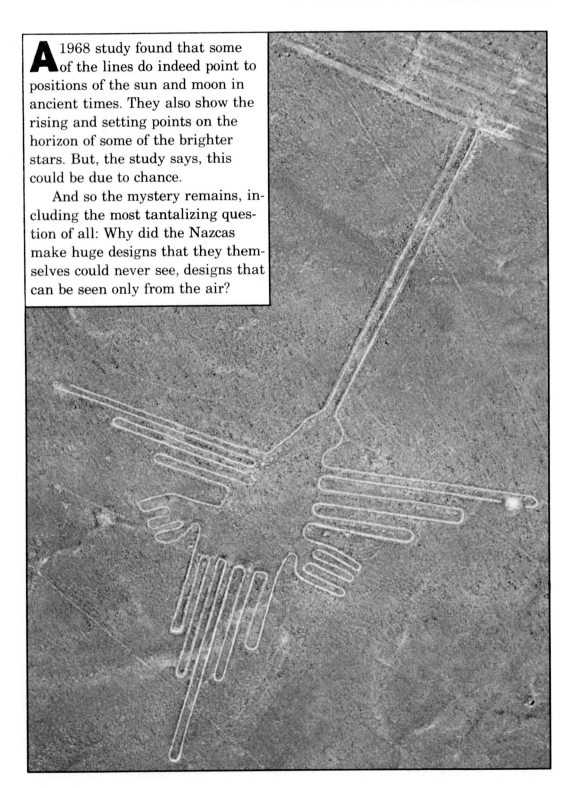

This monkey design measures over a hundred meters across and can only be seen from the air.

For more than twenty-five years Maria Reiche has photographed and charted the lines. She is trying to complete a map of the hundreds of designs and figures.

Ms. Reiche laughs at the suggestion that such markings may have been ancient airfields for visitors from outer space. "Once you remove the stones, the ground is quite soft," she says. "I'm afraid the spacemen would have gotten stuck."

"We can't be sure what their meaning was, but we can be sure they had meaning," says art historian Alan Sawyer. "Most figures are drawn by a single line that never crosses itself. Perhaps it is the path of a maze."

The Nazca lines remained for many years much as their makers designed them. For perhaps two thousand years, a spider 150 feet long lay clearly in the sand. Now it bears the scars of dune buggies, jeeps, and sightseers on foot. A similar fate threatens many of the markings.

For years Ms. Reiche has been committed to saving the lines. The Peruvian government gave 1 million sols (about $23,000) for the purpose.

"I would like to see a viewing tower erected near the Pan American Highway," Ms. Reiche says. "Then visitors will not be tempted to walk on the lines. I used to direct people to the sites. Now I direct them away, before all the ruins are ruined."

And if the lines are destroyed, we may never solve their mystery.

Understanding What You've Read

1. What are the Nazca lines?
2. What are some of the theories that have been developed to explain the mystery of the lines?
3. What kinds of information do archaeologists hope to get from studying the Nazca lines?

Applying the Skills Lesson

1. Suppose you wanted to find out if a particular textbook contained information about the Nazca lines. Which of the following topics would you check in the index?
   a. pottery
   b. Kosok, Paul
   c. Nazca lines
   d. deserts
   e. Reiche, Maria
   f. Peru, government of
2. Give the meaning of each of these words as used in the selection. Use the glossary if you need help.
   a. almanac
   b. plateau
   c. prehistoric
   d. tantalizing

TEXTBOOK STUDY

Using Textbooks

If you know how to use the table of contents and index in your textbook, it will be easy for you to find the pages with the information you are looking for. Once you have found the right page, you can focus on the information presented in the paragraphs. As you read the following textbook excerpt, refer to the sidenotes. They will point out the things to notice in an index.

Using the Index in Social Studies

Subtopics are usually listed alphabetically.

On what page would you find out the population of Southeast Asia?

These words direct you to other listings for Southeast Asia.

How many pages deal with the citrus industry in the southern United States?

South Australia, 352–353

South Carolina, 471; rice growing in, 479; textile industry in, 480

South Dakota, and corn belt, 463; gold in, 487; wheat belt, 465

South Island, New Zealand, 358

South Korea, 276, 327–328

South Pole, 5, 22

South Vietnam, 276, 329, 336–337

Southeast Asia, agriculture in, 330–332; climate, 330; colonial history of, 329–330, 332–333; countries of, 329; people of, 330; population, 329; religions of, 330; rivers of, 330; terrace building in, 36–37; *see also* individual countries; Orient

Southeast Asia Treaty Organization (SEATO), 360

Southern Africa, countries of, 261; *see also* individual countries; Sub-Saharan Africa

Southern states, Appalachia region, 482; cities of, 471–472; citrus fruit growing in, 479–480; climate, 474–475; commercial farming in, 477–478; cotton growing in, 475–477; fishing industry in, 480; food processing in, 480; forests in, 480; fruit and vegetable growing in, 480; growth of, 471–472, 481; industry in, 480; natural resources, 475; as oil and gas producer, 475, 480; peanut growing in, 478–479; ports of, 472; problems of, 481–482; rivers of, 472–474; states of, 471; steel production in, 480; Sugar Bowl of, 479; textile industry in, 480; tobacco growing in, 478; topography, 472

—*World Geography Today*
Holt, Rinehart & Winston

Building Skills

1. According to the index, how many pages in the textbook deal with agriculture in Southeast Asia?
2. Which pages would you turn to for information about food crops in the southern United States?

One Picture Is Worth a Thousand Words . . .
Using Graphic Aids

You've come across graphs, maps, and diagrams while reading, and you know how valuable these graphic aids can be. Graphic aids help you to get more meaning from what you read. They can supply additional facts about a topic or can illustrate the information found in a selection. There are many different kinds of graphic aids. Each one serves a different purpose.

Maps

Maps are drawings of geographical areas. They can show small areas, such as towns. They also can show much larger parts of the earth, such as a continent. There are world maps and maps of the moon and some of the planets. Maps can include a great many details. Look at the map on the next page. What kinds of information are shown on the map?

Nearly every map has a **legend** or **key.** A legend explains the colors and symbols used on the map. For example, if capital cities are starred on the map, the legend may show a star and tell you what it means. The legend also tells you what scale of measurement is used. A legend may help you identify mountains, bodies of water, yearly rainfall, and average temperature. On some maps you'll see colored, dashed, or broken lines. The legend will tell you what these lines stand for. With the help of a legend, you can find out a great deal about a particular place.

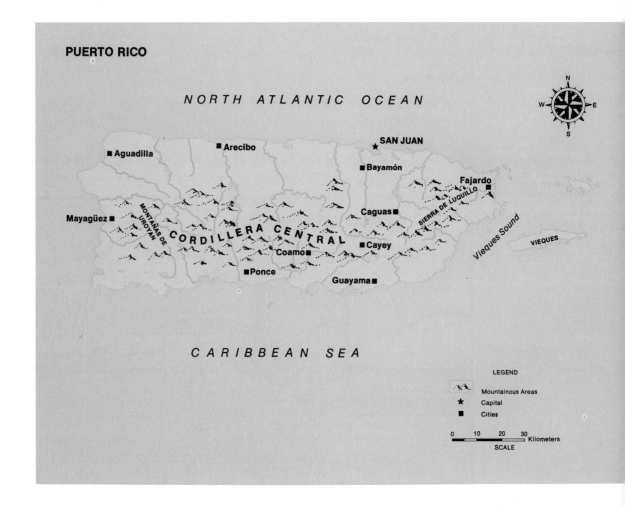

Use the map of Puerto Rico to answer the following questions:

1. What is the capital of Puerto Rico?
2. On what part of the island is the city of Mayagüez located?
3. Arecibo is located in the north-central portion of Puerto Rico. Which city is *closest* to Arecibo?
   a. Aguadilla
   b. Caguas
   c. Fajardo
4. Cordillera Central is
   a. a lake
   b. a mountain range
   c. a large city

Diagrams

A **diagram** is a drawing that shows how the parts of something are arranged. It is usually labeled. Diagrams are especially useful in math and science.

Here is a diagram of the human digestive system. What does the diagram do that a written description cannot do as well?

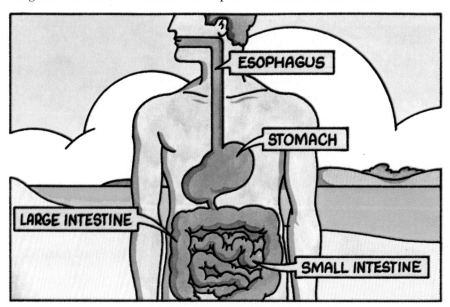

ESOPHAGUS

STOMACH

LARGE INTESTINE

SMALL INTESTINE

Graphs and Tables

Look at the *line graph* below. What kinds of information does it give you?

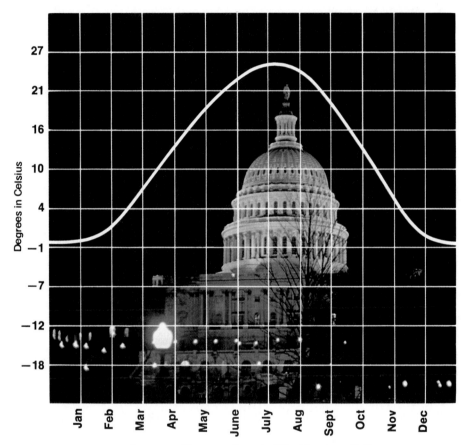

Average Temperature in Washington, D.C.

A **graph** relates two kinds of information. The graph above shows the temperatures in Washington, D.C., during the span of one year. For example, in January, the average temperature in Washington, D.C., is about −1°C. In July, it is about 27°C. What is the average temperature in November? A graph also shows a trend or direction. What happens to the temperature from January to July?

33

A **table** uses rows and columns to list information in a particular order. Look at the table below.

Planets: Distance from the Sun and Number of Moons

Planet	Distance from Sun	Number of Moons
Mercury	60 million km	0
Venus	108 million km	0
Earth	150 million km	1
Mars	228 million km	2
Jupiter	780 million km	14
Saturn	1,434 million km	10
Uranus	2,880 million km	5
Neptune	4,515 million km	2
Pluto	5,910 million km	1

In what order are the planets listed? What kinds of comparisons can you make using the information in the table?

Graphic Aids That Summarize Information

Graphic aids often summarize or illustrate the information already found in a selection. They let you see, in picture or chart form, what you are reading about. Graphic aids help you to understand an explanation or description. Study the map and read the paragraph on the next page. What information from the paragraph does the map illustrate?

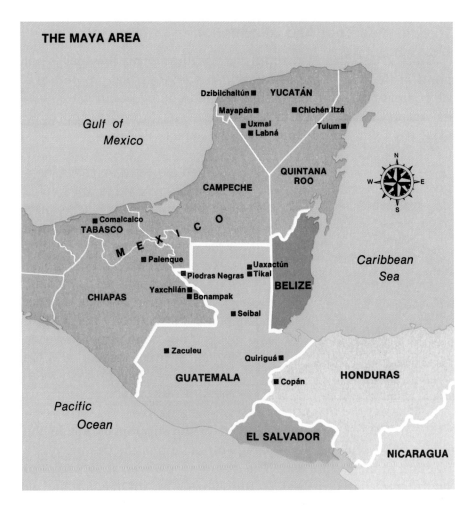

THE MAYA AREA

Dzibilchaltún ■ YUCATÁN

Mayapán ■   ■ Chichén Itzá

Uxmal ■   Tulum ■
Labná ■

Gulf of
Mexico

QUINTANA
ROO

CAMPECHE

■ Comalcalco
TABASCO

M E X I C O

Caribbean
Sea

■ Palenque

■ Uaxactún
Piedras Negras ■ ■ Tikal

Yaxchilán ■   BELIZE
■ Bonampak

CHIAPAS

■ Seibal

■ Zaculeu

Quiriguá ■

GUATEMALA   HONDURAS

■ Copán

Pacific
Ocean

EL SALVADOR

NICARAGUA

● The Maya were a group of people living in Central America between 1400 B.C. and A.D. 1500. Today, all that remains of the Maya are crumbling stone pyramids in several parts of Mexico, Guatemala, and Honduras. Some of the major sites in Mexico are Uxmal, Chichén Itzá, and Labná located near the Gulf of Mexico. Probably the most famous Mayan ruins are found at Tikal, in the jungles of Guatemala. The ruins of Copán, in Honduras, lie at the top of steep mountain slopes. The whole area of Central America—from the Gulf of Mexico east to the Caribbean Sea and west to the Pacific Ocean— is dotted with more than fifty Mayan city sites.

Graphic Aids That Add Information

Graphic aids can also supply you with information that is not found in the text of the selection. Graphic aids that are part of a selection add to your knowledge of the topic by pointing out several related facts. These facts can help you to understand more about what you are reading. Read the paragraph below.

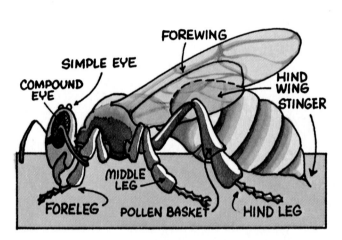

When the word *insect* is mentioned, many people think of a pest. Insects, however, serve us in many ways. The bee, for example, is the only creature on earth that can produce both honey and wax. The praying mantis feeds on other insects, keeping the pest populations under control. Nearly all insects carry pollen from flower to flower. Several insects are the chief food supply of fresh-water fish.

What kind of information given in the diagram is not in the paragraph? Notice that the paragraph mentions the bee only as a producer of honey and wax. The diagram, however, shows some of the different parts of the bee. By referring to the diagram as you read, you can gain a better understanding of one of the insects discussed in the paragraph.

Try This

1. Using the diagram on page 32, list four parts of the digestive system.
2. Use the map on page 35 to answer these questions:
   a. What Mayan ruins have been found in Guatemala?
   b. What is the most northern Mayan ruin?
   c. What Mayan ruin is located closest to a body of water?

VOCABULARY STUDY

The Letter from Lester . . . Synonyms

Lester Zerb wrote a letter of complaint to the Big Burst Sugarless Bubble Gum Company. To make sure the people at Big Burst understood how he felt, Lester underlined some of the words in the letter. He also included a synonym for each underlined word. This is the letter Lester wrote.

Dear Big Burst Sugarless Bubble Gum:

Two weeks ago my <u>ardor</u> for Big Burst Sugarless Bubble Gum was bigger than a Big Burst bubble. However, due to recent <u>circumstances</u>, this love has turned to disappointment. These events I speak of concern your free offer. What a joke! Ha! I thought your company was <u>committed</u> to making people happy. Now I know you are only pledged to making people wait.

Sure, I collected my 12,000 Big Burst Bubble Gum wrappers. Sometimes I had to use <u>drastic</u> measures to get them. I chewed eight packs of gum a day for one week straight! I call that pretty extreme.

Your offer said if I sent in all those wrappers I would get a free prize. Well, where is it?

Send the goods pronto, or I'll never blow another Big Burst bubble as long as I live.

Lester Zerb

Word Play

Find the synonyms that Lester uses to explain the meaning of *ardor, circumstances, committed,* and *drastic.*

Notice how the graphic aids that accompany this selection give you additional information about sharks.

Strange resting places of one of the world's most frightening creatures have been discovered. Follow the author and her team as they go . . .

Into the Lairs of "Sleeping" SHARKS

by Dr. Eugenie Clark

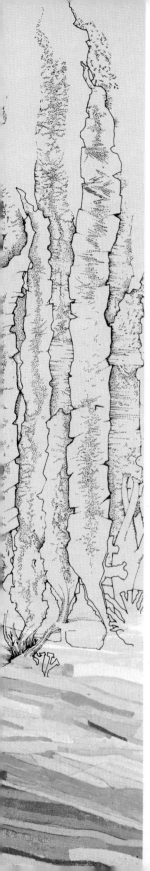

We had been following a requiem shark into a cave off the coast of Mexico's Yucatán Peninsula. Suddenly the shark turned. It swept toward us. My student Anita George and I froze. Moving into the glare of our underwater movie light, the shark stopped two feet short of bumping my face mask.

Spellbound by the light, the shark stood still. Silvery fish with glowing streaks along their backs formed a halo around its head. I could see every part of the shark. I could even see the tiny pores on the snout that allow it to sense changes in electric currents made by water, plants, and other animals.

The shark was female. Her eyes were open. The transparent third eyelid didn't even blink in the glare. Her mouth opened and closed rhythmically.

We could see some two dozen teeth in the front of her lower jaw. Behind each tooth lay four more. These would, in time, push forward to replace the ones in front. By moving its jaws, a shark can change the angle of its biting teeth. I was happy to find that this shark's teeth were not in the biting position.

Like the tiger shark, the requiem belongs to a family of sharks that sometimes attacks people. Why was this one behaving so well? Why was it so quiet, so gentle?

Three years had passed since I first heard of the sea caves off the Yucatán coast. When sharks visit these caves they seem to become strangely "drowsy." The word *drowsy* came from my old friend Ramón Bravo. Ramón is a noted photographer and one of Mexico's leading underwater naturalists. He had never seen these sharks remain still. But he made it clear that in these caves they did remain still. They were not frightened when people came toward them. Nor were they to be mistaken for the lazy nurse sharks which loiter in caves in many parts of the world.

In November 1972, I made a six-day trip to Mexico. I saw sharks but no "sleeping" sharks in the caves.

"Eugenie, I don't know how I can prove to you that sharks sleep in these caves," Ramón told me. "Maybe I have to put them in pajamas and give them an alarm clock." He told me to come back.

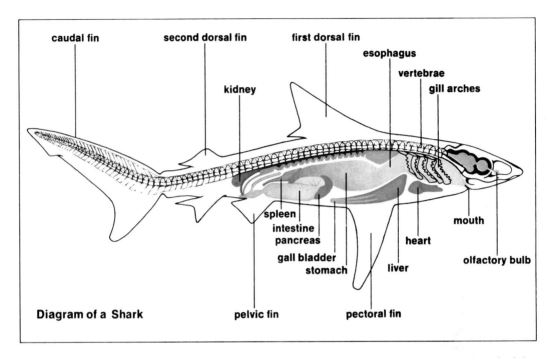

caudal fin · second dorsal fin · first dorsal fin · esophagus · vertebrae · gill arches · kidney · spleen · intestine · pancreas · gall bladder · stomach · liver · heart · mouth · olfactory bulb · pelvic fin · pectoral fin

Diagram of a Shark

So in April 1973, I returned to the caves. I was guided by Carlos Garcia. Carlos had discovered the beautiful caves and their oddly gentle visitors. This time I saw and studied my first "sleeping" sharks. When Carlos first found them, he thought they were dead. He thought he had stumbled onto a graveyard for sharks.

In 1974 I returned to the caves with some of my students from the University of Maryland. We wanted to find out what causes the sharks to become so "sleepy." Anita George was my main assistant. My other students, several visiting scientists, and half a dozen Mexican divers sometimes joined us.

It was on our last field trip that Anita and I met the requiem shark at such close quarters. Ramón and Carlos told us earlier that they had found others. They said that sometimes they were able to touch and even gently lift the sharks without angering them. When the sharks were approached and gently pushed, they might swim away or go back to "sleep."

This was very strange behavior. Why would this shark hide in a cave? It has no natural enemies. Why would it lie there pumping water over its gills? It usually breathes by keeping its mouth open while it swims. This seems easier to me.

To try to find the answer, we tested the water in the cave. We measured how deep and cold it was, how much oxygen and salt it contained, and how fast and in what direction it moved.

We got high oxygen readings even in the deepest parts of the caves. The extra oxygen probably allows the sharks to remain quiet for many hours.

At times, on the floor of the sixty-five-foot-deep cave at La Punta (The Point), we found a spot where the water was a little cooler than elsewhere. Could a different kind of water sometimes flow into the cave? Could it attract the sharks and then make them drowsy?

During the summer of 1974, we made a record of places where the water in the cave had less salt than the water outside. Pat McInturff, another of my students, boldly took a water sample under the very nose of a "sleeping" shark.

At La Cadena (The Chain), we had our first close look at a big "sleeping" shark. This one, like others we saw later, had a slave: a remora. This small fish cleans the shark by removing parasites. "Could these caves be cleaning stations for the sharks?" David Doubilet, our photographer, asked me.

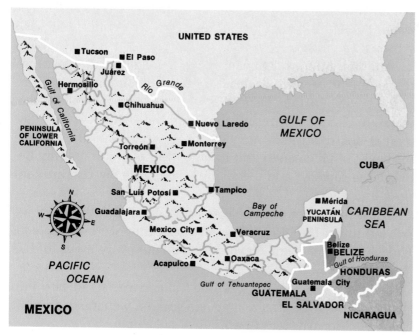

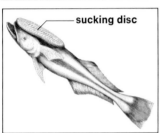

sucking disc

A sucking disc on the top of its head allows the remora to cling to a shark while it removes parasites.

I knew that biologists thought certain fish go into waters with less salt to get rid of parasites. The grip of the parasites is weakened by less salty water. We found that the water in these caves was not as salty as the water outside. Also, the remora can clean a shark better if the shark isn't racing through the water. Maybe the relief a shark feels upon getting rid of pests causes it to behave so strangely.

Another student, Michael Resio, thought that "sleeping" sharks might be getting pleasure from the strange conditions in the caves. Further tests of the cave waters may show that there are chemicals present that drug the sharks.

It seems likely that our "sleeping" sharks are drawn into the caves to be cleaned and to enjoy the pleasant feeling. Between the remoras and cleansing waters, the big fish are kept sleek and shiny.

We kept calling our subjects "sleeping." But the more we studied them, the more we agreed that they were not asleep. The way the "sleepers'" eyes followed our every move told us that they were awake.

Each day we saw a "sleeping" shark we talked late into evening. The night after a large one suddenly charged Anita, it was a wonder we slept at all.

"The shark's tail kicked up so much sand I couldn't see a thing. I thought it really got her," David told me. But Anita was safe.

Anita and student helper Nick Caloyianis said they had each received a terrible slap as the shark turned. It smashed its tail into them, almost knocking off their face masks.

Ramón, who had had the best view, praised Anita. "What a reaction! She hit the shark on its head with her clipboard!"

"I didn't really *hit* it," Anita said. "I used the clipboard to push it away when it came toward me. What else could I do? My back was to the cave wall and both exits were blocked."

The Mexican divers said that sometimes they had seen other kinds of sharks in the caves we checked. They reported seeing a lemon shark and a shark with a longer snout. Ramón thinks this second one might have been a blue shark.

Perhaps in deeper waters or undersea caves in other parts of the world, requiem sharks also "sleep." The more we study the oceans, the more shark "hotels" we might find.

Understanding What You've Read

1. Why is the behavior of the requiem shark at the beginning of the selection so unusual?
2. According to Dr. Clark, why might the sharks be "sleeping" in the caves?
3. What were the results of the water tests that were made in the area of the "sleeping" sharks?

Applying the Skills Lesson

1. Aside from the details given in the selection, what additional facts about sharks does the diagram on page 40 provide?
2. Study the map on page 41.
   a. In what part of Mexico is the Yucatán Peninsula located?
   b. What major bodies of water surround the Yucatán Peninsula?

TEXTBOOK STUDY

Using Graphic Aids

Maps, charts, and diagrams are valuable reading aids. Read the following textbook excerpt. Use the sidenotes to help you see how useful graphic aids can be in your textbook reading.

Using Graphic Aids in Social Studies

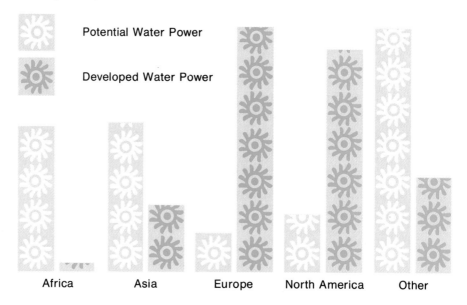

Potential Water Power

Developed Water Power

Africa   Asia   Europe   North America   Other

This graphic aid is called a *bar graph*. Why do you think it is called this? The key in the upper left-hand corner tells what each bar stands for.

A Closing Frontier

The chart on this page gives information about the present development of the world's water resources. The figures are averages. This means that some areas on each continent are above the average figure and some are below it. An average is

Why is it important for you to know that the figures are averages?

one way of comparing information. Using these averages, you can compare water resources for the several areas.

As you can see, the North American continent has developed much more of its water resources than have some of the other continents. This information should not really surprise you, since you live in North America. However, it may surprise you to know that during your lifetime you will probably use about seven million liters of water.

What areas? Look at the places listed on the bar graph.

This paragraph refers to the bar graph. The text and the graphic aid work together to help you understand the topic.

In addition, it is likely that you will also use over five thousand liters of gasoline, eat 450 kilograms of meat, drink thirteen thousand liters of milk, and wear over $6,000 worth of clothing. You will also use many metals, fuels, and chemicals when you buy and operate hundreds of manufactured items.

—Sources of Identity
Harcourt Brace Jovanovich

Building Skills

1. How does the graphic aid help you to understand the selection?
2. In the selection, there is no graphic aid to illustrate the third paragraph. What kind of graphic aid would be useful? Why?

Using Graphic Aids in Science

There are no sidenotes accompanying the following textbook excerpt. As you read, refer to the diagram. It will tell you more about cells. Then answer the questions that follow.

Plant Cells

In many ways, plant cells are like animal cells. Plant cells oxidize foods, use energy, dispose of wastes, grow, and divide. But as you might suspect, they do differ from animal cells in some respects.

Let us look at the diagram of a plant cell. This plant cell has a nucleus and a cytoplasm, just like an animal cell. It also has a cell membrane. But outside the cell membrane there is a *cell wall*. This cell wall contains a plant material known as *cellulose*. Cellulose is not found in the coverings of animal cells.

The Green Plant Cell

The diagram represents a green plant cell. It is the type of cell you might find in green leaf tissue. One very different thing about it is that it contains chloroplasts. In the diagram the chloroplasts appear as a number of small organelles in the cytoplasm. They get their green color from the

substance chlorophyll, which they contain. When a plant looks green you may
be quite sure that it contains a lot of
chlorophyll.

—*Modern Life Sciences*
Holt, Rinehart & Winston

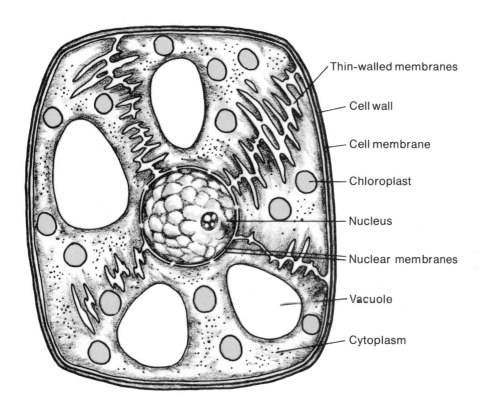

Thin-walled membranes

Cell wall

Cell membrane

Chloroplast

Nucleus

Nuclear membranes

Vacuole

Cytoplasm

Building Skills

1. Some parts of the cell are labeled in the diagram but are not
   described in the text. What are these parts?
2. What other information supplied by the diagram is not given in
   the selection?

SKILLS LESSON

The Most Useful Tool of All . . .
Using the Dictionary

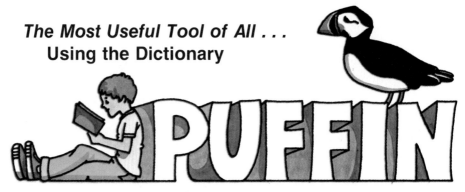

In your reading you come across new words all the time. Sometimes you can figure out the meaning of an unfamiliar word from the context in which it is used. Other times, however, the context may not really help you. So you turn to the dictionary.

Guide Words

Look at the portion of a sample dictionary page below.

---

presto	577	previous

* **pres·to** [pres′tō] **1** *adj.*, *adv*. In music, very quick. **2** *n*. A presto movement or passage.
pre·sum·a·bly [pri·zōō′mə·blē] *adv*. Probably.
pre·sume [pri·zōōm′] *v*. **pre·sumed, pre·sum·ing 1** To take for granted; assume; sup-

pre·ter·nat·u·ral [prē′tər·nach′ər·əl] *adj*. **1** Different from but not outside nature or what is natural; abnormal. **2** Outside nature or what is natural; supernatural.
pre·text [prē′tekst] *n*. A false reason or motive

The two words printed at the top of the page are called **guide words.** The guide words help you quickly find the word you are looking for. The guide word on the left, *presto*, tells you the first word that appears on the page. The guide word on the right, *previous*, tells you the last word on the page. Only words that come alphabetically between *presto* and *previous* are on the page. Why can you expect to find the word *pretend* on this page? Would you find the word *price* on this page?

* From the *HBJ School Dictionary*, © 1977 by Harcourt Brace Jovanovich, Inc. Reprinted by permission.

Entries

Look at the dictionary entry below. What kinds of information can be found in the entry?

> * **fos·sil** [fos′əl] **1** *n*. The remains of a plant or animal of an earlier age, hardened and preserved in earth or rock. **2** *adj. use* Like or being a fossil: a *fossil* fern. **3** *n. informal* A person with old-fashioned notions or ways.

A fossil fern

The boldface word at the beginning of the entry is called the **entry word.** How does the dictionary show that the word *fossil* is divided into two syllables? Next to the entry word, in brackets, is the pronunciation of the word. The definitions, or meanings, of the word are usually the longest part of the entry. How do you know when a word has more than one meaning? How many meanings does the word *fossil* have?

Sometimes a chart, diagram, or illustration appears in the entry. This is another aid in helping you to understand the meaning of the word.

English has adopted many words and parts of words from other languages. Where a word comes from is called its **etymology** or origin. Some dictionary entries contain information about the etymology of a word. Look at the entry below. Where does the word *helicopter* come from?

> * **hel·i·cop·ter** [hel′ə·kop′tər] *n.* An aircraft that is lifted and propelled by big, motor-driven, horizontal rotors and is able to hover and to fly in any direction. ◆ *Helicopter* comes from two Greek words meaning *spiral wing*.

Helicopter

* From the *HBJ School Dictionary,* © 1977 by Harcourt Brace Jovanovich, Inc. Reprinted by permission.

The Ways Words Are Used

How many ways can you think of to use the word *run*? Some ways are: a *run* in a stocking; a *run* of good luck; to *run* an ad in a newspaper. Did you know that there are at least forty different ways to use the word *run*? In the dictionary, a word's usage is often shown by an example after each separate definition.

Study the entry below for the word *break*.

* **break** [brāk] *v.* **broke, brok·en, break·ing,** *n.* **1** *v.* To separate or crack into pieces, as by a blow or pull: Don't *break* the cup; The rope *broke*. **2** *n.* The act of breaking. **3** *n.* A gap, crack, or broken place. **4** *v.* To open the surface of, as with a plow; pierce: to *break* ground. **5** *v.* To put or get out of order; make or become useless: The clock *broke*. **6** *v.* To lessen the force or effect of: The snow *broke* his fall. **7** *v.* To overcome or defeat: to *break* a strike. **8** *n.* A stopping; interruption: to take a *break* from work. **9** *v.* To end or stop: to *break* a silence. **10** *v.* To fail to keep or obey; violate: to *break* a promise; to *break* the law. **11** *v.* To teach to obey; tame: to *break* a horse. **12** *v.* To lower in rank; demote: He was *broken* from corporal to private. **13** *v.* To give or get smaller units of money: to *break* a dollar. **14** *v.* To make or become poor; put or go into debt: Taxes will *break* me. **15** *v.* To make or become known: There may be trouble when the story *breaks*. **16** *v.* To do better than; exceed: The snowfall *broke* all records. **17** *v.* To change suddenly in tone or quality, as a singer's voice. **18** *v.* To dissolve and go away: The clouds *broke*. **19** *v.* To come into being; appear suddenly: The storm *broke*; Dawn is *breaking*. **20** *v.* To force one's way out of; escape from: He *broke* jail. **21** *n.* An escape, as from prison. **22** *n. informal* A chance or opportunity: a lucky *break*. **23** *v.* To change or fall off suddenly: The fever *broke*.

How is usage 1, "Don't *break* the cup," different from usage 22, "a lucky *break*"? Which definition shown in the entry above explains the way the word *break* is used in this sentence: "Let's take a *break* and have lunch"? In this sentence the word *break* means "a stopping; interruption," definition number 8. Knowing several ways in

* From the *HBJ School Dictionary*, © 1977 by Harcourt Brace Jovanovich, Inc. Reprinted by permission.

which a word can be used helps you to gain more understanding of what you read.

Multiple Entries

When you look up some words in the dictionary, you may find what looks like two definitions. Look at the entries below. What do you notice about the definitions of *swallow*?

* **swal·low**[1] [swol′ō] *n.* A small bird having a short bill, long pointed wings, and forked tail, noted for its swiftness in flight.

swal·low[2] [swol′ō] **1** *v.* To make the muscular action that causes (food or liquid) to pass from the mouth, through the throat and gullet, and into the stomach. **2** *n.* The act of swallowing. **3** *n.* The amount swallowed at one time. **4** *v.* To take in, as if by swallowing: The night *swallowed* them. **5** *v.* To hold in or conceal: to *swallow* tears; to *swallow* one's pride. **6** *v.* To endure or submit to: to *swallow* insults. **7** *v.* To take back: to *swallow* one's words. **8** *v. informal* To believe without question or criticism: He will *swallow* any old tale.

The first entry refers to a bird called a *swallow*. The second entry refers to the act of *swallowing*. The two words are completely different even though they are spelled and pronounced the same. Another example is *bat*. *Bat* has three entirely different meanings. Do you know what they are? If not, how could you find out?

Kinds of Entries

The dictionary is a source of many different kinds of information. It can be a good starting point for school reports and studying. An entry in the dictionary that captures your interest can be the beginning of a new hobby or project.

Look at the different kinds of entries shown on the next page. How many different topics do they deal with? What kinds of information do they contain?

* From the *HBJ School Dictionary,* © 1977 by Harcourt Brace Jovanovich, Inc. Reprinted by permission.

cir·cle [sûr′kəl] *n.,* *v.* **cir·cled, cir·cling**
1 *n.* A plane curve all of whose points are equally distant from a point in the plane, called the center. **2** *n.* The area enclosed by this curve. **3** *n.* Something resembling a circle, as a ring, etc. **4** *v.* To make or put a closed curve around: The fence *circled* the field. **5** *v.* To move about in or nearly in a circle: The lion *circled* its prey. **6** *n.* A complete series that repeats over and over: the *circle* of seasons. **7** *n.* A group of people with a common interest or purpose: a sewing *circle*.

Circle

British Isles Great Britain, Ireland, and the small islands surrounding them.
British thermal unit The long form of BTU.
Brit·on [brit′(ə)n] *n.* **1** A member of a Celtic people who used to live in England before the Anglo-Saxon invasions. **2** A Britisher.
Brit·ta·ny [brit′ə·nē] *n.* A region of western France.

British Isles

o·rang·u·tan [ō·rang′ə·tan *or* ō·rang′oō·tan] *n.* A large ape having brownish red hair and extremely long arms, found in Borneo and Sumatra. ◆*Orang-utan* comes from two Malay words meaning *forest man.*
o·rate [ôr′āt *or* ô·rāt′] *v.* **o·rat·ed, o·rat·ing** To speak in a pompous manner.
o·ra·tion [ô·rā′shən] *n.* A serious public speech, usually given at a formal occasion.

Orang-utan, about 54 in. high

dis·cus [dis′kəs] *n.* A heavy disk, now usually of metal and wood, used in athletic contests to see who can throw it the greatest distance.
dis·cuss [dis·kus′] *v.* **1** To talk over or consider; exchange ideas or opinions about: to *discuss* a proposed law. **2** To have or treat as a subject: This chapter *discusses* the American Revolution.
dis·cus·sion [dis·kush′ən] *n.* Argument on or consideration of a subject.
dis·dain [dis·dān′] **1** *n.* Scorn or haughty contempt, especially toward someone or something considered inferior. **2** *v.* To regard as beneath one; scorn; spurn: a rich man who *disdains* his poor relatives; a poor man who *disdains* gifts of charity. See CONTEMPT.

Woman throwing a discus

ac·cor·di·on [ə·kôr′dē·ən] **1** *n.* A portable musical instrument in which wind from a bellows, controlled by keys or buttons, causes metal reeds to sound. **2** *adj.* Looking like the folds in the bellows of an accordion: *accordion* pleats.
ac·cost [ə·kôst′ *or* ə·kost′] *v.* To stop and speak to; speak to first: A stranger *accosted* him.
ac·count [ə·kount′] **1** *v.* To hold to be; consider: I *account* that a lie. **2** *n.* A statement, narrative, or explanation. **3** *n.* A record of money paid out, received, or owing.

Accordion

Roo·se·velt [rō′zə·velt], **Eleanor,** 1884–1962, U.S. lecturer, writer, and diplomat, wife of Franklin Delano Roosevelt.
Roo·se·velt [rō′zə·velt], **Franklin Delano,** 1882–1945, U.S. statesman, 32nd president of the U.S., 1933–1945.
Roo·se·velt [rō′zə·velt], **Theodore,** 1858–1919, U.S. army officer and statesman, 26th president of the U.S., 1901–1909.

* From the *HBJ School Dictionary,* © 1977 by Harcourt Brace Jovanovich, Inc. Reprinted by permission.

Special Dictionaries

Besides dictionaries of the English language, there are rhyming dictionaries, dictionaries of synonyms and antonyms, dictionaries of slang, dictionaries containing only scientific terms, biographical dictionaries, foreign dictionaries, and many others. Next time you are in a library, take a look at these other kinds of dictionaries.

Try This

1. In addition to definitions, what other kinds of information can you find in the dictionary?
2. Use your dictionary to match each word in column A with its etymology in column B:

A	**B**
a. pajamas	1. from an Algonquian word meaning "white beast"
b. moccasin	2. a variation of the word *travail*, meaning "hard work"
c. opossum	3. from a Hindi word meaning "leg garment"
d. Wednesday	4. from the Algonquian word, *mokussin*
e. travel	5. from the Old English *Wōdnes dœg*

3. Use the dictionary entries on page 52 to answer each of the following questions:
   a. What two bodies of water surround Ireland?
   b. Which is larger: the radius of a circle or the diameter of a circle?
   c. What is a discus made of?

VOCABULARY STUDY

The Parasite and the Maze . . .
Meanings from Context

B. Barnaby Baxter is amazing! He can make words come alive. Once he took a musty old book off the shelf, opened it, and read the first word he saw. It was *parasite*. Here's what happened:

"A parasite," said B. Barnaby, "lives off another living thing which it usually injures in the process—like a flea, for instance."

B. Barnaby blinked twice, and a parasite appeared right before my very eyes! Well, the parasite looked pretty uninteresting, so B. Barnaby decided to put a *halo* around it. He blinked again, and a faint glow of light circled the parasite.

"Let's run it through a *maze*," I suggested.

B. Barnaby wiggled his ears, and the most confusing network of passages I've ever seen popped into view. He set the parasite down at the start of the maze. When it didn't move, I was puzzled.

54

"Why doesn't it run through the passages?" I asked.

B. Barnaby chuckled. "There's no reason for it to run. So we'll put a shiny brass *trophy* at the end of the maze. If the parasite successfully runs the maze, it can keep the trophy as a symbol of its victory."

I can hear you out there, laughing and making fun of my story. But don't *scoff* at it. B. Barnaby, the *parasite,* the *halo,* the *maze,* and the *trophy* are all real.

I'm the one who's make-believe.

Word Play

Now, look over the story and find the definitions of each of the five italicized words.

Life in Ancient Egypt was a deep, dark mystery for hundreds of years. We knew very little about one of history's most fascinating civilizations until one man found the . . .

Key to the Unknown:
THE ROSETTA STONE

by James Norman

The key that unlocked hieroglyphic writing and opened the door to Egypt's long history was found in the Nile Delta in 1799. Near the village of El Rashid (called Rosetta by the British), an Arab worker discovered an oddly shaped stone. When it was cleaned, it was found to be covered with strange writing.

The black slab, now known as the Rosetta Stone, was three feet, nine inches high and two feet, four inches wide. It was about eleven inches thick. On its polished surface were three wide bands of carved writing. The top band had fourteen lines of hieroglyphics. The thirty-two-line middle band was not familiar. The bottom band of fifty-four lines was in Greek. Parts of the stone were missing. The upper left- and right-hand corners as well as the lower right-hand corner had been broken off.

Could the stone be valuable? It had the same message in three languages, and one was in a known language, Greek. Could the others be decoded? The stone was sent to the National Institute in Cairo. Its importance was quickly confirmed.

The Greek part was translated into a half-dozen modern languages. The other two scripts were identified. It would seem, with this key at hand, that figuring out the hieroglyphics should be a snap. But no such luck. It took more than twenty years to unlock the Egyptian writing. The triumph of solving its secrets fell to a young Frenchman from Grenoble, Jean François Champollion.

Champollion: Learning to Learn

As a child, Jean François was surrounded by books. His father was a bookseller. His mother read Bible stories to him. They aroused his interest in Egypt and the Pharaohs. A family friend taught him Latin at a very early age.

In the village school, Jean François seemed to be a rather poor student. He was not interested in mathematics and sciences. Languages, however, appealed to him. He soon memorized long passages in Greek and Latin.

In 1801, eleven-year-old Champollion began to study Hebrew. Within a year he stunned the school officers. During an exam he gave a remarkable translation and interpretation of parts of the Bible. A visitor to the school, Jean Baptiste Fourier [zhäN ba(p)·tēst′ foo·ryā′], was also impressed by the boy. Fourier was a noted mathematician and physicist. He had done scientific work in Egypt. He invited Jean François to his home to view his valuable Egyptian collection. The visit, in the fall of 1802, was a turning point in Jean François's life. He was enchanted by the Egyptian artifacts. But he was more interested in the hieroglyphics on the stone tablets.

"Can these be read?" Champollion asked.

Fourier shook his head. "No one has been able to as yet."

Cheeks flushed with ardor, the boy said, "I shall read them. Not yet, but in a few years."

Champollion knew he had to prepare himself for the task. He had to learn everything he could about Egypt and the languages of the Near East. At age thirteen he began studying three more languages: Arabic, Chaldean [kal·dē′ən], and Syriac. He covered the walls of his room with hieroglyphic signs. Since he could not read them, however, he studied everything he could find about Egypt.

When he was sixteen he began his first major Egyptian project. He made a chart and chronology of Egypt under the Pharaohs. During the summer of 1807 he sent the outline to the Grenoble Academy, the most learned institution in the city. On September 1, he read his paper before a group of professors. When he had finished, he was unanimously elected to the faculty.

Champollion continued his studies of Persian, Sanskrit, Arabic, and Coptic. Among all these languages, Coptic enchanted him the most. Within a year he spoke and wrote it so easily that he kept his diary in that language. "I am in fact a Copt," he wrote, "who for his amusement translates into that language everything that comes into his head. I speak Coptic to myself so no one will understand me."

During the year he spent in Paris, Champollion had the chance to see and study a plaster copy of the Rosetta Stone. Silvestre de Sacy, a well-known student of Oriental languages, discouraged Champollion from trying to decode Egyptian scripts. De Sacy told him it was a waste of time, that he could not possibly succeed.

Champollion returned to Grenoble in 1809. At eighteen, he was a professor teaching his former classmates. He also was writing a Coptic dictionary. He felt it would help him in his attack on the Egyptian writing. The book kept growing and growing. When he reached page 1,069, he wrote his brother: "My Coptic dictionary is getting thicker day by day. The author, meanwhile, is getting thinner."

In 1814, Champollion returned to his first love—the Egyptian riddle. In 1821, he worked with the signs from the Egyptian *Book of the Dead*. These were rolls with ritual prayers, poems, and drawings that were buried with the dead. They were supposed to help the spirit of the dead in a safe passage to the afterlife.

By fall, Champollion had done something no one else had ever done. He had translated a "shorthand" form of Egyptian writing, sign by sign, into the form used by Egyptian priests. Then he translated this into hieroglyphics. He now had the proof of the evolution of Egyptian writing.

Shorthand form of the name Ptolemy

On his thirty-first birthday, December 23, 1821, Champollion had a brilliant idea. It was so simple, one wonders why no one else had thought of it. He decided to add up

A page from the Egyptian Book of the Dead

all the different signs on the Rosetta Stone. There were 1,419 Egyptian symbols, but only 486 Greek words. From this Champollion guessed that each sign did not stand for a whole word as was generally believed. There were too many of them. He felt that the signs made words just as our alphabetic letters form words. Thus, many of the signs must stand for sounds. Others must stand for ideas.

Working with names carved in ovals (now believed to be royal names), he noted that there was only one oval-enclosed name on the Rosetta Stone. But it was repeated six times. Its simplest form was this:

But it also appeared as this:

Sir Thomas Young, an English scholar, had already decoded it. It stood for the name of Ptolemy [tol'ə·mē], one of the great kings who ruled Egypt. Like Young, Champollion broke the word down into its sound equivalents. His work notes looked like this:

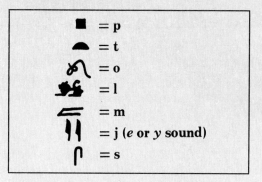

Champollion's phonetic values for the Ptolemy signs

Now Champollion needed proof that the signs really stood for Ptolemy. He wanted proof that these same letters could be applied to a different name with similar letters. He found this proof during January 1822. Champollion received copies of the writing on another Egyptian stone. He quickly spotted the signs for Ptolemy.

But something else excited him—a different name in a royal oval! According to the Greek writing on the stone, the name was Cleopatra, wife of one of the Ptolemys. When he compared the signs in the two ovals, it was clear that some of them matched:

The Cleopatra Oval

Cleopatra's name, with sound values similar to the Ptolemy signs underlined

Building a new line from the Cleopatra oval, Champollion filled in the signs with the letters he already knew.

He had seen that sometimes the ◣ sign was replaced by the 🐟 sign. He figured they both stood for *t*. Thus he was left with two bird signs, a mouth-shaped sign, a right-angle sign, and an odd tenth sign. Champollion knew that in the Greek spelling of *Kleopatra,* as in English, there are two *a*'s. He decided that the birds stood for the *a*'s. Since he now knew the value of most of the signs, he thought the ◣ must stand for the Greek *K* sound. Thomas Young and others had already noticed that one sign always followed the name of a queen, princess, or goddess. It stood for no sound. The only sign left without a sound value was the ◯ sign. Champollion believed it stood for

an *r* sound. Thus *Kleopatra* was decoded. From these two names, he figured out eleven signs that stood for eleven sounds in the Greek alphabet.

In some of the ovals, other signs followed the name of Ptolemy. A careful reading of the Greek on the Rosetta Stone showed Champollion that these were royal titles. They meant "Ever-living, beloved of Ptah." His knowledge of Coptic helped him figure out their sounds and add several more signs to his list. Now familiar names began to appear. The names were famous in history: Alexander, Antonius, Tiberius, Germanicus.

Despite his success, Champollion was not sure how far his keys to Egyptian would work. For a while he feared that only foreign names and titles were written in sound-signs.

Breakthrough!

On the morning of September 14, Champollion received some new writings. Among them he found copies of writing taken from an Egyptian rock temple on the Nile.

Champollion gave a sudden start when he saw the first oval. Clearly, it showed the name of a king. But it was not like any of the Egyptian names he had come across so often.

Oval with the name of Rameses in hieroglyphics

Champollion already knew that the last two signs stood for *ss*. He also knew that the first sign, a circle, was a pictograph for the sun. In Coptic the word for sun was pronounced "Rē." Did the first and last signs in the oval stand for *Rē-?-ss*?

Champollion remembered running across the three-pronged middle sign on the Rosetta Stone. The Greek on the Rosetta Stone showed this sign to mean "birthday," *mise* in Coptic. Just shorten it to *m* and slip it in between *Rē* and the *ss*. *Rē-m-ss*! Was it possible? Could this be Rameses, one of the most famous of ancient Pharaohs?

Then Champollion found another oval that made his brain spin. He instantly knew that it was the name Thothmes [thōth'mās *or* tōt'mās]. Thothmes was another famous Egyptian king.

The name of Thutmosis or Thothmes in hieroglyphics

The system was clear. Champollion had turned the key and opened the door to a history that had been lost for centuries.

With Champollion's key, archaeologists and others have been able to unlock many of the mysteries of ancient Egypt. Even today, much is unknown about this world. But with the key to the Rosetta Stone, the past becomes less and less unknown.

Understanding What You've Read

1. Why was decoding the Rosetta Stone so important to archaeologists studying ancient Egypt?
2. How did Champollion's background and childhood experiences help him in his work on the Rosetta Stone?
3. Why were the names in the ovals so important to Champollion's work?

Applying the Skills Lesson

Use a dictionary to answer the following questions:
1. Where does the Nile flow?
2. What does your dictionary say about Egypt?
3. What is an artifact?
4. Where was Sanskrit spoken?
5. When did Cleopatra live?

TEXTBOOK STUDY

Using the Dictionary

The dictionary is a valuable reference source. In addition to giving you information about specific words, the dictionary can improve your understanding of a subject by supplying you with facts about people, places, and events. Refer to the sidenotes as you read the following excerpt. They identify some of the kinds of information found in a dictionary.

This word can be spelled two different ways.

chlo·ro·phyll or **chlo·ro·phyl** [klôr′ə·fil] *n.* The green substance found in most plants. In the presence of sunlight it converts water and carbon dioxide from the air into sugars and starches.

chlo·ro·plast [klôr′ə·plast] *n.* A part of a plant cell where chlorophyll is found.

chock [chok] **1** *n.* A block or wedge placed to prevent something from moving or rolling. **2** *v.* To hold in position with a chock or chocks.

An illustration can help you understand a meaning. What does the illustration add to your understanding of *chocks*?

chock-full [chok′fŏŏl′] *adj.* Completely full.

choc·o·late [chôk′(ə·)lit *or* chok′(ə·)lit] **1** *n.* Cacao nuts that have been roasted and ground. **2** *n.* A drink or candy made from this. **3** *adj.* Made or flavored with chocolate: a *chocolate* cake. **4** *n.*, *adj.* Dark, reddish brown. ◆ This word comes from a Mexican Indian word. Indians gave chocolate to Spanish explorers in South America and Mexico.

Chocks holding an airplane wheel

This is an etymology. Where does the word *chocolate* come from?

choice [chois] *n.*, *adj.* **choic·er, choic·est** **1** *n.* The act of choosing; selection. **2** *n.* The right or privilege of choosing; option. **3** *n.* The person or thing chosen: the people's *choice*. **4** *n.* A number or variety from which to choose: a large *choice* of articles. **5** *n.* An alternative: He had no *choice*. **6** *adj.* Of very good quality; excellent: *choice* food.

In order to know how to pronounce *choir*, you may have to refer to the pronunciation key. Almost every dictionary has a pronunciation key.

choir [kwīr] *n.* **1** A trained group of singers, especially in a religious service. **2** The part of a church occupied by the choir.

choke [chōk] *v.* **choked, chok·ing,** *n.* **1** *v.* To stop the breathing of by squeezing or blocking the windpipe. **2** *v.* To become suffocated or stifled: to *choke* from smoke. **3** *n.* The act or sound of choking. **4** *v.* To keep back; suppress: to *choke* down anger. **5** *v.* To clog or become clogged: Filth *choked* the pipes. **6** *v.* To stop or hold back the progress, growth, or action of: to *choke* a fire. **7** *v.* To lessen the intake of air of (a gasoline engine). **8** *n.* A device that does this. **— choke up** To be overcome by emotion, nervousness, etc.

choke·cher·ry [chōk′cher′ē] *n.*, *pl.* **choke·cher·ries** **1** A wild North American cherry with a bitter taste. **2** The tree it grows on.

chok·er [chō′kər] *n.* **1** A necklace worn high on the neck. **2** A person or thing that chokes.

chol·er [kol′ər] *n.* An excitable temper; anger.

From the *HBJ School Dictionary,*
© 1977 by Harcourt Brace Jovanovich,
Inc. Reprinted by permission.

Building Skills

1. Sometimes a dictionary uses a word in a number of sentences to help you understand its different meanings. What does the word *choke* mean in the following sentences?
   a. Dorothy was so choked up with happiness, she could barely speak.
   b. "If you keep taking such big bites," said Linda, "you'll choke on your food."
   c. The drain was choked with leaves from the rainstorm.

2. Which of the following are definitions of the word *choice*? Which are examples of the way *choice* can be used in a sentence?
   a. an alternative
   b. the people's choice
   c. choice food
   d. the act of choosing; selection
   e. a large choice of articles

SKILLS LESSON

The Heart of the Matter . . .
Finding Topics and Stated Main Ideas

Suppose you're browsing in an old bookstore. A very dusty book catches your eye. The cover and title page have been torn off. Filled with curiosity, you pick up the book and look through the table of contents. The chapters read as follows:

1. The Cheetah
2. Dark Runner: The Panther
3. Lions
4. Bengal and Siberian Tigers
5. The Leopard

What do you think the book is about? In other words, what topic does the book deal with? Your first guess might be *animals*, but can you be more specific? Look at the list again. You will notice that all the animals are cats. They're not house cats, though. They're part of a large group often called the big cats. The topic of the book, then, is probably *big cats*.

A **topic** is the person, place, thing, activity, or event that a selection is about. You can use the topic of a selection as a clue to what you are about to read.

Finding Topics

The topic of this paragraph is *finding topics*. You knew this because you read the heading in boldface type. Every paragraph, however, doesn't begin with a heading. In order to find the topic you must carefully read all the sentences in the paragraph. Then you have to decide what they are about. What is the topic of the following paragraph?

I have a lucky rabbit's foot. Don't laugh. I'll bet you have a four-leaf clover or an old penny tucked away someplace. Most people just seem to grow up with the belief that an object, a rhyme, or an act like throwing salt over your shoulder can bring good luck. On the other hand, black cats, the number thirteen, and a broken mirror are said to bring bad luck. The fear of walking under a ladder has probably been around almost as long as the ladder itself.

Were you able to discover the topic of the paragraph? It can be stated in one word: *superstitions*. Even though the word *superstition* does not appear in the paragraph, all the sentences except the second one deal with superstitious beliefs.

Recognizing Stated Main Ideas

The topic of the paragraph below is *garlic*. But what does the paragraph say about garlic? The topic alone doesn't tell you anything about it. You have to read the paragraph to find out what it has to say about the topic.

Through the ages garlic has been thought to have amazing properties. In ancient Rome, workers ate garlic because they believed it would make them strong. Because garlic has such a powerful smell, people in the Middle Ages wore it around their necks, hoping to chase away evil spirits. It has been said that when garlic is crushed and rubbed on the skin, it can cure insect bites.

The paragraph tells you the following things about garlic:

1. Roman workers believed garlic would make them strong.
2. People in the Middle Ages thought garlic would chase away evil spirits.
3. Garlic is said to cure insect bites.

Which sentence in the paragraph sums up this information? In other words, which sentence states the main, or most important, idea? It is: "Through the ages garlic has been thought to have amazing properties." Notice that all the other sentences illustrate or support this idea.

To find the **main idea** of a paragraph, first find the topic. Then ask yourself, "What is the most important thing the author is saying about the topic?" Read the paragraph below. See if you can find the sentence that states the main idea.

What part of the United States is famous for its chili and tacos? Where could you feast on fried chicken and black-eyed peas? The regional cooking of the United States offers great variety. A trip to San Francisco would not be complete without a visit to Chinatown to taste the delights of Oriental cooking. Moving southeast from California, you will find the renowned steak-and-eggs breakfast of Texas and the creole dishes of New Orleans. Travel north to upper New England, and Maine lobsters await you.

What is the topic of the paragraph? Which of the following sentences states the main idea of the paragraph?

a. What part of the United States is famous for its chili and tacos?
b. The regional cooking of the United States offers great variety.
c. Travel north to upper New England, and Maine lobsters await you.

Notice that all the sentences in the paragraph support the statement: *The regional cooking of the United States offers great variety.*

Now look for the main idea in the following paragraph.

The tallest pyramid in the world is in the Sahara Desert in Africa. It was built in 2580 B.C. to honor an Egyptian Pharaoh. The Great Pyramid of Cheops stands 144 meters high. It is made entirely of stone blocks. Each one weighs almost 250 kilograms. Measurements have shown that the four corners of the pyramid are directly in line with the four cardinal points: north, south, east, and west. In ways that are unknown to us, the ancient Egyptians were able to raise the pyramid without the use of the wheel. The Great Pyramid of Cheops is a remarkable structure.

Which sentence states the main idea of the paragraph?

a. The tallest pyramid in the world is in the Sahara Desert in Africa.
b. In ways that are unknown to us, the ancient Egyptians were able to raise the pyramid without the use of the wheel.
c. The Great Pyramid of Cheops is a remarkable structure.

Notice that the main idea is stated in the last sentence of the paragraph. Where is the main idea in the paragraph about regional cooking? This should tell you that the main idea can be stated anywhere in the paragraph: in the beginning, middle, or end. Therefore, you have to think about all the facts before you can decide which sentence states the main idea.

How the Main Idea Relates to the Topic

Below you see a list of the three topics and main ideas from the paragraphs you have just read.

Topic	Main Idea
garlic	Through the ages garlic has been thought to have amazing properties.
regional cooking of the United States	The regional cooking of the United States offers great variety.
the Great Pyramid of Cheops	The Great Pyramid of Cheops is a remarkable structure.

It is easy to see that topics and main ideas are worded differently. The topic is usually stated in a word or phrase. The main idea tells you something about the topic. What does the main idea tell you about garlic? What does it tell you about the regional cooking of the United States?

Looking for topics and main ideas helps you focus on what you are reading. It directs your attention to the most important thing the writer is saying in the paragraph.

Try This

1. What is the difference between the topic and the main idea of a paragraph?
2. What is the main idea of the next to last paragraph above?

VOCABULARY STUDY

The "What-Do-You-Mean-by-That?" Game . . .
Multiple Meanings

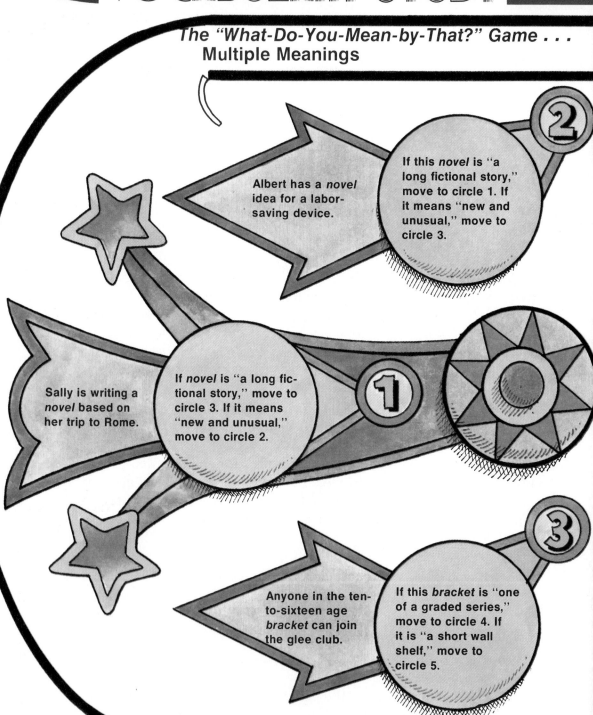

Albert has a *novel* idea for a labor-saving device.

② If this *novel* is "a long fictional story," move to circle 1. If it means "new and unusual," move to circle 3.

Sally is writing a *novel* based on her trip to Rome.

If *novel* is "a long fictional story," move to circle 3. If it means "new and unusual," move to circle 2.

①

Anyone in the ten-to-sixteen age *bracket* can join the glee club.

③ If this *bracket* is "one of a graded series," move to circle 4. If it is "a short wall shelf," move to circle 5.

74

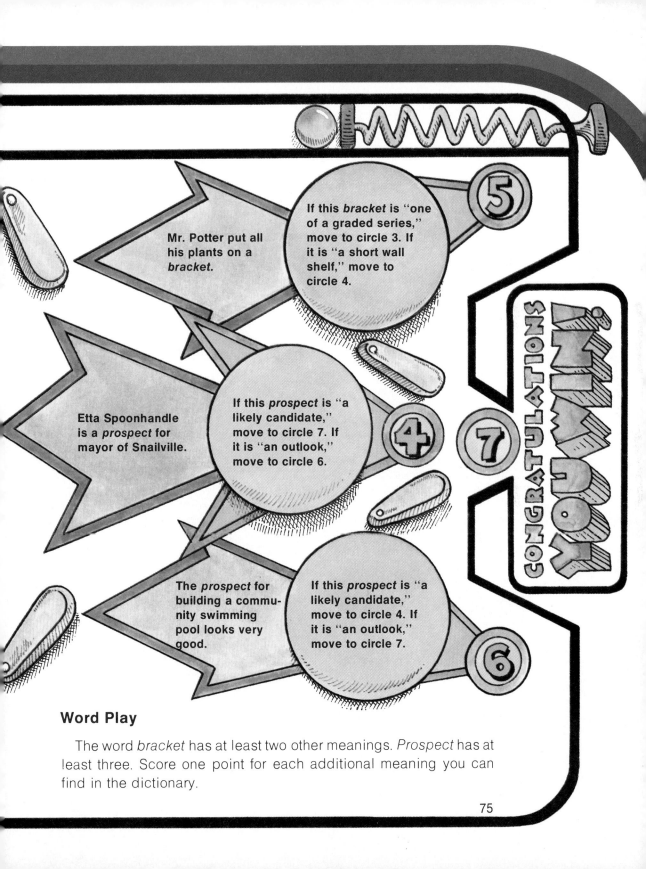

Mr. Potter put all his plants on a *bracket*.

If this *bracket* is "one of a graded series," move to circle 3. If it is "a short wall shelf," move to circle 4.

Etta Spoonhandle is a *prospect* for mayor of Snailville.

If this *prospect* is "a likely candidate," move to circle 7. If it is "an outlook," move to circle 6.

The *prospect* for building a community swimming pool looks very good.

If this *prospect* is "a likely candidate," move to circle 4. If it is "an outlook," move to circle 7.

CONGRATULATIONS YOU WON

Word Play

The word *bracket* has at least two other meanings. *Prospect* has at least three. Score one point for each additional meaning you can find in the dictionary.

As you read the following selection,
notice the topics of the paragraphs.

*People have been fascinated by
the mystery of the Loch Ness
monster for hundreds of years, and
scientists still keep up . . .*

The Search for
Nessie

by Mary Fiore

The clock in the 200-year-old
church tower near Foyers, Scotland,
had just struck nine on the morning
of April 23, 1960. For Tim Dinsdale, standing with his movie camera on the shore of Loch Ness, it was
the most exciting hour of the most
important day in his life. Only a
few seconds before, Dinsdale had
sighted the legendary Loch Ness
monster. Now he was filming it in
the water.

77

The excitement was almost too much to bear. Tim was capturing a legend on film — a legend that had begun in the sixth century. His film would be the first proof that there really is an unknown creature living in the *loch* (the Gaelic word for *lake*) in northern Scotland.

Suddenly, the monster sank beneath the water. Dinsdale waited a few moments to be sure the creature would not surface again. Then he jumped into his car and drove off to have the film processed.

Those few moments of film changed Dinsdale's way of life. It also started the hunt for the creature that has captured the imagination of the world. The film was responsible for setting up the Loch Ness Phenomena Investigation Bureau in 1961. The bureau acts as a conductor for all searches and keeps track of the growing list of sightings.

The Loch Ness monster is said to have been first sighted in the sixth century. Since then, there have been more than 3,000 reported sightings of "Nessie," as the monster is called. People who have seen it describe it as an ugly, shy, greenish-blackish creature, from five to sixteen feet long and from one to five feet wide. It is said to have a snakelike head and a long neck sticking out from a wide, flat body. The body, itself, is reported to have from one to seven camel-like humps.

So far, Nessie has escaped all the research teams. In 1971, I was a member of such a team. We set up offices in Drumnadrochit, a town near Loch Ness. For two weeks we tried to find Nessie — or at least to find out more about it.

Loch Ness is spectacular. It is one mile wide and has an average depth of 700 feet. In some places, the depth is more than 1,000 feet, greater than the height of a 90-story building. The lake is part of a 100-mile crack in the earth running north and south through the Scottish Highlands. It is surrounded by cliffs and hills. From the high roads the water looks blue and clear. From lakeside, it is neither. The water is so dark that divers have trouble seeing anything that is more than twenty feet deep. The icy water can be mirror-smooth. But it can also splash up eight-foot waves at a moment's notice.

Scientists believe that between 5,000 to 10,000 years ago, Loch Ness was part of the North Sea. A change in sea level due to melting at the end of the Ice Age caused a thin strip of land to form. This land separated the lake from the sea. As a result, many creatures were trapped in the lake. Scientists believe their descendants may still be there today. Thus, the Loch Ness monster is most likely not one, but a family of creatures — if it does exist at all.

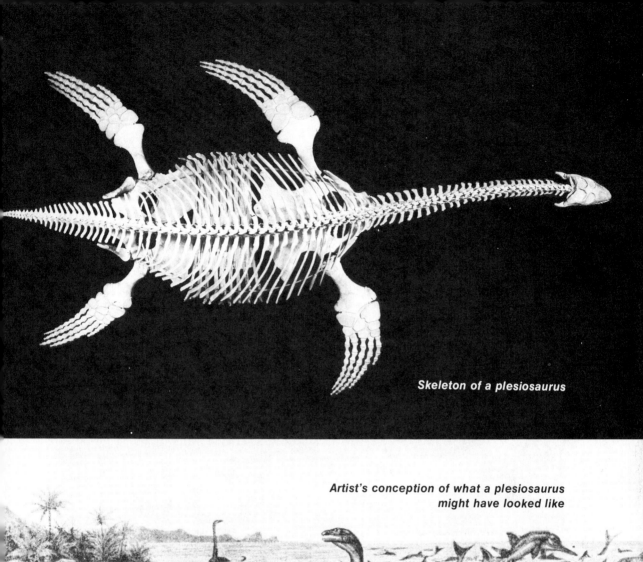

Skeleton of a plesiosaurus

Artist's conception of what a plesiosaurus
might have looked like

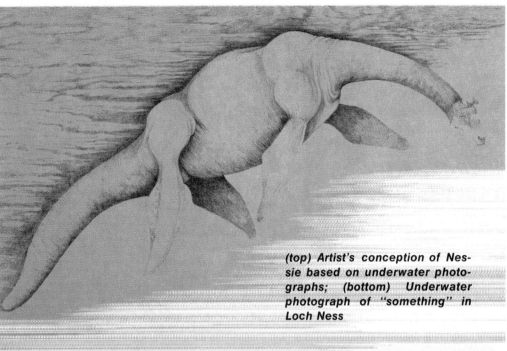

(top) Artist's conception of Nessie based on underwater photographs; (bottom) Underwater photograph of "something" in Loch Ness

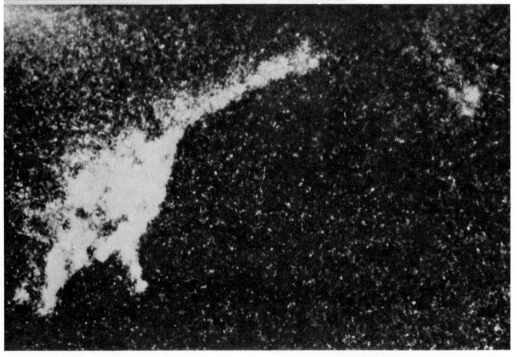

Every day our group would report to Temple Pier, the lakeside office of the Underwater Division of the Loch Ness Phenomena Investigation Bureau. The bureau records only those sightings it feels are without question. More sightings are rejected than accepted. Those made thirty minutes before or after a boat passes are not accepted. The lake is so smooth at times that a ship's wake can ripple for a full half hour after the vessel has passed. The bureau does not want to mistake a ship's wake for Nessie.

All the workers at the bureau are serious about finding Nessie. Perhaps the most serious is Tim Dinsdale. He gave up a job with a company that makes airplane engines to head the Surface (picture-taking) Division. This, of course, was after he took his eye-opening film of "something" swimming in the lake.

Dinsdale's film shows a creature with its head and neck sticking up about six feet above the water. It is swimming away from where Dinsdale was standing. In the film a bus can be seen on the opposite shore. The monster, perhaps scared by the bus motor, turned and swam back toward Dinsdale. Then it ducked under the water, leaving only a foamy wake.

The bureau's Underwater Division was headed by electrical engineer and diver Robert Love. While I was there, Love and a group of divers from Plymouth, England, were trying to raise the wreck of a 100-year-old ship.

One day I was at the pier when the divers surfaced. When we saw the first diver we sensed something had happened. He tore the oxygen hose from his mouth and yelled, "I stepped on something!" Seconds later the other diver bobbed to the surface and shouted the same thing.

"What do you think you stepped on?" I asked.

"I don't know," one diver answered. "But whatever it was, it was big!"

A group of scientists from Massachusetts was at the pier with sonar equipment for underwater tracking. As I was talking to the divers, one of the scientists rushed up and asked if they had seen anything. The sonar, he said, had picked up something big in the area.

Could the divers have brushed against each other or against the mast of the ship? They felt they were too far apart to have hit each other. They also thought it unlikely that they had both hit the mast. "I'd like to think it was Nessie," said one of the divers. "Then again, I'm not so sure. I've got to go down again tomorrow."

Each diver carried a knife in a case below his right knee. A knife

What was swimming in Loch Ness? Just visible are several "humps" breaking the surface of the water.

would probably not be used on Nessie unless it were a matter of life or death. The creature is protected by British law. Both a fine and a possible prison term have been set for anyone who harms it. This is to keep cranks from poisoning the water or throwing in dynamite — both pretty drastic ways to find Nessie. There is a reward for finding Nessie. It can only be paid, however, if the creature is found alive and well.

Among our own group's tools, one of the most interesting was a camera for taking pictures in the dark. We brought it along because 80 percent of all sightings of Nessie have taken place at or just before dawn.

Each morning at four, two members of our group made a sonar-boat run of the lake. The night was particularly chilly when my turn came. During the run, I sat in the cabin and watched the sonar screen. The screen shows every-

thing in its path, from a small fish to caves along the shoreline. Studies had shown that whenever Nessie was picked up on the screen, all fish in the area disappeared. Whether they were frightened or eaten by Nessie remains to be seen. When Nessie disappeared from the screen, it was thought to have swum into a cave.

We had no luck on my run. The following night, two team members were waiting on board the boat. Suddenly one of the underwater lights at the pier began to do a strange dance. Down, down the light went, then up, as if it were caught on something that was trying to shake it loose. Finally, the light came loose and floated to the surface. It had been ripped from its bracket. Had it been caught on Nessie? The two men on the run were certain it had.

Just what is Nessie? There are several ideas. Bob Love believes that Nessie is a very large eel. Eels can fold up like an accordion. This could account for the camellike humps. Another novel idea is that Nessie is a meat-eating, sea going mammal sometimes called a cowfish. A third idea is that Nessie is a plesiosaur, a large fish-eating reptile that lived about 65 million years ago and which should be extinct. However, a large living fish from about the same time was discovered in 1947.

Why hasn't anyone found Nessie? One reason is that there is not enough money. The bureau has had to use wits in place of dollars to make its own tools and underwater flash cameras. But, in November 1971, scientists from London University said they had seen a family of monsters like Nessie in Loch Morar, the deepest lake in Britain. Shortly after the Morar sightings, the Loch Ness Phenomena Investigation Bureau received more money. It is now searching with better tools.

Nessie itself may help to solve the mystery. A new power plant at the village of Foyers has forced Nessie to give up its favorite spot in the lake. The creature now goes to Urquhart Bay, six miles north of Foyers, where it has been seen surfacing time and again.

So chances of solving the centuries-old mystery are better than ever. All who have helped in the search know there is some creature in Loch Ness. We would love to be there when it is finally found.

Understanding What You've Read

1. Why was the film made by Tim Dinsdale considered important?
2. What are some of the ways investigators are trying to prove Nessie's existence?
3. Why is the existence of Nessie still only a theory and not a fact?

Applying the Skills Lesson

1. What is the topic of the last paragraph on page 78?
2. Find the paragraphs that deal with the following topics:
   a. a description of Loch Ness
   b. a description of Nessie
   c. the job of the Loch Ness Phenomena Investigation Bureau

TEXTBOOK STUDY

Finding Topics and Stated Main Ideas

You've learned that most paragraphs have a topic and a main idea. The main idea is the most important thing that the author says about the topic. Read the following textbook selection. Use the sidenotes to help you find the topics and main ideas.

Finding Topics in Science

This sentence states the main idea of the paragraph. What is the topic?

Blood clots are produced by both chemical and physical changes in the blood. The clotting of blood involves bodies called *platelets*. Platelets are irregularly shaped, colorless bodies. They are much smaller than red blood cells. A blood protein called *fibrinogen*, the mineral calcium, and vitamin K are also involved in the clotting of blood.

The topic of this paragraph is how blood clots form. Which sentence helps you find the topic?

How does a blood clot form? As blood escapes from a blood vessel, the platelets disintegrate. They release a substance which causes changes in fibrinogen. As a result, *fibrin* forms. Fibrin is insoluble microscopic threads. These threads form a mesh, or net, which traps blood cells among its fibers. This forms a clot which prevents further bleeding. As the clot dries, it forms a scab. Both vitamin K and calcium must be present for blood to clot. Therefore, a deficiency of vitamin K or calcium in the diet can be harmful. Lack of vitamin K or calcium reduces the rate at which blood clots.

How do these sentences relate to the topic of the paragraph?

Blood clots can occur inside the body as well as on the skin. For example, a black-and-blue mark that forms under a

bruise is caused by a blood clot. Sometimes a blood clot forms inside a blood
vessel. One kind of heart attack is caused
by a blood clot in a coronary artery.

— Focus on Life Science
Charles E. Merrill

Building Skills

1. Why do you think the words *blood clots* at the beginning of the
   selection are printed in boldface type?
2. Which of the following states the topic of the last paragraph in
   the selection?
   a. the causes of heart attacks
   b. where blood clots form
   c. bruises

Finding Stated Main Ideas in Social Studies

The following textbook excerpt is not accompanied by sidenotes. As you read, look for the topics and stated main ideas. Then
answer the questions that follow.

Cool Clear Water

The first summer rainfall in the Kalahari
is the biggest event of the year. Everyone
looks forward to it. Wild fruit becomes
available and helps the Bushmen build
up their ever-scanty food supply. But,
most of all, rain means that the dry salt
pans soak in the water. The misery of
looking for water and finding none is
past.

Water is so valued here that Bushmen
put it in ostrich eggs, which they fill

through a small hole. They hide these eggs in the sand. They leave nothing to mark the spot, but they know where the eggs are. The Bushmen have many ways of finding water. When they know of a place, they will put a long hollow reed down into the dry ground and suck up the water. These holes are called "sip water" holes. The water in these areas would be lost by digging.

Because they cannot farm with such a water supply, the Bushmen are nomadic hunters and gatherers. When the game in the area disappear, they move on. When they search for water, the Bushmen follow the antelope. When they are hungry, they follow the vulture.

— Sources of Identity
Harcourt Brace Jovanovich

Building Skills

1. What is the main idea of the first paragraph in the preceding selection? What details support the main idea?
2. How are the main ideas of the three paragraphs related? What clue does the heading of the selection give you?

SKILLS LESSON

Figure It Out . . . **Finding Unstated Main Ideas and Recognizing Details**

Like the scientists in this cartoon, there are times when you have to study the details in order to figure out what something is all about. In many paragraphs the main idea is not stated in one of the sentences. To find the main idea, first find the topic of the paragraph. Then ask yourself: "What is the author saying about the topic? What is the most important idea that ties all the sentences together?"

Read the following paragraph. What is the main idea?

Airplane travel may be fast and comfortable, but it can only be used for long distances. Walking, however, is perfect for a short trip. A car may be convenient, but it's expensive. Walking or hiking costs only the price of a pair of shoes. Also, you'll never find yourself stuck in a traffic jam. Because trains run along certain routes, they don't always go where you want to go. Your feet can take you anywhere. Walking is good exercise and a chance to take a good look at the world around you.

What is the topic of the paragraph above? The paragraph talks about different kinds of travel, but only one kind, walking, is dealt with throughout the paragraph. Now, what is the author saying about walking? Notice that every sentence either states the disadvantages of another means of travel or shows the benefits of walking. So the main idea of the paragraph is: *Walking is a good means of travel.* Can you think of another way to state the main idea?

Finding the Main Idea from Supporting Details

In a well-written paragraph, the main idea is supported by details. A **detail** is a phrase or sentence that supplies information about the main idea. Read the following paragraph carefully. Look for the main idea. Pay close attention to the supporting details.

In Hunza, Pakistan, in the Himalaya Mountains, the average person lives to the age of ninety. It is not unusual to find hundred-year-old people still doing the same kinds of work they have always done. One woman from a town in the Caucasus Mountains (U.S.S.R.) was said to have been 168 at the time of her death. Vilcabamba, Ecuador, is 1,600 meters above sea level. The people are quite healthy and do not often need a doctor. Twice as many Vilcabambans as North Americans live past a century.

In order to state the main idea—*long life spans have been found in many mountainous places*—you would have to read the paragraph and find the supporting details. Which details tell you about different places in the world? Which details add to the idea that the different places have mountains? Notice that all the details support the main idea.

Read the paragraph below and look for the main idea.

Early in his career, Jules Léotard, a French circus performer, found his costumes too confining. So he made a one-piece elastic garment that became known as the *leotard*. The fourth Earl of Sandwich once asked his servants to bring him cold roast beef between two pieces of toasted bread. The first *sandwich* was born! The *zeppelin*, or lighter-than-air ship, was named after its designer, Count Ferdinand von Zeppelin. In 1893, George Washington Gale Ferris set out to build the largest wheel in the world. Today at fairs and carnivals you can see examples of the ride that now bears his name.

Which of the sentences below states the main idea of the paragraph you just read?

a. Europeans are great inventors.
b. People's names are the origin of many English words.
c. Given enough time, people will find solutions to their problems.

What Details Are Important?

Suppose your purpose in reading the paragraph above was to find out where the word *leotard* came from. Which details would be important? Only the first two sentences give you information about the word *leotard*. All the other details, therefore, are unimportant to your purpose. As you read, you won't always be interested in all the details. The details that relate to your purpose are the details that are important to you.

As you read the following paragraph, look for the details that describe Banneker's connection with Thomas Jefferson.

Benjamin Banneker (1731–1806) was an eighteenth-century scholar and scientist. He made many important contributions to America. Despite his limited opportunity for education, he became a farmer, writer, astronomer, mathematician, and inventor. He wrote an almanac and made clocks. He also worked as a surveyor and helped lay out the boundaries of the District of Columbia. Banneker was influential in helping people in high governmental posts to become aware of the need to abolish slavery. Thomas Jefferson was impressed by Banneker's talents. First he sent a copy of Banneker's almanac to the Royal Academy of Sciences in Paris. He then recommended Banneker to a governmental surveying position.

Adapted from *The World Book Encyclopedia.* © 1975 Field Enterprises Educational Corporation.

Notice it is only the details in the last two sentences that describe Banneker's connection with Jefferson. What details would be important if you were looking for information on these two topics: *Banneker's work for the abolition of slavery* and *Banneker's work as a surveyor?*

Read the paragraph that follows. Which detail tells you what hieroglyphics on a doorway might have meant?

A *hieroglyphic* is a picture or a symbol, often carved in stone, that stands for a word or sound. Many ancient peoples used hieroglyphics in the same way we use our alphabet. They recorded all kinds of events, such as a good harvest or the crowning of a new king. Hieroglyphics found on the doorway of a house could have identified the owner. When written on tomb walls, they usually told a story of the dead person's life, death, and funeral.

The detail that tells you what hieroglyphics on a doorway might have meant is stated in the fourth sentence: "Hieroglyphics found on the doorway of a house could have identified the owner."

Try This

1. Find the main idea of the paragraph on hieroglyphics above.
2. What details support the main idea in the paragraph on Banneker?
3. What details in the last paragraph on page 89 explain the origin of the word *sandwich?*

91

The Contest . . . Prefixes and Suffixes

"Step right up, folks, and Marcos the Magician will surprise you with his prefix tricks!"

"But," said Wilma the Wizard, "I will work wonders with suffixes!"

"Is that so?" said Marcos. "Well, I challenge you to a contest. Suppose we start with the word *history*."

"*History,*" cried Wilma, "is 'recorded events of the past.' Add the suffix *-ic*, meaning 'relating to,' and you get *historic*, 'relating to history.' "

"Hold on," said Marcos. "I can add the prefix *pre-*, meaning 'before,' and come up with *prehistoric*, 'relating to the time before recorded history.' "

"What about *expense*?" someone yelled.

"*Expense* means 'cost,' " said Wilma. "Take off the last *e*, add the suffix *-ive*, and you have *expensive*, 'having a high cost.' " Wilma grinned proudly.

"Don't get your hopes up," said Marcos, glancing at the scoreboard. "The prefix *in-* can mean 'not.' That makes the word *inexpensive*, 'not having a high cost'!"

"*Act,*" said a little girl in the front row.

"That's easy," said Wilma. "The suffix -ion means 'the result of a process.' Therefore, an action is 'the result of an act'! It's up to you, Marcos."

"I know. I'm thinking."

"How about the prefix re-, meaning 'against'?" suggested Wilma. "A reaction is 'an act done in response to or against another act'!"

"Sure, sure," said Marcos. "But the prefix re- also means 'again,' as in the word REMATCH!"

Word Play

How many words can you make by adding the prefixes and/or suffixes on this page to the root words *spell*, *hero*, *place*, *correct*, and *test*?

93

THE

Look for the details to help you find the main ideas of the paragraphs in this selection.

WARRIOR ANTS

by Dee Brown

Arthur Loveridge's battle began one July morning in
Tanzania, Africa. At about eight o'clock Loveridge
stepped outside his house and saw thousands of flying
beetles. They seemed to fill the air like a dark cloud. As a
naturalist, Loveridge was surprised to see fierce, red ants
attached to many of the beetles, biting their hind legs.

Later, Loveridge discovered about half a dozen long
lines of these ants. They marched across the ground and
disappeared into cracks at the base of the house. All
along the lines of march, groups of ants attacked crickets
and grasshoppers. They slashed off the grasshoppers'
legs and tore at them with large, powerful jaws. From his
knowledge of insects, Loveridge guessed he was being invaded by a small army of driver ants.

When Loveridge went back inside, he was surprised to find drivers roaming about his kitchen in search of household prey. His first concern was his collection of butterflies, birds, tortoises, and crocodiles. He had spent months gathering them. He soaked balls of paper in a special acid and stuffed them into the cracks where the ants were entering. Then he swept out the drivers that had already entered his kitchen. He piled grass over the heap of ants, poured kerosene over the grass, and set it on fire. Within fifteen minutes, all that remained were a few scattered ants.

Loveridge relaxed. He believed he had won the battle. But the main body of driver ants usually marches after dark. Loveridge was in for another attack.

The Second Army

It was nine o'clock in the evening. Loveridge was reading. Suddenly, he heard faint noises. At first he thought nothing of it. When he went to his bedroom later, however, he was shocked by what he saw. The walls were a moving mass of driver ants. They covered everything—the bookcase, the shelves, the chest of drawers.

Loveridge soon discovered that this second army of drivers was after plant beetles. The beetles had flown into his bedroom to get away from the drivers. Plant bugs give off a powerful smell when they are annoyed. Usually this smell saves them from attack. But to the drivers it was a challenge.

For two days Loveridge battled the drivers. He was helped by several Africans. Together they shoveled hot ashes into the drivers' holes. They set out meat as bait. When the meat was covered with ants, Loveridge drowned the ants in oil and water. He wrote later, "We destroyed several thousand in a few minutes with the greatest of ease."

At the end of the second day, the drivers appeared to be losing the battle. Loveridge decided he could safely return to sleeping in his bedroom. First, however, he filled pans with water and placed one pan under each leg of his bed. He also covered the bed with a mosquito net.

The Attack Strengthens

Loveridge was awakened at about two-thirty in the morning. A crocodile was wildly splashing in its pen. Most of the animals had been moved outside the day before, but Loveridge thought the crocodiles could protect themselves. The tortoises had also been left in their pen.

Loveridge lifted the mosquito net and reached for his lamp. An ant was on the lamp handle. Loveridge turned up the light and saw that the walls and floors were crawling with driver ants. His pillow was covered. Two single lines of ants—one outside and one inside—were moving up the mosquito net.

Loveridge turned up the mattress to tuck the net in further. He managed to stop the inside stream. He started to put on his slippers and saw that they were covered with ants. He checked the pans of water under the legs of his bed. A living bridge of ants stretched across one of them. This was how the other ants were getting to the bed. Loveridge quickly unscrewed the cap of the lamp and splashed enough oil on the bridge to cause it to fall. A thin coat of oil formed on the water beneath.

After treating the other pans in the same way, Loveridge hurried to look after his young crocodiles. He found one of the cages filled with driver ants. The crocodile inside was turning round and round in the water. It flipped from back to belly and thrashed with its tail. The edges of the pen were lined with ants. They threw themselves upon the crocodile whenever its struggles brought it near one of the sides.

Loveridge reached one arm inside the cage. A shower of drivers leaped upon it. He was able to grab the crocodile's tail, lift the reptile out, and toss it to what he thought was safety. At once a swarm of ants circled the crocodile. Again, Loveridge hurried to its aid. He moved the crocodile to a drinking tank some distance away. When he returned to the cage, he discovered the other crocodile had already been killed by the drivers.

Just then, Loveridge heard an uproar in the tortoise pen. "The ground that lay between me and the tortoises," he wrote in his diary, "was so alive with drivers that I turned back." He thought the tortoises probably had crawled under the rocks in their pen. He would not be able to get to them anyway.

The End of the War

So far the battle had lasted two days and nights.
Loveridge had grown used to living with the warrior ants.
He decided to return to his bedroom and seek shelter
under his mosquito net. He tore off all the bedding that
might be hiding his enemies. As he sat in the center of his
bed beneath the net, he thought over the situation.

A column of ants was wandering to and fro on the top
of the net. Twenty or thirty more crawled around the
sides. "I picked these off one by one," wrote Loveridge,
"killing them as I did so. I got rid of the column on the
ceiling of the net and shook off the ones on the outside."

At dawn Loveridge crept from his mosquito netting.
He hurried outside and called his helpers. He wanted to
begin an attack before daybreak, when the drivers
would return to their holes. The meat baits placed in
the yard the evening before were crawling with ants.
Loveridge wrote, "It is difficult for one who has never
seen drivers to conceive of the way in which they pile
themselves one upon another." Loveridge dropped the

baits into oil and water. Then he set fire to the hay in the crocodile's cage, which was a moving mass of ants.

Loveridge was relieved to find all of his tortoises alive, though some were suffering badly. For the first time, Loveridge and his frightened helpers wondered if they should leave while they still had the chance. The ant army had stopped in the grass some thirty feet from the cleared yard. Their whispering movement sounded across the deepening dusk.

Loveridge waited, but the ants never came any closer. Had these new armies received a message from the drivers who had been battling Loveridge for days? Had there been a council of war? Had the final battle proved so deadly that the soldier leaders decided to turn back? No one will ever know. But when Arthur Loveridge entered his house late that night, he didn't find a single driver ant. And the next morning, the armies of warrior ants had vanished from the lonely African landscape.

Understanding What You've Read

1. How did Loveridge first discover he was being attacked by an army of ants?
2. In what ways did Loveridge try to fight off the driver ants?
3. Arthur Loveridge was a naturalist—a person who studies plants and animals. How did his background affect the way he dealt with the ants?

Applying the Skills Lesson

1. Find the main idea in the first paragraph on page 96. What details support this idea?
2. Find the details from the third paragraph on page 100 that support the idea, *Loveridge worked hard to save one of his crocodiles.*

TEXTBOOK STUDY

Finding Unstated Main Ideas and Recognizing Details

Details can be important or unimportant to you, depending on your purpose for reading. As you read the following textbook selection, the sidenotes will help you recognize the details you need to solve the problems.

Recognizing Important and Unimportant Details in Mathematics

Which details do you need to solve the problem?

1. Two hundred adults and three hundred students attended a school play at Vaux Junior High School. Adult tickets cost $1.50 and student tickets cost $1.25. How much money was collected in ticket sales? The seventh-grade class that performed the play had $285.50 in expenses. How much profit did the class make?

2. June averaged 12.7 points per game in 20 basketball games. How many points did she score in all?

3. Harold can read newspapers at the rate of 475 words per minute. How many words could he read in an hour?

Why are these details important? How will they affect your answer?

4. In a 24-hour automobile race, one team of drivers averaged 172.34 miles per hour for the first 20 hours. Then they were forced out of the race by mechanical problems. How far had they driven?

5. Pressure is force per unit of area. A submerged diver is under a pressure of 99.88 grams per square centimeter per meter of depth. That is, a diver 2 meters under the surface is under a pressure of 199.76 grams per square centimeter. What

This detail helps you figure out how to do the problem.

104

is the pressure on a diver at 30 meters?

6. Michael sells popcorn in the theater lobby for 50¢ and 75¢ with butter. How much did he make on Sunday when he sold 102 boxes, 64 of them with butter?

Why must you know both prices to solve the problem?

—Heath Mathematics
D. C. Heath

Building Skills

1. Problem number 4 has a sentence with an unimportant detail. Which detail is it?
2. Problem number 1 asks two questions. Which detail from the first question do you need to solve the second question?

Recognizing Main Ideas and Details in Social Studies

There are no sidenotes accompanying this textbook excerpt. As you read, look for the main ideas and details. Then answer the questions that follow.

Suppose that twenty young people about your age found themselves stranded on a tropical island in a remote area of the South Pacific Ocean. Several of the young people have explored their new environment already. They have just returned to report to the group that there is no sign of human life anywhere on the island. All anyone can see are palm trees, wilderness, and the wide blue ocean beyond. Everyone realizes that the group is completely on its own.

"We've got to find some food and fresh water," someone says as soon as everyone is gathered together. Others disagree. "We've got to build some shelters to live

105

in first." Still others claim that being rescued is more important, and that everyone should help build a huge bonfire to signal any passing boats or airplanes. "Get sticks and dry stuff. Hurry!" they shout.

— Sources of Identity
Harcourt Brace Jovanovich

Building Skills

1. What details in the first paragraph of this selection describe the setting?
2. Which of the following states the main idea of the second paragraph?
   a. These people don't agree on how to deal with their problem.
   b. Food and water are more important than shelter.
   c. The people who are stranded on the island should build a fire to signal for help.

SKILLS LESSON

Beginnings, Middles, Ends . . .
Recognizing Different Kinds of Paragraphs

You have seen how details in a paragraph relate to each other and to the topic. Different kinds of paragraphs also work together to introduce, make transitions between, develop, and summarize the ideas of a topic. Recognizing the different kinds of paragraphs in a selection will help you to understand what you are reading.

Paragraphs That Introduce

An **introductory paragraph** is easy to find. It often comes first in a section or chapter. The following is the first paragraph from a chapter in a history book. What can you tell about introductory paragraphs from this example?

Although he had very little schooling, Alexandre Dumas became one of France's greatest writers. He was born in 1802, the son of a general in the French Revolution and a woman from Santo Domingo. When Dumas was twenty, he set out to make his fortune in Paris with only fifty-three francs in his pocket.

Based on the information in the paragraph, you can expect the chapter to be about the life and works of Alexandre Dumas. Thus, an introductory paragraph can state the topic of the entire selection.

Sometimes, however, introductory paragraphs look like this:

Can you remember your dreams? Are your dreams in color? Do you see familiar people and places in your dreams? Do you wake up after a dream feeling excited or frightened or very happy?

What is the topic of the selection introduced by this paragraph? Even though the writer uses questions instead of statements, you can tell that the topic is *dreams*. What is the main idea of the paragraph? Is it stated or unstated? What do the questions tell you about the kinds of information in the selection?

Read the introductory paragraph below. What do you think the selection that follows it will be about?

There was nothing but water for miles around us. We could not see the smallest piece of land anywhere. How lonely we all felt as the boat rocked gently on the rising and falling waves.

The selection could deal with crossing the Atlantic or fishing in the ocean. It might be about loneliness, or even pirates. In the above example, the introductory paragraph does not give you any clue about the topic of the selection. Instead, the author has used the introductory paragraph to get your attention and to set the scene.

Paragraphs That Develop

A **developmental paragraph** further explains an idea that was introduced in the paragraph that came before it. A developmental paragraph adds more information by using examples or descriptive details.

Read the paragraphs below about Wilma Rudolph.

The day Wilma Rudolph, a young woman from Tennessee, made the 1960 Summer Olympic team, her hopes were high. She wanted a medal. When the games were over, Wilma had more than a medal. Once a cripple, she had become the first American woman to earn three gold medals in track.

When Wilma was a child, an illness kept her in bed for many months. When she recovered, the doctors told her there was little chance she would ever walk again. But giving up was not Wilma's style. She and her family would not accept the facts. They decided to change them.

Which idea presented in the first paragraph is developed in the second paragraph? The first paragraph states that Wilma was once a cripple. The second paragraph explains how she became crippled. Which sentences supply this information?

Now read the third paragraph:

Each week Wilma went to a doctor for therapy on her legs. Her family helped at home with heat treatments and special exercises. Wilma wore special shoes to strengthen her feet.

Which idea introduced in the second paragraph is developed in the third paragraph?

Paragraphs That Make Transitions

Sometimes a paragraph is needed within a selection to make a transition between ideas or to connect more than one idea. Thus, a **transition paragraph** does not have a topic or a main idea. It often has a key word or phrase that tells you the paragraph is linking two ideas. Clues such as *As a result, Therefore, As you can see,* and *Thus* often begin a transition paragraph.

Read the paragraph that follows. What two ideas does it connect?

Thus, we see how a hurricane forms over a large body of water. Now let's look at what happens when the hurricane moves toward a land mass.

Does the transition paragraph give new information? Notice that the first sentence refers to something that has already been discussed in one or more earlier paragraphs. What topic was discussed in the passage that came before the transition paragraph? Notice, too, that the transition paragraph gives a hint about the information that follows. What will probably be discussed in the paragraphs that come after the transition paragraph?

Paragraphs That Summarize

Read the **summary paragraph** below.

We have seen many ways in which people throughout history have tried to measure the passing of time. The modern atomic clock is a far cry from the sundial, the hourglass, and the water clock. But the idea of counting minutes and hours has not changed. People were, and perhaps always will be, interested in the flow of time.

Based on the information in the paragraph above, what topics do you think the selection is about? What ways of measuring time were discussed? What is the purpose of the summary paragraph?

Like many transition paragraphs, summary paragraphs often begin with a key word or phrase. Some examples are: *In conclusion, As we have noted, To review,* and *We have seen that.* The summary paragraph is one of the most important paragraphs in a selection. It brings together or reviews the most important ideas in the selection.

Try This

1. Why is the last paragraph above a developmental paragraph?
2. What is the function of an introductory paragraph?
3. What is the function of a summary paragraph? Why do you think the summary paragraph often comes at the end of a selection?
4. Read the sentences below. In what kind of paragraph are you most likely to find each of the following?
   a. Another example of a bird that cannot fly is the penguin.
   b. As you have seen, there were several major events that led to the American Revolutionary War. But there were also two other situations that indirectly influenced the colonists' decision to fight.
   c. Let us now review the most important ideas presented in this article.

VOCABULARY STUDY

Say Something in Scientific . . .
Greek and Latin Roots

Yes, it's true, America! Now *you* can speak the fabulous language of Scientific! Your very first lesson teaches you that some English words get their meanings from Greek and Latin words. In no time at all you'll be saying scientific words like *anthropologist, hieroglyphic,* and *artifact.* Listen to these unrehearsed interviews:

Ms. L.: My aunt is an anthropologist. Before I learned to speak Scientific, I didn't know what she did. Now I know that the Latin *anthropo* means "human being." *Logy* is Greek and means "the study of." So an *anthropologist* studies the growth and development of human beings.

112

Robin M.: Since I took the course in Scientific, I'm chock-full of unusual words. Last week I said *hieroglyphic* at a party, and everyone asked for my autograph. I explained that the Greek *hiero* means "sacred." *Glyphein* is also Greek and means "to carve." Hieroglyphic writing uses pictures to stand for ideas. The ancients usually carved hieroglyphics on stone.

The W. Family: Until we took the course in Scientific, we made spoons. Now we make artifacts. The School of Scientific Language taught us that the Latin *arte* means "by skill." *Factum* means "thing made." So an *artifact* is "a simple object—usually a tool or ornament—that has been made with great skill." Just look at our spoons . . . I mean artifacts . . . now!

Word Play

Match each Latin or Greek word with its correct meaning.

anthropo	sacred
arte	thing made
factum	human being
glyphein	by skill
hiero	the study of
logy	to carve

As you read, look for the paragraphs that develop the various ideas presented in the selection.

Now that we have information about the possibilities of life on other planets, some people are taking a closer look at . . .

The Case of the UFO's

by Andrea Balchan

It was June 24, 1947. Kenneth Arnold was flying his plane in the area of Mount Rainier, Washington. At about two o'clock in the afternoon, the sky was sunny and clear. Arnold was looking out the window, enjoying the view. Suddenly, he says, he saw a bright flash on the wing tip. About twenty-five miles away, nine shining objects seemed to be skipping across the sky like stones across a pond. Each of the objects appeared to be about the size of a small plane. They flew together, turning at the same time,

114

almost as if linked by an invisible chain. They darted around the mountain peaks. They dipped up and down, shining brightly in the sun.

At first, Arnold thought the objects might be some kind of jet airplane. But he couldn't see any tails on them, and they weren't moving the way planes move. In fact, they didn't look like anything Arnold had ever seen before. He reported his strange experience to the press and the U.S. Air Force. The press called them "flying saucers."

Since Kenneth Arnold's experience in 1947, people in South America, Europe, Asia, and different parts of the United States have reported sighting unidentified flying objects, or UFO's. Flying objects of many different shapes and sizes have been described. Many were said to be "very bright" objects that moved and sometimes turned "very fast." Some were high in the sky. Others seemed to float in the air just above the ground. Several witnesses claimed to have been able to photograph the UFO's.

Some UFO's Identified

In 1947, the U.S. Air Force organized Project Blue Book. A small group of people were assigned to record all UFO reports and conduct investigations to gather as much information as they could. Project Blue Book checked out thousands of UFO sightings. In most cases, the objects could be identified.

On one occasion, several people in six Midwestern states saw flaming objects shoot through the sky. Later, a chunk of metal was discovered half buried in a street in Wisconsin. Scientists identified it as a piece from the Soviet satellite *Sputnik IV*, which had broken apart in space and burned as it reentered the earth's atmosphere.

Many UFO's were discovered to be *meteors*. These are huge hunks of rock or metal that enter the earth's atmosphere from space. Others turned out to be weather balloons, comets, and the planet Venus, which at certain times of the year is very bright.

Quite often people have simply been fooled by *mirages*—tricks played on the eyes by odd conditions in the atmosphere. For example, a faraway mountain peak can seem to be floating in midair. This occurs when cold air near the ground has a layer of warmer air above it. The cold air is denser, or more closely packed, than the warmer air. As light strikes the cooler air, it is bent, and the top of the mountain looks higher in the sky than it really is.

Scientists have explained a great number of UFO's as *swamp gas*. When swamp weeds and grasses rot, they produce a gas that is often trapped in the frozen swamp during the winter. In the spring, when the ground begins to thaw, the gas is released. It pops and cracks as it leaves the ground. Sometimes it shimmers and glows in colorful patterns. Scientists believe that it is this light that is often mistaken for a UFO.

These are only a few explanations for UFO's. The list includes such familiar things as airplanes and even birds! But several hundred of the UFO's reported to the Air Force have still not been explained. About a quarter of these reports were impossible to check without more information. Other UFO's, however, were described in detail by people who said they had time to watch them for many minutes.

Three photographs of UFO's; two are fakes, one is unexplained. (top) Cloud formations; (bottom right) A cut-out drawing superimposed on a photograph; (bottom left) The real thing?

(top left) These unexplained objects were visible for several minutes; (top right) UFO over California — the object was traveling very fast when the picture was taken; (bottom) After carefully studying these objects, the Air Force announced they were "natural phenomena."

Scientists Don't Agree on UFO's

Some years ago, the Air Force asked scientists at the University of Colorado to study unexplained reports of UFO's. The scientists concluded that all the sightings could be explained as stars, satellites, optical illusions, and weather phenomena. This ended the Air Force's twenty-year UFO study. It did not, however, end people's reports of UFO sightings.

Scientists who take UFO's seriously state that many reports have come from people with some scientific and technical training. An airplane pilot, for example, would not be likely to mistake a meteor or a satellite for a UFO. It is also hard to believe that a scientist would make up a UFO story just for the fun of it. Several people have asked that their names be kept secret, so obviously they were not seeking publicity.

Visitors from Another Planet?

Could UFO's carry visitors from another planet? This question constantly faces UFO researchers. The Air Force says it has found no proof to support the theory that UFO's are evidence of other civilizations. Though many scientists believe that life exists on other planets, they do not think it possible that these beings have found a way to travel to the earth. So the UFO question remains unanswered — at least for now.

Understanding What You've Read

1. What explanations have been offered for supposed UFO sightings?
2. How did the Air Force investigate UFO sightings?
3. According to the selection, what are some of the arguments for the existence of UFO's?

Applying the Skills Lesson

1. What idea presented in the first paragraph on page 116 is further developed in the second paragraph?
2. What kind of paragraph is the last one in this selection?

Is it real or just a tall tale? Someday all our questions may be answered about . . . THE CREATURE CALLED BIGFOOT

by William Wise

While you are reading the following selection, look for introductory, transition, developmental, and summary paragraphs.

Ape Canyon got its odd name in 1924. That summer, five prospectors were camping some sixty miles south of Tacoma, in Washington's Cascade Mountains. One day—so goes the story—a band of huge, apelike creatures came out of the woods without warning. The prospectors hurried back to their cabin. They locked themselves inside while the screaming invaders threw rocks against the walls. The attack lasted several hours. Then, as suddenly as they had come, the strange, hairy giants melted back into the woods.

The prospectors returned to civilization and told people of their adventure in the canyon. Most listeners scoffed at the tale. There were, however, a few local townspeople who accepted the story. They remembered others who claimed to have seen a large, apelike animal in the neighboring wilderness. Some had found giant footprints—footprints of an animal that walked on its hind legs like a human being. By the mid-1920's, tales of a subhuman creature called *Bigfoot* had become widespread. Many people felt certain the animal was more than just a myth.

Sasquatch and Jacko

The incident at Ape Canyon stirred fresh interest in Bigfoot. Soon more questions were being asked. Had the five men really seen the animals, or had they simply made up a tale? If Bigfoot did indeed exist, what kind of animal could it be? Could huge, nearly extinct primates still live in small numbers in the thick forests stretching from northern California to British Columbia?

Of course there were no final answers, and the debate raged on. Those who believed Bigfoot existed could point to a number of strange facts. For one thing, some of the stories about it were centuries old. Long before the first trappers and prospectors had come to the region, local Native Americans were certain that a race of heavy, apelike animals lived in the neighboring mountains. They called them *Susquatch* [sas'kwôch'] and had made them a part of their tribal lore.

The puzzling affair of Jacko occurred in British Columbia. In the early 1900's, a railroad line was being extended through the wilderness. One day, some of the workers returned to camp with a strange trophy. A newspaper story at the time said the workers had captured a creature that could truly be called half human and half beast. *Jacko,* as the animal was named, stood five feet tall.

Some people felt sure Jacko was a young Bigfoot. Unfortunately, Jacko was not brought down from the mountains to a place where scientists might have studied it. Either the workers allowed it to return to the wild, or it died while still in captivity. As a result, the chance to learn more about it — and perhaps Bigfoot as well — was lost.

Monster Tales and Legends

The story of Jacko, the tales of Sasquatch, and the adventure of the five prospectors in Ape Canyon still failed to convince most people that Bigfoot was real.

After all, the doubters pointed out, Bigfoot was not the first monster that some people had believed in. During the Middle Ages, people lived in fear of terrible dragons that flew through the air. They were afraid of centaurs that were supposed to be half human and half horse.

Some American colonists, too, believed in monsters. For example, there was the sea serpent of Gloucester [glos'tər], Massachusetts. According to the story, the serpent appeared in the harbor one sunny day and swam back and forth for almost an hour. Afterward, a number of experienced seafarers swore they had seen the beast.

If Americans could believe in the Gloucester Sea Serpent, said the skeptics, why be surprised by their belief in a Sasquatch or Bigfoot? This did not mean the animal really existed. Soon the public would realize the truth and lose interest.

Proof of Bigfoot?

For some reason, the Bigfoot tales refused to die. In 1958, more than thirty years after the five men had reported their Ape Canyon adventure, a road was built through the wilderness of northern California. Time and again, during the course of their work, members of the crew found huge footprints in the soft earth around their camp. As these discoveries were reported, interest in Bigfoot flared up again.

One of the new investigators was Roger Patterson. For nine years, using every moment he could spare from his job, Patterson searched the wildest sections of northern California for traces of the huge animal. Then, in October 1967, while he and a friend were riding through the wilderness, their horses suddenly reared in panic and threw them. Even as he fell, Patterson spotted the cause of the trouble. A short distance away stood a tall, apelike animal.

As the animal moved off into the brush, Patterson picked himself up, aimed his 16mm camera, and ran after it. He managed to shoot seven feet of shaky film before the animal disappeared. The film showed a hairy, apelike creature running with bent knees. The short film was spliced into a twenty-minute movie about Bigfoot.

When Patterson's film was shown to the public, some called it a fake. But several Hollywood technicians said the seven-foot strip might well be genuine. It could have been faked only at great cost to the makers, who would not be likely to recover their expenses. During the five remaining years of his life, Patterson did receive a good sum of money from the movie. After his death, however, his friends insisted that all the profits had gone back into further efforts to find Bigfoot.

A frame from Roger Patterson's puzzling film — even after hours of study, no one can say for sure exactly what it was that Patterson photographed.

The Search Goes On

A number of other investigators are still looking for Bigfoot. There is John Green, a former publisher who lives in British Columbia. The author of two books about Sasquatch, Green says he's found almost 1,000 people who say they have seen either the huge animal itself or some of its footprints. Another investigator is Peter Byrne, once a game hunter in India. Byrne made three trips to the Himalayas, hoping to track down the Abominable Snowman. He believes the chances of finding Bigfoot are much better.

Bigfoot seems more active than ever. In the 1970's, Richard Brown, a high school teacher from Oregon, was returning to his trailer. It was dusk, and as he turned into the trailer park, he saw a nearby field lit up by the headlights of two cars. Standing in the light, claims Brown, was "something big and real."

Brown, an experienced hunter, hurried into camp and found his rifle. It had an eight-power scope. Through this, at a distance of about 150 yards, he was able to see the animal clearly. It was hairy, muscular, and as he said later, neither an ape nor a bear. Brown released the safety catch. However, he could not bring himself to shoot the creature, which he later said, "seemed more human than animal." After about five minutes, it wandered up a hillside and vanished.

Brown called the sheriff's office. When the officers investigated, they found deep, twenty-inch-long footprints resembling those of a human. It was estimated that they had been made by an animal about ten feet tall, weighing between 600 and 800 pounds.

Was the animal really Bigfoot? Probably not, most experts would say. One scientist, when asked for an opinion, said, "It's a question of the number of animals necessary to maintain any living species. Taking the fact that you need a lot of them, it's very unlikely we wouldn't have found one, especially in an area like the United States."

Some "Monsters" That Were Real

Quite possibly the experts are right about Bigfoot. In similar circumstances, however, they have sometimes been wrong. Just over a hundred years ago, European travelers in Africa kept hearing reports of a huge creature, half human and half ape, that lived nearby. Scientists laughed at such "superstitions," until the gorilla was found to be a fact and not a myth.

So the question of Bigfoot remains unanswered. However, we can be sure that during the next few years, at least, investigators will be searching for more clues to the ancient mystery of Sasquatch — or Bigfoot — America's famous and elusive monster.

Genuine Sasquatch footprints? The plaster cast at the left measures over thirty-eight centimeters.

Understanding What You've Read

1. Is Bigfoot the first monster reported in America? Explain your answer.
2. Why did Jacko and the creature seen by Richard Brown seem to be evidence that Bigfoot actually exists?
3. In this selection, you are told about many people who claimed to have seen Bigfoot. In your opinion, which people offered the best proof of the claim? Explain your answer.

Applying the Skills Lesson

1. What is the purpose of the introductory paragraph of the selection? Where is the topic of the selection first introduced?
2. What idea introduced in the seventh paragraph on page 122 is developed by the two paragraphs that follow it?

Recognizing Different Kinds of Paragraphs

Paragraphs serve different kinds of purposes. Some introduce and develop a topic. Others connect one or more ideas or events. Still others summarize information that has already been discussed. As you read the following textbook excerpt, refer to the sidenotes. They will help you to recognize the relationship of the paragraphs.

Recognizing Different Kinds of Paragraphs in Science

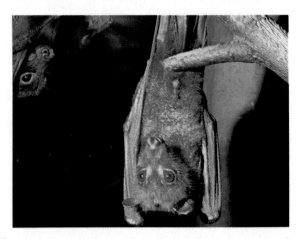

This paragraph introduces the topic of *bats*. It gives you general information about them.

Have you ever seen a bat flitting around at dusk? A bat is a small mammal that looks something like a flying mouse. The wings are thin, leathery membranes extending from the arms and long fingers in front to the small hind feet and tail. Hanging by their hind feet from trees, roofs, and sides of caves, from rafters or in barns, bats sleep during the day. But at dusk they come out and spend the night catching flying insects.

How are these sentences related? Can you see how the last sentence in the first paragraph is a "bridge," or transition, to the topic of the second paragraph?

How does a bat catch a flying insect, particularly at night? By experimenting with bats, biologists have discovered that bats accomplish this by a kind of "animal *sonar.*" (Sonar is a method ships use to determine their distances from objects by sending out sound waves and catching the echoes bouncing back.) Bats make high, shrill cries in short bursts, or pulses, constantly while in flight. You cannot hear these sounds because they are pitched too high for most human ears to hear. When the sound waves hit an object — even a tiny insect — the waves bounce back to the bat's sensitive ears. The bat apparently can determine from the returning echo where the insect is located, and how far away.

Which details describe how bats catch insects?

Fruit bats, or "flying foxes," are much larger than insect-eating bats. Fruit bats live in Africa, Australia, and parts of Asia. One kind of fruit bat has a body 30 centimeters (a foot) long and a wingspread about five times as long as its body. These bats live on fruits, as their name suggests.

What topic does this paragraph deal with?

— Life: A Biological Science
Harcourt Brace Jovanovich

Building Skills

1. Which of the following statements is true about the paragraphs in the selection you just read?
   a. Each paragraph discusses a different kind of bat.
   b. All three paragraphs describe one particular kind of bat.
   c. The first and second paragraphs discuss bats in general, and the last paragraph focuses on a particular kind of bat.
2. What information might be included in a summary paragraph for the selection?

Books About the Unknown

Other Worlds, Other Beings by Stanley W. Angrist. T. Y. Crowell, 1973. *Here is a fascinating discussion of the probability of life on other planets. The author also speculates about what this alien life might look like.*

The Egyptians by Isaac Asimov. Houghton Mifflin, 1967. *Asimov provides a colorful picture of life in an ever-changing Egypt — from prehistoric times to the present.*

The Search for Bigfoot: Monster, Myth, or Man? by Peter Byrne. Acropolis, 1975. *In this engrossing book, the author, a former big-game hunter, presents footprints, photographs, and other evidence to support his theory that Bigfoot exists.*

Ancient Monuments and How They Were Built by Daniel Cohen. McGraw, 1971. *This interesting book discusses the Nazca lines as well as Stonehenge and other ancient monuments.*

Aku-Aku by Thor Heyerdahl. Rand McNally, 1958. *This is the author's personal account of his experiences on Easter Island.*

Strange Monsters and Great Searches by George Laycock. Doubleday, 1973. *The author presents and examines evidence for the existence of Bigfoot, the Loch Ness monster, and other elusive creatures.*

Easter Island: Land of Mysteries by Peggy Mann. Holt, Rinehart & Winston, 1976. *Included is interesting evidence that attempts to solve the mysteries surrounding the giant stone statues of Easter Island.*

Walking Catfish and Other Aliens by Charles E. Roth. Addison-Wesley, 1973. *Curiosities in the animal world, such as the walking catfish; the fire ant whose sting causes a burning sensation; and the nutria, a water-dwelling rodent, are explored.*

Investigating the Unexplained by Ivan T. Sanderson. Prentice-Hall, 1972. *Here is a chapter-by-chapter examination of unexplained mysteries, such as the Bermuda Triangle, UFO's, and Bigfoot.*

MEETING THE CHALLENGE

SKILLS LESSON

For Example . . . Organization by Example

Walk through a large sporting-goods store. Look around you. You'll probably notice that each kind of equipment is located in a different department. Skis, boots, poles, and ski clothing are in one section. Golf bags, clubs, and golf balls are in another. Thus, the store is organized by *kind of sport.*

The information in paragraphs, too, follows a logical order. This makes it easier for the reader to understand the information presented.

One kind of organization authors use is **organization by example.** That is, the author makes a statement and gives examples to support it. This statement is the main idea of the paragraph. The examples are **details** that support the main idea.

Read the paragraph below. What is the topic? What is the main idea?

Most land mammals are good swimmers. For example, the raccoon thinks nothing of jumping into the water when it becomes necessary for safety. The rat can swim great distances and tread water for three days. Cats generally steer clear of water. Yet, they can swim with great ease and grace.

The topic of the paragraph above is *land mammals*. What is the most important thing the author says about land mammals? It is: "Most land mammals are good swimmers." This is the main idea. It is stated in the first sentence. The details that support the main idea are *examples* of land mammals that are good swimmers. How many examples does the author give? What are they?

The second sentence begins with the words *for example*. These words are a clue that the paragraph is organized by example. Other word clues are *for instance, namely,* and *such as.*

Read the following paragraph. Find the topic and main idea. What examples support the main idea? Look for the word clues.

Vegetation in the New River area is made up of a wide variety of trees. White cedar, for instance, is found along the New River and many of its tributaries. River birch and sycamore grow in great numbers. Silver maple, black willow, and American elm are found along the river's edge.

The topic of the paragraph above is *vegetation in the New River area*. What is the main idea? It is stated in the first sentence. The phrase *for instance* is a clue that the paragraph is organized by example. How many examples of different kinds of trees does the author list?

Finding Examples Without Word Clues

Not all paragraphs have word clues to tell you they are organized by example. In such cases, first find the main idea. Then look for the examples that illustrate the main idea.

Read the following paragraph. What is the main idea? What examples illustrate the main idea?

Students at all grade levels in Kenya are helping to build the nation. Pupils in the primary schools learn modern farming methods. High school students study to become teachers and civil servants. College students receive training for jobs in medicine, government, and business.

The main idea of the paragraph is stated in the first sentence: "Students at all grade levels in Kenya are helping to build the nation." The author gives three examples:

- Primary school pupils learn modern farming methods.
- High school students study to become teachers and civil servants.
- College students prepare for jobs in medicine, government, and business.

Try This

Read the paragraph below. Answer the questions that follow.

Recent efforts to save our threatened wildlife have seen a number of successes. In this country, for instance, there are now more deer than when the first settlers arrived in the 1600's. Another example of wildlife preservation is the dramatic increase in the number of bison. There were only 551 in 1889. Today there are between 25,000 and 30,000 head.

1. What is the main idea of the paragraph?
2. What examples does the author give to support the main idea?
3. What word clues signal these examples?

VOCABULARY STUDY

The Right Person for the Job . . .
Greek and Latin Roots

"I looked over all your applications, but I can't decide who is best for the job. Please tell me something special about yourselves."

"Mr. Nautical here. I'm Greek. I come from *naus*, meaning 'ship.' If the job is on the sea, it has to do with me — because I'm Nautical."

"Hi. My name is Manipulate. I'm from the Latin word *manus*, meaning 'hand.' I can do the job with my hands."

"Surely I'm better. My name is Logical. I'm from *logos*. That's Greek for 'reason.' Since I'm Logical, I think things out quite reasonably."

"You'll do better with me. I'm Literally. My Latin root is *littera*, meaning 'letter.' I'll follow all of your instructions 'to the letter.'"

136

"You all have good qualities, but I can only hire one of you."

"Excuse me, but I haven't been interviewed. I have all the qualifications that you're looking for and several more. Perhaps you've heard of me."

"Heard of you? Why, you're famous! You're the only one for the job! Otto, show Dictionary to its new office."

Word Play

1. If *astro* means "star," what is an *astronaut*?
2. If the prefix *il-* means "not," what does *illogical* mean?
3. *Manacles* are (a) handcuffs, (b) foot cuffs, (c) shirt cuffs.
4. Suppose you took this direction literally: *Reach for the moon.* Would you (a) stretch your arms up as high as you could or (b) set high goals for yourself?

As you read this selection, notice the examples the author gives to support her statements.

An American woman goes to Africa to observe mountain gorillas. She imitates their feeding habits and learns their calls. She even touches them! For Dian Fossey, it's all a part of . . .

Making Friends with Mountain Gorillas

by Dian Fossey

Two black hairy arms circled the tree trunk. A moment later a furry head appeared. Bright eyes peered at me through the ferns.

I was on a branch of another tree, just downhill from the gorilla who stared at me. We were both in a forest on Mount Visoke [vē·sō′kā] in Rwanda, Africa. This is where I have been studying wild gorillas.

The face was familiar. It belonged to Peanuts. He is one of my favorite gorillas and a member of one of the groups I have studied closely. These groups have grown used to my being among them.

Peanuts was wearing a look that I think of as "fun and games." I have learned to know that look in gorillas. They wear it when they want to stay near me for a while.

Slowly I left the tree. I got down into the thick leaves on the ground. There I made feeding noises to let Peanuts know everything was all right.

The moments that followed are among the most memorable of my life.

Peanuts left his tree. He strutted a bit before he began to come toward me. Being a showman, he beat his chest, threw leaves into the air, swaggered, and slapped the leaves around him. Then suddenly he was at my side. His look said that he had entertained me. Now it was my turn. He sat down to watch my "feeding" but didn't seem very impressed. So I changed activities. I scratched my head noisily, making a sound familiar to gorillas — who do a lot of scratching.

Almost right away, Peanuts began to scratch. Then I lay back in the leaves to appear as harmless as possible. Slowly I held out my hand. I held it palm up at first, because the palms of an ape and a human are more alike than the backs of the hand. When I felt he knew what my hand was, I slowly turned it over and let it rest on the leaves.

139

Peanuts seemed to think awhile about taking my hand. Finally he came a step closer. He put out his own hand. Gently, he touched his fingers to mine. As far as I know, this was the first time a wild gorilla had ever come so close to "holding hands" with a human being.

Peanuts sat down and looked at my hand a moment longer. He stood up and showed his excitement by a whirling chest beat. Then he went off to join his group. I showed my own happy excitement by crying.

My handshake with Peanuts came after more than three years of studying the mountain gorilla. The animal is the largest of the great apes. It is now very rare, and extinction is a real danger.

My goal was to take up where other students of wild mountain gorillas had left off. I wanted to know how they acted alone and in groups. I wanted to watch them from close up. And I wanted to do so in a way that did not affect them. To do this, I decided to act like a gorilla.

One of the first things I learned was that mountain gorillas are among the gentlest of animals. In some 3,000 hours of watching, I saw only a few minutes of aggressive action. These happened only when a young gorilla came too near me and its parents became excited.

One day I was in a tree taking pictures of a gorilla group. Bravado, a young male, tried to climb past me down the trunk. He seemed to think I was in the way and should move. When he got very close, I decided it was time to turn my back to him. Just as I got a good hold on the tree, I felt two hands on my shoulders, pushing down. Gorillas often push down on each other when they want the right of way on a narrow trunk.

Not wanting to fall, I refused to move. After another moment of gentle pushing — only a small bit of the mighty shove he could have given me — Bravado moved back. He beat his chest, then jumped out onto a side limb. He hung there by two arms, bouncing deliberately. He knew his weight would break the branch and make a loud snapping noise. The branch broke with a crash. Bravado landed eight feet below, where he calmly began feeding.

In my years of study, I have watched nine groups of gorillas. For close-up meetings, however, I chose just four.

Gorilla groups have from five to nineteen members; the average is thirteen. Each group is ruled by a strong male leader — a silverback. The male becomes a silverback as he gets older. The hair on his back turns from black to silvery gray. There may be one or more lesser silverbacks in the group. Then come younger mature males (blackbacks), females, juveniles, and infants.

Early in my study I decided that one of the best ways to help the gorillas accept me was to make the sounds they make. I learned that there is more to gorilla sounds than just roars, screams, and *"wraaghs."*

One animal might show feelings of well-being by making a "belch sound" like *"naoom, naoom, naoom."* This brings a chain of similar sounds from nearby animals. Sometimes I crawled secretly among a feeding group and began a belch sound. It would be answered by the animals around me.

The belch sound is the most common sound, but it is not the only one. The "pig grunt," for example, is a harsh, short sound to keep order. A silverback will use it to settle a squabble or to order his group to move on. Females also use it, in a softer tone, to control their infants.

The "hoot bark" is most often heard when an animal is curious or alarmed. When sounded by the silverback leader, it usually brings the quick attention of the group.

My main interest was to use these sounds to gain acceptance by the gorillas. That way, I could carefully study their behavior.

Why do gorillas go where they go? Do their routes stay the same or do they change? How many gorillas are still alive? What is their present territory? I have strong reasons for wanting to know. For if we are to save the mountain gorilla, we must find the answers to these questions.

Understanding What You've Read

1. Why did Dian Fossey decide to act like a gorilla?
2. What was one of the first and most important things Dian Fossey learned about gorillas?
3. Why do you think previous students of gorillas did not get as close to them as Dian Fossey did?

Applying the Skills Lesson

1. What are some examples of the sounds gorillas make? What do each of the sounds mean?
2. Give three examples that show gorillas are gentle creatures.

Karen Casper cannot get around
without a wheelchair or crutches.
Yet she has won several medals
and trophies in sports events.
Her courage and determination
show us . . .

A CHAMPION'S SPIRIT

by Celeste Callahan

"If life shortchanges you in one department, it's likely to give you a full hand someplace else." Karen Casper's fingers comb through the long hair that frames her face. Her shoes point toward a pair of crutches leaning against the sofa. Lying on the floor are trophies, medals, ribbons, newspaper stories, and pictures. "At least that's what Babe Didrikson said."

A young woman, crutches, and trophies: strange companions. But nineteen-year-old Karen, from White Bear Lake, Minnesota, is a sports champion. The gold medals are from international wheelchair games and from the Paraplegic Pan-American Games.

Karen was about nine months old—the age at which most babies begin to walk—when her parents discovered that she couldn't stand up without crying. Careful hospital tests showed nothing. One day Mrs. Casper noticed a lump on Karen's back. Another test was made right away. The test showed that Karen had a rare kind of cancer.

Her parents were told that Karen had about six months to live. But the Caspers refused to accept the death sentence. They began to take Karen to special doctors. The doctors tried a new kind of treatment for such cancers. It worked, and Karen became the first American to live through the disease.

Karen's illness left its mark, however. Nerve cells in her legs had been destroyed. Karen has never walked.

"In that way, I'm lucky." She grins, fixing the brace hidden by jeans. "I never had to accept a change. A high school friend of mine was a cheerleader; she's now a quadriplegic. She broke her neck doing a backflip when she was fourteen years old. For her, life ended with the wheelchair. For me, life has always been the wheelchair."

More Active Than Most People

What is life like on crutches or in a wheelchair? You make do. You don't know anything else. You've been given these cards, so you play them. "There were seven of us children running around. I'm next to the youngest. My parents didn't have time to single me out for pity," she recalls.

Today, even with the "hardware," Karen carries on like any other person. In fact, she's more active than most. She has been a Campfire Girl for ten years. She sings with the church choir. She has a "HaniHam" radio license to communicate with other disabled people. ("Hani" stands for handicapped.) She also drives a car, using hand controls.

Through on-the-job training for high school credit, Karen got a job in telephone sales at a department store. She still works there each day after school. She helps at her father's candy store and plays wheelchair basketball once a week. Her team is the Rolling Gophers. Since graduation from high school, Karen has taken general courses at the local community college.

And she dates. "Oh yeah, I . . . uh . . . keep company." Her brown eyes flash amusement. "I'd say 50 percent of the guys I date are paraplegics, partly because of our mutual interest in the wheelchair games and partly because—well, they understand. The others I date, the able-bodied, or 'AB's,' are older, more mature. It takes someone mature to see through a handicap to the person on the other side."

Camp Courage

Although Karen is matter-of-fact about her capabilities, her life is hardly easy. "One incident stands out above all others," Karen recalls. "To this day it still burns me up." The big brown eyes begin to narrow. "One time a couple of years ago, I went roller skating with my friends. Yes, roller skating. I had to decide whether just to

hear about my friends' adventures or to run with them. I paid my money, got skates fitted—big enough to fit over the braces—and got out on the floor. I'd made it around once, using my crutches in ski-pole fashion. Then the owner came out and told me to leave! I was a hazard! That incident made me question whether I was doing the right thing, trying to be like everyone else."

It was then that Karen discovered wheelchair sports at Camp Courage. Wheelchair games are held by the National Wheelchair Athletic Association. The NWAA includes paraplegics and amputees in just about all major track and field events, from racing to shotput. It also gave Karen the chance to go to the championship games in New York City, Mexico, and England.

"I don't care for field events. So, other than shotput I've stuck with track," says Karen, who weighs 100 pounds and can lift a 150-pound weight. "I was groomed for the sixty-yard dash. I practiced by wheelchairing to school every day." But her specialty is swimming. "Without the wheelchair," she quickly adds. Her laugh is easy.

Karen swims without the use of her feet and legs. Her times are half as fast as those clocked in regular women's high school competition: 45.7 seconds compared to 29.5 seconds for the fifty-yard freestyle.

144

"At first I was really scared. I mean, I'd always been a pretty good swimmer. But large-scale competition would—well, maybe I wouldn't do as well out there. And it's a hard thing to admit your limitations."

Yet, from England Karen brought home one gold medal and two bronze ones. In Peru she placed in all seven events she entered. In Mexico City, as the youngest member of the American team, she won medals in three swimming events. She holds five national records and one world's record. "But that one's probably broken by now," she adds.

More Aware

Karen hopes to get a job helping other handicapped people. "That's what being handicapped does—it makes you more aware of the difficulties of others," she says.

"Laws and building codes are doing great things for the handicapped. Special parking places, ramps, and doors are important—as is the opportunity to work. But now that the public is more aware of the handicapped, attitudes must change. We want to be recognized as people," says Karen, the Twin Cities' Outstanding Handicapped Youth and regional runner-up in the Miss Wheelchair America contest. "I want a job typing because I can type, not because I'm handicapped."

Karen was once shy about learning her limitations. Now she wants to reach her potential. To each new challenge, she says, "You don't know until you try."

Understanding What You've Read

1. How did Karen Casper's parents discover she was ill?
2. How does Karen feel about life in a wheelchair?
3. How did Karen train for track events?

Applying the Skills Lesson

1. The author states that Karen is "more active than most people." What examples support this statement?
2. On page 144, the author states that Karen's life is "hardly easy." What example does Karen mention to illustrate this?

TEXTBOOK STUDY

Organization by Example

Textbook authors often use examples to illustrate points they want to make. Read the following textbook excerpt. Refer to the sidenotes and the illustrations. They will help you see how the selection is organized by example.

Organization by Example in Science

Types of Misuse. Natural resources are misused in three ways: (1) a resource is wasted, such as when a catch of fish is allowed to spoil; (2) a resource is made useless, such as when an oyster bed is polluted by sewage; (3) a renewable resource is so badly damaged that it cannot be renewed, such as when dams prevent salmon from swimming to their breeding grounds.

What is this an example of?

Soil can be misused in all three ways. It may be wasted by being used for unprofitable crops. It may be made useless by improper farming. It may be permanently ruined by gully erosion.

The top photograph shows badly misused soil. It contains little humus and probably lacks the minerals needed by plants. The original humus decayed without being replaced. Discuss what may have happened to the minerals in this misused soil.

Here the author asks the reader to give several examples.

This soil is not permanently damaged. How may the humus be restored? How may the minerals be replaced? Will the renewal be expensive?

146

Study the photographs.
What is each photograph
an example of?

The center photograph shows farm land that has been more badly damaged. Describe the possible history of this land. Why will this land never be fit for crops again except at great cost? What can the land be used for? What processes will renew the topsoil?

Discuss the bottom photograph in terms of the three types of misuse. How might the misuse have been prevented? How can this resource be restored, at least in part?

— Exploring Life Science
Allyn & Bacon

Building Skills

1. What three examples of the misuse of soil are given in the second paragraph of the selection?
2. What example of a wasted resource does the author give in the first paragraph? What phrase tells you that the author is stating an example?

Organization by Example in Mathematics

This textbook excerpt is not accompanied by sidenotes. Look for the main ideas and supporting examples. Then answer the questions that follow.

The Vocabulary of Geometry

A fish tank has many examples of geometric figures. The corners are examples of **points.**

Points A, B, C, and D all lie in the same **plane.** A plane is a flat surface that has no end.

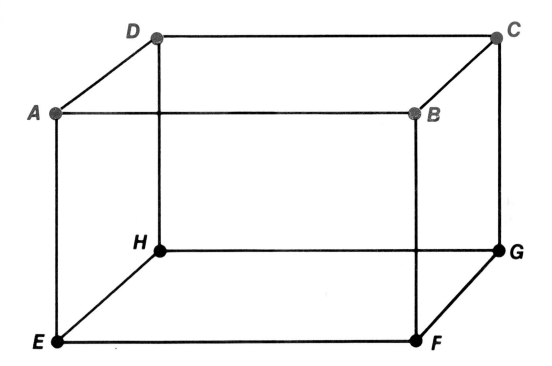

Each edge of the tank is an example of a
line segment. Find line segment AB (A$\overline{B}$).
The **endpoints** are A and B.

— Growth in Mathematics: Silver
Harcourt Brace Jovanovich

Building Skills

1. What are the three examples of geometric figures found in the
   diagram of the fish tank?
2. Which of these sentences states the main idea of the textbook
   selection?
   a. A fish tank has many examples of geometric figures.
   b. A plane is a flat surface that has no end.
   c. The endpoints are A and B.

SKILLS LESSON

Just Like Clockwork! . . . Recognizing Time Clues

Below are three photographs. At what time of day or year was each one taken?

Look carefully. You should notice several clues: a dark sky and lighted streetlamps, the kind of sport being played, the hands of a clock.

When you read, you should also look for clues that tell you when things happen. Being able to recognize these **time clues** will increase your understanding of the information that is presented.

Dates as Time Clues

Dates are the easiest kind of time clues to recognize. Read these sentences:

In 1970, women aquanauts began their mission in the Tektite II project.

Matthew Henson reached the North Pole on April 7, 1909.

The dates *1970* and *April 7, 1909,* are time clues that tell exactly when each event occurred. In the sentence that follows, however, the date is not exact.

Severe storms in the late 1860's sank several ships on the Great Lakes and the Mississippi River.

You aren't told exactly when there were storms. Instead, you are given a general time period. The time clue "the late 1860's" is an *approximate date.* It generally refers to the years 1867 to 1869.

Another example of a time clue that indicates a general time period is found in this sentence:

Thousands of years ago, humans discovered that tools and weapons could be made from copper.

The phrase "thousands of years ago" covers a very large period of time. It is used because, in this case, it is not possible to be more exact. Do you know why? When authors refer to events such as the discovery of fire or the invention of the wheel, the time period can only be approximated.

Single Words as Time Clues

Dates are not the only kinds of time clues that tell you when things happen. The following recipe is for a dish called "Egg on a Raft." Read the recipe and look for the time clues.

151

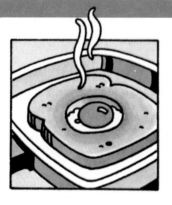

First, cut or break out a two-and-a-half-inch hole in the center of a slice of bread. Then, butter both sides and brown on one side in a frying pan. Turn the bread over. Next, break an egg into the hole, cover the pan, and cook until the egg is done. Finally, if you want, turn the bread over again and cook the top of the egg lightly.

The words *first, then, next,* and *finally* are time clues that tell you when to do each step. The steps are listed in **chronological order.** That is, the step that should be done first is listed first, the second step is listed second, and so on.

There are many other single-word time clues. Read the paragraph that follows. Find the time clues. Is the paragraph organized by chronological order?

Yesterday we started to make plans for our hike. We soon discovered, however, that there was a great deal to be done. Today two members of the group went to town to buy extra supplies. If all goes well, we should be on the trail tomorrow.

The four time clues in the paragraph above are *yesterday, soon, today,* and *tomorrow.* Notice that the events described in the paragraph are listed in chronological order.

Phrases as Time Clues

Phrases, or groups of words, can also serve as time clues. Read this paragraph. What phrases tell you when each event occurred?

Three days after take-off, the *Apollo 13* spacecraft was damaged by an explosion to the service module. At that moment, the lives of three astronauts depended on the small lunar landing module. Its air, water, and batteries were the men's lifelines during the last three days of the flight.

Three phrases in the paragraph are time clues. They are "three days after take-off," "at that moment," and "during the last three days of the flight."

Sometimes you can use time clues to infer information that is not directly stated in a selection. For example, in the paragraph above, you can figure out how long the *Apollo 13* mission lasted. Note that the explosion occurred *three days* after take-off. Immediately, the astronauts made use of the facilities in the lunar landing module. They did this for the last *three days* of the flight. Thus, the flight lasted six days (3 days + 3 days = 6 days).

Now read the following paragraph. Note the time clues. In what year was the Pan-American Expo held?

On July 14, 1853, the New York World's Fair opened at the Crystal Palace in New York City. The state did not host another major fair until forty-eight years later, when the Pan-American Expo was held in Buffalo.

There are two time clues in the preceding paragraph: "July 14, 1853" and "forty-eight years later." If you add forty-eight years to 1853, you can figure out when the Pan-American Expo was held in Buffalo: 1901. The time clues also show that the events in the paragraph are told in chronological order.

Try This

1. Which time clue in the following sentences is exact? Which is approximate?

    Judy arrived in Rome on May 10. A few days later she already felt at home.

2. Read the paragraph below. Then answer the questions.

When Phillis Wheatley arrived in the United States in 1761, she was twenty-two years old. Only six years later she wrote her first poem.

   a. What time clues are given in the paragraph?
   b. Are the events in the paragraph told in chronological order? How can you tell?
   c. How old was Phillis Wheatley when she wrote her first poem?
   d. In what year was Phillis Wheatley born?

VOCABULARY STUDY

The Letter from Big Burst . . . Synonyms

Dear Mr. Zerb:

Thank you for writing to Big Burst Sugarless Bubble Gum. We especially like to receive <u>whimsical</u> letters from our customers. It is not often that we get a note that is so amusing.

It <u>astounded</u> us to learn that you saved 12,000 gum wrappers. We were truly surprised. We can't figure out what we'll do with the wrappers you sent us, but your effort is <u>memorable</u>. In fact, something that notable cannot go unrecognized.

So we at Big Burst have <u>nominated</u> you "Chewer of the Year." You were chosen 20 to 1 by the Bubble Gum Board. Congratulations.

Big Burst Sugarless
Bubble Gum

Word Play

Match the words in Column A with their definitions in Column B.

A	B
whimsical	shocked, surprised
astounded	chosen, appointed
memorable	fanciful and amusing
nominated	worth remembering

Noticing the time clues as you read this selection will help you follow the sequence of events.

What kind of person would you choose to go with you on a dangerous adventure? Arctic explorer Robert E. Peary chose Matthew Henson and four guides to stand with him . . .

AT THE POLE

by Floyd Miller

They planned to reach the North Pole in five marches. How many marches had they made in the twenty-two years together? Two thousand? Four thousand? They didn't know. But five more marches seemed now so very few. Surely, nothing could prevent them from reaching the Pole.

At midnight on April 2, Matthew Henson left camp with his team to break trail. Following him came Ootah, one of the Eskimo guides, then the main party with Admiral Peary. Henson and his team marched for ten hours. Then he made camp and, with Ootah, built the igloos for the overtaking party. They had covered thirty miles.

They took only a few hours' sleep and were off again on the morning of April 3. The weather was clear and calm. They covered twenty miles and made camp.

Again they took only the minimum amount of sleep, and shortly after midnight on April 4 they were again moving forward. There was one disturbing development: the temperature kept rising. Also, the tides of the approaching full moon were at work. The opening of major leads was to be expected at any moment. In fact, the entire polar cap might become fragmented, and this gave urgency to their marches. They could be trapped by open waters and be unable to return south to shore. But that was not what quickened their pace. They feared that they might be cut off from their prize to the north.

As they reduced their supplies of food and fuel, they were able to press on, believing they made greater speed. Actually, they were so exhausted that they were just able to keep the pace.

On the evening of April 4, Peary took a sighting with the sextant. It was a long and difficult operation, particularly because of the condition of his eyes. Both he and Henson were suffering from snow blindness. This made it torture to remove the heavily smoked glasses and look with naked eyes into the instrument. After a long and careful look, and figuring with pencil and paper, he said, "We're at 89 degrees."

They were one degree from the Pole! Sixty miles away was the prize.

They started north, driving the dogs at a trot. On the night of April 5, they were completely played out and had to make camp and sleep. When they awoke, measurements showed them at 89 degrees and 25 minutes. They were thirty-five miles from the Pole. With any luck, they could make it in a single march. Surely they had earned some luck.

Robert Peary (left) and Matthew Henson

The next march was begun before midnight on April 5. The sky was overcast. Very little snow lay upon the ice — so little that it had been difficult to make igloos at this camp. The air temperature had risen to fifteen below zero, which decreased the friction of the sledge runners on the ice but increased the danger of leads.

Henson went forward to break trail. After a run of what he estimated to be fifteen miles, he waited for Peary and the others to join him, and they had tea. They now believed themselves ten miles short of the Pole. A final march! Henson snapped his long whip above the ear of his king dog and cried "*Huk!*" The sledge moved forward with the hissing of steel on ice, a sound that seemed to have been in his ears for a lifetime. Ootah moved his sledge in behind Peary's. Ooqueah, Seegloo, and Egingwah prepared to follow.

Henson trotted beside his sledge, feeling a mounting excitement. His exhaustion, his frozen flesh, his sore eyes were all forgotten in the drama of each yard gained. In this fever of the final chase he also lost some of his judgment. There could be no other explanation of what was about to happen.

Henson came to the edge of the lead that had only recently frozen over with young ice. His team drew up and waited for his order. Normally he would have scouted east or west to find firmer ice, but he could not stand the thought of such a delay. He viewed the young ice and decided it would hold. "*Huk!*" he cried, and he snapped the whip.

After a few yards onto the ice it was clear they were in trouble. The thin sheet began to sag beneath their weight. The dogs crouched to their bellies and whimpered, but Henson refused to turn back. "*Huk!*" he cried. And as they advanced, he walked spread-legged to distribute his weight.

A new sound came to his ears. He looked down to see that the sledge runners were cutting through the sheet of ice and throwing up a wet wake of bubbles. He cried out frantically to the dogs and threw his weight against the sledge in an effort to get it on firm ice. But his pressure was fatal. It broke the ice beneath his feet, and he went down. For a moment the furs kept him afloat. Then he felt the searing pain of the water pouring into his boots. He began striking out, clutching for something solid, but the thin ice broke beneath his flailing arms. The pain swept through his body.

Henson was filled with a wild anger against the fate that had brought him within a few miles of the Pole, only then to destroy him. But there was nothing he could do.

Suddenly, his descent was checked. Then, by some miracle, he began to rise in the water. He felt himself being lifted clear of the water and dropped down on firm ice, like a beached fish. He looked up into the calm, brown face of Ootah, who still gripped him by the back of his fur jacket.

Without a word the guide went methodically about the work to be done. He tied up the dogs and pulled off Henson's boots to put his feet against his own warm, dry belly. Then he began to beat the ice out of Henson's bearskin pants. When the feet were warm, he got dry boots from the sledge and helped Henson into them.

There was no way Henson could thank his friend for saving his life. This was a normal and almost routine act on the trail.

Henson accepted a deserved scolding from Ootah and busied himself untangling his team. The main party had now caught up with them, and it was discovered that Peary, too, had gone through the ice, though not so badly. He had changed his fur boots and was walking quickly to keep the circulation going in his feet.

Peary led the combined party a few miles north, then called a halt. He said to Henson in a matter-of-fact voice, "Matt, this may be it. We'll take an observation."

There was a wind blowing and Henson knew what had to be done. With his snow knife he built a snow windshield. Then he took the instrument box and bedded it firmly in the snow on the sheltered side. He threw down a fur skin. The skin would partly protect Peary's eyes from glare during the observation. It would also keep the snow from melting due to body heat and unsettling the instrument box.

They normally found their latitude by measuring how far the sun was above the horizon. Now, however, the horizon could not be seen. Gray sky blended into gray ice without anything to mark where one or the other ended. It was therefore necessary for Peary to make an artificial horizon.

He placed a small wooden trough on top of the instrument box and filled it with mercury. He had been carrying the mercury next to his body to keep it from freezing. Then he made a "tent" from two panes of glass. He placed the tent over the trough to prevent air currents from distorting the sun's reflection in the mercury. He removed his dark glasses. Painfully blinking his inflamed eyes, he lay down on the rug. Finally, he grasped the sextant firmly in his hands.

By propping himself on his elbows, he was able to look through the eyepiece and into the mirrors. A few adjustments would bring the sun's image down until it touched the upper edge of its own reflection in the trough of mercury. Peary sat

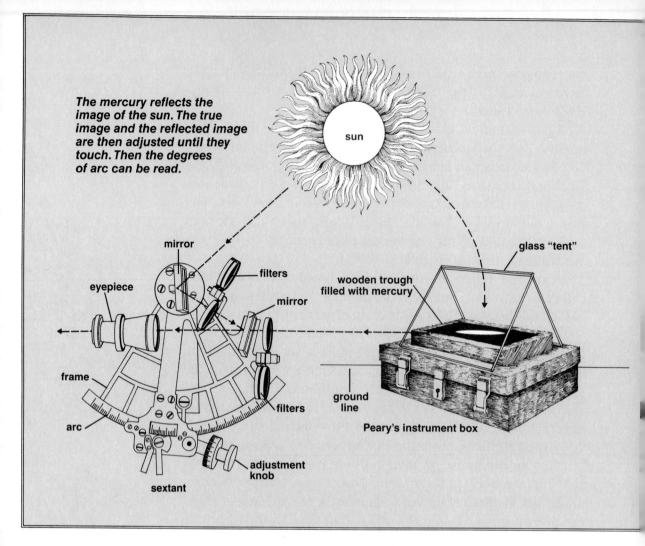

The mercury reflects the image of the sun. The true image and the reflected image are then adjusted until they touch. Then the degrees of arc can be read.

sun

mirror

filters

eyepiece

mirror

glass "tent"

wooden trough filled with mercury

frame

arc

filters

ground line

adjustment knob

sextant

Peary's instrument box

up to read the degree of arc shown on the sextant. Using figures from a nautical almanac and a table of logarithms, he did some quick calculations.

He looked up at Henson and in a voice flat with exhaustion said, "89 degrees and 57 minutes."

They were three miles from the Pole.

The Pole was a tiny spot covered by a vast sea of drifting ice. No instrument available to Peary could locate it with complete accuracy. The errors inherent in his method meant that he might at this moment be on top of the Pole. Then again, he might be three miles away in any direction. In all practical terms they had reached their goal.

162

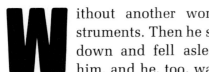ithout another word Peary packed up his instruments. Then he surrendered to his body. He lay down and fell asleep. Henson lay down beside him, and he, too, was instantly asleep.

Seegloo, Egingwah, Ooqueah, and Ootah stood about in bewilderment. This was the place, the goal, the prize? They had traveled all those miles for this? But it was no different from the sea and the ice and the sky 100 miles south, or 200, or 400! What had driven these two sleeping men to spend a lifetime reaching this spot? Was there something here their eyes did not see? They asked each other these questions and could find no answers. They sensed that they would never understand. They, too, lay down and went to sleep.

When Henson woke up, he saw Peary sitting motionless beside him. He remembered where they were—at the North Pole—and he cried out to Peary in sheer joy. Peary turned bloodshot eyes toward him and said in a dead voice, "I'll take Egingwah and Seegloo and make more observations."

Something seemed to have gone out of the man. He was on the verge of a physical breakdown, but it was more than that. The flame that had helped him overcome all pain and sacrifice seemed to have been snuffed out. Henson had hoped for a response equal to his own mood of joy, but he didn't find it then or later. For a time he thought Peary was angry with him. He tried to think back on what he might have done wrong. But he could come up with nothing. Peary had always been silent with him, but he had expected some demonstration of comradeship or triumph at this high point in their lives. He found its absence puzzling.

He might have understood if he had seen the words Peary had written in his diary that day immediately after awakening. They were:

. . . The Pole at last. The prize of three centuries. My dream and goal for twenty years. Mine at last! I cannot bring myself to realize it. It seems all so simple and commonplace.

The attitudes of Peary and the Eskimos were not so very different, after all.

Taking two Eskimos and a double team, Peary made marches in several directions, each time taking observations and entering the results in his journal. At the end of the day he wrote:

. . . I have taken thirteen single, or six-and-a-half double, altitudes of the sun at two different stations in three different directions, at four different times, and to allow for possible errors in the instruments and observations, have traversed in various directions an area of about eight by ten miles across. At some moment during these marches and countermarches, I had for all practical purposes passed over the point where north and south and east and west blend into one.

Now, at last, Peary was ready for some ceremony. He named their camp "Camp Morris K. Jesup," after the president of the American Museum of Natural History and also of the Peary Arctic Club.

From beneath his fur jacket he removed the patched and sweat-soaked American flag he had carried for so many years. Then from his sledge he withdrew an amazing collection of other flags. He gave one each to Seegloo, Egingwah, Ooqueah, and Ootah. As they lined up before Peary's camera, Henson stood in the middle holding the American flag. The others were holding the Delta Kappa Epsilon fraternity flag, the Navy League flag, the Red Cross flag, and the World Ensign of Liberty and Peace, a flag created by the Daughters of the American Revolution.

"Plant the Stars and Stripes over there, Matt," Peary called.

Henson carried the flag to a small mound of ice and drove the staff into the hard surface. Then he asked the Eskimos to join him in three cheers.

"Hip, hip, hooray," came the cry of voices with strange accents. "Hip, hip, hooray," urged on Henson. "Hip, hip, hooray," came the final chorus. The words were caught by the wind and blown south. Every direction was south.

It was now April 7. The spring tides were due the last of April. After that, when the leads opened, they would not close again until after fall. And land was over 400 miles away.

To make it home they would have to double-march all the way. This meant starting out in the morning, covering the distance previously made by one day's march north, having tea and lunch, and covering a second march. Failure to meet this schedule by so much as a single march could only increase the danger of the trail being destroyed by shifting ice and impassable leads opening between them and land.

Before setting out, Henson saw that all the dogs were double-rationed and that all the harnesses and sledges were in good repair. All equipment not necessary for travel was left behind. All they carried were food, fuel, tools, weapons, and clothes. The trail was made. The igloos that had already been built waited to shelter them each night. Their only enemies were the warm weather and their own failing strength.

"We're ready, sir," Henson said to Peary.

The commander nodded and stepped out on the trail to lead them south. He walked alone. Into line behind him fell the five sledges with their drivers walking and crying orders to the dogs.

Peary set a fast pace, but within the hour he staggered and almost fell. He righted himself and with supreme effort marched on. Again he staggered. Henson ran forward to grab him and hold him upright. The face of his commander, black and crusted from frost and sun, streamed with tears that froze as they ran. His eyes were almost blind, and the pain was unbearable. Not only had his eyes given out, but his entire body sagged against Henson. All the iron had gone out of it. He was an old and sick man.

"Egingwah!" Matt cried. "Bring the sledge. Fast!"

When the sledge came up, they hurriedly transferred its load to the other sledges. Then they placed Peary carefully upon it and covered him with furs. In this way he traveled southward, protesting loudly. Each morning he left camp early to walk ahead on the trail. When the sledges caught up with him, however, he had used up his small measure of strength and allowed himself to ride.

On April 9, after two days on the trail, a gale descended upon them. Fortunately it was from the north-northeast and to their backs.

The leads were beginning to widen and were occurring more often. Yet they continued to be covered with new ice that could support the lightened sledges and smaller teams. By April 10 the dogs were beginning to show the effect of double marches. Several of them were worn out and had to be destroyed. Thirty-five dogs were left—seven to a sledge.

The sun was more dazzling each day, and everyone had trouble with his eyes. To take off the goggles would have meant immediate blindness. They were reaching older and heavier ice floes. Travel was more difficult but safer. The chief worry now was the Big Lead. Would it be open or closed? If they found it open, they were doomed.

By April 18 the dogs were almost lifeless from the driving pace and had to be given a rest and double rations. But land clouds could be seen ahead. The Big Lead was near. The dogs were reduced to thirty.

On April 20, just as they were approaching the Big Lead, Peary became feverish. His throat ached and he could not sleep. Yet he continued.

On April 21 they came to the Big Lead. It was frozen over, and they passed safely. Two days later they reached land.

Understanding What You've Read

1. What details in the selection show that Peary, Henson, and Ootah made a good team?
2. What three problems were caused by the severe weather conditions at the North Pole?
3. How did Peary feel as he neared the Pole? How do you know?

Applying the Skills Lesson

1. Starting from April 2 and using dates as time clues, determine how long it took the expedition to reach the Pole.
2. Are the dates of the expedition exact or approximate?
3. Reread the last two paragraphs on page 160. What words are time clues that tell the order of the steps Ootah followed to save Henson after he fell through the ice?

Recognizing Time Clues

Recognizing time clues is important to your understanding of textbook material. As you read the following textbook excerpt, refer to the sidenotes. They will help you identify the time clues.

Recognizing Time Clues in Science

How old was Spallanzani when he performed his test?

Note the difference in heating times between the groups of flasks.

Is this time clue exact or approximate?

In 1768, Lazzaro Spallanzani (1729-1799) tested the idea that microbes were formed by spontaneous generation. Spallanzani was an Italian biologist. He placed broth in several green flasks. He sealed some flasks with corks. The remaining flasks were left open. Some flasks of both groups were heated for a few minutes. The remaining flasks of both groups were boiled for an hour. Spallanzani believed that boiling would kill the microbes already in the broth.

The flasks were allowed to stand for several months. Then the broths were examined with a microscope. Microbes were found in all the unsealed flasks. No

168

microbes were present in flasks with cork seals that were boiled for an hour.

Problem

Explain the result of Spallanzani's experiment. Almost all organisms need oxygen to live. Why might Spallanzani's result not have been accepted by other scientists?

Louis Pasteur (1822-1895) was a French scientist. He performed experiments which finally disproved the theory of spontaneous generation. He boiled broth for several hours. Then the broth was placed in flasks with S-shaped necks. The curved necks trapped dust particles. Thus, dust was kept from entering the flasks. Dust particles, like other matter, carry microbes. The flasks were allowed to stand for months and even years. But microbes were not found in the broth.

How old was Pasteur when he died?

Note how long Pasteur boiled the broth.

How long was the broth kept in the flasks?

The experiments of Spallanzani and Pasteur showed that microbes are not produced by spontaneous generation. No case of spontaneous generation has ever been proven to be true! Thus, scientists believe that every living thing comes from another living thing.

—*Focus on Life Science*
Charles E. Merrill

Building Skills

1. How long after Spallanzani's death was Pasteur born?
2. Which scientist—Spallanzani or Pasteur—allowed the experimental flasks to stand the longest?

SKILLS LESSON

Time and Time Again . . .
Recognizing Time Relationships

The pictures below show the launch of a satellite. However, they are not in the correct time order. Study the pictures. Which was taken first, second, and last?

Look how high up the satellite is in each picture. The further away from earth the satellite is, the later the picture was taken. The picture of the satellite when it was closest to the ground was taken first.

Very often, authors describe events out of chronological order. Noticing the time clues will help you recognize the correct time order. Read the following paragraph. Find the time clues. Are the events described in the order in which they happened?

In March 1959, the submarine *Skate* smashed its way up through the ice at the North Pole. This was the first time any ship had been on the surface at 90° N. Less than a year earlier, *Skate* had made an underwater crossing there. But it was not the first ship to do so. Another submarine, the *Nautilus,* had crossed beneath the North Pole nine days before that.

The time clues in the paragraph above are:

- March 1959
- less than a year earlier
- nine days before

Notice that the events are not described in chronological order. The most recent event is mentioned first. The time clues, however, help you understand the correct order of events.

Now read the encyclopedia article that follows. Are the events described in the order in which they happened?

GIBSON, ALTHEA (1927-   ) became one of the world's greatest women tennis players. She was one of the leading women amateur players from 1950 to 1958. Gibson won both the women's U.S. national singles title and the British national singles title (the Wimbledon) in 1957 and 1958. She also played on the winning U.S. teams in the Wightman Cup meets for American and British women's teams both years.

Althea Gibson was born in Silver, South Carolina, and grew up in New York City. She began playing amateur tennis in the early 1940's. She retired from tennis in 1958 and became a professional golfer.

Adapted from *The World Book Encyclopedia.*
© 1975 Field Enterprises Educational Corporation.

Notice that the first time clue given in the first paragraph is the year when Althea Gibson was born: 1927. The article then mentions the years 1950 to 1958 when Gibson was considered one of the leading amateur tennis players. In the second paragraph, the article refers to "the early 1940's," when Gibson began playing amateur tennis. This information is followed by her retirement from tennis in 1958. Thus, the events presented are not in the order in which they happened. By paying attention to the time clues — the dates — you can keep track of the proper order of events.

Time Differences

Recognizing the correct order of events may not give you all the information you need to understand time relationships. You may also want to know how much time passed between two events.

The three events discussed in the following paragraph are not in chronological order. The time clues, however, are keys to recognizing the correct order. As you read the paragraph, use the time clues to help you figure out the actual chronological order. Then figure out how much time passed between events.

On April 12, 1961, Russian cosmonaut Yuri Gagarin broke the space barrier. He became the first person to circle the earth successfully in a spacecraft. The event would have greatly pleased the two Frenchmen who, in 1783, proved that human beings could sail skyward in a hot-air balloon. But a hot-air balloon does not have a mechanical power source. That did not come until 120 years later when the Wright brothers gave birth to true flight. They launched their mechanically propelled airplane from a hillside in North Carolina. Flight time: twelve seconds.

The time clues given in the paragraph are: "April 12, 1961," "1783," and "120 years later." These clues are all you need to figure out the order of events:

- first hot-air balloon flight with human passengers (1783)
- Wright brothers' first flight (120 years later)
- first space flight with human passenger (April 12, 1961)

172

Now, how much time has passed between these three events? You already know that there are 120 years separating the first hot-air balloon flight and the Wright brothers' flight. To find out the date of the Wright brothers' flight, add 120 to 1783: 1903. How much time passed between the Wright brothers' flight and Yuri Gagarin's flight? Subtract 1903 from 1961: fifty-eight years. What is the time difference between the first hot-air balloon flight and Yuri Gagarin's flight?

Try This

Read the paragraphs below. Note the time clues. Then answer the questions that follow.

Composer Scott Joplin never lived to see the successful production in 1973 of his first opera, *Treemonisha*. He died in 1917. During his life, Joplin had written dozens of songs in a new style called ragtime. These songs set millions of toes tapping all over the world.

Joplin was born in 1856 and wrote his most famous piece, "Maple Leaf Rag," at the age of forty-three. He predicted that the song would make him "King of Ragtime," and it did. Pieces like "The Easy Winners" and "The Entertainer" (1902), "Palm Leaf Rag" (1903), and "The Cascades" (1904) soon followed. By the time of his death he had written or been coauthor of fifty-two works.

1. Not all of the events in the paragraphs are in chronological order. Using time clues, determine the order in which they actually happened.
2. What are Joplin's birth and death dates?
3. How much time passed between Joplin's death and the production of his first opera?
4. How old was Joplin when he died?

VOCABULARY STUDY

Alfonso . . . Meanings from Context

Alfonso is usually a very *aggressive* cat. Believing he is a fierce jungle animal, he boldly chases anything that moves. But Alfonso folds up like a pack of cards when he meets his mighty enemy, the vacuum cleaner. Since he thinks that the vacuum cleaner is going to gobble him up, he quickly plans his escape *strategy,* step by step. First he watches the path of the vacuum cleaner. Then he checks to see if there is enough room to make his getaway. He waits until the vacuum cleaner has its "back" turned. Then suddenly, Alfonso is off like a rocket. As he reaches the safety of the kitchen, he is bursting with joy. He is *elated.* Once again he has been *victorious* in his battle with the vacuum cleaner.

Word Play

1. Which word best describes an *aggressive* person? (a) pushy, (b) calm, (c) shy
2. Another word for *strategy* is (a) power, (b) plan, (c) escape.
3. What is another way to write this sentence: *The victorious runner was elated?* (a) The slowest runner was annoyed. (b) The winning runner was overjoyed. (c) The fastest runner was employed.

In the following selection, the events described are not in chronological order. Look for the time clues that will help you see the correct order.

All twelve-year-old Maria Pepe wanted to do was play Little League baseball. But she learned that just wanting to do it demanded . . .

A SPECIAL KIND OF COURAGE

by Geraldo Rivera

By the bottom of the third inning, the baseball game had been turned into a rout. In the Hoboken, New Jersey, Little League contest, the home team was the Young Democrats. They were on the short end of a nine-to-one score against the team backed by local businessman C. C. Casalino. Despite the lopsided score, the old wooden bleachers of Stevens Park were still packed. Carmen Ronga, coach of the trailing Young Democrats, thought it was one of the largest crowds he could remember. He didn't want to disappoint them. He walked up and down in front of the bench clapping his hands.

"C'mon, c'mon, let's go, fellas. . . . We can still pull this one out of the fire." But after the Young Democrats failed to score in the third inning, Coach Ronga did some shuffling.

"Okay, we're making some changes," he said, pulling the lineup sheet from his back pocket.

He benched many of his starters and brought in the reserves. The Little League has a rule that everyone on the team must play at least three innings of each game and get to bat at least once.

Ronga then made his big move. He brought in a new pitcher. He knew the new pitcher could throw hard, but he feared that the big crowd had made her nervous.

"Okay, Maria. This is it. Go out there and blast it past them."

The first batter went down swinging. From the stands the crowd roared its approval. Maria had struck him out. Both sides remained scoreless after that. The game ended in a nine-to-one victory for the C. C. Casalino team.

"But wasn't Maria great?" Coach Ronga smiled. "I'm going to make her the starting pitcher in

next week's games against the Hoboken Elks."

The Young Democrats lost these two games to the Elks by lopsided scores. But Maria had won another victory. She had gained the respect of her teammates and coach.

"Her fast ball is as good as or better than any of the boys'," said her coach. "And she's not a bad hitter, either."

But then the bombshell hit. The national office of Little League, Inc., of Williamsport, Pennsylvania, responded to the news of Maria's entrance into the formerly all-boy league. They took away the charter and canceled the league insurance, not only for Maria's team, but for the entire Hoboken league. Ten teams, with 200 ballplayers, were affected by the action.

James Farina, the sponsor of the Young Democrats, was faced with losing Maria or the whole league.

"They had me over a barrel," Farina explained later. "I didn't want to drop her from the team, especially after she showed us all how well she could do once she had the chance. But the national office didn't just kick our team out of the league. They knocked out the whole Hoboken city league! We didn't want to jeopardize 200 other kids who play Little League baseball in this town."

It's Not for Girls?

Maria Pepe grew up in Hoboken. She had been playing sandlot baseball in the city with the boys long before she joined the Little League. The Pepe family lived in the ten-story Church Towers, one of Hoboken's largest buildings. From a window of their seventh-floor apartment, Maria's mother could watch her playing baseball in the vacant lot across the street.

From about the age of five, she would shyly ask the boys in her building if they would let her play. She had to ask quite a few times. But she kept asking and was finally given a chance to get into a ballgame. After that, the boys never objected. Maria was a good ballplayer. And on the roughly drawn baseball diamonds of the city's vacant lots, all that really counted was whether or not you were a good ballplayer.

In the spring of 1972, Maria came home with some papers for her parents to sign. It was Saturday, the only day her father was off from work. He and Mrs. Pepe were sitting in the kitchen.

The papers Maria handed them were her Little League application forms. She told them she wanted to try out for a team called the Young Democrats. Her father was astounded. He took his eyeglasses off and put the newspaper down. "But, honey," he said, as he rested one arm on his daughter's shoulder, "the Little League is for boys. They aren't ever going to let a girl play." Maria was an obedient child. Though she was disappointed, she was ready to accept any reasonable decision. But she was curious.

"But, Daddy, what if I can play better than the boys can?"

"That doesn't count, sugar. It's for boys, not for girls."

"Why?"

Mr. Pepe thought for a while. Unable to come up with a logical answer, he turned to his wife. "You tell her."

"It's just always been that way," she said. But the answer wasn't satisfactory to Maria. It didn't sound right to her parents either. Maria explained that Coach Ronga had told her she could attend the tryouts. If she was good enough, she could play.

All she really needed now was her parents' permission.

Maria's father told her that they would give it some thought. As twelve-year-olds almost always do, Maria happily accepted this "maybe" as a definite "yes."

"You know something?" said her father after she had gone. "She's right." Smiling, he picked up the application forms and leafed through them.

"I don't know," said Mrs. Pepe. "What if she gets hurt?" She was worried about the roughneck boys Maria would be playing against.

"Aw, c'mon . . . she's been playing ball with the same kids since she was this high." Maria's father held his hand at about the level of the tabletop. "The only difference now is that she'll have a uniform."

Maria's parents were almost ready to give their consent. However, they thought it wise to wait a few days. During that time, Mr. Pepe spoke with Coach Ronga.

"What's the story, Carmen? You going to let her play?"

"Yeah, sure we're going to take her. She's better than half the boys in the league."

With that assurance, Mr. and Mrs. Pepe gave their consent.

A Wave of Controversy

So Maria was there on the first day of the tryouts for the league.

As expected, she easily made the team. From the start of the season, however, her position in the lineup caused controversy.

One of the benefits of all this talk was the increase of local interest in Little League games. There were more spectators in the stands. Reporters and photographers were on the field. Word even traveled to the national office—and that was the beginning of the end of Maria's career in organized baseball. The national office canceled the Hoboken league's charter.

The following day, Maria decided to throw in the towel. "It was just that I didn't want to hurt all the other kids' chances to play ball," she explained. "And I already figured that I'd caused people enough trouble. . . . I just didn't think it was fair anymore."

Later in the same week, a women's group filed a suit against the National Little League. The suit charged that the league had acted unfairly. The league, it said, uses public land for the games and had discriminated against Maria because she was a girl.

The Pepe family learned about the lawsuit when a reporter for the *Hoboken Evening News* called, asking for a comment.

"Well . . . I approve of the action," Mr. Pepe said to the reporter. "Not only for Maria, but for all the other girls who might want to play." He paused just long enough to wink at Maria, and continued. "Maria and Mrs. Pepe and I don't want to jeopardize the other kids' chances of playing ball—no way. But if the ladies bringing the case feel it's right, then I say go ahead. They even have women jockeys nowadays, don't they?"

A spokesman for the national office announced that a court fight would prove useless. He pointed out that a federal court in Boston had just thrown out a lawsuit filed by a team in Newton, Massachusetts. This team had also tried to challenge the "boys-only" rule.

During the following week, Frank Yacenda of the State Division of Civil Rights announced that medical opinions were being sought. The opinions would decide whether girls between the ages of eight and twelve were physically inferior to boys in that same age group. But Maria's attention was diverted by another telephone call.

The VIP Treatment

"Hello, Mr. Pepe? My name is Jackie Farrell. . . . I work with the New York Yankees. Listen, on behalf of Mike Burke, the president of the club, and Ralph Houk, the skipper, and all the fellows on the team, I'd like to invite Maria to spend a day with the Yanks. Yes, that's right, we'd like her to be a Yankee for a day, . . . come to the stadium, meet some of the guys, have lunch with the team, and then, of course, watch the game. It's against the Tigers. . . . No, no, I'm not kidding."

Maria was overjoyed. "You mean it, Dad? You really mean it? I'm going to meet the Yankees?"

The following Saturday, Jackie Farrell drove out to the Pepes' apartment to pick up the entire Pepe family and take them to Yankee Stadium.

During the ride, Maria was bubbling. "Mr. Farrell, can I really meet Mel Stottlemyre? How about Bobby Murcer? I can?" Each time she received a "yes," she would squeeze, shake, or pound her brother or sister. "Did you hear that, Mark? Did you hear that, Michele?"

The hour ride from Hoboken, New Jersey, to the Bronx, New York, was endless. But when they finally reached Yankee Stadium, it was strictly red carpet. Maria and her family were whisked into the club offices. Maria stared at all the photographs of the past Yankee teams. "Look! That's Mickey Mantle. And that's Yogi Berra. Whitey Ford! I wish I was a lefty. There's Joltin' Joe DiMaggio . . . and the Babe! And that's Lou Gehrig."

"Would you like to meet a few of our more recent ballplayers, Miss Pepe?" asked Mike Burke.

"Oh, would I!"

Burke took Maria's hand. The whole Pepe clan followed as he led the way through the stadium and out onto the playing field.

The rest of the day was a whirl of thrilling experiences for Maria. She got her picture taken with all her heroes. She received a signed baseball, a batting helmet, a tour of the Yankee dugout, and an armload of books about the team.

The only disappointment of the entire beautiful day was the score. Detroit beat the Yanks two to one.

One reporter asked Maria how she felt about what was happening to her. She answered with, "I just want to play ball."

Victory?

A few weeks later, a hearing was held before the State Division on Civil Rights. It produced some very unexpected results. The evidence showed that girls between the ages of eight and twelve could play baseball with no greater risk of injury than boys in the same age group.

Sylvia B. Pressler was the division hearing officer. She ruled that the league had been unfairly acting against Maria and against all other New Jersey girls who wanted to play Little League ball.

"The Little League," wrote Mrs. Pressler, "is as American as hot dogs and apple pie." She added that there was no reason "why that piece of Americana should be withheld from Maria or any other girl."

Maria eagerly listened as her mother read the newspaper reports of her legal victory. "Hurray!" she shouted.

"We won! We won!" yelled Mark and Michele.

By the time Mr. Pepe came home from work, the excitement had died down. When he heard the good news, however, he knocked on the girls' bedroom door and went in to congratulate Maria.

"Not bad. Not bad. How do you feel about the whole thing now? Do you think it was worthwhile?"

"Of course she does," said Mark.

"But what do you think, Maria?" asked her father.

"I'm happy, Daddy," she said softly. "I'm mostly happy for all the other girls who'll get the chance to play."

"But what about you, sugar— aren't you happy for yourself?"

"I guess so, Daddy, but . . ."

"But what, Maria?"

"I'm too old to play!"

Sadly enough, the victory had come too late. At thirteen, Maria Pepe was already over the Little League hill. She was no longer eligible to play.

The next spring, fifty girls joined the 175 boys who turned out to register for the Hoboken Little League.

In June 1974, officials of Little League, Inc., in Williamsport announced that they would "defer to the changing social climate." The league would permit girls to play on its teams. The statement added that the board of directors felt it would be "imprudent for an organization as large and as universally respected as the thirty-five-year-old Little League to allow itself to become embroiled in a public controversy."

On December 26, President Ford signed a law that officially opened the Little League baseball program to girls.

When girls were admitted at last, the action rated only a small item in the back pages of the newspapers. And nobody even called Maria for a comment.

Understanding What You've Read

1. In what ways did Maria show courage in playing Little League baseball?
2. How did Maria's parents react when they learned of her desire to join the Little League? Why?
3. How did Maria feel about the controversy surrounding her entrance into Little League?
4. What was the result of the civil rights suit filed against the National Little League?

Applying the Skills Lesson

Put the following events in the order in which they happened.
1. Girls are officially permitted to play on Little League teams.
2. Maria quits the Little League.
3. Maria decides to join Little League.
4. Maria visits the Yankees.
5. The Hoboken league loses its charter.
6. A lawsuit is filed against the National Little League.

TEXTBOOK STUDY

Recognizing Time Relationships

Information in textbooks is not always presented in chronological order. In such cases, look for time clues to help you understand time relationships. Read the textbook selection that follows. Refer to the sidenotes. They will help you recognize the time relationships.

Recognizing Time Relationships in Science

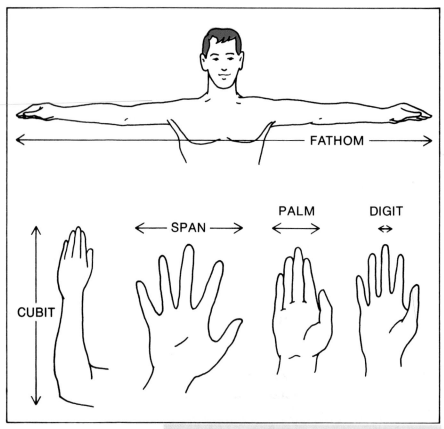

FATHOM

SPAN

PALM

DIGIT

CUBIT

Pay attention to the illustration of a span. This measurement is referred to in the selection.

What is the length of your desk in your hand spans?

When you measured the length of your desk top in spans, you used a unit that is not standard. Today we use standard units that always mean the same distance. The size of a standard unit is set by law.

To what period does this time clue refer?

It didn't take long for people to learn what you just found out. Parts of the body aren't good standards for measurement. They vary from person to person. This problem led to setting standards that could be used by everyone.

King Edward I of thirteenth-century England ordered the use of an early standard master yardstick. Made of iron, it was called the iron ulna. It was about a yard long. A foot was one third as long as the ulna. An inch was only one thirty-sixth of the ulna or one twelfth of the foot. The standards of this system of units changed many times over the years. Finally, in 1824, the English Parliament standardized the yard.

When was an early kind of yardstick called the *iron ulna* in use?

About how long did it take to standardize the yard?

During the early 1800's the French government set up a new system of measurement. They called it the metric system. Its basic unit of length was the meter. The meter was supposed to be one ten-millionth of the distance from the North Pole to the equator.

Approximately what years are covered by this time clue?

—*The Natural World/1*
Silver Burdett

Building Skills

1. Use time clues to choose the phrase that best completes the following statement: The French government set up a standard system of measurement (a) long before the English; (b) long after the English; (c) about the same time as the English.
2. How do you know the selection on the preceding page was not organized according to chronological order?

Recognizing Time Relationships in Social Studies

The following textbook selection tells about the history of Brazil through the words of an imaginary person. Although the speaker is imaginary, the information is factual. The selection is not accompanied by sidenotes. Read the selection. Then answer the questions that follow.

"I was born 70 years ago near Salvador. But my story started before that. My grandparents had been slaves on a sugar plantation. Years ago, Brazil was one of the world's main sugar producers. Portuguese settlers had taken huge tracts of land from the Indians. By 1530, the Portuguese were carving sugar plantations out of the forests along the coast of northeastern Brazil. These plantations prospered for many years.

"Not until 1888 were slaves freed in Brazil. And in the next year, Brazil became an independent republic, completely free from Portuguese rule. By that time, the sugar plantations had worn out the soil. As a new nation, Brazil had no money to start new farms or factories in the northeast. People moved away. The old plantation houses stood empty in the midst of barren fields that had once been thick with sugar cane.

"My parents thought about leaving the northeast. Instead they moved near Salvador. My mother washed clothes for other people; my father unloaded ships on the docks. When I grew up, I knew I wanted to leave.

"But I had a problem," Cecilia continued. "I had fallen in love with a man who didn't want to leave Salvador. But my mind was made up. I left without him. That's when I came to São Paulo—over forty years ago.

"São Paulo was very different in those days. It was much smaller. We had none of these big roads or tall buildings. But I remember those times as good years."

—People, Places and Change
Holt, Rinehart & Winston

Building Skills

1. When did Brazil become independent?
2. How many years passed between the time when the Portuguese were carving sugar plantations out of the forests to the time when slaves in Brazil were freed?

SKILLS LESSON

Like It or Not . . .
Organization by Comparison and Contrast

Look at these two pictures. How are they alike? How are they different?

Both show a race. However, one is a track meet, whereas the other is a sack race. The racers in the first picture are adults; in the second, they are children. A closer look at the details reveals other differences.

The process of seeing likenesses and differences is called **comparison and contrast.** When you make a **comparison,** you look for ways in which things or people are both alike and different. When you make a **contrast,** you look only for the differences.

Finding Comparisons and Contrasts

Sometimes authors organize information by comparison and contrast. Read the following paragraph. What is being compared or contrasted?

Krakatoa was completely re-covered by plants within a few years after the volcanic explosion. But plantlife was slow in coming to Surtsey after its volcanic activity. Krakatoa is a tropical island. Plants grow very quickly in its warm, wet climate. On the other hand, the island of Surtsey is located in the north. Thus, the growing season is short, and there are fewer kinds of plants.

The author is contrasting the two volcanic islands, Krakatoa and Surtsey. They are different in several ways. First, plantlife returned quickly to Krakatoa after the volcanic explosion. It was slow to return to Surtsey. Second, Kratakoa is tropical. Surtsey is located in the north. Third, the author suggests that Krakatoa has a long growing season due to its climate. The author states that Surtsey's growing season is short. Fourth, there are fewer plants on Surtsey than on Krakatoa.

The islands have one similarity. Do you know what it is?

Clues to Comparison and Contrast

There are a number of words and phrases that signal comparisons and contrasts. In the following paragraph, two states are being compared. Read the paragraph. Look for the words and phrases that signal the comparisons.

New Hampshire and Vermont are sometimes called twin states. Located in the eastern United States, they are shaped almost exactly alike. Both have towering mountains and thick pine forests. Their climates are also quite similar. Generally, winters are cold and summers are mild.

Notice that the author uses the phrase "almost exactly alike" when comparing the shapes of Vermont and New Hampshire. What comparison does the word *both* signal? What phrase shows that the author is comparing the states' climates?

Other words and phrases that can signal comparisons and contrasts are: *same, unlike, different from, similarly, rather than, as opposed to,* and *also.*

Unstated Comparisons and Contrasts

Sometimes an author doesn't use clues to signal comparisons and contrasts. You can, however, see likenesses and differences by noticing the details. Pay attention to the details as you read this selection. What is being compared?

Florida's ocean breezes whine through the deserted tower on Cape Canaveral's Pad 14. This is where John Glenn rocketed into space in February 1962, to become the first American to orbit the earth. The tower sways in the wind. Tangled weeds are sprinkled with bits of rusting steel. Decaying cables are wrapped around the tower's feet.

On nearby beaches thousands once stood to cheer humanity's reach to the moon. Now turtles have taken over again. Rattlesnakes sun themselves on empty launch pads. Small deer dart into clearings to feed. Alligators cry out for the space workers who used to feed them marshmallows and doughnuts.

It was from Pad 19 that the Gemini astronauts rose on ten missions. Today, the orange tower lies useless. The once-gleaming white room, where so many astronauts had their last look at earth before lift-off, now houses wild rabbits.

In these paragraphs the author compares launch pads 14 and 19 at Cape Canaveral as they look *today* to the way they looked in the *1960's*. The phrases "John Glenn rocketed into space," "thousands once stood," and "workers who used to feed them [alligators] marshmallows and doughnuts" refer to the past. What phrases describe the launch pads today?

Comparing the Unfamiliar to the Familiar

When authors describe an idea they think may be unfamiliar to the reader, they often compare it with something the reader is likely to know. For example, do you know what a hydra is? Read the following paragraph. To what familiar objects does the author compare the hydra?

190

A *hydra* is a small animal with a soft, tubelike body. Its mouth is at one end of the "tube" and is surrounded by tentacles that resemble cooked spaghetti. The animal looks somewhat like a rope whose strands have begun to unwind.

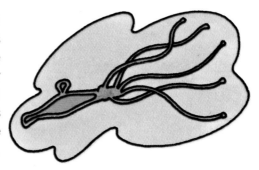

The author compares the hydra's body to a tube. This is an object the reader is likely to know. The comparison makes it easier for the reader to picture something that may be unfamiliar. What other familiar things does the author use as comparisons in describing the hydra? Could you draw a hydra based on this description?

Try This

Read this paragraph. Then answer the questions that follow.

I was about to use a Para-Plane, the most sophisticated parachute around. It looks nothing like an ordinary spherical parachute. It's rectangular and flat, and it measures only ten feet by twenty feet. Resembling the cross section of an airplane wing, the Para-Plane has a curved upper surface and a flat lower surface.

Although the Para-Plane has 25 percent less supporting surface than an ordinary parachute, it descends at about the same rate. Unlike a conventional chute, however, this "flying mattress" has a forward air speed of twenty-five to thirty miles an hour. It can even be slowed to under five miles an hour for a soft landing.

1. How is the Para-Plane different from the ordinary parachute?
2. How is the Para-Plane similar to the ordinary parachute?
3. To what two familiar objects besides the parachute does the author compare the Para-Plane?
4. Identify three words and/or phrases from the paragraph that signal a comparison.

VOCABULARY STUDY

The Wonder Word Jackpot . . . Multiple Meanings

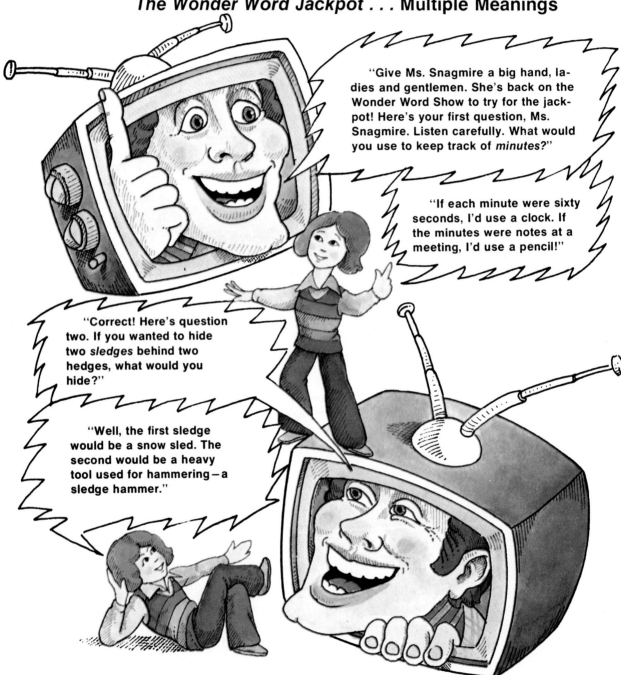

"Give Ms. Snagmire a big hand, ladies and gentlemen. She's back on the Wonder Word Show to try for the jackpot! Here's your first question, Ms. Snagmire. Listen carefully. What would you use to keep track of *minutes*?"

"If each minute were sixty seconds, I'd use a clock. If the minutes were notes at a meeting, I'd use a pencil!"

"Correct! Here's question two. If you wanted to hide two *sledges* behind two hedges, what would you hide?"

"Well, the first sledge would be a snow sled. The second would be a heavy tool used for hammering—a sledge hammer."

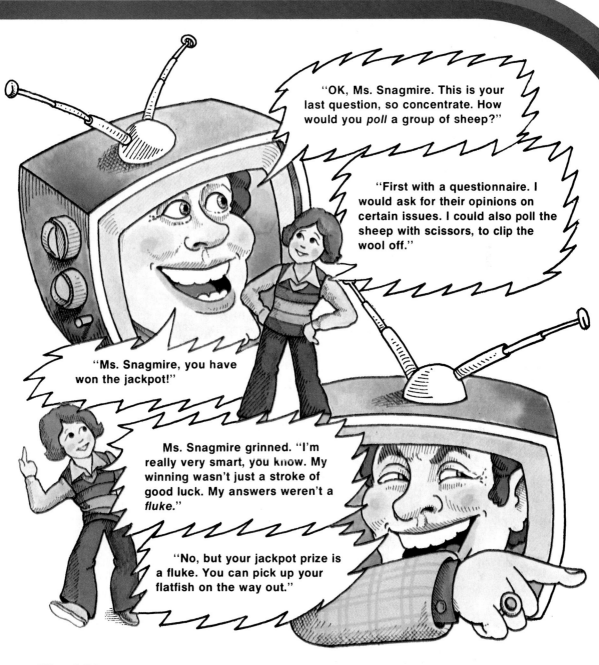

Word Play

Give at least one meaning of *fluke, minutes,* and *poll* that is not given above. You may use your dictionary.

Notice how the author of this selection uses comparisons and contrasts
to make the unfamiliar familiar.

*On June 4, 1966, two young Englishmen left Cape Cod in a
rowboat and headed out to sea. Their goal was . . .*

Rowing the Atlantic

by Captain John Ridgway *with* James Atwater

I suppose there is nothing more pointless than to try to row across the Atlantic. It is pointless in a commercial sense. But the trip made sense to me. I'm an experience-seeker.

I was born out of my time. I'm very much a dreamer. I grew up imagining myself doing things like climbing Everest or sledding to the South Pole or canoeing down the Amazon. But most of these things had been done when I became a man. That's why I jumped at the idea of rowing the Atlantic when I heard that someone was planning to do it. It was exactly right. I could afford it—it only cost me about $1,500 altogether—and it was a proper test for Sergeant Chay Blyth and myself.

I was always looking for ways to test myself, to see what I could stand up to. So when I heard in 1965 that Dave Johnstone was planning to row across the Atlantic, I volunteered to go along with him. There were other volunteers, and Johnstone and I never did get together. Then, next spring, I read that he was planning to make the trip with someone else. I became determined to beat them.

Although I wanted Chay to go with me, I didn't feel that I could ask him. But he came up to me one day and said, "I hear you're looking for someone to row across the Atlantic. I'm your man."

And I said, "All right, it's settled." Just as quickly as that. We didn't even have to shake hands on it.

194

Chay not only had never been on the sea, he didn't even know how to row. I had never done any serious ocean rowing. But this lack of experience didn't worry us. We believed that rowing skill would be secondary. More important would be the determination to survive. We knew we could survive. We don't quit. We always finish. That's what our lives are all about.

We got together $600 to buy a plywood dory and decided to leave from Cape Cod. I had read about the marvelous fishermen on Cape Cod who had used dories years ago. I practically prayed that some of these people would still be alive. And some of them were.

They came forward, eager to help. Several of them took us out on Pleasant Bay for rowing lessons. They built up the deck of our dory about fourteen inches to give the cockpit more protection against the waves. Thick pieces of oak were added to reinforce the hull.

To keep us attached to the boat, the Cape Codders worked out a system of harnesses hitched to twenty-foot safety lines. These were long enough so that we would not be caught under the dory if it turned over. We carried a compass, which was mounted in front of the rower nearest the bow. We had four radios. One was a coffee-grinder set that had to be cranked when you wanted to send a message. We carried a transistor receiver to pick up the exact time for accurate navigation.

We had foul-weather clothes that eventually became so worn we had to tape them together. To keep out the cold, we brought along heavy warm-up suits and plastic-coated blankets.

We had fresh fruit, vegetables, and eggs. When they were gone, we ate dehydrated army rations, which were stored in plastic boxes and lashed to the inside of the cockpit. We carried a gallon of water a day per person for sixty days— about a half a ton of water. It turned out to be far too much.

Before we left, the Cape Codders didn't give us any tips for survival on the water. I think we impressed them with our determination to survive. We didn't make any pretense of being boat handlers. But the people who really knew weren't worried about the rowing. The rowing was nothing.

So on Saturday, June 4, the Cape Codders shook our hands, escorted us out to the fringe of the North Atlantic, and left us on our own. We weren't afraid. We were just glad to be getting on with it.

Even when the sea was absolutely calm, life in our dory was wretched. *Rosie* (the *English Rose III*) was only twenty feet long. Watertight compartments at each end reduced our living space to an area of about ten feet by five feet. On our first night, we found that the open cockpit was so cluttered with lashed-down gear, there was no place to stretch out. Our sleeping had to be done in a bent position. Our knees were drawn up, and the backs of our necks rested on some equipment, usually one of the spare oars. We often woke up with headaches.

We cooked our meals of dehydrated British army rations on a small camping stove fired by compressed gas. We had to learn to sleep, row, eat—to exist—in wet clothes. We were constantly soaked by rain and waves. A canopy rigged upon a metal frame covered about half the cockpit. This gave us only minimal protection, however.

On the second day, it began to blow. By the third, we learned what an Atlantic gale is like. We put out our sea anchor and holed up under our canvas. Twice that night, Chay called out in his sleep for us to hold on. For the first time, we heard the great storm waves coming at us, the thunderous crash somewhere in the darkness, and then the silence as the waves re-formed.

Early on, we talked mainly about getting to the Gulf Stream. But we were obviously making little progress in those first few days, and we became very dejected. On June 9, I figured we were only about 100 miles off the coast of Maine.

On June 15, we met the *Winchester,* a trawler out of Boston, and received some shattering news. After twelve days we were only 180 miles east of Boston. In fact we had come only about 120 miles from Cape Cod. Either on this day or soon after, I calculated that at that rate, we wouldn't reach England until March.

Up to that point Chay and I both had been sleeping at night. Now we began to take turns rowing all night long — two hours of rowing, two hours of sleep, and so on. We had such a mania to keep rowing, we tried not to lose one stroke. When we changed over, one man would be poised to take the oars so that we lost no momentum at all. It sounds kind of ridiculous now, but it worked. At five in the morning we ate a hot breakfast, and then both of us would begin to row. We'd take a five-minute break every hour, but we'd alternate them so that one man was always pulling.

We never felt that sense of aching loneliness that comes over some people in small boats on the sea. We talked all the time. In fact, we could hardly wait for the morning so that we could begin talking again. We never argued. That, of course, would have been disastrous. We knew each other so well, we didn't have to try not to argue. We just didn't. Nor were we ever bored. There never was enough time to do everything that had to be done, such as mending our clothes and keeping the cockpit shipshape.

On June 17, after rowing through dense fog for three days, we began to hit great swells with wide valleys between them. This must have been the edge of the continental shelf. We were really on the deep sea then, and we thought, what in the world is this going to be like in a storm?

While we were shrouded in fog, we had our first terrible fright. Softly at first, but growing steadily louder, was the *thump-thump-thump* of the diesel engines of an enormous

197

ship. As it drew closer, we heard the great rush of it through the water, but we couldn't tell where the monster was coming from. There were no lights, and the sound enveloped us in the fog. I blew our pitifully small foghorn a couple of times, and then gave up. We just sat there, staring wildly around us at the gray fog, waiting to be destroyed. Then, suddenly, the thing roared past us, still without showing a single light, and the *thump-thump-thump* receded. Our escape had been a fluke, and we slumped back in relief as the swells from the wake lifted our boat.

On June 19 the fog cleared, and we set off again in pursuit of the Gulf Stream. Sharks prowled around us for the first time. One chased its tail around and around, just like a puppy. Then, on June 22, we experienced our second great fright. We had just finished reorganizing the boat and were relaxing in the sun. Chay said, "Why don't you go for a swim?"

I said I really didn't want to, and I slipped the oars into the oarlocks. I was tired, and I began to row gently. But as we slid quietly away, there it was. I've never seen a fin like that. It was so big, it kind of drooped over, and it was all battered and scarred. The front was curved like the conning tower of a submarine. We moved away, and the shark swam slowly, keeping its head in the shade of the boat. Its fin was about ten feet back in the water. I suppose that shark would have finished me if I had gone swimming. After that, we gave up the idea of taking a dip for the rest of the trip.

From time to time, we saw other sharks following us, great

dark brown shapes in the gray water. They'd nose their heads under the boat—I guess because we were the only shadow on the sea, and we were moving slowly enough for them. We could feel the vibrations when some of the sharks scratched their backs on the bottom of the boat.

Our logs during this period show how the strain of the trip was beginning to get to us. Chay wrote:

We have been out three weeks now, and I am getting a bit depressed. Mainly, I think, because of lack of westerly winds. . . .

Food plays a large part in our lives. We try to alter the flavor by a series of concoctions. Jam with rice pudding or cheese. Rice with meat blocks. Mixed vegetables. . . . Our sole spice is pepper, and now even that is wet. Mashed potatoes—we used to cook them on their own—now go into thickening the stews. Soup cooked with biscuits. Coffee—black and white, with and without sugar, and the same with cocoa. This cocoa is our luxury. We are beginning to feel the lack of sleep.

The wind switched to the west after a while, and *Rosie* swept on like a surfboard. We made 150 miles in five days. And we were in the Gulf Stream, or as close to it as we ever got. I suppose this really was the turning point of the whole trip. We had proved to ourselves that we could make progress even on shortened rations and with the wind sweeping around to the east to blow us backward.

We had complete confidence in the boat and in each other, and we were prepared for a six-month voyage, if necessary.

This was our game, really—a contest of endurance. We knew we could win it.

We rowed on, one man at the oars all night long. Chay was rowing on the night of July 4 when the wind began to build steadily. I was sleeping—curled up miserably on the floor of *Rosie*. Suddenly, I was shocked awake. Cold seawater had flushed me out from under the canopy like a stream of water from a fire hydrant.

"It's a 'whiteout'!" Chay screamed. I was fighting to get my bearings when a second monstrous wave hit us. *Rosie* was lifted by the sea and tossed along through the white spray as though we were shooting rapids. The water sparkled like snow in the sun.

I took over the oars, and Chay went under cover. The next two hours became one of the great moments of my life. My safety and my life had been taken out of my hands. There was nothing I could do except sit back and watch what was happening. *Rosie* would soar up on a great wave and slide down the slope. The stern rose up until I could see the silhouette of the rudder against the sky.

The sounds of the storm and the boat were an orchestra. It was wonderful. I'm sure I was sitting there with a great grin on my face.

The sheer vastness of the Atlantic and the sky made us feel humble. Many of the little things that used to worry us before the trip seemed so petty now. We talked of our wives and our parents, and how much we wanted to see them.

By now, we were down to 2,700 calories a day, and when we weren't talking about our wives, we were talking about food. We began to plan our celebration dinner with our wives in London with such elaborate care, the discussions went on for nearly fifty days.

All through the trip we had looked forward to reaching 40 degrees west, the spot at which we took our final course for home. We made good progress as we neared the fortieth parallel, clipping off about thirty miles a day. Then the wind began to blow from the east. It was as though the fortieth had become a great fence in the sea. We'd approach it and be blown back, approach it again and be blown back again.

We calculated that we had just enough rations to make England, but the easterly winds caused an agonizing reappraisal. We decided to accept rations from the next ship that stopped. Was it a mature decision? Or was it chicken?

This was also the time when the strain of the voyage really began to tell on us. I wrote in my log:

I have known fear many times in my life, and indeed I have often striven to develop a situation that provided fear in both boxing and parachuting. I have never known anything like this — this cannot be over tomorrow, or for many tomorrows. Somehow it is like being rubbed down with sandpaper.

Tonight we lie and wait. Nothing could save us if we get into difficulties. No ship could get us off these seas if it arrived in time. We are completely at the mercy of the weather. All night the wind screams louder and louder, and the sound of the sea grows. . . . Slowly we are overtaken by an enormous feeling of humility and a desire to return to try and live a better life.

Later I noted: "Today I was sick of the whole business."

We began to hate the seawater as though it were acid. After a while we tried to do everything we could to keep it from getting on us. Of course we couldn't. The feeling was something like the unpleasant sensation you have when you get a noseful while swimming, only it lasted all the time, and the feeling was all over our bodies. We hated the stuff.

During this period we also cut down to about 1,000 calories a day, and food became an obsession. I used to cut up my ration of cheese into little bits and let each one literally melt in my mouth. For a while Chay would put a candy in his mouth with its wrapper on. Then he would take the paper off with his tongue to make the sweet last longer.

Then, finally, on July 23, we crossed the 40 degree mark. Six days later we were hit by a hurricane. But as our rations ran lower, the easterly winds returned. I wrote in my log:

It is hard to describe how depressing it is to row all day, head into the wind when you are a thousand miles from home, knowing full well that at the end of the day, after all the toil, you will still be a thousand miles from home.

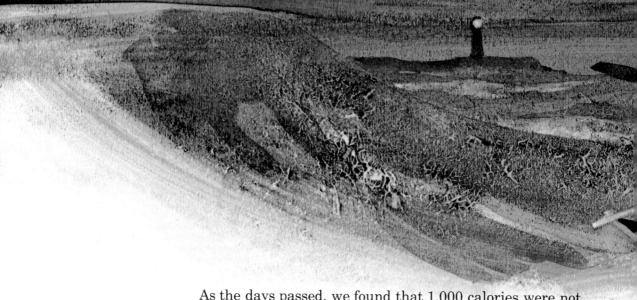

As the days passed, we found that 1,000 calories were not enough to keep us going. On August 13, a British tanker stopped and graciously offered us the stores we so desperately needed.

At the time, we were too far south for the British Isles. We turned north, and in a few days we were struck by a terrific storm from the south. It drove us on like a speedboat. In a week's time we moved from a spot along the coast of France to a spot opposite the middle of Ireland. The cold became a serious problem. Once again we were battered by easterly winds and chilling rains. Our clothes and blankets were now disintegrating. I began to suffer from boils and an irritating rash that spread over my body. Both Chay and I had salt-water sores on our hands and wrists.

We were aiming for the center of Galway Bay, almost the midpoint of the coast of Ireland. And then suddenly, after all the days of easterly winds, a storm rose out of the west and hurled us toward Ireland. We covered 250 miles in a week. Seaweed and cork and other signs of land began to appear on the ocean.

We knew that the west coast of Ireland was very rugged, with cliffs coming straight down into the water in many places. We decided, quite matter-of-factly, that if we hit the cliffs, at least one of us might drown. To serve as floats, we lashed together two watertight containers with everything we thought we would need, including rations and flares.

On the morning of Saturday, September 3, the wind suddenly shifted from the west to the south. I saw a thin line

above the horizon. "That's it over there," I said very quietly. We tried to keep a check on our emotions throughout the trip.

Chay said, "Are you sure?"

"Yes, I'm quite certain," I replied.

But Chay still refused to look. He said he'd wait until we got closer. A gale was beginning to build, and the land disappeared for another hour and a half. When it reappeared, there was no mistaking it. I persuaded Chay to look. "Oh, yes," he said. "That's definite."

Neither of us felt any real elation at that point—just a relaxed feeling that we were nearing the end of our very long voyage. As we drew closer to Ireland, it became more apparent what a horrifying landing we were going to make. The gale was rising steadily, dashing waves halfway up the great cliffs that rose out of the water. We were headed directly for the four Aran Islands. I decided to head for the sheltered side of the third island. It had a lighthouse.

Trying to beat the storm and pulling for home was the second great moment of the trip for me. Once again our fates were out of our hands. We could simply enjoy watching to see what would happen next. We sang at the tops of our lungs against the howling wind, just for the pure joy of it.

We made the sheltered side of the lighthouse, but the gale was blowing so hard that the waves splashed around both sides of the island. In an hour's time, rowing as hard as we could, we made only about a hundred yards. By then, though, we were certain we weren't going to die. We had come so far, it just wasn't going to happen.

Finally two men from the lighthouse waved us toward the other small island. We started to head that way when we spotted a lifeboat with seven or eight men coming after us. Neither Chay nor I wanted to be helped, especially at this point, so Chay said, "Ignore them — keep rowing."

The lifeboat circled us. The men kept asking us if we wanted a rope. After a while we decided that we couldn't just tell them to push off. So we finally accepted the rope and transferred to the lifeboat for the last lap.

When we landed at the dock, we staggered around a bit, unable to clench our hands for the handshaking. To our astonishment, we discovered that we had beaten Johnstone. He was still somewhere at sea.

We've been described as national heroes, but I think that's only because the press is calling us that. The newspapers and magazines, not the deed, have made us heroes. The actual rowing of the Atlantic turned out to be easier than we expected.

Some of the newspaper posters in England read, **"The Boys Who Beat the Atlantic."** But Chay and I felt that we were lucky to get away with it. No, we didn't beat the Atlantic. It let us go.

Understanding What You've Read

1. Why did John Ridgway and Chay Blyth want to row the Atlantic?
2. What are two problems that Ridgway and Blyth encountered during their trip across the Atlantic?
3. What does the author mean when he says, "No, we didn't beat the Atlantic. It let us go"?

Applying the Skills Lesson

1. Compare the reactions of Ridgway and Blyth when they finally spotted land at the end of the trip.
2. Compare the reactions of Ridgway and Blyth to food after they had cut back to a daily ration of 1,000 calories.

As you read this selection, notice the ways in which Arthur Mitchell's background and training differed from those of other dancers.

It made no difference that he was poor. It was through hard work, determination, and talent that success came to . . .

Arthur Mitchell, Dancer

by Nicholas Pease

A grim and sweating Arthur Mitchell was lined up with the other dance students, doing stretching exercises. When the teacher yelled for them to begin, Arthur bent his body into a wide curve, his hands almost touching the floor.

"Again!" demanded the teacher. Arthur bent over even farther. He'd been exercising for hours, and every muscle ached. OK, so it hurts, he said to himself. But didn't it hurt just as much when you were carrying trash all morning, then shoveling the walk, then doing your paper route, then . . . ?

"Again!"

Arthur stretched harder, trying to remember what an honor it was to be a student at the New York High School of the Performing Arts. Yet his mind kept going back to what the head of the school had told him: He'd never make it as a dancer. He was strong, but his body was too stiff for a professional dancer.

"Again!"

With a tremendous effort, Arthur stretched farther than before. Suddenly he doubled up and crumpled to the floor. A pain like a knife wound shot through him. He had torn several muscles.

But later, as he limped painfully home, he wasn't thinking of giving up. Instead, he was filled with a cold, steely determination. Never mind the torn muscles. Never mind the stiffness. He *would* become a dancer, and a great one!

Born into a poor family in 1934, Arthur Mitchell knew hard work and misfortune. His parents were kind and loving, but the Depression was on. Jobs were hard to find. His father just barely made a living doing odd jobs of backbreaking work. Arthur helped him almost as soon as he could walk.

Such a difficult life might have crushed another person. But for Arthur it had had the opposite effect. As if in defiance, Arthur developed a warm, outgoing personality and a healthy sense of fun. This made him a natural leader among his school friends. When the opportunity presented itself, it also made him a gifted, natural performer.

Arthur loved nothing better than to dance. His energy and expressiveness were well known to his friends. One night at a junior high school dance, those talents brought about a major change in his life. One of his teachers was impressed with his dancing and suggested he try out for the High School of the Performing Arts.

Arthur didn't know that the school's judges were used to seeing highly polished classical performances. He prepared for the tryout by learning an old-time song-and-dance act. He appeared wearing a top hat and tuxedo and did a soft-shoe number to the tune of "Steppin' Out with My Baby." It was hardly what the judges expected. Arthur's smooth, graceful style, however, quickly won them over. He was accepted.

There was still one big problem. Arthur's muscles had tightened from years of heavy labor—lifting, hauling, pulling. It was nearly impossible for him to perform the free-flowing movements of ballet and modern dance. This was why the head of the school had suggested he quit. Arthur's torn muscles were the result of his fierce determination.

And Arthur was not through trying. When his injuries healed he resumed practice. He improved rapidly. When he graduated he was named the school's most accomplished dancer.

Bennington College offered him a scholarship, but Arthur graciously refused. He had received a better offer —a chance to study under the great choreographer George Balanchine at the New York City Ballet.

Arthur knew it was only a study scholarship. He would have to prove himself before he got the chance to join the ballet company. So far, no black dancer had made it. If Arthur were to succeed, he knew he would have to be better than the others.

Arthur decided he would have to work twice as hard as everyone else.

And work he did. Over the next three years, while the other dancers were turning off alarm clocks or brewing coffee, Arthur was already in the studio warming up. While they dragged themselves home, exhausted after their first or second class, Arthur was getting ready for his third. While they were relaxing, he was taking additional lessons from his good friend and teacher, Karel Shook. With whatever energy he still had, he worked to support his family.

But one question was constantly haunting him. Could he, a black dancer, win a starring role? The answer came in 1955, when Arthur was asked to join the New York City Ballet. He was given the leading role in Balanchine's *Western Symphony*. The sight of a black performer brought gasps of surprise from the opening-night audience. But Arthur's dazzling leaps and brilliant turns soon brought gasps of admiration. Many thought he was twice as good as anyone who had ever before danced the role.

Successes followed one another rapidly as Arthur proved he was equal to any role. He could be grand and stately in a serious ballet. He could be delightfully whimsical in a comedy. With each new part, he added a personal touch to the movements. He created a distinctive style that others tried hard to match. In 1957 Balanchine paid him a great honor by staging *Agon,* a ballet created just for Arthur. In 1962 Arthur won fame as Puck, the playful elf, in a ballet based on Shakespeare's *A Midsummer Night's Dream.*

With victories like these, Arthur might have been content with riches and fame, both of which he had. But he wasn't. Now he wanted to help other blacks succeed in the dance world. He wanted no less than a whole new art form — black ballet.

With his usual, incredible energy, he pushed ahead with his dream. He left the glamour of the New York City Ballet and, with Karel Shook, rented an empty garage in Harlem. This was to be their school. They had four professional dancers, thirty students, and a wooden platform for a stage. The Dance Theater of Harlem had begun to take shape.

It usually takes several years for a dancer to learn the complicated moves of classical ballet. Arthur felt, however, that if ballet were based on the dance and music already a part of their culture, black dancers could learn faster. He began holding classes morning, noon, and night. He challenged his students to match his fast pace. Inspired by his leadership, the young people progressed quickly. Arthur was learning that besides his very great talents as a performer, he was a very fine teacher as well.

One of his aims in setting up the school was to help as many young, promising dancers as possible. Students were accepted for little or no tuition. The school would have to pull itself up by its own bootstraps. Students would have to make the scenery, costumes, and other equipment.

The plan worked. Within a few months there were over 400 students, Larger quarters were now needed. So the Dance Theater of Harlem moved into a neighborhood church. It became a project for the whole community. Neighbors and well-wishers helped out whenever they could.

Among the dance forms studied were ballet, tap, and modern dance. Students learned instrumental music, stage sets, design, and costuming. Meanwhile, Arthur was busy creating new ballets based on African tribal rituals and jazz.

Glowing reports on the Dance Theater's work began to appear in the newspapers. But because of the fast growth of the school, money was still a problem. There never seemed to be enough. Arthur made appeals to wealthy people and businesses. At last he talked one group into matching whatever money the Dance Theater could raise itself.

That was the break Arthur was looking for. He set up a performing tour for his best dancers. They visited large and small towns all over the country. They scored a huge success at the Jacob's Pillow Dance Festival in Massachusetts and another at New York's Guggenheim Museum. Then it was on to the Caribbean Islands and Europe, always to wildly cheering audiences. The result was a permanent home for the Dance Theater in a restored warehouse just a few blocks from where Arthur grew up.

The Dance Theater of Harlem now performs a full season of dances in New York. Some people place it among the world's best companies.

For its founder and guiding spirit, Arthur Mitchell, the days of performance are over. But he still teaches, directs, choreographs, manages, and plans. More than anyone else, he has helped to create a new means of expression for black artists and a new source of enjoyment for people all over the world.

Understanding What You've Read

1. What effect did growing up in the Depression have on Arthur Mitchell?
2. Why wasn't Arthur satisfied with the riches and fame of a successful dancer?
3. How did Arthur Mitchell raise money for the new Dance Theater of Harlem?

Applying the Skills Lesson

1. In what ways was Arthur unlike other dance students?
2. How does Arthur Mitchell's work today differ from his earlier work as a performer?

TEXTBOOK STUDY

Organization by Comparison and Contrast

Textbook authors often use comparison and contrast to organize information. Recognizing these comparisons and contrasts will help you understand the material. Read this textbook selection. Use the sidenotes as keys to the comparisons and contrasts.

Organization by Comparison and Contrast in Language Arts

One of the first things you'll usually do when you write a story is to establish the setting. The *setting* tells the readers when and where the story takes place. Usually the setting is made clear at or near the beginning of the story.

Some writers give only a brief description of the setting. Here are three story beginnings that establish the settings quickly and briefly:

The author asks you to compare these three settings.

Paris has a grief of its own on some nights in December. . . .

— Kay Boyle, "Art Colony"

You can also compare and contrast the three writing styles.

It was late and everyone had left the café except an old man who sat in the shadow the leaves of the tree made against the electric light. . . .

— Ernest Hemingway, "A Clean, Well-Lighted Place"

It was mid-morning — a very cold, bright day. Holding a potted plant before her, a girl of fourteen jumped off the bus in front of the Old Ladies' Home, on the outskirts of town. . . .

— Eudora Welty, "A Visit of Charity"

Other writers describe the setting in great detail. Here is the description of Maycomb, the setting of the novel *To Kill a Mockingbird*:

Maycomb was an old town, but it was a tired old town when I first knew it. In rainy weather the streets turned to red slop; grass grew on the sidewalks, the courthouse sagged in the square. Somehow, it was hotter then: a black dog suffered on a summer's day, . . . Men's stiff collars wilted by nine in the morning. Ladies bathed before noon, after their three-o'clock naps, and by nightfall were like soft teacakes with frostings of sweat and sweet talcum.

People moved slowly then. They ambled across the square, shuffled in and out of the stores around it, took their time about everything. A day was twenty-four hours long but seemed longer. There was no hurry, for there was nowhere to go, nothing to buy and no money to buy it with, nothing to see outside the boundaries of Maycomb County. But it was a time of vague optimism for some of the people: Maycomb County had recently been told that it had nothing to fear but fear itself.

—Harper Lee, *To Kill a Mockingbird*

—*Growth in English*
Laidlaw Brothers

How is this description of a story setting different from the descriptions quoted on page 212?

Building Skills

1. Look at the quotation from *To Kill a Mockingbird*. To what are the ladies of Maycomb compared? What clue word signals the comparison?
2. What is similar about the way Kay Boyle, Ernest Hemingway, and Eudora Welty developed their settings?

Organization by Comparison and Contrast in Science

There are no sidenotes accompanying this textbook selection. Read the selection. Then answer the questions that follow.

Life in a Swiftly Flowing Stream

Mountain streams and ponds both contain fresh water, but that is about as far as the similarities go. If we compare them with land environments, a pond and a mountain stream are about as different as a forest is from a desert. Why is this so?

Pond water is warm most of the year. A mountain stream is fed by melting snow and is usually cold. A pond is usually stagnant—that is, the water is not mixed and churned. Most ponds are fed new water only by creeks or by seepage of ground water from the surrounding land. A mountain stream rushes toward the valleys below and is mixed violently, thrown into the air, and churned by its swift flow, usually over rocks. Thus the water becomes mixed with a great amount of air. A mountain stream is usually crystal clear, whereas a pond is generally muddy.

— Life: A Biological Science
Harcourt Brace Jovanovich

Building Skills

1. How are streams and ponds similar?
2. In what ways are streams and ponds different?
3. What word clues (if any) signal the comparisons and contrasts in the selection?

SKILLS LESSON

Tell Me Why . . . Organization by Cause and Effect

There is an old folktale of a little Dutch boy who, when passing a dike, noticed a small leak. He quickly sized up the situation. The leak was bound to get bigger if it wasn't plugged up. So the boy poked his finger into the hole and lo and behold! The flow of water stopped instantly. The Dutch boy probably was not even aware that he was illustrating a **cause-and-effect relationship:**

The boy poked his finger in the hole (the cause) and the flow of water stopped (the effect).

In a cause-and-effect relationship, the action that *brings about* an event is the **cause.** The **effect** is the event that occurs as a *result of* the particular action. You can identify causes and effects by asking yourself two questions. First, "What happened?" Your answer will be the *effect.* Second, "Why did it happen?" The answer to this question is the *cause.*

Read the three sentences that follow. In each case, what is the cause and what is the effect?

1. Several cars skidded because the pavement was icy.
2. The professor asked a very difficult question, so only a few students raised their hands to answer it.
3. Because the Rite-Fine Pencil Company didn't pay its bill, the electric company stopped its service to the factory.

What happened in sentence 1? "Several cars skidded." This is the effect. Why did several cars skid? "The pavement was icy." This is the cause.

In sentence 2, what happened when "the professor asked a very difficult question" (the cause)? "Only a few students raised their hands" (the effect).

Notice that in sentence 1, the effect is stated first. In sentence 2, the cause is stated first.

What was the effect of the Rite-Fine Pencil Company's failure to pay the electric bill?

One Cause, Several Effects

Sometimes one event (the cause) can have several effects. For example, suppose a hurricane strikes a town along the coast. Its effects might be:

severe flooding   many people left homeless
uprooted trees   downed power lines
damaged homes   landslides

When you read about such events, finding all the effects that relate to the cause can help you understand what happened and why. When authors write about such events, they often organize the material by cause and effect. This makes it easier for you to note the relationships.

In the following paragraph, the author has organized the information to show how a single event had several effects. Read the paragraph. What is the cause? What are the effects?

217

On Halloween night in 1938, Orson Welles presented the science fiction novel *The War of the Worlds* as a radio news broadcast. Before the program began, Welles explained to the audience that the "news" was pure fiction. However, many listeners tuned in late and missed Welles's introduction. As a result of the broadcast, thousands of people thought that the Earth was being invaded by Martians. They panicked. They took to the streets, hoping to flee the cities by whatever means they could. Traffic was at a standstill. Telephone lines were jammed. The following day, headlines such as "The Night the Martians Landed" appeared in the newspapers. Records of the broadcast followed soon after. The number of science fiction movies increased at a tremendous rate.

The paragraph above is organized to show a cause-and-effect relationship. The emphasis is on the large number of events (effects) that resulted from a single cause, the 1938 broadcast of *The War of the Worlds*. Eight effects of the broadcast are mentioned. What are these effects? Notice that the author uses the phrase "as a result" to introduce all the effects of the broadcast.

Chain Reactions

Very often one event results in another event which in turn causes still another event. Thus, an event is both an effect and a cause. This is called a **chain reaction.** Read the paragraph that follows. Notice that the author has organized the information to show this kind of cause-and-effect relationship.

There has been very little rain this year. As a result, the grain crop is smaller than usual. A smaller crop means that grain will be in demand. A large demand causes wholesale grain prices to rise. Therefore, all products made from grain will cost the consumer more money.

Notice that the cause of the small grain crop is the lack of rain. What is the effect of a small grain crop? It is that grain will be in demand. What is the effect of a large demand for grain? What is the effect of a rise in wholesale grain prices?

Try This

Read this paragraph. Then answer the questions that follow.

Oregon has many forests. Thus, lumber, paper, and furniture have become the state's three largest industries. Oregon's vast forests also provide homes for a large population of beaver—the master architect of the animal world. For this reason, Oregon has been nicknamed "The Beaver State."

1. What sentences in the paragraph develop a chain reaction?
2. What event mentioned in the paragraph is both a cause and an effect?
3. For which event mentioned in the paragraph is more than one effect given?
4. What caused lumber, paper, and furniture to become Oregon's three largest industries?

VOCABULARY STUDY

Maxwell's Words . . . Prefixes

When Maxwell cut three words into pieces with his plastic scissors, he wasn't worried. He knew that his sister Natalie would paste them all back together.

"What did the first word mean?" she asked angrily.

"It meant 'to break up into separate parts.' "

Natalie picked up the word *integrate*. "This means 'to unite,' " she said. Then she taped it to the prefix *dis-*. "*Dis-* can mean 'to do the opposite.' So the opposite of unite is *disintegrate*. Next definition."

Maxwell grinned. "Righto! This word means 'to make another estimate about the worth of something.' "

"*Appraise* means 'to judge the worth of something,' " said Natalie. "The prefix *re-* means 'again.' " A small piece of tape did the rest: *reappraise.*

"Definition number 3!" Maxwell announced with delight. " 'Lacking good judgment.' "

"Well, that certainly describes you!" snapped Natalie. "So pay attention. *Prudent* means 'having good judgment.' The prefix *im-* means 'not.' Tape them together and you get *imprudent,* 'NOT having good judgment'! There! We're done!"

Maxwell chuckled softly. "Not quite," he said, and he reached into his pocket for another list of words.

Word Play

1. If you put a sugar cube in hot tea, does it *integrate* or *disintegrate?*
2. If the worth of a diamond is estimated for the first time, is it *appraised* or *reappraised?*
3. If Waldo Dumbcookie does eighty kilometers an hour in a twenty-five-kilometer zone, is he *prudent* or *imprudent?*

As you read this selection, look for the cause-and-effect relationships.

For four years Shirley Chisholm represented her community in the New York State legislature. Then she took on an even more difficult task. This is the story of how she became . . .

The Congresswoman from Brooklyn

by Susan Brownmiller

In 1968, the New York State legislature changed some of the Congressional District (CD) lines in Brooklyn, New York. One of the new districts became known as the Twelfth CD. Even before the boundaries of the "new Twelfth" were made public, the neighborhood of Bedford-Stuyvesant, in the heart of the Twelfth CD, was buzzing with the news. A representative in Congress from Bedford-Stuyvesant! Who would the new representative be? Whom would the Democrats choose as their candidate? Would there be a primary fight? Who would be nominated by the Republicans? What would the Liberal and Conservative parties do?

One evening in February, after Shirley Chisholm had returned to Brooklyn from her week's work in Albany, she received a surprise visitor.

"Mrs. Chisholm," said an elderly woman standing on the doorstep, "my friends and I know what you've been doing for us up there in Albany. We want you to run for Congress from this neighborhood. We collected this money, and we want to give it to you for a campaign contribution."

223

Vote for Chisholm

Shirley was flabbergasted. She invited the woman inside the house.

"It isn't much," said the woman, handing Shirley an envelope. "We don't have much to give. But it's a beginning, and we're going to go out and collect more."

Inside the envelope Shirley found $9.62—all in coins. She hugged the lady tightly. "I know what this money means to you," she whispered. "We'll make it together—you and I."

After the woman had left, Shirley carefully wrapped the envelope of coins in a handkerchief and put it away in the top drawer of her dresser.

"I'm going to keep this envelope always," she said to her husband Conrad, "just the way it is."

"I've been wondering when you were going to start thinking about that Congressional seat," Conrad replied.

"Oh, I've been thinking about it, all right."

"Your Assembly District is the heart of the new Congressional District," Conrad pointed out. "It seems to me that you'd be the logical choice of the party leaders."

A few evenings later, Conrad came home to find Shirley poring over a set of large books.

"I see you wasted no time in getting hold of the election rolls," he said with a grin.

"It's fascinating, Conrad. You can tell so much about a neighborhood just from looking at the names of the registered voters."

"You've always gotten along well with all kinds of people," said Conrad, as he leafed through the pages.

"There's something else here, Conrad. It appears that there are thousands more women voters in this district than men."

"That is interesting," Conrad agreed. "The women voters have always been fierce about you, Shirley. The Twelfth CD is looking better all the time."

The following week, Shirley Chisholm announced that she was running for Congress. Shortly afterward, another legislator from Bedford-Stuyvesant, State Senator William C. Thompson, declared that he was also in the race. A few weeks later, James Farmer, founder of the Congress of Racial Equality and a well-known civil rights leader, declared himself a Republican candidate.

"What are you going to do about it?" Conrad asked.

"I'm going to call a campaign meeting for tomorrow night. It's not only going to be a tough primary fight, it's going to be a battle right up until November."

Shirley had asked her old friend Wesley Holder to be her campaign manager. Everyone agreed that Shirley's base of strength was her own Fifty-fifth Assembly District. That was the district she represented in Albany. Everybody in the neighborhood knew her.

"First things first," Holder had said to Shirley. "Our first job is to win the Democratic primary. If you take the primary, you'll have no trouble winning the general election. This district has always been heavily Democratic."

"What about the other sections of the new Twelfth CD where they don't know me personally?" Shirley asked. "Have you figured out a battle plan?"

"You're going to get a group of your supporters together," Holder said excitedly. "They'll fan out over the whole district with shopping bags full of campaign leaflets. You, Shirley, will be out on a sound truck a good deal of the time. You'll acquaint the voters with your personality and your stand on the issues."

"I guess we'll be wanting bumper stickers, too," Conrad put in. "Signs that say 'CHISHOLM FOR CONGRESS.' The bumper stickers and the leaflets and the sound truck will take a lot of money, though, won't they?"

"Most of the money will be raised from people in the Twelfth CD who want to see Shirley Chisholm in Congress," Holder said thoughtfully.

Shirley's campaign organization got under way. Speaking to voters from the top of a sound truck was nothing new to Shirley Chisholm. Her races for the state assembly had given her plenty of experience.

Chisholm for Congress

"I really like to campaign," Shirley told Conrad one weekend evening. She had spent the entire day making street-corner speeches to voters in the new Twelfth CD. "The people really listen to what I have to say. It's important to get close to the voters—to let them see you and to shake their hands."

"Ladies and gentlemen, this is fighting Shirley Chisholm coming through," she would announce in a firm, strong voice. Her opening statement over the loudspeaker and the sight of campaign cars covered with Chisholm stickers were usually enough to draw a crowd.

By the time Shirley had finished her speech, the crowd would generally triple in size. Her campaign staff would hand out about 2,000 leaflets. Then Shirley would climb down from the sound truck and begin shaking hands.

"Judging from the response, I don't think I'm doing too badly in this campaign," Shirley said to Conrad after a particularly successful afternoon. But she didn't want to admit she was worried. Her long-time ally, Tommy Fortune, had told her that most of the other political leaders in the new Twelfth CD considered State Senator Thompson to be an easy winner.

"But what do you think?" Shirley had asked Fortune.

"Well," he replied, "I think you'll make it."

The third candidate in the primary race, Dollie Robinson, didn't bother Shirley. "Some people think that Dollie's going to cut into my vote because she's a woman," Shirley told Conrad. "But I don't think so. Dollie's from the same part of the district as Willie Thompson. I think they're going to hurt each other—not me."

At last June 18, primary day, rolled around. Shirley's supporters had worked hard to get out the vote. But by the time the polls closed in the evening, only about 12,000 registered Democrats had gone to the voting booths. The turnout had been small, but the important question was: Which candidate had gotten the most votes?

At Shirley's campaign headquarters, Wesley Holder sat at a desk with long sheets of paper in front of him. As the poll watchers brought in the results from each small election district, he entered the figures in three columns labeled Chisholm, Thompson, and Robinson.

Finally, Holder stood up and chalked the totals on a big board:

CHISHOLM	5,680
THOMPSON	4,907
ROBINSON	1,848

A roar went up from Shirley's campaign workers. Shirley Chisholm had won the Democratic nomination for Congress!

But only half the battle had been won. The other half—the general election in November—still remained.

When Shirley and Conrad went home late that night, they had a very serious matter to discuss. Shirley's health had run down during the hard months of campaigning. She and Conrad knew that she would have to enter the hospital for an operation. She had postponed it as long as she could.

Shirley went into the hospital in July. In August she was back on her feet, working but weak.

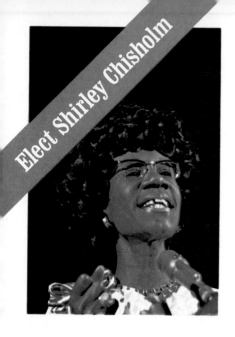

Elect Shirley Chisholm

The National Democratic Convention was held in Chicago at the end of August. Shirley decided not to attend. She felt the trip would not be good for her health. But something happened to make her change her mind. Tommy Fortune called from Chicago to say the Democrats wanted to elect her National Committeewoman from the State of New York. It was an important party office. Still weak, Shirley was bundled onto a plane and flown to Chicago for the honor.

Back in Brooklyn, Shirley's campaign organization began preparing for the general election in November. Shirley's major opponent was James Farmer. He had gotten both the Republican and the Liberal party nominations.

Campaign manager Holder gave Shirley his ideas on the kind of campaign they needed to wage. "Farmer's strategy is going to be that you're a gracious lady with the right ideas, but that the Twelfth Congressional District needs a man for the job."

"My research turned up the fact that there are about 12,000 more women voters registered in this district than men," Shirley said. "Farmer's strategy might just backfire."

Shirley was still recovering from her operation. She couldn't do as much rugged street campaigning as she had for the primary. The few speeches she did give were at indoor meetings.

By contrast, her opponent's campaign was loud and noisy. Farmer's campaign managers used bongo players to drum up a crowd for the candidate's street meetings.

Whenever Shirley and Farmer met face to face for a debate, however, her positions were just as strong as his. The people who listened knew that she could do more than just hold her own with him.

Election day 1968 finally arrived. The lines at the polling places were long. The voters often had to wait more than an hour before they could cast their votes.

Shortly before midnight there no longer was any doubt about the outcome of the race. Shirley Chisholm had won!

She had been overwhelmingly elected by the people in her district. She would represent them in the United States Congress in Washington.

Back at campaign headquarters, a victorious Shirley Chisholm greeted her supporters. A cheer arose in the crowded hall as she made her entrance.

Yes, with the help of these close supporters, she had won. But the victory was truly hers. She had worked for many years to reach her goal.

Understanding What You've Read

1. What interesting discovery did Shirley Chisholm make before the primary when she looked at the election rolls in her district? Why was this discovery so important?
2. What evidence does the selection give that Shirley Chisholm waged a tough campaign for the Democratic primary?
3. What was Farmer's strategy in the general election?

Applying the Skills Lesson

1. What caused Shirley Chisholm to change her mind about attending the National Democratic Convention?
2. Was the effect of Farmer's strategy in the general election what he intended? Explain your answer.

As you read the selection that follows, notice that some events produce more than one effect.

A woman who has perhaps done more than anyone else to help rid her people of age-old problems is . . .

ANNIE DODGE WAUNEKA, NAVAJO CRUSADER

by Marion E. Gridley

In December 1964, the Presidential Medal of Freedom Awards were presented by President Lyndon B. Johnson. This is the highest award that can be presented to citizens in peacetime. Only those who have made outstanding contributions are chosen.

When the name Annie Dodge Wauneka was called, a tall, stately woman stepped forward. All eyes were upon her. Mrs. Wauneka was the first Native American to be honored with the Medal of Freedom.

Annie was born on a Navajo reservation, the daughter of one of the Navajos' great leaders, Henry Chee Dodge. He was the first chairman of the Tribal Council and held the office for more than eight years.

As soon as Annie could walk, she helped herd her father's sheep, as was the custom among her people. When she was eight years old, her father sent her to the government boarding school for Native Americans at Fort Defiance, Arizona.

While Annie was in first grade, the terrible flu epidemic of World War I hit, and many Navajos died. Annie escaped with a mild attack. When she was fully recovered, the school nurse showed her how to clean the lanterns every morning so that they could be placed in the hospital's halls and rooms. Annie did all that she could to help. The experience, still vivid in her mind today, was probably the spark that ignited her great interest in Navajo health.

When she had finished fifth grade, Annie's father sent her to a school in Albuquerque [al′bə kûr′kē]. For the first time, she discovered that there were other Native Americans besides Navajos. Among her closest friends were many Pueblo girls. Annie learned to speak English as did all the students. Now she could communicate with both her teachers and the other students, regardless of which tribe they belonged to.

When Annie was thirteen, her father was named chairman of the newly formed Tribal Council. Soon after, he visited the Albuquerque Indian School to speak to the children. Annie listened carefully as he talked about the need to educate Native Americans. She was very proud, and her father's words would prove to be a great influence in her life.

Annie finished her schooling with the eleventh grade. This, however, did not end her education. She continued to learn throughout her life in every way she could. After leaving school, she continued to herd sheep and goats and care for the livestock on her father's ranch. When she married George Wauneka, she and her husband settled down and began to learn the business of successful cattle ranching.

Annie worked closely with her father in his duties as tribal chairman. She attended many meetings and listened to the long discussions. In this way, she came to understand the problems affecting her people and the reasons for their extreme poverty.

Chee Dodge often began his speeches with comments on the hardships the Navajos had suffered. He always said that this suffering had been caused by a lack of education. He tried to impress upon his people, over and over, that education was the key to their future.

When Annie first attended these meetings, she was very shy. However, her father encouraged her to voice her opinions. "Do not be afraid to speak your mind," he said. "But never lose your respect for your elders or for the old people who have lived before you. If it were not for them and their courage, you would not be here."

Chee Dodge was very strict with his daughter. He insisted that she concentrate on the exact meanings of words so that she could accurately interpret them to Navajos and non-Navajos alike. He had been one of the first Navajo interpreters, and Annie saw how his deep understanding of language had earned him the respect of all.

Annie and her husband continued to run the ranch. But more and more, her father gave her tribal jobs and responsibilities. He trusted her completely. She began to see how one works for an ideal. She also learned about politics.

Although Annie had always been close to her father, she became even closer during the last days of his life. Shortly before he died, he said to her, "Do not let my straight rope fall to the ground. If you discover it dropping, quickly pick it up and hold it high."

After her father's death, Annie became determined to hold the straight rope high. She worked for her council chapter and continued to act as interpreter. When she was chosen secretary, one of her tasks was to interpret for Navajos who were in hospitals. Four years later, she became the first woman elected to the Tribal Council.

Annie was appointed chairwoman of the council's Health and Welfare Committee. When the Surgeon General of the United States set up the Advisory Committee on Indian Health, Mrs. Wauneka was invited to become a member.

To get her health crusade under way, Annie concentrated her energies on tuberculosis. She visited hospitals and homes. She talked with the patients. She tried to persuade patients who had run away from the hospitals to return and continue treatment.

She taught and encouraged better health habits and advised people to improve their living conditions. She influenced the Tribal Council to set aside money for a home-improvement program. "Dirt floors must become a thing of the past," she said. "Sanitation must be improved. There must be a good and adequate water supply, and there must be running water in the homes."

In desert areas, water is scarce, and sometimes it is of poor quality. The sicknesses caused by these conditions became one of Annie's major concerns. She campaigned so strongly that a bill was finally passed authorizing the Public Health Service to build, improve, and extend sanitary facilities for Native Americans. Later, the Tribal Council gave money to those Navajos who wanted to follow the new health provisions.

These were great victories. With more financial help, many new homes were built on the reservation. They were neat, compact houses with bright roofs, wooden floors, and small outhouses a proper distance away. Often a hogan remained nearby for those who preferred to live in the old way or for sacred ceremonies.

Mrs. Wauneka started her own radio program. She broadcast health information in the tribal language.

Everything Annie Wauneka did brought results. Tuberculosis was so greatly reduced among the Navajos that it is no longer a major concern. More and more Navajos now seek medical and hospital care. Medicine men work with the doctors as respected partners. Mrs. Wauneka was able to win them to her cause by using a language they understood and by relating it to their needs. She was also able to help the doctors appreciate and understand the place of the medicine man in Navajo life.

Mrs. Wauneka became known throughout the country for her health-care work. She was honored by the Western Tuberculosis Association for her efforts to free her people from sickness. She was named Arizona's Woman of Achievement by the Arizona Press Women's Association. She received the Josephine B. Hughes Memorial Award for promoting the health and welfare of her people, and of the country as a whole. She received the Indian Achievement Award for her great humanitarian services.

She was appointed to the governor of New Mexico's Committee on the Aging and to many other health groups. She attended a meeting on Native American

health problems in Alaska and often went to conferences in Washington, D.C. She was able to start a reservation eye-ear-dental-care program.

Like her father, she stresses the need for education. This interest is second only to her interest in Navajo health.

Mrs. Wauneka understands the loneliness of the child away at school. She believes that parents and schools must work together to educate children.

"Parents must have a say in where schools are to be located," she says. "Children should be allowed to remain closer to home.

And their parents should have a close tie with their schools.

"Nothing is wrong with the Navajos except poor education," she states. "We are fifty years behind the rest of the country. We want to keep our children near us. We don't want to send them miles away to a school where we cannot look after them. But until things change, we must accept the education that we have, for it is the answer to our problems."

Mrs. Wauneka could, without criticism, turn now to a more quiet life. But she has no intention of retiring. Instead, she works closely with the Tribal Council on the Advisory Committee, reviewing concerns and making recommendations.

When a new seventy-five-bed hospital opened on the reservation at Shiprock, New Mexico, Mrs. Wauneka was an honored guest. The chief of the U.S. Public Health Service introduced her with these words: "No one person has done more than Annie Dodge Wauneka to spread a wide understanding of health among Native Americans. No one has encouraged them more to take an active part in the health services."

And Annie smiled her beaming smile and answered, "Over the years, I learned that one failure— or even a half-dozen failures— should never be the end of trying. I must always try again, and I will continue to try as long as there is breath to do so."

Understanding What You've Read

1. How did Annie Dodge Wauneka probably first become interested in Navajo health?
2. What are her feelings toward Navajo education?
3. What did Annie Wauneka's father mean when he said, "Do not let my straight rope fall to the ground. If you discover it dropping, quickly pick it up and hold it high"?

Applying the Skills Lesson

1. According to Chee Dodge, what was the cause of much of the Navajo suffering?
2. What were some of the effects of Annie Wauneka's efforts to improve the health of Native Americans?

TEXTBOOK STUDY

Organization by Cause and Effect

Information in textbooks is often organized by cause and effect to show how events or ideas are related. As you read the textbook selection that follows, use the sidenotes as keys to the cause-and-effect relationships.

Organization by Cause and Effect in Social Studies

The United States has only 5 percent of the world's people, but those people account for 40 percent of the world's yearly use of resources. Resource use in the United States will be even greater **if** its population and standard of living continue to rise.

Does *if* signal a cause or an effect?

As a result of this nation's high level of development, the supply of resources in the United States is getting smaller. Unlike water and air, which are naturally recycled or renewed, some resources are nonrenewable. They are gone after they are used, unless people recycle or renew them.

In this sentence, what is the cause and what is the effect?

If people in the United States continue to use some mineral resources as they have in the past, and if new sources of these minerals are not found, many of them will be gone within a few years. Judging from the supplies that are available to the United States now, if no new resources are discovered, zinc will last 20 years, lead 25 years, iron ore 350 years, and coal 450 years.

According to the author, what will be the effect if no new mineral resources are discovered?

—Sources of Identity
Harcourt Brace Jovanovich

Building Skills

1. According to the first paragraph of the selection, what would be the effect if the United States' population and standard of living continue to rise?

2. What phrase in the second paragraph signals an effect?

Organization by Cause and Effect in Language Arts

There are no sidenotes accompanying this selection. Read the selection carefully and look for the cause-and-effect relationships. Then answer the questions that follow.

Middle English: 1100-1500

Old English had developed slowly over about six hundred years. Then new conquests began that marked the end of Old English and the beginning of Middle English.

In 1066, England was once again invaded. This time it was by the Normans from the northern part of France. Their leader, Duke William, earned the title "the Conqueror" as he and his army defeated the English in battle.

Once again, conquest brought with it a new language. French took the place of English for the rulers of England—the educated and merchant classes. Although the common people still spoke English, their speech began to reflect the presence of the conquerors. As they worked and traded with the French, French words began to replace many of their English ones.

—Language for Daily Use: Silver
Harcourt Brace Jovanovich

Building Skills

1. What effect did the 1066 invasion have on the English language?
2. Why was Duke William given the title "the Conqueror"?

SKILLS LESSON

Sort It Out . . . Mixed Patterns of Organization

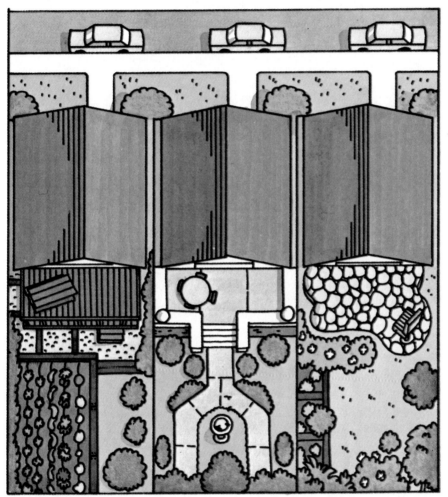

In the previous skills lessons, you saw how information can be organized by examples, time, comparison and contrast, and cause and effect. In many cases, however, authors use more than one pattern of organization when presenting information. For example, the paragraph that follows is organized by time and by cause and effect. As you read, look for the time clues. Is the information presented in chronological order? What are the cause-and-effect relationships?

Ghana, the first great African empire, began about 1,600 years ago. Most of its people were farmers, but some were miners who dug gold out of Ghana's mountains. By selling the gold to North Africa and the Middle East, Ghana became wealthy. The country used this wealth to build strong armies. It conquered weak tribes and other countries. But wars also hurt Ghana. Many men were lost in battle. Thus, the strength of the nation was threatened. The people began to leave and form separate tribes. By the year 1200, ancient Ghana's power came to an end.

Notice that the paragraph talks about Ghana's history. The events are described in chronological order. The first time clue given is the phrase "about 1,600 years ago." Approximately what date would that be? To find out, subtract 1,600 from the present date. (Since these dates are only approximate you can round off the number to the nearest ten.) Ghana's empire began in about A.D. 380 — or the second half of the fourth century. The last sentence has another time clue: "the year 1200." How many years did Ghana's empire last? Subtract 380 from 1,200. All the other events occurred during that 820-year period.

The paragraph also is organized to show cause-and-effect relationships. What was the cause of Ghana's wealth? The third sentence tells you that Ghana became wealthy by "selling gold to North Africa and the Middle East." What effect did wars have on Ghana?

By using two patterns of organization, the author is able to provide the reader with a great deal of information and illustrate different kinds of relationships.

Now read the following paragraph. What two patterns of organization do you notice?

As a rule, buildings constructed before World War II are safer than modern buildings because they were built brick by brick and floor by floor. The floors are thick, sometimes constructed of one solid foot of concrete. The windows open. Air-conditioning units serve one or two floors apiece, not the whole building. Commercial buildings, divided into small offices, have floor-to-floor fire-resistant walls, so if a fire breaks out in one area, it's likely to stay there. Of course, there is no such thing as a completely fireproof building. However, these older buildings are generally more resistant to fire, and less dangerous to their occupants, than the more modern ones.

You should have noticed that the author sets up a contrast between pre– and post–World War II buildings. What characteristics of pre–World War II buildings are mentioned? How are post–World War II buildings different? What word clues show that the paragraph is organized by comparison and contrast?

In addition to comparison and contrast, the paragraph also illustrates cause-and-effect relationships. For example, the first sentence states one of the causes of pre–World War II building safety. What word clue signals this cause? Notice that the fifth sentence states that one of the effects of fire-resistant walls is to keep the fire contained in one area. What word clue signals this effect?

Try This

Read the paragraph below. Then answer the questions.

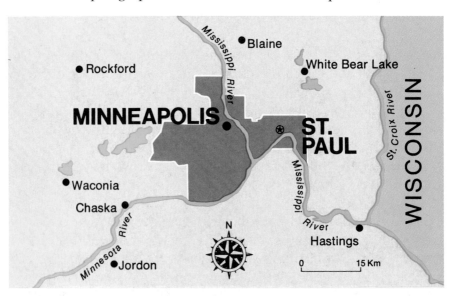

    Minneapolis, Minnesota, and St. Paul, Minnesota, are known as the "Twin Cities." Indeed, they are very much alike in certain ways. The area of Minneapolis is 153 square kilometers as compared to 152 square kilometers for St. Paul. Both cities are located close to the Mississippi River. The two cities boast several industries. Minneapolis, for instance, is a major electronics-computer manufacturing center and is the headquarters of the nation's four largest grain millers. St. Paul's important industries include publishing, electronics, and livestock. Another example of the cities' similarity is in population. Minneapolis ranks first in the state; St. Paul ranks a very close second.

1. What two patterns of organization were used in the paragraph?
   a. cause and effect and comparison and contrast
   b. examples and comparison and contrast
   c. time and cause and effect
2. What word clues in the paragraph signal the two kinds of organization used?

VOCABULARY STUDY

Grandma, What's a Concoction? ... Suffixes

WELL, NOW, A CONCOCTION IS SOMETHING YOU CONCOCT, LIKE A BANANA-STRING-BEAN-WALNUT SUNDAE TOPPED WITH WHIPPED CREAM.

AND WHAT'S A DEPRESSION?

A DEPRESSION IS CAUSED WHEN YOU DEPRESS SOMETHING. SUPPOSE WE'VE MADE THAT CONCOCTION, AND I POKE MY FINGER INTO THE WHIPPED CREAM TOPPING. I'VE MADE A DEPRESSION IN THE CONCOCTION.

I THINK I UNDERSTAND NOW. WHAT'S A DISTORTION?

AH HA! A DISTORTION IS SOMETHING THAT YOU DISTORT. LET'S SAY I USE MY FIST TO SMASH OUR CONCOCTION. YOU NOW HAVE A TERRIBLE DISTORTION OF THE CONCOCTION. ANY QUESTIONS?

YES, JUST ONE. WHAT DO WE DO WITH THIS MUSHY BANANA-STRING-BEAN-WALNUT CONCOCTION? IT'S NOT FIT TO EAT.

OH, GOODNESS, YOU'RE RIGHT. WE SHOULDN'T HAVE ADDED THE WALNUTS.

Word Play

Make up a story to explain each of the following unusual events:

- why Phinias Poker became famous when people tasted his new *concoction*
- what created the mysterious *depression* in the middle of Crab Apple Park
- how ace reporter Marcia Smunk's news story became a *distortion* of facts

As you read the selection that follows, notice the different ways in which the factual material is organized.

A single moment on a battlefield shattered a young man's arm but not his dream of becoming an artist. This is the story of . . .

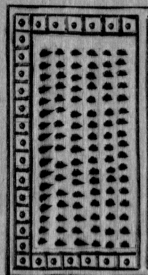

"Self-Portrait"

Horace Pippin's Struggle to Create

by Romare Bearden *and* Harry Henderson

On a spring day in 1937 two old friends walked through West Chester, a small town near Philadelphia. They were artist N. C. Wyeth and art critic Dr. Christian Brinton. In the window of a shoe-repair shop they saw a painting with strong, flat colors. It had been done on thick board instead of canvas. The shape of several items seemed to be cut deeply into the painting. Its simple, charming quality caused the men to inquire about its creator.

"Oh, that was painted by Horace Pippin, a black man with a bad arm," said the shoemaker. He paints all the time. He asked if he could put it in my window. He said, 'Maybe someone would like to buy it.' He certainly needs the money."

Interested, Brinton went to Pippin's home. He was greeted at the door by a tall, dignified, sad-faced man whose right arm hung limply at his side. Pippin reached over with his left arm to grab his right wrist. He lifted his right arm to shake hands. Brinton felt the strength and life in Pippin's right hand. "My arm got hurt in the war," said Pippin simply.

Pippin showed Brinton several of his paintings. All had the same brilliant colors painted flatly on boards. Brinton also saw some unfinished paintings — boards with outlines of figures burned into them. Pippin explained that he drew on a board with a red-hot poker. He showed Brinton how he had to grasp his limp right arm in his left when painting with a brush on canvas. But when he used a poker, the heavy iron supported his hand so he could manipulate it. Brinton was impressed by both the man and his work.

Draw Me and Win a Prize

Horace Pippin was born in West Chester, Pennsylvania, on February 22, 1888. He discovered very early in life that he could draw. At school he would print a word and then draw a picture to illustrate it.

One day he saw a magazine advertisement with a cartoon of a funny face. "Draw me — and win a prize!" it said. Horace made a drawing and sent it in. A week later he received the prize — six crayons, a box of water colors, and two brushes. Horace was elated. He began drawing and coloring pictures of what he saw in the village: houses, stores, trees, and animals. He also copied pictures from Sunday School books.

Each year the Sunday School held a festival. Everyone was asked to contribute something to be sold. Horace bought a yard of cloth and cut it up into six pieces. Then he cut the edges of the pieces to make them look like doilies. On each he drew a Biblical scene. He colored them brightly and took them to the festival as his donation. By noon, every doily had been sold. Horace was overjoyed.

A month later, as Horace was on his way to school, a woman called to him from a doorway. "Aren't you Horace Pippin?"

"Yes, ma'am."

"Are you the one who made the doilies?"

"Yes."

"Well, you certainly made some bum things," she said. She pulled a few pieces of fringed cloth from the pocket of her apron. "This had a picture when I bought it at the festival. Then I washed it, and this is all I have — a plain piece of cloth."

"But you're not supposed to wash it," protested Horace. "It's only a crayon picture. It washes right off."

Horace's feelings were hurt. The woman had implied that he had cheated her. Over forty years later, he still remembered the hurt.

When Horace was fourteen, he got a job at a farm owned by a man named James Gavin. One night Mr. Gavin fell asleep while reading his paper. Horace sketched him as he slept and put the drawing on the kitchen table.

"Who drew this?" asked Mr. Gavin when he saw the sketch.

"I did," said Horace.

"That's a very good drawing. You ought to go to school to really learn. You have the talent."

"Yes, sir," said Horace. "But I have no money."

"Well, maybe I could send you," said Mr. Gavin.

But before the idea could be followed up, Horace was called home. His mother was very ill and had almost no money. "Don't worry," he said, "I'll be able to get a full-time job. I'm a good worker."

So, at fifteen, Horace Pippin went to work. He unloaded coal. Then he worked at a feed store. When he was eighteen, he took a job at the local hotel. Later he packed and loaded furniture vans. In 1916 he went to work for a brake-shoe company, hoping to become a molder in its foundry.

Wounded in Action

When the United States entered World War I, Horace joined the army. This had extraordinary meaning for him, as did everything that happened to him as a soldier. More than twenty years later he wrote about his army life in four autobiographical essays.

Horace joined a unit of black soldiers that reached France in December 1917. There, his unit was transferred to the French command as the 369th Regiment and put into action. For three months they took a terrible pounding from the German troops.

Pippin worked to become a good soldier. Soon he was made corporal. Still he found time now and then to sketch his friends and the war-torn landscape.

As a corporal, Pippin served at a lonely listening post far out in no-man's-land. His job was to report enemy movement and protect the main body of troops against surprise attacks. Men assigned to the outpost were often killed.

One night Pippin's company was moved to a new section of the front lines. They were told they were going "over the top" at daybreak. Shortly after dawn, following heavy enemy fire, the company climbed over the top of the trenches and charged.

"The snipers were plentiful," Pippin later wrote. "I remember spotting a shell hole, and I made a run for it. Just as I was within three feet and getting ready to dive in, I was hit in the shoulder."

Pippin fell into the shell hole among three other soldiers. One bound his wound. Then they left him. When Pippin tried to crawl out, however, enemy shooting drove him back.

Two stretcher-bearers eventually found Pippin. They carried him out of the hole and laid him beside a path. "It started to rain that morning about nine. It rained all day. At night it increased. My stretcher was full of water. At about ten o'clock I knew that help was coming. I could hear them splashing in the mud. Some nearly stepped on me." Finally the new troops sent their stretcher-bearers to take Pippin to a first-aid station.

When Pippin was finally taken to a base hospital, little could be done for his wounded arm. He was sent to America on a hospital ship and discharged on May 22, 1919. "My right arm was bound to me. I could not use it for anything," he later recalled. Every man in the 369th Regiment was awarded the *Croix de Guerre* [krwä′ də gâr′] for heroic services. Its soldiers and officers had spent 191 days in the front lines, five days more than any other U.S. troop. Pippin was proud of this all his life.

Pippin went back to West Chester to his family. He thought that getting used to life with a shattered arm would be easier there. The government provided a small disability pension. Clearly there was little work he could do.

He met Jennie Ora Feather-stone Wade, a widow with a young son, and a year later they were married. Jennie Pippin took in wash to help support the family. Horace got odd jobs from time to time.

But Horace missed working at things he knew how to do. Mostly, however, he missed being able to draw. He thought of the pictures he had done in France and wished he still had them. He would have been able to show people what it was like in the war. Sometimes by holding his right arm in his left hand, he could support his right hand long enough to sketch a few lines. But his hand usually smudged the drawing.

Finding the Way

One day, in the winter of 1929, Horace Pippin watched the poker in the kitchen coal stove grow red-hot. It gave him an idea. He re-moved an oakwood leaf from the dining-room table. He set it up so that its rough bottom side was fac-ing him. Then he took the red-hot poker in his right hand. Holding that hand with his left, he began to burn an outline into the board. It showed a lonely, bent man leading

a horse. The horse pulled a two-wheeled covered wagon through the snow. Other burned lines represented the edge of the woods and the darkness of the night. In the foreground Pippin added a fallen log with twisted branches. At the bottom he burned in the title, "Losing the Way." Then he added "by Horace Pippin." He had created a picture despite his limp arm. He had freed himself.

Use of the poker strengthened his arm muscles. He was proud of his "invention," as he smilingly called his drawing with the poker. The burnt wood panel was the basis of one of his most famous paintings. The theme was something he had thought about for years—the coming of peace on the battlefield. He called it "The End

of the War: Starting Home." He worked on it for three years, piling one coat of paint on top of another. At last it was so thick with paint that it looked almost carved. And instead of an ordinary picture frame, Pippin carved grenades, tanks, bombs, rifles, bayonets, and gas masks into the heavy frame.

Pippin once wrote:

How I Paint: The colors are very simple, such as brown, amber, yellow, black, white, and green. The pictures . . . come to me in my mind, and if to me it is a worthwhile picture, I paint it. I go over that picture in my mind several times and when I am ready to paint it I have all the details that I need. I take my time and examine every coat of paint very carefully to be sure that the exact color I have in mind is satisfactory to me. Then I work my foreground from the background. That throws the background away from the foreground—in other words, bringing out my work.

These words show a deep understanding of painting and Pippin's strong drive to create, despite his injured arm. It took a very patient person who was willing to search endlessly for the right color, design, and composition.

A Style Emerges

Pippin had painted for nearly nine years before Dr. Brinton saw his work. He was thankful for Brinton's friendship and interest in him and his paintings. However, fame itself did not impress him.

After Pippin had done a portrait of Dr. Brinton, the art critic tried to tell him how to paint. Pippin coolly rejected his advice. The only advice he accepted was that of young Robert Carlen. Carlen had been an artist before

"John Brown Going to His Hanging"

becoming an art dealer in Philadelphia. Carlen gave Pippin his first one-man show in 1940. He also supplied him with materials and kept in close contact with him.

Pippin accepted an invitation to attend the Barnes Foundation art school. He left after taking only a few classes, however. "My opinion of art is that a person should have a love for it and should paint from the heart and mind. To me it seems impossible for another to teach one of art."

Pippin's work was displayed at the Downtown Gallery in New York and at major shows in Chicago, San Francisco, and Pittsburgh. Yet, he remained an isolated and lonely artist. He met other black artists at exhibitions of his work, but he always returned quietly to West Chester.

Like many other black artists, Pippin was attracted to the life of John Brown. Pippin's grandmother had told him many times of having been present when John Brown was hanged after he tried to start a rebellion among the slaves in the South. This led Pippin to paint a series of three paintings of Brown— reading his Bible, on trial, and on his way to be hanged.

In "John Brown Going to His Hanging," nearly all the spectators face the wagon which is carrying Brown to the gallows. In the foreground, looking at the viewer with a face that is both sad and angry, is a black woman. She has turned her back on the hanging of John Brown. Many people believe that she represents both Pippin's grandmother and black people in general.

Pippin yearned more than ever for an end to wars and fighting. In the past he had painted scenes from the Bible. With World War II in full fury, he began a painting that showed different animals lying side by side in peace. Called "The Holy Mountain," it represented Pippin's hope for peace among all people.

Later he wrote of "The Holy Mountain":

The world is in a bad way at this time. I mean war. And men have never loved one another. There is trouble every place you go today. Then one thinks of peace. . . . To think that all the animals that kill the weak ones will dwell together, like the wolf will dwell with the lamb, and the leopard shall lie down with the kid and the calf and the young lion. . . .

Pippin's career as a recognized painter lasted barely ten years. Yet in that short time, he overcame the handicap of his war-shattered arm and, without training, established himself as a master of color and design.

"Holy Mountain II"

Understanding What You've Read

1. How did Horace Pippin win his first prize in drawing?
2. How did using the poker help Pippin create pictures?
3. What themes did Horace Pippin treat in his paintings?

Applying the Skills Lesson

Listed below are the major kinds of organization used in this selection. Find examples of each kind in the text.

1. cause and effect
2. time
3. comparison and contrast

TEXTBOOK STUDY

Mixed Patterns of Organization

Recognizing different patterns of organization will increase your understanding of textbook material. As you read the following textbook selection, use the sidenotes to help you identify the kinds of organization used.

Mixed Patterns of Organization in Language Arts

Pondering the Facts

Words like *great* and *worst* and *most* usually have a context for the speaker, but they rarely have much *real* meaning for the listener. **For example,** which sentence in each of the following pairs actually tells you something?

This phrase introduces the examples.

What are these examples of?

1. a. He's a great person.
   b. He helps me with my math whenever I get stuck.
2. a. That river has the worst pollution of any in the whole state.
   b. Statewide tests show that the percentage of industrial wastes in that river is extremely high.
3. a. Our team is the most powerful in school history.
   b. This year the average weight of our offensive line is 179 pounds, and the average weight of our defensive line is 185 pounds.

What pattern of organization is used in this paragraph?

In each sentence pair, the first sentence is a statement of opinion; the second is a statement of fact. Each opinion states what the speaker thinks. Each fact states something that can be checked.

Most of us have opinions about one thing or another. Putting those opinions into words is an important side of using your language. Sometimes, however, opinions are too readily accepted as facts. Moreover, before forming an opinion, the facts should be examined carefully. Part of the thinking process is to arrive at opinions based on facts.

—Patterns of Language
American Book Company

Building Skills

1. What two ways of organizing are used in the selection?
2. Which examples support the idea that *great, worst,* and *most* rarely have much real meaning for the listener?

Books About Meeting Challenges

Reading, Writing, Chattering Chimps by Aline Amon. Atheneum, 1975. *This book discusses how a psychologist attempted to teach chimpanzees to communicate using sign language, plastic symbols, and a computer.*

Dance by Jack Anderson. Newsweek, 1974. *This book describes the history of ballet, the great ballet companies of the world, choreographers, and dancers.*

The Impossible Voyage by Chay Blyth. Ballantine, 1973. *The author recounts his ten-month solo voyage aboard a fifty-nine-foot ketch.*

Seventeen Black Artists by Elton C. Fax. Dodd, 1971. *The author describes the lives of black American painters, sculptors, and photographers.*

The Boy Who Sailed Around the World Alone by Robin Lee Graham. Golden Press, Western Pub., 1973. *In this account, the sixteen-year-old author discusses his adventures on his around-the-world sea voyage.*

American Indian Women by Marion E. Gridley. Hawthorn, 1974. *Biographies of several influential Native American women as well as fascinating information about Native American culture are included.*

Fighting Shirley Chisholm by James Haskins. Dial, 1975. *This is the story of Shirley Chisholm and her Congressional career.*

Peary to the Pole by Walter Lord. Harper & Row, 1963. *The story of Peary's conquest of the Arctic is described through exciting narrative and fascinating old photographs.*

Women in Sports by Irwin Stambler. Doubleday, 1975. *Twelve women and their sports are discussed. Included are speed skating, diving, and gymnastics.*

Connie's New Eyes by Bernard Wolf. Lippincott, 1976. *This is a beautifully written true story of how a young girl successfully copes with her blindness.*

THE GREAT OUTDOORS

SKILLS LESSON

The Big Picture . . . Writing Topical Outlines

WOW! THAT'S SOME NOVEL YOU'VE WRITTEN.

WHAT DO YOU MEAN, "NOVEL"? THIS IS ONLY MY OUTLINE.

Long reading selections may contain a great deal of information that is organized according to **topic.** Suppose an article is about famous fictional characters. It might have the following topics: *detectives, heroes and heroines,* and *villains.* The author may then discuss examples of fictional detectives, heroes and heroines, and villains. These examples would be the **subtopics.** An outline of such an article would look like the one that follows.

Famous Fictional Characters

I. Detectives
   A. Sherlock Holmes
   B. Charlie Chan
   C. Nancy Drew
II. Heroes and heroines
   A. Tarzan
   B. Wonder Woman
   C. Robin Hood
   D. Zorro
III. Villains
   A. The Dragon Lady
   B. Professor Moriarty
   C. Fu Manchu

Notice that in an outline, topics are listed with Roman numerals. Subtopics take capital letters.

For the selection outlined above, **details** about each character would be listed by number under the appropriate subtopic. Adding details, the first part of the outline would look like this:

Famous Fictional Characters

I. Detectives
   A. Sherlock Holmes
      1. Created by Arthur Conan Doyle
      2. Solved many cases that baffled Scotland Yard
      3. Good friend Dr. Watson

The details usually are not written as complete sentences.

Now, suppose the author includes details that support other details. For example, the first detail in the outline states that Sherlock Holmes was created by Arthur Conan Doyle. If the selection gives facts about Conan Doyle, they would be listed in the outline as follows.

I. Detectives
  A. Sherlock Holmes
    1. Created by Arthur Conan Doyle
      a. 1859–1930
      b. English novelist
      c. Practiced medicine
    2. Solved many cases that baffled Scotland Yard
    3. Good friend Dr. Watson
      a. Kept a diary of Holmes's cases
      b. Assisted in cases with his medical knowledge

Which detail in the above outline is not supported with additional facts? To whom do details 3a and 3b refer?

Note: Sometimes you will only be able to list one important detail for a subtopic. When this is the case, the detail is not numbered.

Outlining a long reading selection can help you in many ways. First, it gives you a clear picture of how the information is organized. Second, writing the outline helps you understand and remember the information. Third, once you have an outline, you can use it as a study aid in the future.

Recognizing Topical Organization

Now you're ready to do an outline. Read the following selection. Refer to the sidenotes. They will direct your attention to the topics, subtopics, and details.

Ancient Reptile: The Crocodile

The first two paragraphs are the introduction. What topic do they discuss? This topic will be listed in your outline as I.

Crocodiles are members of the reptile family. Some reptile branches have died out over the years. Others have survived since the age of the dinosaurs.

Reptiles fall between fish and mammals, since some are born live and others hatch from eggs. All reptiles have back-bones. They are *cold-blooded*. This means they cannot control their body temperature and stay active in the winter. Thus, they must live in warmer parts of the earth.

What details explain the term *cold-blooded*?

The crocodile has a long, cigar-shaped body. It has short legs and a powerful tail. The tail is used for swimming and protection. The hide of the crocodile is very tough. The snout is long and narrow. The teeth are very sharp, and the feet are webbed.

These three paragraphs deal with the topic *characteristics of crocodiles.* What three subtopics are discussed?

Crocodiles are found in warm countries where the temperature changes by only a few degrees. They spend most of their time in large bodies of shallow water.

The crocodile feeds on small animals such as fish and birds. Sometimes it will attack larger animals. It will approach the animal slowly and then rush forward suddenly with a snap of the jaws. Because the crocodile cannot chew, it must swallow large chunks of flesh.

The following is a partially completed outline of the selection you just read. Complete the outline with the missing topics, subtopics, and details.

Ancient Reptile: The Crocodile

I. Reptiles
   A. History
      1. _____
      2. _____
   B. Characteristics
      1. Between fish and mammals
      2. Have backbones
      3. _____
         a. _____
         b. _____
         c. _____
II. Characteristics of crocodiles
   A. _____
      1. Long, cigar-shaped body
      2. Short legs
      3. Powerful tail
         a. _____
         b. _____
      4. _____
      5. _____
      6. _____
      7. _____
   B. Location
      1. _____
      2. _____
   C. _____
      1. Usually on small animals
      2. _____
      3. _____

The first topic discussed in the selection about crocodiles is *reptiles*. It can be broken down into two subtopics. Subtopic *A* is the *history* of reptiles. What details are given about the history of reptiles? First, some reptile branches have died out. Second, some branches have survived since the age of the dinosaurs. These two details should be listed by number under the subtopic *history*.

Subtopic *B* is *characteristics* of reptiles. The selection gives three general characteristics of reptiles: (1) They fall between fish and mammals; (2) They have backbones; and (3) They are cold-blooded. What details further explain detail number 3?

What is the next topic discussed in the selection? It is *characteristics of crocodiles*. It can be broken down into three subtopics. What do the first three details under subtopic *A* describe? They describe the *physical appearance* of crocodiles. What other details about the appearance of the crocodile are given? What details describe the crocodile's tail? What two details should be listed under subtopic *B, location?* Subtopic *C* is *feeding*. Notice that the detail listed in the outline describes what the crocodile eats. What other details deal with feeding?

This outline is rather detailed. But not all outlines must, or should, have this much information. The length of the outline will depend upon: (1) the length of the selection, (2) how much information is in the selection, and (3) your purpose for making the outline.

Try This

The following is the first part of a long article about *unusual plants*. Read the article. Note the topical organization. Then complete the partial outline that follows.

Unusual Plants

Perhaps the most unusual kind of plant is the *insectivore*. This is a plant that feeds on insects. Venus's flytrap is probably the best known. It eats insects too large to escape its "prison-bar" grip. The plant has several kidney-shaped lobes that look like an open book. Trigger hairs extend from the lobes. If an insect lands on the lobes and touches one of the trigger hairs, the lobes snap shut. Digestion begins a few minutes later.

The butterwort is found in bogs and wet ground. Insects are attracted to the plant's short, thick, sticky-haired leaves. When the prey touches down, the edges of the leaves roll up. This traps the insect.

Unusual Plants

I. Insectivores

    A. _____

        1. Several kidney-shaped lobes

        2. _____

        3. _____

    B. _____

        1. In bogs and wet ground

        2. _____

            a. _____

            b. _____

VOCABULARY STUDY

The Case of the Missing Words . . .
Suffixes

Inspector Le Beau arrived at the scene of the crime, and the three worried suffixes met him at the door.

"Our words are missing!" they cried.

"Are there any clues?" asked Le Beau.

"Yes," said *-ize*. "I mean 'to cause to be formed into,' as in *rubberize*, 'to cause to be formed into rubber.' "

"I am 'the quality, state, or degree of something,' " said *-ity*. "For example, the word *equality* means 'the state of being equal.' "

"My definition," said *-able*, "is 'capable of,' as in the word *reachable*, 'capable of being reached.' "

Le Beau noted the facts on a pad. Then, suddenly, he spotted three sentences peeking out from behind a bookcase.

1. Water will *crystal* when the temperature reaches 0°C.
2. Years ago, the rocket was a fantasy; today it is a *real*.
3. If you study, you will find that every test I give in this course is *pass*.

"Success!" cried Le Beau. "The words you are looking for are hiding in these sentences. *Crystal, real,* and *pass* all need suffixes. Case closed," cried Le Beau, and he disappeared into the foggy London night.

Word Play

Are you as clever as Le Beau? Add the suffix *-able, -ize,* or *-ity* to the three words mentioned by Le Beau to make the sentences correct. Remember, the spelling of a root word may change when a suffix is added.

Look for topics, subtopics, and details as you read this selection. Then think about how you would arrange them in an outline.

To some people, the Everglades seems no more than a swamp. But to those who know its wonders, the Florida Everglades is truly . . .

A Park of Life

by Patricia Lauber

Early summer's noonday sun blazes out of a cloudless blue sky. Its heat stills the park. Almost everywhere the animal world has taken refuge; in trees and holes and burrows, under leaves and stones. Only in the water is there movement, and it is slow.

In Taylor Slough, which resembles a large clear pond, fish are swimming. A large-mouthed bass lazily pursues a little sunfish. Big, cigar-shaped garfish wiggle past. A large turtle waddles across the bottom. What looks like a waterlogged tree trunk comes to life and begins to swim. It is not really a tree trunk, but an alligator. An anhinga perches motionless on a distant tree branch overlooking the slough. Its head is turned sideways and its four-foot-wide wings are spread in the sun. Even in the most quiet hours of the most quiet season, there is always something for the patient watcher to see in Everglades National Park.

Tucked in the southern tip of Florida, Everglades is the third largest national park. It is nearly twice the size of Rhode Island. Everglades, like other national parks, is an area of wilderness set aside to remain in its natural state. But in one way it is different. Other parks were established to preserve natural features of the land. Everglades was established to protect the many forms of life within its boundaries. It has no snowcapped mountains, no geysers, no giant canyons, no glaciers. This is a park of life; of birds, mammals, fish, reptiles, amphibians, and plants.

For this reason, strange as it may seem, a new visitor is likely to feel disappointed. The big park is flat and open. During part of the year, much of it lies under a foot or two of water. Most visitors, used to more spectacular views, see nothing at first. Everglades yields its treasures slowly, and the park's quiet charm grows on its visitors.

During the course of a year, more than 300 different species of birds can be seen in the park. Some are native to south Florida. Others are migrants, flying north or south with the seasons and perhaps wintering in the park.

There are many familiar land birds—towhees, cardinals, blue jays, meadowlarks, red-winged blackbirds, bobwhites. Wild turkeys may be seen near live oaks, where they find and eat acorns. Sometimes a pileated woodpecker can be heard chopping a hole in a tree trunk.

Birds of prey are numerous. There is the owl, a night hunter swooping down to catch a mouse, rabbit, or insect. There are vultures, whose circling flight signals a death on the ground. Hawks hunt small mammals, frogs, and lizards. About thirty pairs of bald eagles nest in the park. Most are on mangrove islands in Florida Bay.

All the familiar shorebirds can be found. Terns and gulls fish the coastal waters. Long-legged sandpipers and plovers stalk their food on the tidal mud flats. Ducks and coots float on marshes and lakes.

The park has many big water birds. Easily spotted, they are the star attractions. One is the anhinga, seen in tree-fringed fresh-water ponds and sloughs. The anhinga is sometimes called the water turkey, perhaps because of its glossy dark feathers. It is also known as the snakebird. Only its small head and long slender neck show above the water when it swims, giving it the appearance of a swimming snake. The anhinga stalks its prey underwater, spears it with a quick thrust of the bill, and carries it to shore.

Among the many wading birds, the roseate spoonbill is the most eye-catching. It feeds by wading in shallow water and swinging its bill back and forth in the mud. Minnows, shrimp, insects, and other living organisms found in the mud are eaten. Mud and other lifeless matter are washed out.

Many kinds of herons can be seen in the park. Among them are the great white and the great blue heron, two of the largest wading birds in North America. They are stately and slow-moving. They often stand motionless in shallow salt water, poised to strike at shrimp, fish, and other prey.

The brown pelican is impossible to mistake. It has a huge wingspan of six and a half feet and a long, flat, pouched bill. Brown pelicans are common in areas where fishing boats come in and handouts are plentiful. They can be seen in clusters, feeding near the docks or resting on pilings. They are, however, excellent fishers themselves. A brown pelican will fly over shallow water until it sees a suitable fish. Then it will execute a power dive, plunging into the water with a noisy splash and scooping up the fish in its pouch.

Given the richness and variety of its birdlife, the park seems rather poor in mammals. There are only about thirty species. The reason for this great difference is that birds can fly. They can readily cross land and open water barriers. For land mammals a sea is seldom passable without the help of people. This is why relatively few mammals have reached the southern tip of Florida.

Compared with the rest of the continent, the Florida peninsula is new land. It has been above water for only a few thousand years. Its animals and plants have spread into Florida from other regions. Birds, traveling by air, have come from both the north and south. Mammals, traveling mostly by land, have come chiefly from the north.

Except for one or two kinds of bats — air travelers from the south — all the mammals are species known in eastern North America. There are rabbits, squirrels, mice, shrews, skunks, mink, otters, wildcats, panthers, black bears, gray foxes, white-tailed deer, raccoons, and opossums.

The wildcat looks like an overgrown house cat with a short tail. It is often seen in early morning or early evening. Deer are numerous and can be seen around dawn or twilight, when they are out feeding. Raccoons are everywhere: robbing garbage cans, fishing, catching fiddler crabs, climbing trees for fruit, stealing eggs from nests. Otters are seen in many of the fresh-water areas, where they feed mostly on fish, snakes, frogs, turtles, and some-

times baby alligators. With their sleek, streamlined bodies and short legs, otters are more at home in the water than on land; they are strong, graceful swimmers.

Like the mammals, most of the reptiles and amphibians in south Florida belong to species that came from the north. An exception is the crocodile, which—like a few species of frogs and lizards—reached south Florida from the West Indies.

The reptiles of the park include lizards, turtles, snakes, alligators, and crocodiles. Of these, the alligator is the easiest to see, and one that park visitors find the most fascinating. This long, dark creature is one

of the few living relics of the vanished age of dinosaurs.

More than a million people visit the Everglades each year. They come for pleasure and recreation and to return to nature. Here they can experience what much of south Florida was like before the coming of European settlers. The park preserves a small part of the great wilderness that once stretched across the center of south Florida.

Understanding What You've Read

1. Why is the Everglades called "a park of life"?
2. What is an anhinga? Why is it also called a snakebird?
3. Why does the Everglades have fewer species of mammals than birds?

Applying the Skills Lesson

1. What three major kinds of life are discussed in the selection?
2. What details would be included under the subtopic *shorebirds* in an outline of this selection?
3. Using the information given in the selection, complete this outline of the section on mammals.

II. Mammals
   A. Population
      1. About thirty species
      2. _____
   B. Kinds
      1. _____
         a. Resembles overgrown house cat
         b. _____
      2. Deer
      3. _____
      4. Otters
         a. _____
         b. _____
         c. _____

Look for the many different forms and uses of the cactus described in the selection. Think about how you would organize this information in an outline.

What's your image of the desert? A big wasteland with little or no signs of life? Then you'll be surprised when you explore . . .

Saguaro,
Forest of Unreality

by Leslie Payne

Saguaro National Monument is the desert's answer to the giant redwood forests of California. It is located in Pima County, just outside Tucson, Arizona. The monument was created in 1933 to preserve about ninety-nine square miles of beautiful, rugged land. The park is divided into two sections. The larger, original area is fifteen miles east of Tucson in the Rincon and Tanque Verde mountains. The other section is seventeen miles west of the city in the Tucson Mountains. It has America's most luxuriant growth of rare saguaro cactus and a striking stand of ironwood trees.

The giant saguaro is quite unusual. It may grow to a height of fifty feet and live to be well over a hundred years old. Nature designed the saguaro to be a good water-storage tank. Its holding ability is second only to the barrel cactus's.

The saguaro has no leaves to lose moisture. The green-gray accordion-folded trunk is covered with lines of spines. The roots are close to the surface and may spread as far as fifty feet in all directions. They suck every drop of water into the trunk, which expands as it fills. In very dry years, the plant may be only a narrow column. Even branch growth is controlled by rainfall. Depending on the amount of water, the branches may range from small knobs to lengths of twenty feet.

The waxy-white saguaro blossom is the state flower of Arizona. It blooms on the tips of the branches, appearing in May and ripening into fruit in June. The Papago tribe celebrates the harvest feast and new year at the time of the ripening.

The juicy watermelon-red pulp of the fruit is delicious fresh or dried. Saguaro preserves are sold in some of the local shops. The Papagos make a kind of butter from the seeds or grind them into chicken feed. They use the fiber of the saguaro for building. Woodpeckers bore holes into the trunks in their search for insects and water. When these holes dry and harden, the Papagos remove them and use them for drinking vessels.

Desert animals also make use of this versatile plant. Birds nest in the woodpecker holes. A small desert owl may peer sleepily out as you pass by. The whitewing dove feeds on the seeds during the fruiting season.

In early spring the desert bursts into life with an explosion of color. The desert floor wears a carpet of wildflowers—scarlet, yellow, pink, and magenta. Butterflies flit from blossom to blossom. Honey bees busily hum. The surrounding mountains frame a picture that is not easy to forget. The air is pure and clear and sweet with the smell of new life. Lucky hikers may catch a glimpse of curious little coyotes or a javelina (wild pig) family hurrying into the distance.

The monument has many interesting plants besides the giant cactus. Sprinkled throughout the area are graceful palo verde trees, with their green trunks and spiny branches. There are also many other kinds of beautiful cactuses and shrubs.

Returning to the desert at night is well worth the drive. When the moon is bright, another side of the desert's beauty appears. The scene remembered from daytime is gone. In its place is the eerie world of a haunted forest. Twisted cactus arms seem to reach out. Their spines, like iron spikes, grab and tear at clothing. Big shadows flicker and disappear at the whim of the breeze. The soft call of a night bird blends with the coyote's chilling cry. Mountain shapes, friendly in daylight, now look dark and scary. The visitor feels transported back to the dawn of time, when all was primitive and unexplained.

Understanding What You've Read

1. What are some of the different kinds of plants and animals found in Saguaro National Monument?
2. Why is the saguaro a "good water-storage tank"?
3. In what ways do the Papagos use the saguaro?

Applying the Skills Lesson

Refer to the selection to complete the following outline.

The Saguaro Cactus

I. Characteristics
   A. Some over a hundred years old
   B. Size
      1. _____
      2. Growth controlled by rainfall
         a. _____
         b. _____
   C. Water storage
      1. _____
      2. _____
      3. _____
      4. _____
II. Uses
   A. People
      1. Fruit
         a. _____
         b. _____
      2. Seeds
         a. _____
         b. _____
      3. Fiber
         _____
      4. Trunk
         _____
   B. Animals
      1. _____
      2. _____

TEXTBOOK STUDY

Writing Topical Outlines

Many textbook selections are organized by topic. Making a topical outline of these kinds of selections can help you understand and remember the important information. As you read this textbook excerpt, refer to the sidenotes. They will help you focus on topics, subtopics, and details that might be included in an outline.

Writing Topical Outlines in Language Arts

Voice Characteristics

What is the first thing you notice about a stranger's speech? Your initial reaction is to the *sound of the voice.* You may enjoy listening to it or you may find it unpleasant. Perhaps you have heard the expression "____'s voice gets on my nerves." In addition to causing an unfavorable reaction, a sharp, shrill voice, for example, or a slow, muffled, weak voice will detract from what is being said. Perhaps the most important single characteristic of effective speech is *good voice quality.* There are four qualities of voice to consider.

This sentence alerts you to the topics discussed in the selection.

Pitch

What topic will be listed in your outline as I?

Pitch is the "highness" or "lowness" of a sound. The pitch of your voice is determined by the length, thickness, and tension of your vocal cords. You have no control over the length and thickness, but you can control the tension. When the vocal cords are too tense, they may produce unpleasantly high tones. Try to speak easily and without strain.

Volume

Volume is the loudness or softness of a sound. Having to listen to a voice that is too weak or soft is tiring to people. Listening to one that is too loud is annoying. Therefore, you should try to control the volume of your voice. Adjust it to suit your purpose and the place where you are speaking.

What details will you include in your outline under the topic *volume*?

Tone

Tone is the quality of harshness or smoothness of a sound. The tone of your voice is the way your voice sounds. If your friends say that you sound as if you talk through your nose, you have the problem of nasality. There are only three nasal sounds in English: **m, n,** and **ng.** No other sound should be produced through the nose. Try this sentence, which has no nasal sounds: *Ted is outdoors.*

This is a subtopic. What details would you list under this subtopic?

Block your nostrils and say the sentence again. If you do *not* have a nasal problem, you should feel no pressure of air through the nose. All breath should come through the mouth.

Inflection or Flexibility

Inflection, or flexibility, is the rising and falling of a voice. A person who has no inflection speaks in a *monotone.* Your voice should help to express the meaning of words and sentences. Keep your voice flexible, not static and monotonous. To

Notice that each topic directly relates to the title of the article, "Voice Characteristics."

create inflection in your speech, change your pitch, speed, and volume according to your meaning.

— *Language for Daily Use: Silver*
Harcourt Brace Jovanovich

Building Skills

1. What four topics would be listed in an outline of the section you just read?
2. Complete the outline that follows based on the information given in the selection.

Voice Characteristics

I. _____
    A. Definition: highness or lowness of a sound
    B. Vocal cords
        1. Length, thickness, tension — pitch
            a. Length and thickness — not controlled
            b. Tension — controlled
        2. _____
II. _____
    A. Definition: loudness or softness of a sound
    B. Effect on people
        1. _____
        2. _____
III. _____
    A. Definition: _____
    B. Nasality
        1. _____
        2. _____
IV. _____
    A. Definition: _____
    B. No inflection — *monotone*
    C. _____

SKILLS LESSON

Do You Have the Time? . . .
Writing Chronological Outlines

Suppose you decided to write your autobiography. Where would you begin? Well, you might start with the earliest event you can remember and work forward to the present. If you did, the story of your life would be told in **chronological order,** or the order in which the events occurred.

The information in many articles is organized by chronological order. For example, an article may discuss important events in history or milestones in sports. To outline this kind of selection, you could write a **chronological outline.**

The Standard Chronological Outline

Study the chronological outline that follows. How is it different from a topical outline?

Arctic Explorers

I. Eighteenth century
   A. 1700–1749
      1. Great Northern Expedition surveys Siberian Arctic coast (1733–1740)
      2. Vitus Bering sights Alaska from sea (1741)
   B. 1750–1799
      James Cook—from Bering Strait to Icy Cave, Alaska, and North Cape, Siberia (1778)
II. Nineteenth century
   A. 1800–1849
      1. Ferdinand von Wrangel completes survey of Arctic Coast (1820–1823)
      2. John Franklin seeks Northwest Passage (1845)
   B. 1850–1899
      1. Fridtjof Nansen crosses Greenland ice cap (1888)
      2. Salomon Andrée attempts to reach North Pole (1896)

Notice that instead of topics, the major headings in a chronological outline are **general time periods.** Some examples of general time periods are *the Mesozoic Era, the fifth century,* and *1900–1950.*

The general time periods in the outline above are *centuries.* They are listed next to Roman numerals. What time period do you think would be listed in this outline as III? Each century has been divided into fifty-year periods. The centuries could also be divided into ten- or twenty-year periods. Specific dates are listed with each detail.

The following selection is organized chronologically. As you read, refer to the sidenotes. They will point out some things to watch for when you write your outline.

Ice Cream

Ice cream has delighted us for hundreds of years. But it didn't start out as the dessert we know today. During the reign of Nero (A.D. 54–68), Romans enjoyed snow flavored with honey, juice, and fruit.

At the beginning of the thirteenth century, explorer Marco Polo brought the first sherbet to Europe. While traveling in the Far East, he had tasted a sweet, icy treat made with milk. He was very impressed and returned home with the recipe.

Ice cream began to take on some of its present characteristics around 1560. Honey and milk were combined and then frozen. The dessert was called "the flower of milk" or "cream." By 1670, "iced creams" had caught the fancy of the general public. They were beginning to be served in Paris cafés.

Americans gave ice cream an added boost. In 1846, Nancy Johnson invented the first hand-cranked ice-cream freezer. Five years later, Jacob Fussel opened the first ice-cream plant.

Throughout the early 1900's, soda fountains introduced frappés, sundaes, and other ice-cream concoctions. The ice-cream cone was born in 1904. The sandwich was developed in 1924. During the first half of the 1970's, the United States produced over 3 billion gallons of ice cream.

The years A.D. 1–99 are the first century. The author discusses events that occurred between the first and twentieth centuries.

What details would you list in your outline for the thirteenth century?

To what century does the year 1560 refer?

In what year did Jacob Fussel open his ice-cream plant?

What details would you list in your outline for the twentieth century?

283

Although the information in the selection is presented in chronological order, several centuries are left out. For example, the author "jumps" from the first century to the thirteenth, and then to the sixteenth. What other century has been left out? Notice, however, that the selection covers almost 2,000 years! How would you divide this time period for an outline? One way is:

I. First century
II. Thirteenth century
III. Sixteenth century
IV. Seventeenth century
V. Nineteenth century
VI. Twentieth century

This is the most obvious form for the outline. Yet, most of the events described in the selection happened after the fifteenth century. So, you might want to organize your outline like this:

I. First through fifteenth centuries
II. Sixteenth through twentieth centuries

Other Chronological Outlines

You will sometimes find that information is organized out of chronological order. However, this will not affect your chronological outline. Just use the time clues in the selection to help you rearrange the information in chronological order. Then write the outline.

Some selections have time clues and are written in chronological order. However, they do not necessarily refer to specific dates or time periods. The authors may use phrases such as *early in her career, a short time later, when he was in college,* and *after they were married.* In such cases, you can organize your outline according to **stages** or **events.**

Look at the following sample outline.

George Washington

    I. Youth
   II. Education
  III. Early jobs
  IV. Military career
   V. Career in government
  VI. Presidency
 VII. Retirement

The outline is chronological because it identifies stages spanning a certain amount of time in Washington's life. These stages are listed in chronological order. Subtopics and details are also listed in chronological order *even though the author may not have given specific dates.*

Try This

Read the selection that follows. Then complete the outline.

Milestones in Television

In 1969, 100 million people watched a man set foot on the moon. In 1955, the show that was to become television's longest-running western, "Gunsmoke," was aired for the first time. Six years earlier, "Captain Video," the first science fiction program, made its appearance.

In 1985, television will be sixty years old. Throughout its history, it has entertained, informed, excited, and educated the world.

Television began in the 1920's with the invention of the iconoscope by Dr. Vladimir Zworykin. No doubt, he would have been delighted with the introduction of cable TV just fifty years later. Television was still in the experimental stage in 1928, and programs were broadcast three days a week.

Believe it or not, TV's first star was a cartoon character. Felix the Cat was shown to viewers in 1930.

Television blossomed in the 1940's and 1950's. For the first time, in 1947, four cities watched the World Series on television.

Weekly programing got into full swing with "The Life of Riley" (1949), "The Today Show" (1952), and "Howdy Doody" (1947).

The Nixon–Kennedy debates in 1960 were a great milestone for television. Although the 1952 Presidential nominations and the 1954 Army–McCarthy hearings had been televised, never before had two candidates for President discussed political issues face to face to such a large audience.

The seventies, too, brought major changes to television: the "twelve-foot" screen, educational programing, and broadcasting via satellite.

Milestones in Television

  I. 1920–1929
    A. _____
    B. Experimental programs broadcast three days a week
 II. _____
    Felix the Cat first TV star
III. _____
    A. World Series first broadcast
    B. _____
    C. _____
    D. _____
 IV. _____
    A. _____
    B. _____
    C. _____
    D. _____
  V. 1960–1969
    A. _____
    B. _____
 VI. 1970's
    A. _____
    B. The "twelve-foot" screen
    C. _____
    D. _____

Aesop's Jokes . . . Multiple Meanings

Aesop Guffaw, the famous comedian, has a new act. Here's a sample of his jokes. Do you get the punch lines? Use the definitions to help you.

I visited my cousin Doris last week and found her wearing a ten-gallon hat and sitting on top of the stove. When I asked her what she was doing, she said she wanted to see what it was like to live on the *range*.

range: (a) a cooking stove
       (b) an open area over which livestock roam and feed

Uncle Max is a terrible cook. He never understands the recipe. Yesterday he tried to *strain* the peas by making them lift weights.

288

strain: (a) to injure by overuse

(b) to save the solid pieces while the liquid passes through

Grandpa Zach used to be a sailor. I gave him a dark blue teacup for his birthday, and now he goes around telling people he owns a navy *vessel.*

vessel: (a) a large boat

(b) a bottle, cup, or bowl for holding something

Word Play

Which definition above, (a) or (b), is correct for the italicized words as they are used in these sentences?

1. As we flew over the *range,* we could see grazing cows.

2. The ancient *vessel* had a broken handle.

3. Eddie *strained* a muscle trying to move the couch.

The headings in this selection identify important events in Carver's life. Use them to help you decide on topics for an outline.

He showed farmers how to keep the soil healthy. He used sweet potatoes, soybeans, and peanuts in new ways. He taught people to respect nature. This is the story of . . .

George Washington Carver, Pioneer Ecologist

by Shirley Graham *and* George D. Lipscomb

In October 1896, George Washington Carver left his teaching post at Iowa State University. He had been invited to teach at Tuskegee Institute in Alabama by Booker T. Washington, the president of the school.

When Carver arrived at Tuskegee, he had a big job ahead of him. The agriculture department had no laboratory and no equipment. Many students had been assigned to the department—known as "the farm"—as punishment. At first they were uninterested in what Carver had to teach. But Carver had a way of creating interest. Here is how one student described Carver's method:

My very first recollection of him was my first morning in his class. Before going right into the subject at hand, he gave us about ten minutes of general talk. I remember his words so well. Looking hard at us, he said, "Young people, I want to beg of you, always keep your eyes and ears open to what nature has to teach you. By so doing you will learn many valuable things every day of your life."

Word went out among the students that the new teacher was "different." Those who had been sent to "the farm" for punishment decided to remain.

290

Breaking New Ground

One morning Carver said, "Today we're going to do something that has never been done before. We're going into town to find the things we need for our laboratory. We'll look through every scrap heap. We'll go to people's houses and ask for old kitchen utensils that can't be used. We need containers of all kinds, and lamps, and pans in which to cook."

Carver showed the class pictures of laboratory equipment. From a box he extracted tubes and small glass cases. "These are the kinds of things we need. Let's go!"

It was an exciting hunt. The students had caught Carver's crusading spirit. They searched alleys, raked through trash and dump heaps, and gathered hollow reeds from the swamp. When evening came, they met with all their findings. Carver praised each one. What he could not use at once, he set aside for use later.

Carver had been assigned a twenty-acre patch of "no-good" ground. Hogs rooted among the weeds and rubbish. But with the help of his students, Carver managed to clear it. Then he asked for a two-horse plow. No one at the school had ever seen a two-horse plow, but Dr. Washington approved the request. When the plow arrived, Carver hitched it up and began to turn the soil. Local farmers slapped their thighs and rocked with laughter. The idea of a professor plowing! Even his students were a bit embarrassed. But he was good-natured about it, even joking with the people who gathered around.

Carver asked the students to bring him mud from the swamps and leaf mold from the woods. He plowed these under. Then he told them to clean the barns and bring the "drippings." The farmers were surprised when, after all this work, Carver planted cowpeas instead of cotton.

When the students harvested only stringy cowpeas with one miserable pea in each stalk, they were disgusted. All this for something to throw to the hogs! But the teacher surprised them.

That evening they all sat down to a delicious meal prepared by their professor. Afterward Carver explained that each dish had been prepared from cowpeas!

Early Fame

Word of the remarkable professor quickly spread. His classes grew in size. In the spring he said to his students, "I've been rotating crops on our land. It has been rested, refreshed, and enriched. Now we'll try cotton."

Long before the cotton was ready to pick, farmers came from near and far to gaze in wonder at the perfect stalks. When Carver harvested a 500-pound bale of cotton from one acre, everyone regarded him with deep respect. Never had such a thing been done in that part of the country!

Meanwhile, Carver was getting acquainted with the neighborhood. Each morning at four, he arose and went to the woods or swamp. That spring, he discovered that Alabama had a greater variety of trees than all of Europe—twenty-two species of oak, pine, and spruce—all valuable woods. And he found more wildflowers than he had ever known existed!

When the country people saw Carver gathering plants and scooping up different kinds of soil, they called him a root doctor and came to him with their aches and pains. Recognizing that most of them were suffering from pellagra, Carver prescribed wild grasses and weeds which were rich in vitamins. He showed the people how to brew teas from certain roots. He cooked weeds that grew beside the road and let the people taste them. The people praised Carver, bowed, and called him "Doctor."

When asked, Carver gave advice freely. He lectured and wrote pamphlets. In simple language, he explained to the people the connections between plants and animals, soil and rain, air and sun. He tested many soils, and because he never threw anything away, jars full of clay collected in heaps.

A Discovery

One morning, Carver was lost in thought as he headed for the swamp. Spreading branches of trees lined with Spanish moss shut out the sun. Tangled vines stretched across the marshy ground. Mosses slushed underfoot. Carver was completely preoccupied with the beauty all around him, when suddenly his foot caught on a vine and he fell flat into a mudhole. He was not hurt, and he scrambled up quickly. He wiped away the sticky mud with his handkerchief, but the stains remained. When he looked at the handkerchief, he saw that it was a brilliant blue! He tried rinsing the cloth in the water. Everything washed out except the blue coloring.

Carver excitedly hurried back to the laboratory. Forgetting about his dirty appearance, he reached for a basket of clay he had been saving. After arranging a tray, he dumped a handful of red clay on it, smoothing it out with his palm. Then, tilting the tray a little, he held a dipper of water above it and allowed the water to drip slowly over the clay. Small rocks and grit washed away. Carver emptied the dipper and, tilting the tray in the opposite direction, repeated the process.

He did this until a thin, pasty coating of red remained on the tray. He touched it lightly with his finger and smeared it across a sheet of paper. Holding the paper close to the window, he studied it a long time.

"Paint!" he cried. "The people down here are walking on paint. Good paint. Durable paint."

For several days and nights he worked alone. He carefully separated his clays according to colors and washed them clean. With intense heat, he reduced the clay to the finest powder. He mixed the powder with oils and with water, first hot and then cold. He tested the samples on wood, on canvas, with a brush, and with his fingers. When he finally told his students what he had discovered, they were amazed.

Sometime later, Carver was asked to speak about soil improvement at a new church near Montgomery. He learned that the people of the community could not afford to buy paint for their church, and they were concerned that the coming rains would ruin the new wood.

In a few days, a little wagon drew up in front of the church. Carver and several students climbed down, unloaded pails of blue paint from the wagon, and went to work. By the next weekend, the community had a bright, newly painted church. And when the rains finally came, the paint neither cracked nor peeled.

A New Crop

That spring the cotton was in full bloom. Many of the farmers had taken Carver's advice. They had "rested" their acres with sweet potatoes or cowpeas. They had enriched their soil with fertilizer. Then they had planted their cotton, and they looked forward to the best harvest in many years. Money would at last be plentiful; good times had come to Alabama.

But when they arose one morning and looked out across their fields, they gasped in horror! In one night, the lovely blossoms had turned brown and were falling to the ground. The leaves had yellowed and the stalks drooped. The dreaded boll weevil had arrived, and the entire cotton crop was doomed. Nothing could drive out this terrible pest until it had its fill. Billions of eggs would be left, which could only be flushed from the soil with the strongest of poisons. But these poisons would also kill the young cotton seeds.

Carver heard the cry that had gone up all around him. He had a few acres of cotton, but his peanut vines stood green and sturdy in the sun. The boll weevil hadn't touched them! Here was food for thought. Already, he knew much about the peanut. He organized his facts and took his findings into the countryside. "Plow under your cotton!" he told the farmers. "Spray the soil with poison, and one month later plant peanuts."

But people were not comforted by Carver's words.

"Peanuts!" they said. "Peanuts are food for hogs, and they're good to chew. But all our income crop is gone. We're ruined!"

"No! No!" Carver grew more emphatic. "The peanut is an ideal food. Plant peanuts!"

He prepared a bulletin and sent out hundreds of copies. The bulletin gave details on cultivating, harvesting, and preparing peanuts for market, and included a few facts about peanut hay.

The farmers read, listened, and grew hopeful. Perhaps everything was not lost. After all, the things this man from Tuskegee had told them before had turned out well. They took Carver's word and planted peanuts.

The first crop was good. Anything that hadn't been sold at the market was used according to Carver's instructions. By this time Carver had sent out other bulletins describing several ways of preparing peanuts as food. There were recipes for making peanut bread and cake, "mock" chicken, sausage, cheese and roast, candies, and ice cream.

And so more farmers planted peanuts.

But there was no market for peanuts. No one in the North had ever heard of cooking peanuts, and they had all the bags of salted peanuts they wanted. Since sellers were well supplied, the price of peanuts fell to almost nothing. The plants rotted in the fields. Disaster again faced the farmers of Alabama, and this time it was because a "fresh young upstart from over Tuskegee way" had told them to plant peanuts!

Yes, Peanuts!

Carver was deeply hurt. He withdrew to his laboratory, shut the door, and refused to see anyone. He blamed himself completely. He had made a terrible mistake. He should have foreseen this disaster.

Carver called for heaped-up bushel baskets full of peanuts. When they arrived, he shut the door again. Some people saw his light burning throughout the night. They brought him trays of food which he scarcely touched. To those who tapped lightly on his door, he called out sharply, "Go away. I'm busy!"

Several days and nights had passed when Carver staggered from the laboratory, climbed the stairs to his room, and fell across his bed. He slept until dawn the next day. He arose, took his usual walk in the woods, returned, and ate a hearty breakfast. Only then did he say to his few selected students, "Come with me!"

The students followed close at his heels. When they entered the laboratory, they could only stare at the many bottles and containers on the table. Where had he gotten milk and cheese? As he pointed out other articles, their wonder grew. There were about two dozen products in all. And every one had been made from peanuts. But this was only the beginning. Before his death, Carver had developed 300 new products from the peanut alone.

With his eyes now opened to new possibilities, Carver was able to develop more than a hundred products from the yam: flour, starch, tapioca, breakfast foods, stock foods, numerous dyes for silk and cotton, ginger, vinegar, mucilage, ink, and much later, synthetic rubber!

During World War I, the United States government learned that Tuskegee Institute, thanks to Carver's genius, was saving two pounds of wheat a day. Tuskegee was using sweet-potato flour with wheat flour and, upon testing, enjoying a better loaf of bread than before. The government sent for Carver, and he went to Washington. Sweet-potato flour was soon helping to feed millions of American soldiers and their allies.

Today in Enterprise, Alabama, you can find a monument to a bug. These words are written on the monument: "Profound appreciation of the boll weevil and what it has done as a herald of prosperity."

The boll weevil had driven the farmers to raising peanuts! But then, the real honor goes to Carver. He gave Southern farmers an alternative to cotton, and he gave us all a new respect for nature. In an age of fewer natural resources, we appreciate Carver's achievement more than ever. He was truly a pioneer ecologist.

Understanding What You've Read

1. How did Carver get equipment for his laboratory?
2. How did Carver discover that the clay in the swamp could be made into paint?
3. Why did the people of Enterprise, Alabama, build a monument to the boll weevil?
4. Why was Carver so admired by the students at Tuskegee Institute?

Applying the Skills Lesson

Suppose you were going to write a chronological outline of the selection you just read.
1. What period of time in Carver's life does the selection discuss?
   a. from childhood to his death
   b. his years at Iowa State University
   c. his years at Tuskegee Institute
2. Which topics would you include in an outline?
   a. youth
   b. the first year at Tuskegee
   c. Carver becomes a "doctor"
   d. Carver discovers paint
   e. Carver develops peanut products
   f. marriage
   g. army life
   h. Carver's later successes
3. Based on your answers to question 2, what details would you include under each topic?

Writing Chronological Outlines

Textbook selections that discuss events often can be outlined in chronological order. The textbook excerpt that follows is one example. As you read, refer to the sidenotes. They will point out the time clues that can help you write a chronological outline.

Writing Chronological Outlines in Social Studies

Flying Machines

1903 is the earliest date mentioned. Note the span of years covered in the selection.

Is the information presented in chronological order?

There had been interest in aviation in the United States from the time Orville and Wilbur Wright flew their first motor-powered aircraft at Kitty Hawk, North Carolina, in 1903. Technological changes during the early years of the 20th century improved the flying machine.

Then, on the morning of May 20, 1927, Charles A. Lindbergh took off from Roosevelt Field in New York for Paris in his airplane, the "Spirit of St. Louis." Americans followed his progress by radio and newspapers as he made the first nonstop solo flight across the Atlantic Ocean.

When Lindbergh returned to the United States, he was greeted with thou-

sands of telegrams and honored with parades. He also received the Congressional Medal of Honor.

Women were among the pioneers in aviation. Amelia Earhart made a nonstop flight across the Atlantic Ocean in 1928. She also attempted to fly around the world in 1937, but she and her plane were lost over the Pacific Ocean. Ellen Church became the first flight attendant (or stewardess, as the job was called) in 1930. For the job she had to be skilled in nursing.

The first regularly scheduled passenger service between Boston and New York began in 1927. By 1932, there were several commercial airlines regularly carrying passengers in planes that traveled at speeds up to 150 miles an hour.

—America! America!
Scott, Foresman

What other details will you list in your outline for 1927?

Building Skills

Complete the outline below and at the top of page 300, based on the information in the selection.

I. 1900–1919
   1903

   _____

II. 1920–1929
   A. _____
      1. Lindbergh makes first nonstop solo flight across Atlantic
      2. _____
   B. 1928

   _____

III. 1930–1939
   A. _____
      Ellen Church becomes first flight attendant
   B. 1932

      _____

   C. 1937

      _____

Writing Chronological Outlines in Science

This textbook selection is not accompanied by sidenotes. As you read, look for the chronological organization. Then complete the outline that follows.

White pine and hemlock trees do not grow as fast as many other species, but they grow to be quite tall. They also can survive in moderately shaded places. They must, however, have a fairly moist soil. The settlers found pine and hemlock forests in many portions of the United States, where the environment favored their survival.

What happens when the trees of such a forest are cut down? Does a new forest of white pine and hemlock start growing again? Not at all. Rather, a long succession begins. During the first two or three years, the ground is largely covered with weeds. Here and there grasses begin to appear. Time passes, and young trees begin to rise above the grasses and weeds. These young trees are a mixture of ashes, birches, soft maples, poplars, and various other species. Young white pines and hemlocks are also growing, but more slowly.

After 10 to 15 years the fast-growing trees and bushes shade the area. The weeds and grasses gradually disappear because they can no longer get the sunlight necessary for growth. The trees are in competition with one another for this all-important sunlight. The young white pines and hemlocks survive because they can get along with only a little sunlight.

Forty or fifty years later the young forest is still a mixture of tree species. Here and there, the shade-tolerant white pines and hemlocks can be seen. These trees slowly begin to win out in the competition. Their success is due to two factors. First, they are adapted to the existing conditions of life, and second, they finally tower above their competitors, and these competitors cannot tolerate the shaded conditions in which they now live.

A hundred years, or perhaps 150 years later, the original forest is restored. This can only happen, however, if people do not interfere with the succession, and if the environment does not undergo marked change. Then, once again, the white pines and hemlocks dominate the forest, which may appear much as it did years before. It is now what we call a *climax forest*.

—*Modern Life Science*
Holt, Rinehart & Winston

Building Skills

Complete the outline that follows based on the information in the selection you just read.

Forest Succession

I. First nine years
   A. _____
   B. _____
   C. _____
      Birches, soft maples, poplars, etc.

II. Ten to fifteen years
   A. Fast-growing trees and bushes shade area
   B. _____
   C. _____
   D. White pines, hemlocks survive

III. Forty to fifty years later
   White pines, hemlocks begin to win out
      1. _____
      2. _____

IV. One hundred to 150 years later
   _____
      1. _____
      2. Climax forest

SKILLS LESSON

The Same and Yet Different . . .
Another Look at Topical Outlines

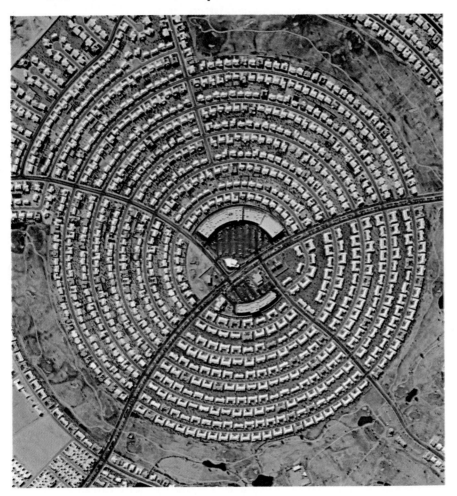

Not all selections are organized by topical or chronological order. How then do you outline a selection organized by comparison and contrast? What if the author seems to "bounce" back and forth between one topic and another? How do you outline information that is mostly examples? If you study the facts presented in an article, regardless of their organization, you'll find you can still write a topical outline.

Organization by Comparison and Contrast

It is fairly easy to recognize topics when the information is presented through comparison and contrast. Just ask yourself this question: "What two (or more) things is the author comparing?" Each of these persons, events, objects, or ideas becomes a topic in your outline.

In outlining a selection organized by comparison and contrast, first skim the selection. Find the topics that are being compared. List the topics beside Roman numerals. Be sure to leave space for subtopics and details. Then go back and read the selection more carefully. Complete the outline as you read.

Read the following selection. Then complete the outline.

Chief Gods in Mythology

Ancient peoples did not always understand many of the forces of nature. So they developed gods and goddesses.

In Egypt, the chief god was Ra, lord of the sky. In Greece, it was Zeus; and in Rome, Jupiter.

Ra took many forms. Sometimes he was shown as a child, a man, or a snake. In contrast, Zeus was always drawn as a bearded man with long hair. He often carried a thunderbolt. Pictures of Jupiter show him younger than Zeus. He carried three thunderbolts. Unlike Zeus and Jupiter, Ra was not always young. Sometimes he was an old man with trembling hands. But Ra's power could not be denied. He was responsible for creating the universe and ruling the world.

Zeus, too, ruled over humankind. He also protected the weak. At first Jupiter was the god of light. He then became the controller of wind, rain, thunder, and other natural events. Finally, Jupiter was the protector of Rome and most powerful of all Roman gods.

Chief Gods in Mythology

I. _____
   A. Appearance
      1. Child
      2. _____
      3. _____
   B. Powers
      1. _____
      2. _____

II. _____
   A. Appearance
      1. _____
      2. _____
   B. Powers
      1. _____
      2. _____

III. _____
   A. _____
      1. Younger than Zeus
      2. Carried three thunderbolts
   B. Powers
      1. _____
      2. _____
      3. Protector of Rome and most powerful Roman god

To complete the outline, ask yourself these questions:

- *What three topics are discussed in the selection?* They are *Ra, Zeus,* and *Jupiter.* Each topic is listed next to a Roman numeral.
- *What two subtopics are discussed for each topic?* They are the *appearance* and *powers* of each god. These subtopics are listed next to capital letters.
- *What details describe each subtopic?* In other words, what did each god look like? What were his powers? These details are listed with numbers or small letters.

Organization by Example

You can use a topical outline when a selection gives examples to illustrate a main idea or point the author wants to make. If the examples are discussed in great detail, they may become the topics of your outline. If they are mentioned briefly, they may be subtopics or even details in the outline. The structure of your outline will depend upon:

- how much discussion is given to each example in the selection
- whether all the examples illustrate a single point the author is making
- whether the examples illustrate different points the author is making

For instance, in a selection, an author may make several points about clothing through the ages: (1) It has been made out of different kinds of materials; (2) It has been used for different purposes; (3) It has changed greatly. If the author gives examples to illustrate each point, the points are the topics. The examples are the subtopics.

Clothing

point   I. Materials
                 A. Animal skins
examples { B. Cotton
                 C. Synthetics

point   II. Purposes
                 A. For protection
examples { B. In jobs
                 C. As decoration

point   III. Changes
                 A. Women's clothing
examples { B. Men's clothing
                 C. Children's clothing

If, however, the author makes only one point about clothing and gives examples, the examples become the topics.

Kinds of Clothing Materials

    I. Animal skins
   II. Cotton
  III. Synthetics

Read the following selection. How many points is the author making? What examples illustrate each point?

You can find a cave system in nearly every state. For example, one of the largest is Mammoth Cave in Kentucky. A river runs through the cave twenty-seven meters below the surface. Famous for its huge chambers and beautiful formations is Carlsbad Caverns in New Mexico. Each evening in the summer, hundreds of bats swarm out of the cave to feed on insects. Bear Gulch Cave is part of Pinnacles National Monument in California.

There are many different kinds of caves. Perhaps the most well known is the limestone cave. The longest passageways and largest chambers are found in limestone caves. Here one can see salamanders, blind fish, and transparent crayfish. Lava tube caves are really empty tubes through which hot, liquid rock has forced its way to the surface. A glacier cave is formed inside or beneath a glacier.

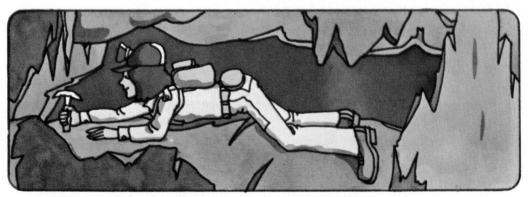

The author of the selection makes two points: (1) You can find a cave system in nearly every state; (2) There are many different kinds of caves. These statements are also the main ideas of the first and second paragraphs. The author supports each statement with examples. What examples illustrate the first point? The second point? Suppose you wanted to outline the selection. What two topics would you list? What subtopics would you list under each topic?

Try This

Read the selection that follows. Decide what kind of organization the author uses to present the information. Then complete the outline.

For hundreds of years, people have tried to find ways to predict the future. The most elaborate of the ancient methods is astrology. Unlike palmistry, crystal-ball reading, and consulting oracles, astrology involves research and writing. The astrologer must first figure out the positions of the stars and planets on the day the person was born. The astrologer then draws up a horoscope or chart.

In contrast, the other three methods do not even consider outside forces. The palmist usually does no writing. The skin lines on a person's palm are examined and then "read" for the meanings they are said to contain. The crystal-ball reader doesn't interpret anything. The individual's future supposedly appears as a picture within the glass ball.

Astrologers and palmists can, in a sense, be trained. The crystal-ball reader, however, supposedly has "natural gifts." He or she is able to see images that others cannot.

The oracle, used mostly by the ancient Greeks, was also "naturally gifted" and was thought to speak directly with the gods. The oracle delivered general information about the near future.

Similarly, crystal-ball readers also "see" into the near future. Their predictions, however, are more specific than the oracle's. On the other hand, palmists and astrologers are said to be able to predict events dozens of years away.

Ancient Methods of Predicting the Future

I. _____
   A. Research and writing
      1. Figures out positions of stars and planets for person's birthday
      2. _____
   B. _____
   C. _____
II. _____
   A. "Reads" skin lines on person's palm
   B. _____
   C. _____
III. Crystal-ball reading
   A. _____
   B. _____
   C. _____
IV. _____
   A. Used mostly by ancient Greeks
   B. _____
   C. _____
   D. _____

VOCABULARY STUDY

Interview with Zim Three . . . Antonyms

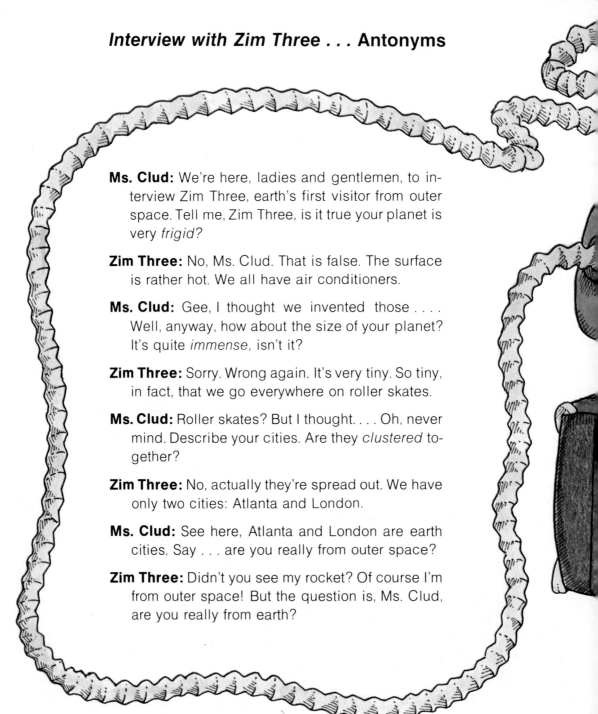

Ms. Clud: We're here, ladies and gentlemen, to interview Zim Three, earth's first visitor from outer space. Tell me, Zim Three, is it true your planet is very *frigid?*

Zim Three: No, Ms. Clud. That is false. The surface is rather hot. We all have air conditioners.

Ms. Clud: Gee, I thought we invented those . . . . Well, anyway, how about the size of your planet? It's quite *immense,* isn't it?

Zim Three: Sorry. Wrong again. It's very tiny. So tiny, in fact, that we go everywhere on roller skates.

Ms. Clud: Roller skates? But I thought. . . . Oh, never mind. Describe your cities. Are they *clustered* together?

Zim Three: No, actually they're spread out. We have only two cities: Atlanta and London.

Ms. Clud: See here, Atlanta and London are earth cities. Say . . . are you really from outer space?

Zim Three: Didn't you see my rocket? Of course I'm from outer space! But the question is, Ms. Clud, are you really from earth?

Word Play

What word or phrase means the same as each of the following?

1. frigid: (a) true, (b) freezing cold, (c) warm
2. immense: (a) huge, (b) false, (c) blooming
3. clustered: (a) blown up, (b) invented, (c) grouped together

In this selection, factual information about the otter is combined with personal observations. As you read, think about how you would organize the information in a topical outline.

Many wild animals are beautiful but fragile creatures. It is illegal to shelter most wild animals without a state permit. Here a person who knows and respects wildlife tells you about her family's adventure with . . .

An Orphan of the Wild

by Rosemary K. Collett *with* Charlie Briggs

Pippa came to us in the spring of 1965 quite by accident. We spotted her one spring evening racing across the fields behind our house. At first we thought she was a black cat. But the undulating way she ran quickly told us she was an otter. My son Clark, then a teen-ager, ran across the field to confirm our identification. Soon he came back carrying Pippa.

Kitten-sized, she was terribly frightened and sopping wet. Clark reported that she had been heading toward the dead end of the canal on our street. Thinking she wanted to go in the water, he had caught her and put her in. Somehow she had managed to struggle back to the shore, piping pitifully and shivering.

Since she seemed to be alone, frightened, and lost, we assumed she had come from an otter colony in the swampy land west of our house. We lived in a small "undeveloped" development—open country and grassy lots cut by canals connecting to the Gulf of Mexico. She could have come from anywhere.

Otters must have something on which to dry themselves or they will get sick. Their beautiful outer coat of dark brown is waterproof hair. Their undercoat, however, is soft and woolly and soaks up water like a sponge.

We took her in the house and I put her on the couch, on a foam-rubber pillow with a hot-water bottle under it. I dried her off with a towel. Our next move was to call the vet. He knew nothing about otters, but by good luck his visiting associate knew something about mink.

The mink vet asked about Pippa's symptoms. We told him she could not stand and was trying to drag herself along on her belly. He said he was sure she had a disease common to mink called hard-pad disease. He said it was almost always fatal. The only treatment was to keep her warm, dry, and quiet, and three times a day rub her foot pads with lanolin. The disease hardens the pads of the feet, he said. It makes them so tender and painful the animal cannot walk or bear any weight.

We started treating Pippa. For days she lay on the couch, sleeping most of the time. She awoke only to call to be let outside—just like a house-trained dog.

This went on for about a week. After that she improved rapidly. We put a dish for her by the refrigerator, next to the family dog and cat bowls. Pippa soon learned to drag herself off the couch and go for food and water. She enjoyed canned cat food but would fight for table scraps.

Once she was healthy again, our education in otter ways really began. We already knew all her otter noises. Otters will

pipe and whistle like a bird. This means they are unhappy, frightened, or uncomfortable. They also can grunt like a frog. And they can literally chuckle and giggle almost like a human, as Pippa did when she was tickled or feeling happy.

At night Pippa stayed outside in a rabbit cage we had placed there for her. By this time we had learned to fill the cage with fresh hay or dried grass from the meadows. She liked to sleep, burrow, and practice drying herself in it. She had a nontippable crockery water bowl and a heavy dish for her cat food, though by now she was eating anything, including all the fresh fish she could get.

First thing in the morning, she was brought inside the house. She stayed there all day and was the delight of the household. She lived in the house much in the same way other pets do, eating and playing with her toys and with members of the family. She enjoyed sitting on our laps. She had a rubber mouse on which she liked to pounce heartily to hear the squeaking sound it made. Then she would pick the mouse up and either drop it in the water bowl or carry it about the house until she tired of it or decided to hide it.

We put her in her cage at night and when we had to go away. She didn't like to be alone in the house. She did, however, seem to like the outdoor cage and considered it her own personal den. Even though she could open the button latch whenever it suited her, she seldom left the cage until we came for her.

Pippa loved to play all kinds of games of her own invention. We had a coffee table with a raised rim around it. One day she found some marbles that the boys had left there. She discovered that by standing on her hind legs and holding one of the marbles with her forepaws, she could pad around the table, "shooting" the marbles with her nose and banking them off the rim. When she was very small, "otter billiards" was one of her favorite games. It held her attention longer than anything else.

Pippa was fond of the dog's water bowl. She brought sea-grape leaves and twigs of assorted sizes to it. She dropped them in the bowl and stirred thoroughly with great care. The neighborhood children loved this game. They called it "making otter soup." Pippa enjoyed showing off for the children and anybody who came by.

As she grew older, Pippa settled on a regular diet of raw chicken necks and raw fish, plus table scraps. These scraps might include corn, green beans, tomatoes, chili, vegetable soup, and perhaps pork chops and roast beef. She especially loved all kinds of seafood.

She became very fond of my husband, Jack, and decided he was her favorite. Her pet game with him was to pounce into his lap when he came home from work and sat down in his armchair. She would get that "I'm-going-to-do-something-funny" look in her eye and start to push between his back and the chair. The game was for Jack to lean very hard against the chair and try to prevent Pippa's passage behind his back. She was very strong, and she always won, coming out giggling on the other side.

When we thought she was old enough to learn to swim, Jack "taught" her. We took her to the canal across the street. She liked to wade in the shallows and play with stones and fiddler crabs, but she showed no interest in swimming or hunting.

Jack waded in deep enough to start swimming, and Pippa began to chirp anxiously. She became worried about him as he ignored her and frolicked in the water. She edged farther and farther out, her feet left the bottom, and suddenly she was swimming!

From then on, Pippa went to the canal every day by herself. She began to spend more and more time there, though we never saw her catch anything. When I would hear her coming home from the canal, I always ran to fetch her towel. I wanted to dry her as much as I could before she got on the rugs. She dried off somewhat on the canal banks, but I still worried about the rugs.

Pippa's old, ragged towel had a fist-size hole in it. She would run toward me when I held it up, leap through the hole, and then twist and turn until she rolled herself up in the towel. This was her favorite way of drying.

As the summer wore on, Pippa began spending entire days at the canal. She seemed to be invisible, and would not answer a call until late in the evening. Then she would appear from the water, or from one of the many "nests" she had made in the tall grass along the banks, and frolic madly around Jack's legs. We all knew she would soon go off on her own, but we assumed only she would know when she was ready.

She was ready that August. We were preparing for a trip and were worried about leaving her alone in the neighborhood. We made arrangements to board her at a kennel in the country. We took her cage out there first, put a new lock on the door, and set it in a wooded area behind the kennel owner's home. We stocked up on frozen fish and chicken necks. The day we were ready to take her out there, we also packed her ragged towel, her water bowl, a mattress she had made from dried grass, and several of her squeaky rubber toys.

At the kennel, we put Pippa in her old, familiar cage with all her things. We also gave her a large, fresh fish. She immediately began to eat her fish, ignoring the barking kennel dogs. We stood around woefully, hating to leave. Finally, however, we did, with many instructions to her keepers. That was the last time we ever saw her.

While we were gone—the third day, in fact—Pippa gnawed through the cage wire and headed into the surrounding saw grass and swamps. We went out there every evening for a week, calling Pippa's name and searching the ditches and canals for a trace or a footprint. We never found any.

I was glad in a way. It was time for Pippa to leave us, and after all, we had left her first. We had always worried that when she grew more mature she might become aggressive and cause trouble in our "civilized" neighborhood.

I like to think that she went back to her native territory, to the place where she was born and the weedy streams she loved so well.

Understanding What You've Read

1. How did the family first meet Pippa?
2. In what ways did the Colletts help Pippa survive?
3. How did the author feel about Pippa returning to the wild?

Applying the Skills Lesson

Suppose you wanted to write a topical outline of the selection you just read.

1. How is the selection organized?
   a. by cause and effect
   b. by comparison and contrast
   c. by example
   d. by time order
2. Which of these topics would you include in a topical outline of the selection?
   a. Pippa's games
   b. otter characteristics
   c. Pippa's otter colony
   d. Pippa's escape
3. What subtopics would you list under the topics *Pippa's games* and *otter characteristics*?
4. What details would you list under the subtopic *speech sounds*?

As you read this selection, think about how you would organize the information about estuaries in a topical outline.

Perhaps the most exciting places to see water life are . . .

Where Rivers Meet the Sea

by Laurence Pringle

Salt Water

Fresh Water

Where Salt Water Meets Fresh Water

As rivers flow to the sea, their fresh water mixes with salty seawater. The place where these waters combine is called an estuary.

For a variety and abundance of plant and animal life, estuaries are among the richest places on earth. They are homes for long-legged herons and egrets. Gulls and terns fly overhead. Scallops, oysters, crabs, and starfish live beneath the waters. Many kinds of ocean fish spend part of their lives in estuaries. Grasses and other marsh plants grow in the shallows along the water's edge.

One of the largest estuaries in the world is Chesapeake Bay, on the east coast of the United States. It is 195 miles long and covers almost 3 million acres.

At one time, the bay was a wide river valley. Then, about 10,000 years ago, the sea level rose. Salt water filled part of the valley. Thus, scientists call Chesapeake Bay a "drowned" river valley. Many other estuaries are also drowned valleys.

Salt Water and Fresh Water

The amount of salt in the water of an estuary varies. Where the estuary empties into the ocean, there are thirty to thirty-five gallons of salt in every thousand gallons of water. Upriver, at the other end of the estuary, the water has almost no salt. The salt content increases steadily as the water flows to the open sea. Salt water is heavier than fresh water, so the water near the bottom is saltier than the water close to the surface. Thus, estuary water is "layered."

Animal life in the estuary depends on the amount of salt in the water. Starfish need salt water. They live only in the ocean or in the saltiest part of the estuary. Other kinds of animals need less salt. Some sea worms, crabs, and oysters can live where there are only five gallons of salt in a thousand gallons of water. They are found where the water is almost fresh, far from the sea.

In the springtime, rivers are full of rainwater and melted snow. Great amounts of fresh water flow into the estuary. It becomes less salty. During these times, some of the fish, crabs, and other animals may move closer to the sea. Clams and other animals that move very little close their shells and live off stored food. They may die if a flood of fresh water lasts a longer time than does their food supply.

Since rivers carry less water in the summer, the whole estuary becomes saltier. Salt water therefore reaches farther upriver. Consequently, sea animals may swim, crawl, or drift farther upriver.

The Food Chain

Rivers carry food—bits of leaves and other plant parts—into the estuary. More food comes from tiny plants called algae that drift in the water. Other kinds of algae grow in the mud and on the stalks of salt-marsh grass.

The greatest source of food for all estuary animals is the grass itself. Some of it is eaten by grasshoppers, other insects, and mud crabs. However, most of the grass is eaten after it dies. Tiny plants called bacteria and fungi feed on dead grass and break it down into smaller bits called detritus.

Twice a day the tides flow in and out of the marshes. Bits of detritus are carried off by the tidal currents. Together with algae, detritus is the most abundant and important food in the estuary.

The water in an estuary is like vegetable soup. Many estuary animals eat this soup. Oysters, clams, and mussels strain food from the water. An oyster, for example, pumps eight gallons of water through its gills in an hour. Detritus, algae, and tiny animals are caught in the oyster's gills and pushed into its mouth.

These plant-eating animals eventually become food themselves. Mussels, clams, and crabs are eaten by raccoons and mink along the edges of the estuary. Snails, crabs, shrimp,

and fish are pulled from the water by birds. Plant-eating animals are also eaten by many kinds of large fish.

When a bird or large fish dies, its energy and food value are not lost, either. Part of it may be eaten by another animal, or it may rot, releasing its nutrients in the water or mud. The ever-mixing estuary waters help keep nutrients from being carried out to sea. These valuable materials may be taken into the roots of a plant as food. And the plant becomes food for an animal once more.

Estuaries offer an adventure for the explorer. One minute you may be hiking through the tall, waving grasses. The next minute you may be up to your waist in gooey mud. But in the grass and mud you can see the daily drama of the estuary, the place where rivers meet the sea.

Understanding What You've Read

1. How was Chesapeake Bay formed?
2. Why is marsh grass an important source of food?
3. Suppose salt water and fresh water were the same weight. What do you think would be some effects on animal life in the estuary? Use the diagram on page 319 to help you decide.

Applying the Skills Lesson

Use the information given in the selection to add details to this topical outline.

I. Estuary water
   A. Salt water
   B. Fresh water
II. Land animals
   A. Birds
   B. Mammals
III. Sea animals
   A. Salt water
   B. Fresh water
IV. Plants
   A. Kinds
   B. As food

TEXTBOOK STUDY

Another Look at Topical Outlines

Information in textbooks may not always be organized by topic. Sometimes it is organized by comparison and contrast or by example. However, you can still write a topical outline for these kinds of selections. Read the following textbook excerpt. The sidenotes will help you see topics, subtopics, and details that can be included in an outline.

Writing Topical Outlines in Science

Date palms and coconut palms will be subtopics in your outline. What is the topic?

Date palms are common plants in the oases of deserts. Scattered over the Arabian, Sahara, and other deserts of North Africa, the Middle East, and Asia are certain areas where underground water or springs make human settlements possible. In these oases date palms provide food and cool shade.

Coconut palms, on the other hand, require a large amount of moisture, either from underground water or a very large yearly rainfall of at least 100 centimeters (40 inches).

Tropical islands and tropical coastal areas are often bordered with coconut palms. Can you guess why? Of course. There is underground water near the edges of oceans and seas, so coconut palms do well there. The way in which coconut palms spread from one island or one shore to another is interesting. Perhaps you have noticed that the trees often lean out over the water. The fruits (coconuts) are covered with a tough, waterproof coat, and they are light enough to float. From the trees leaning out over the water's edge, coconuts drop into the water and are carried hundreds or even thousands of miles by winds, waves, and ocean currents. Eventually, a coconut may be washed up on the shore of an island far from the tree upon which the coconut developed. When conditions are right, the embryo plant within the coconut produces a root that breaks through the shell and grows down into the sand, using the stored food in the *single* cotyledon (the coconut "meat") for the necessary materials and energy to produce new plant cells. A tiny stem pushes up into the air, turns green, and starts manufacturing food. Finally, after many years, another great coconut palm stands at the border of the sea.

Banana "trees" are quite different from palm trees, although they, too, send out leaves only at the top of a single, unbranched stem. Banana plants have no tough, woody outer rind like those of

What details will you list under the subtopic *coconut palms*?

What two main things are being contrasted in this selection? They will be the topics in your outline.

palm trees. They are actually herbaceous plants. However, turgor pressure inside thick-walled cells makes the stem of a banana plant strong and rigid. In addition, the support of the plant is aided by the "trunk," which consists in great part of long leaf-stalks wrapped tightly around the stem.

Where should you look to find the meaning of this term?

What does the palm tree grow from?

Another difference between bananas and palms is that bananas grow from football-sized underground bulbs. The banana trees that are grown for their fruit do

326

not produce seeds. The next time you eat a banana look for seeds. You will find tiny dark dots that are only the *vestiges* [ves′tij·iz], or remains, of seeds. The ancestors of modern bananas were capable of reproducing themselves from seeds, but not the modern banana.

—Life: A Biological Science
Harcourt Brace Jovanovich

Building Skills

Complete the outline below based on the information given in the selection.

I. Palm trees
   A. Date
      1. _____
      2. Provide food and cool shade
   B. _____
      1. Found in tropical areas
      2. Grow from coconut fruit
         a. _____
         b. Light enough to float
         c. _____
         d. _____
II. Banana "trees"
   A. _____
   B. Herbaceous
   C. Stems strong and rigid
   D. _____
   E. Grow from bulbs
      1. _____
      2. _____

SKILLS LESSON

Once Over Lightly . . . Skimming and Scanning

Cindy and Peter went shopping for birthday presents for their mother. Cindy knew that she wanted to get her mother warm gloves. Peter wasn't sure what he wanted to buy. Cindy went directly to the glove counter, not bothering to see what else the store had to offer. Peter looked around quickly to see what was displayed on each counter. He didn't look too carefully at first. He only wanted an idea of the kinds of things he might find in the store.

Just as you shop differently for different purposes, you can read differently, depending on what you want to know. If you want a general idea of what a selection is about, you might **skim** it. When you skim you are following Peter's method. You are looking just closely enough to get a sense of what's there. If you are looking for specific information in a selection, you can **scan** it. When you scan, you are following Cindy's example. Like her, you are going directly to what you want and ignoring the rest.

Skimming a Selection

You skim a selection to get a general idea of its contents. Skimming saves time. After you have skimmed the selection, you may find that it isn't necessary to read it thoroughly. You may have already learned all you need to know, or you may have discovered that the selection isn't suitable to your purpose.

To skim a selection, look at the title first. Then go to the illustrations and captions if there are any. Does the article have an introductory paragraph? A summary paragraph? Are there subheads that identify the topics? All these things can be found quickly, without really reading at all. They can tell you a great deal about the selection. If you still need more information to get a sense of what the article is about, look for main ideas. Often, main ideas are stated at the beginning of paragraphs, so you might try reading the first sentence of each paragraph before looking any further.

Try skimming the selection that follows.

Preparing Materials for Recycling

Before bottles, jars, cans, and even papers can be sent to be recycled, they must be specially prepared. You can do most of the preparation yourself.

Wash the cans, bottles, and jars. Remove the paper labels. Some bottles have metal sealing rings around their necks. These, too, should be removed.

Many collection centers ask you to crush aluminum cans. Flattened cans are easier to store and transport.

Finally, you can help sort the materials for recycling. If there is a collection center in your neighborhood, it probably has separate bins for each glass color. Bottle makers do not want different colors mixed together, because mixing them ruins the color of the new glass. Scientists are developing machinery that automatically sorts the glass by color. However, until these machines are perfected, your help is needed.

Your collection center may also ask you to separate paper products for recycling. Some centers want only newspapers. Others accept all kinds of paper. Any kind of paper can be recycled unless it contains plastic. Just as bottle makers do not mix different colors of glass, papermakers do not mix different kinds of paper.

What is the topic of the selection? How long did it take you to find it? Probably just a second. The title states the topic very clearly. What is the main idea of the selection? It is: *There are special ways to prepare materials to be recycled.* What are these different kinds of materials? Notice how much information you can learn by skimming.

Now read the selection more slowly. Note the additional details you learn by a more thorough reading.

Scanning for Information

When you only want to find specific information in a selection —a name or a date, for example—you can scan the selection. Suppose you are interested in facts about preparing glass for recycling. You can glance through the preceding article very quickly, looking for key words such as *glass, bottle,* and *jar.* Only when you spot these words should you slow your pace and read carefully.

Try scanning the next selection. Look only for specific facts about Project Oceanology.

Career Education

Many critics of American schools say students need better preparation for earning a living in the real world. Educators have begun to develop programs to answer this need. "Career education" is the umbrella title for all such programs.

Schools are now experimenting with a number of approaches to career education. One approach is to teach students about the working world in a traditional classroom setting. Other programs try to recreate the actual work situation.

There are signs that such programs are catching on. In several schools throughout the nation, students are getting a taste of the working world during the school day. In Connecticut, for example, about 10,000 students each year have taken part in "Project Oceanology." Their classroom is a fifty-foot boat on which they learn about careers related to the ocean. These careers include fishing, environment, chemistry, navigation, and marine biology.

Which sentences contain the information you were looking for? What key words did you use to find the information?

Now go back and read the selection more slowly. What other topics are discussed in the selection?

Try This

1. Scan this lesson for the specific things to look for when you skim a selection. What paragraph contains this information?
2. In which of the following situations would you use skimming? In which would you use scanning?
   a. You want to get a general idea of what a particular magazine article is about.
   b. You want to find out if today's newspaper has a story about last night's soccer match.
   c. You're in a restaurant and you've been given a menu. You want to find out the kinds of dishes that are served.

VOCABULARY STUDY

Aesop's Jokes, Act II . . . Multiple Meanings

Aunt Bertha loves *scallops*. For lunch yesterday, she ate a sandwich and the entire border of her bedroom curtains.

scallop: (a) one of several half circles used as a design or border
(b) a small shellfish

My nephew Gladstone has never had much courage. But since he took a job as a sand salesman, I have to admit he's been showing a lot of *grit*.

grit: (a) small, hard particles of sand, stone, etc.
(b) courage

My brother Rupert thought he wasn't getting enough exercise, so he started running at an outdoor track. He took a pair of old shoes and put some *spikes* on them. The shoes are OK, but the spikes are a problem. Every time he runs, he trips over the fish tails.

spike: (a) one of several metal nails set in the sole of a shoe
(b) a young mackerel

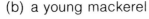

Word Play

What is the correct definition for each of the italicized words?
1. *scallops* you might sew
2. the *grit* on the floor of a sculpture studio
3. *spikes* an athlete could wear

Skim the selection to find out what the title means. Then read the selection more slowly for the specific details.

Tens of thousands of auks lived along the coasts of the North Atlantic 400 years ago. Uncontrolled hunting began . . .

AND THEN THERE WERE NONE

by Mark Wexler

In 1534, a French sea captain reported that his men had killed more than a thousand "northern penguins" in a single day. But the bird to which the captain referred was not a penguin at all. It was the great auk, which at one time nested safely by the millions from Newfoundland to Scandinavia. Today the only specimens are in museums.

Like the penguin, the great auk could not fly but was a powerful swimmer. Each season, a female laid only one enormous egg, measuring about five inches long. Fully grown, a great auk stood three feet tall.

Originally, the great auk's largest nesting ground was an island off the eastern coast of Newfoundland. But by the early 1800's, fishermen had completely destroyed them. They used the birds' bodies for food or rendered them into cooking oil.

While the Napoleonic wars were raging across Europe, ships were sailing from Reykjavik, Iceland, to nearby Penguin Island, the second largest great-auk nesting colony, to kill the birds for food. There, using only large sticks, sailors slaughtered the proud birds by the thousands. Then, in the spring of 1830, another terrible blow struck the few great auks still at Penguin Island. The island just disappeared beneath the frigid ocean waters. Most of the surviving great auks took refuge on the small island of Eldey. This island was not far from where their home had been.

But Eldey was not to remain their home for long. The birds had become famous in Europe. Collectors paid immense sums for great-auk skins throughout the 1830's. In 1844, Carl Siemsen of Reykjavik, an agent for prospective buyers, offered a large cash reward in hopes of getting just a few more skins of the almost-extinct bird. A daring Icelandic fisherman answered the challenge and went to Eldey with a small crew. There, he looked for and finally discovered two great auks. He promptly killed them both. Soon after, he returned to Reykjavik to collect his reward: 100 crowns ($60) for the last two great auks on earth.

Understanding What You've Read

1. Why do you think auks were called northern penguins?
2. What factors led to the death of the great auks?
3. Why was Carl Siemsen willing to pay a large sum of money for more auk skins?

Applying the Skills Lesson

Scan the selection to find:
1. the height of a fully grown great auk
2. the original location of the auk's largest nesting ground
3. what happened to the auk's nesting ground at Penguin Island
4. the dollar equivalent of 100 crowns

What does the author mean by "A World in a Jar"? Skim the selection to find out.

How does the weather affect the plants and animals around us? You can find out some answers for yourself by creating . . .

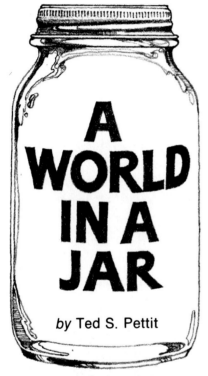

A WORLD IN A JAR

by Ted S. Pettit

We all know how weather affects us. We generally spend more time indoors during the winter than during the summer. We wear different clothes, we may eat different foods, and we enjoy different activities. Obviously weather and climate—the weather over a long period—have a tremendous influence on our everyday life as well as on our seasonal activities.

Weather and climate also have a tremendous influence on wild animals. To a very large extent, weather and climate determine what animals live in a given area, when they live there, or even whether any animals live there at all.

We know that some birds migrate south in the fall and north in the spring. We know that some mammals sleep out the winter in hibernation. We know that some fish are more easily caught at higher temperatures than at lower temperatures; and some theories suggest that fish bite best when the barometer is falling. Through a few do-it-yourself projects you can see how weather and climate influence animals.

You will need two mason jars for the projects. Both jars should be the same size, one gallon if possible. The jars should have screw tops. A screw top on a mason jar has two pieces—the rim that screws on the jar and the flat surface that serves as a lid. Remove the lids and glue the rims together along the outside top edge. When you screw the jars into the glued-together rims from either side, you will have one container with two parts.

Drop some flies into one of the jars. Then screw the jars together. Put the container on its side, in a place where both jars will get the same amount of light. Try to avoid direct sunlight.

Watch the flies for about an hour. They should fly back and forth from one jar to the other. If they don't, stand the jars up and note what happens. If the flies head for the top jar, turn the jars over and see if they go back to the top. If they stay in the bottom jar, turn the jars over and see whether they return to the bottom.

Next, use some black paper or heavy black cloth and cover one jar so that it is dark inside. See what effect this has on the flies. Do they have a preference for the dark jar or the light jar? Now move the cover to the other jar. Do the flies prefer to stay where they are?

Try the same experiment with other kinds of insects.

Tape a thermometer to the inside of each jar. Position the two thermometers so you can read them from the outside.

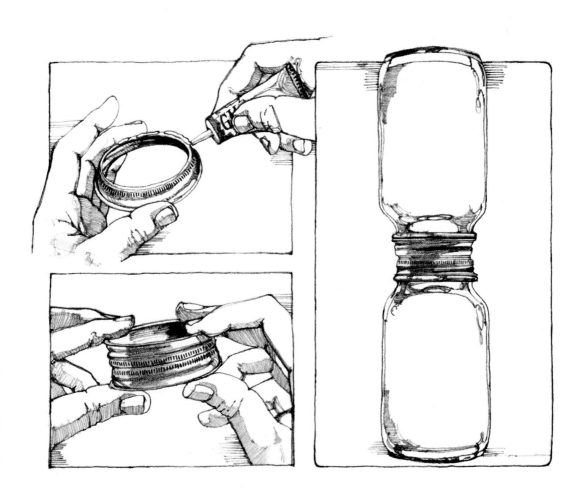

Put the flies, beetles, or other insects inside one jar. Hold a lighted candle under one jar to raise the temperature in the jar. Move the candle back and forth so that the heat will not crack the glass. Does the heat have any effect on the insects? Does their behavior reflect the change in temperature? To increase the temperature difference between the two jars, wrap a piece of wet cloth around the unheated jar and place it in front of a fan.

Now try a combination of light and temperature. Cover one jar with cloth so it is dark inside. Raise the temperature in the other jar. Try all the combinations and watch for the effects.

Next you can add the element of humidity. Soak a piece of paper towel or a small sponge and squeeze out most of the water. Place it in one jar along with the insects. Wait a few minutes and see if it has any effect. Use the information you obtained in the previous experiments to make the flies move from one jar to the other. See whether they react the same way now that you've introduced humidity.

Combine all the elements—light, temperature, and humidity—in one project. Create one warm, dark, humid jar and one light, dry, cooler jar. Then create a cool, dark jar and a light, humid jar. There are several other combinations you can experiment with. Each of them will show something about how insects react to climate.

Understanding What You've Read

1. What are some examples of the effects of weather and climate on animals?
2. Suppose you find some insects that do not prefer cold over warm or wet over dry climates. Would you expect such insects to be more or less widespread than insects that do prefer one climate over another? Why?

Applying the Skills Lesson

Scan the selection to find out:
1. the materials you will need for the experiments
2. some of the different kinds of "climates" you can create inside the jars

TEXTBOOK STUDY

Skimming and Scanning

As you know, you can skim a textbook selection to get a general idea of the kinds of information it contains. Or you might scan a selection to find a specific detail. As you read the following textbook excerpt, refer to the sidenotes. They will point out things to notice when skimming and scanning.

Skimming and Scanning in Social Studies

When you skim, notice the graphic aids. What kinds of information are provided by the map?

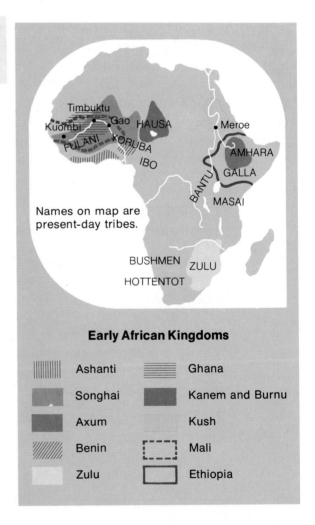

Names on map are present-day tribes.

Early African Kingdoms

|||||||	Ashanti	=====	Ghana
	Songhai		Kanem and Burnu
	Axum		Kush
////	Benin	[- -]	Mali
	Zulu	[ ]	Ethiopia

African Civilizations

As various groups within Sub-Saharan Africa became powerful, they were able to spread their influence to other peoples of the region.

The kingdom of Kush was described by a Greek historian in the fifth century B.C. Its capital was at Meroe in what is now Sudan. The ironworks that flourished at Meroe were so huge that a British scholar has described that city as the Birmingham of ancient Africa. (Birmingham is an iron-manufacturing city in England.) Meroe flourished from about 550 B.C. to A.D. 200. From it, the technology of ironworking spread through Sub-Saharan Africa.

Skim to find out what the selection says about this city.

The civilization at Axum, in what is now Ethiopia, started at roughly the same time. It developed to a point where its merchants became familiar figures in the Middle East and South Asia.

Scan the preceding paragraph to find out when the civilization at Axum began.

Other empires rose at different times in other parts of Sub-Saharan Africa. In what is now Rhodesia, the huge walls of Zimbabwe stand to this day. They show the power of the people who ruled there.

The western Sudan also had several powerful African empires. Among these was Ghana, which reached the height of its power around A.D. 1000. An Arab writer tells that Ghana could put 200,000 soldiers in the field in A.D. 1066. This is the same year that William the Conqueror invaded England with about 25,000 soldiers.

The selection discusses three empires in the western Sudan. Scan the selection to find out their names.

The great emperor of Mali, another great empire of western Africa, made a journey to the holy cities of the Middle East in 1325. He and his party flooded Cairo with so much gold that the price of gold had still not recovered twelve years later. Later still, in the early 1500's, the emperor of Songhai and his armies were able to gain control of an area almost as large as the continental United States.

—World Geography Today
Holt, Rinehart & Winston

Building Skills

Scan the selection to find the answers to these questions:
1. Where were the kingdoms of Kush and Axum located?
2. When did Ghana reach the height of its power?
3. What was the name of an old city in Rhodesia?
4. When did the emperor of Mali visit the holy cities of the Middle East?

SKILLS LESSON

Short and Sweet . . . Summarizing

Hi Jay,
Having a great time!
Went to the beach today
with Jeannie, Jackie, and
Mickey. Had a picnic.
Then did some scuba
diving. Yesterday we
visited an old shipyard
and boarded a real
sailing schooner.
See you soon.
Eileen

Jay Carroll
446 Vernon Pl.
Chicago, IL. 60604

Did you ever write down the high points of a trip on a postcard? Can you get everything you want to say into a three-minute phone call? If so, you know the importance of a good summary.

A **summary** is a brief statement that includes the main ideas and key points of a selection. Being able to summarize what you read is important because it:

- helps you gain an understanding of the material
- helps you remember the important information
- provides you with a study aid for the future

The first step in making a summary is to read—and be sure you understand—the selection. This means identifying the topics and main ideas. It also means finding the definitions of any unfamiliar words. Then ask yourself, "How many important points does the author make?" "What are these points?" A summary is always shorter than the original article. So, you will want to look for the "essentials." Descriptive details and examples often are not part of the summary.

A summary is written in your own words. There is one exception. This is when you directly quote the author. Otherwise, rephrase the information for your summary. Rephrasing is always a good idea because to do it, you first have to understand the information.

The length of your summary depends on the amount of important information in the article. The summary of a chapter in a textbook may be three or four paragraphs. The summary of a newspaper article may be one paragraph. Very few summaries are only one sentence.

Read the following selection. The sidenotes will point out some important information to include in a summary.

The Sun

This is an important fact about the sun.

The source of life on earth is 150 million kilometers away. It is the giant ball of hot gas called the sun. But the sun is just one of billions of stars in the sky. The sun is 109 times the diameter of the earth. Yet,

Why is this fact important?

scientists call it "medium sized." Betelgeuse, the bright red star in the constellation Orion, is 580 times the size of our sun.

The sun has been "burning" for over 4 billion years. It should continue to do so for billions of years more.

344

It is the sun—with the help of the moon—that creates tides. The sun also allows green plants to grow. Green plants use sunlight to make oxygen. One-fifth of the air we breathe is oxygen. The sun also controls our weather and supplies us with vitamin D. Were the sun just a little farther away, there probably would be no life on earth.

The key facts to note in this paragraph tell why the sun is important to us.

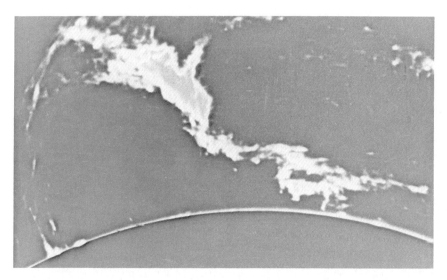

Here is a summary of the selection you just read. Notice that it includes only the most important information about the sun.

The sun is a medium-sized star, 150 million kilometers from earth. It controls tides, stimulates the growth of green plants, controls our weather, and is the source of vitamin D.

The two-sentence summary combines information from several sentences in the original. What sentences in the selection were combined to make sentence 1 in the summary? Why doesn't the summary include information about the composition of our air?

Read the following selection. What is the topic? What key points would you include in a summary?

The number of farms in Canada has been dropping steadily in recent years. On the other hand, the amount of crops and livestock produced has been growing steadily. Also, the size of the individual farm has grown. Farmers can till more land and produce more crops because machines do the work.

In Newfoundland and British Columbia, about two-thirds of the farms today average 70 acres. In the other Maritime Provinces, most farms have 70 to 129 acres. In the Prairie Provinces, most farms have from 240 to 499 acres.

The selection makes three points about farms in Canada: (1) The number of farms has dropped; (2) Production of crops and livestock has risen; and (3) The size of the farm has grown. These three points should be included in a summary. Note that the information given in the second paragraph only gives examples to illustrate the points made in the first paragraph.

A summary of the selection would look like this:

Recently, the number of Canadian farms has been dropping. Yet individual farm production and acreage have been on the rise.

What statements in the original were rephrased in the summary? What statements were combined into one sentence in the summary?

Try This

Read the selection below. Then answer the questions that follow.

There are many other energy sources besides the familiar coal, gas, and oil. For many years, especially in the Midwest and in Holland, windmills have been used as a means of pumping water. Windmills are one form of "clean" energy, because nothing is burned. They are powered by wind. Recently, large-scale efforts have been undertaken to use windmills to make and store hydrogen.

Solar-heating devices are also on the increase as a way of warming houses. Space probes have shown us that solar panels are both clean and efficient. Now, blueprints for building a solar home are available. Some states are experimenting with solar energy to power factories and small communities.

Proposals have also been made to harness the power of the tides in places where conditions are favorable. In New Zealand, Iceland, and the Far West, "natural" or geothermal heat is being considered as an energy source. This heat is being released constantly through volcanic forces inside the earth.

1. What is the topic of the selection?
   a. windmills
   b. coal, gas, and oil
   c. clean energy sources
   d. water power
2. Which of the following are the most important points of the selection?
   a. Coal, gas, and oil are sources of energy.
   b. Windmills are being used to pump water and to make and store hydrogen.
   c. Windmills are powered by wind.
   d. Solar devices are now being used to power homes and factories.
   e. Tides and geothermal heat are being considered as energy sources.
   f. Geothermal heat is released through volcanic forces inside the earth.
3. Which of the two paragraphs that follow is the better summary of the selection? Why?

   Windmills, solar devices, tides, and geothermal heat are potential sources of clean energy. Windmills are being used to pump water and to make and store hydrogen. Houses and factories are being heated by solar panels. There have been a number of proposals to make use of tides and geothermal heat as energy sources.

   Coal, oil, and gas are not the only sources of energy. For many years, windmills have been used as a means of pumping water. Space probes use solar panels as energy sources. They are both clean and efficient. Solar panels can heat homes, factories, and entire communities. Proposals have also been made to harness the power of tides. New Zealand, Iceland, and the Far West are experimenting with "natural" or geothermal energy.

VOCABULARY STUDY

Lester's Reply to Big Burst . . . Synonyms

Dear Big Burst Sugarless Bubble Gum:

I have a funny feeling you didn't understand my first letter. Maybe I wasn't <u>emphatic</u> enough. This time I'm going to be more forceful: WHERE'S MY FREE GIFT? Your offer said if I sent in my gum wrappers, you would forward my gift <u>promptly</u>. Well, not only didn't my Big Burst surprise arrive quickly, it didn't arrive at all!

What's holding up the show? Is your factory in a <u>distant</u> part of the world? It can't possibly be as far as Antarctica, or you'd be making frozen food instead of bubble gum.

This is your last chance, Big Burst. If you don't send my free gift, I'm going to start chewing carrots instead of your old dumb gum.

Lester Yerb

Word Play

Reread Lester's letter and find the synonyms he used for each of the underlined words.

Read this selection. Look for the main ideas that would be included in a summary.

Can garbage be useful and attractive? Before you answer, read . . .

TAKING ACTION
The Story of Mount Trashmore

by Betty Miles

350

A few years ago, Virginia Beach, Virginia, was a flat, sandy city near the ocean. And like every other city, Virginia Beach had a problem: garbage disposal.

It costs a lot of money to collect garbage, dump it, and then burn it. A dump full of burning waste looks ugly and smells bad. Its smoke pollutes the air. The waste does not burn entirely, and rats are attracted to it. The dump makes an ugly, useless scar on the land.

So some people in Virginia Beach came up with an idea. "Let's do something useful with our trash," they suggested. "Let's pile it up, cover it with dirt, and make ourselves a mountain."

Trying something new is always risky. It can be expensive to find out if an idea will work. Fortunately,

Virginia Beach received money from the U.S. government to carry out the experiment. If it worked in Virginia Beach, perhaps other parts of the country could benefit.

Virginia Beach already had a town dump, and this is where the townspeople decided to put the mountain. The swampy land was drained and flattened, and roads to the area were built.

Then the trash was spread out over the dump. The trash wasn't only food scraps like orange peels, watermelon rinds, and coffee grounds. It wasn't only paper trash like boxes, newspapers, and paper bags. This trash included every-thing: buckets, tires, broken stoves, car parts, old toys, and table legs.

A layer of dirt about twenty inches thick was piled on top of the trash. A machine called a com-pactor rolled over the dump, tightly packing the trash and the dirt into a solid block. This became the first layer of the mountain. Every day, loads of trash were dumped, spread out, covered with soil, and com-pacted. The mountain grew.

After five years, 640,000 tons of trash, and a million dollars, the mountain was finished. It measured 800 feet long, 300 feet wide, and stood 68 feet high. The top of the mountain was broad and level. It

wasn't much of a mountain, but it was something special in flat Virginia Beach.

The mountain remained nameless until someone came along and dubbed it "Mount Trashmore." The name became official when it appeared on the Virginia Beach map.

Grass now grows on Mount Trashmore. There are bicycle trails, paths, and picnic shelters. Plans call for tennis courts and an outdoor theater. There are boating and fishing on an artificial lake nearby.

What did Virginia Beach gain from the Mount Trashmore experiment? It disposed of its waste for two dollars a ton, instead of the burning price of seven to thirteen dollars a ton. It got rid of an ugly dump.

Virginia Beach also welcomed visitors from cities all over the world who came to learn about Mount Trashmore. And one winter, when a surprise snow fell, Virginia Beach got its very first ski slope.

Of course, people in Virginia Beach are still making garbage and trash, and the city still has to get rid of it. So they have begun to build a new mountain, which will grow from the garbage and trash of the next twenty years. And perhaps someday, flat Virginia Beach will be able to brag about its mountain chain.

Understanding What You've Read

1. What are two disadvantages of garbage dumps?
2. What does Mount Trashmore look like? What are some ways in which people use it?

Applying the Skills Lesson

Make a summary of this selection by following these four steps:

1. Review the paragraphs on page 351 that state the problem Virginia Beach had. Think of one short statement that describes the problem.
2. Review the paragraphs that state the action taken by the people of Virginia Beach. Think of one statement that describes the action.
3. Review the paragraphs that tell the results of the action. Think of a statement that describes the results.
4. Write these statements in paragraph form.

Why are the Lakotas lovers of nature? The answer to this question will help you summarize the selection.

The Lakotas, known also as the Sioux, roamed the plains. In describing their style of living, Chief Luther Standing Bear says that a Lakota has always been . . .

A LOVER OF NATURE

by Chief Luther Standing Bear

The Lakotas loved the earth and all things of the earth, the attachment growing with age. The old people came literally to love the soil. They sat or reclined on the ground with a feeling of being close to a mothering power. It was good for the skin to touch the earth. The old people liked to remove their moccasins and walk with bare feet on the sacred earth. It was the final abiding place of all things that lived and grew. The soil was soothing, strengthening, cleansing, and healing.

That is why the old Lakotas still sit upon the earth instead of propping themselves up and away from its life-giving forces. For them, to sit or lie upon the ground is to be able to think more deeply and to feel more keenly. They can see more clearly into the mysteries of life and come closer in kinship to other lives about them. . . .

Kinship with all creatures of the earth, sky, and water was a real and active principle. For animals and birds there existed a brotherly feeling that kept the Lakotas safe among them. So close did some of the Lakotas come to their feathered and furred friends that, in true brotherhood, they spoke a common tongue.

The old Lakotas were wise. They knew that one's heart away from nature becomes hard. They knew that lack of respect for growing, living things soon leads to lack of respect for humans, too. So they kept their youth close to the softening influence of nature.

Understanding What You've Read

1. How do the Lakotas feel about animals and birds?
2. How do you think the Lakotas would feel toward people who do not respect living, growing things? Explain your answer.

Applying the Skills Lesson

1. Refer to the selection to find the answers to the following three questions.
   a. Why do the Lakotas love the earth?
   b. How does this love extend to other living things?
   c. How does their feeling affect the way they behave?
2. Use your answers to question 1 to summarize the selection.

Note the main idea in the first paragraph. It will help you summarize the selection.

Do you live near a smoky factory? Do you smell the fumes from buses or cars?
Be careful,
because . . .

FRESH AIR WILL KILL YOU

by Art Buchwald

Smog, which was once the big attraction of Los Angeles, can now be found all over the country, from Butte, Montana, to New York City, and people are getting so used to polluted air that it's very difficult for them to breathe anything else.

I was lecturing recently, and one of my stops was Flagstaff, Arizona, which is about 7,000 feet above sea level. As soon as I got out of the plane, I smelled something peculiar.

"What's that smell?" I asked the man who met me at the plane.

"I don't smell anything," he replied.

"There's a definite odor that I'm not familiar with," I said.

"Oh, you must be talking about the fresh air. A lot of people come out here who have never smelled fresh air before."

"What's it supposed to do?" I asked suspiciously.

"Nothing. You just breathe it like any other kind of air. It's supposed to be good for your lungs."

"I've heard that story before," I said. "How come, if it's air, my eyes aren't watering?"

"Your eyes don't water with fresh air. That's the advantage of it. Saves you a lot in paper tissues."

I looked around and everything appeared crystal clear. It was a strange sensation and made me feel very uncomfortable.

My host, sensing this, tried to be reassuring. "Please don't worry about it. Tests have proved that you can breathe fresh air day and night without its doing harm to the body."

"You're just saying that because you don't want me to leave," I said. "Nobody who has lived in a major city can stand fresh air for a very long time. He has no tolerance for it."

"Well, if the fresh air bothers you, why don't you put a handkerchief over your nose and breathe through your mouth?"

"Okay, I'll try it. If I'd known I was coming to a place that had nothing but fresh air, I would have brought a surgical mask."

We drove in silence. About fifteen minutes later he asked, "How do you feel now?"

"Okay, I guess, but I sure miss sneezing."

"We don't sneeze too much here," the man admitted. "Do they sneeze a lot where you come from?"

"All the time. There are some days when that's all you do."

358

"Do you enjoy it?"

"Not necessarily, but if you don't sneeze, you'll die. Let me ask you something. How come there's no air pollution around here?"

"Flagstaff can't seem to attract industry. I guess we're really behind the times. . . ."

The fresh air was making me feel dizzy. "Isn't there a diesel bus around here that I could breathe into for a couple of hours?"

"Not at this time of day. I might be able to find a truck for you."

We found a truck driver and slipped him a five-dollar bill, and he let me put my head near his exhaust pipe for a half hour. I was immediately revived and able to give my speech.

Nobody was as happy to leave Flagstaff as I was. My next stop was Los Angeles, and when I got off the plane, I took one big deep breath of the smog-filled air, my eyes started to water, I began to sneeze, and I felt like a new man again.

Understanding What You've Read

1. Why did the author find the air unusual in Flagstaff, Arizona?
2. What are some of the things the author says about fresh air versus smog? Does the author really feel this way? Explain your answer.
3. How did the author react when he reached Los Angeles?

Applying the Skills Lesson

Which of the following best summarizes the selection?
1. It's better to breathe polluted air than fresh air.
2. Through humor, the author is pointing out that people who constantly breathe polluted air become used to it and its damaging effects on the body.
3. When the author went to Flagstaff, he felt sick. However, his health improved when he was able to breathe exhaust fumes from a truck.

TEXTBOOK STUDY

Summarizing

Making a summary of textbook material is one way to help you understand and remember information. A summary can also be a useful study tool. As you read the following textbook excerpt, refer to the sidenotes. They will point out the kinds of information that should be included in a summary.

Summarizing in Social Studies

Your summary will include the reasons why there is famine in the Sahel.

This is an important point. It states one reason why there is famine in the Sahel.

This is an example used to illustrate a point the author is making. Should this example be included in your summary? Why or why not?

Famine in the Sahel

The Sahel is a dry land, with little rain. It is covered with a thin blanket of grass and thorny bushes. Many of the people who live in the region raise cattle, sheep, and goats.

But the desert—the Sahara—is spreading southward, perhaps as fast as 30 miles a year. The grass and bushes of the Sahel are giving way to sand. In the early 1970's, the great herds of the Sahel began dying off. The people began dying, too.

What happened? From 1968 to 1973, there was much less rainfall than usual. Another problem is that the herds of the Sahel had been growing much larger, because of government programs to improve the health of the animals. The larger herds ate too much grass. These and other things caused the spread of the desert. During 1973, 40 percent of the cattle, sheep, and goats in the Sahel died—along with 100,000 people.

Governments and other organizations in the richer nations of the world have shipped huge amounts of food to the

Sahel. Hundreds of thousands of lives have been saved. Yet the big problems of the Sahel are not yet solved. And some of its people continue to die as the desert spreads southward toward them.

Which statement in this paragraph explains what is being done to stop the spread of famine?

— The Human Adventure
Addison-Wesley

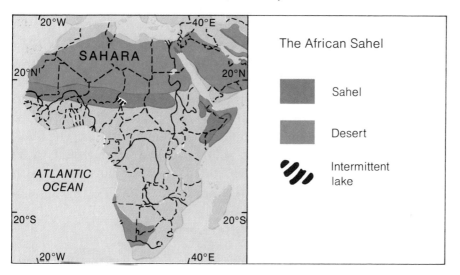

The African Sahel

Sahel

Desert

Intermittent lake

Building Skills

Which of the following is a better summary of the selection? Explain your answer.

The southward spread of the Sahara is causing famine in the Sahel. Grazing land is being replaced by sand and decreasing the food supply for the herds. At the same time, less rainfall has limited plant growth, while the animals made healthier by government programs are consuming more grass. Other nations have begun sending food supplies to the people of the Sahel.

The Sahara Desert is spreading. People in the Sahel are suffering from a great famine. Since healthy animals eat more grass, desert area is increasing. Decreasing rainfall lowers plant growth.

Summarizing in Language Arts

This textbook excerpt is not accompanied by sidenotes. As you read the selection, look for important points to be included in a summary. Then answer the questions that follow.

The Origin of Language

Where did language come from? If we knew the answer to that question, we would also know a great deal more than we do about civilization. Since spoken language developed long before written language, we have no written records to tell us what really happened. Instead of written proof, we have theories. The nicknames scholars have often given these theories, however, show how much faith they have in them.

The "Bow-wow" Theory

One theory is that language began when people started to imitate sounds. This is sometimes called the "bow-wow" theory, after the sound a dog makes. In

English, such words as *murmur, pop, purr, whiz, snarl,* and *squelch* are clearly imitations of natural sounds. However, only a very small number of words in any known language falls into this group. Most words seem to have no relationship to the sounds of nature.

The "Pooh-pooh" Theory

Still another theory holds that people have always made certain noises in certain situations and that our languages are based on these responses. Such sounds might be "Ugh!" "Hey!" "Ouch!" and "Humph!" The theory is sometimes called the "pooh-pooh" theory. Although there may be some truth in it, it, too, explains only a very few words.

— Language for Daily Use: Silver
Harcourt Brace Jovanovich

Building Skills

Which of the following statements would you include in a summary of this selection?

1. Nobody knows where languages come from.
2. There are no written records to tell us how spoken language developed.
3. There are many theories about how language developed.
4. The "bow-wow" theory states that people imitated sounds.
5. Dogs say "bow-wow."
6. *Murmur, pop,* and other words imitate sounds.
7. The "pooh-pooh" theory states that people have always made certain noises.
8. The origin of many words cannot be explained by these theories.

SKILLS LESSON

Who? What? When? Where? Why? . . .
Taking Notes

When you take notes, you use many of the same skills you use for outlining. You look for topics. You word them in a way that will help you remember them. You look for the relationship among topics, subtopics, and details.

However, there are a few differences between outlining and note-taking. First, you don't always have to take notes on everything in a chapter or an article. The kinds of notes you take will depend upon your purpose for reading the selection and the things you want to be sure to remember. Second, there is no special format for note-taking. Third, since you usually take notes as you read, you can use your own personal shorthand.

Using Question Words

When newspaper reporters cover a story, they want to be sure they include all the important facts. Five questions help them do this: *Who? What? When? Where?* and *Why?* If you write down the answers to these questions as you read, you will have a set of notes that includes most of the important information in the selection.

Suppose you wanted to take notes on an article about miniparks. While reading, ask yourself: "*What* are miniparks?" "*Who* builds them?" "*Why* are they built?" "*Where* are they found?" Look for the answers to these questions as you read the following selection.

In the last ten years, many parts of New York have changed. Low-rise buildings in the business district have been replaced by skyscrapers. Old buildings in waterfront districts are being torn down to make room for high-rise apartments. Empty lots in residential areas are being turned into miniparks by block associations. A minipark is a small outdoor area set aside for relaxation. It may have benches, trees, and playground equipment.

City agencies are changing zoning laws to encourage builders to create space for miniparks in business districts. As one excited builder says, "The minipark attracts more tenants to the area than anything else."

Your notes on the selection might look like this:

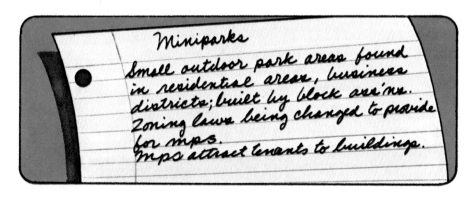

Since your notes should be brief, it is not necessary to write complete sentences. You can also use abbreviations. What do the abbreviations *ass'ns* and *mps* stand for in the notes at the bottom of page 365? Which phrase answers the question *What?* Which phrase gives information on *where* miniparks are found?

An important point to remember when taking notes is to *use your own words.* To rephrase an idea in your own words, you must first understand it. And, of course, one of the main reasons for taking notes is to increase your understanding of the material.

Sometimes you may want to include an exact quotation in your notes. The original phrase or sentence might be a very good way of wording an idea. If you decide to quote something directly, be sure you use quotation marks and note the source.

Taking Notes on Several Topics

Very often, a selection gives information on several different topics. However, authors do not always present each topic separately. To help you group your notes according to topic, first identify the topics. You might want to skim the selection and jot down the topics. Or you could list each new topic in your notes while reading the selection at a slower rate. In either case, be sure to leave room under each topic to write down the details you find.

Read the following selection. What topics are discussed? What information would you include in your notes under each topic?

The tropical rain forest has warm temperatures year round. In a temperate forest, found north and south of the tropics, the climate changes with the seasons. There, winter temperatures can fall below freezing. Rainfall averages 75 to 150 centimeters a year, but it is not constant. In the tropical rain forest, it rains nearly every day.

Rain, sunlight, and high humidity stimulate the growth of a wide variety of plants in the tropical rain forest. Among these are the aerial plants which do not grow in the ground. Instead, they are found on the limbs and trunks of trees. The orchid is one example of an aerial plant. This flower could never survive in a temperate forest, which is home to evergreen trees such as pine, fir, and spruce.

Parrots, monkeys, and snakes are common in the tropical rain forest. Animal life in the temperate forest includes moose, squirrels, and grouse.

Two topics are discussed in the selection. They are *the tropical rain forest* and *the temperate forest.* You might want to list these topics side by side in your notes and then jot down important information under each topic as you read.

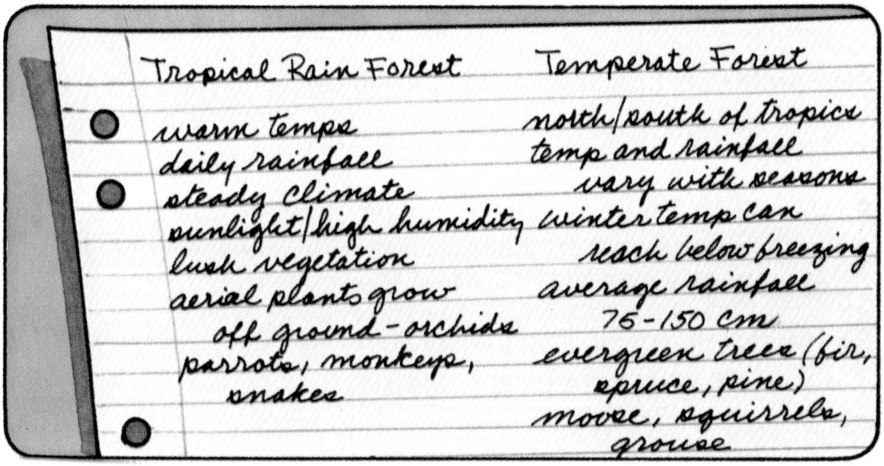

Tropical Rain Forest
- warm temps
- daily rainfall
- steady climate
- sunlight/high humidity
- lush vegetation
- aerial plants grow off ground—orchids
- parrots, monkeys, snakes

Temperate Forest
- north/south of tropics
- temp and rainfall vary with seasons
- winter temp can reach below freezing
- average rainfall 75-150 cm
- evergreen trees (fir, spruce, pine)
- moose, squirrels, grouse

You may decide to arrange your notes differently from those shown above. For example, you could list the topics vertically on your paper, leaving a space between them for the important details. The arrangement you choose usually will depend on the number of topics discussed and the amount of information given for each topic. Be sure to keep your notes on the different topics separate from one another.

Try This

1. Which details in the preceding selection on tropical and temperate forests would you include when taking notes on the topic *aerial plants?*
2. Suppose you wanted to take notes on this skills lesson. What topics would you want to be sure to include in your notes?

VOCABULARY STUDY

The Tomb of the Latin Magician Dentist . . .
Etymologies

Sir Jason: We've found it, Sir Harold! The tomb of the ancient Latin magician dentist!

Sir Harold: How can you be sure? All the words written on the tomb walls are Latin.

Sir Jason: Tut, tut, Sir Harold. I can read Latin. Look at this word: *predict*. The prefix *pre* means "before," and in Latin, *dicere* means "to say."

Sir Harold: Oh, I get it. To *predict* is "to say something will happen before it happens." Very clever. But what about this word: *revive?*

Sir Jason: The prefix *re-* means "again," and the Latin word *vivere* means "to live." Thus, *revive* is "to live again" or "to bring back to life."

Sir Harold: Bravo, Sir Jason! Magicians have the power to predict the future and revive people. But you have no clues that this chap was a dentist.

Sir Jason: Oh, yes I do—this word *extract,* from the prefix *ex-*, meaning "out," and the Latin *trahere*, meaning "to draw." When you *extract* something, like a tooth, you draw it out.

Sir Harold: I say, Sir Jason, good job! But what are you going to do now that you've located the tomb of the Latin magician dentist?

Sir Jason: I'm going to make an appointment, of course. My tooth is killing me.

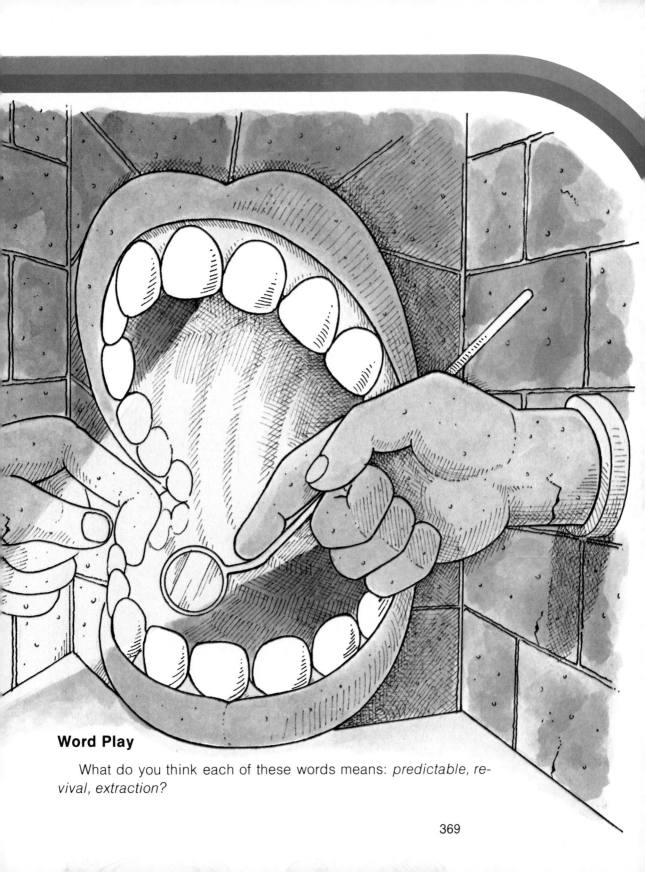

Word Play

What do you think each of these words means: *predictable, revival, extraction?*

As you read this selection, look for the answers to the five questions, *Who? What? When? Where?* and *Why?*

A remarkable woman lives in Brooklyn. Her concern for the environment has inspired the planting of hundreds of trees in her neighborhood. It is no wonder that she is known as . . .

The Tree Lady

by Benita Korn

"Neighborhoods need to be taken care of just like gardens and lawns."

For twenty-two years, Mrs. Hattie Carthan has lived in New York's Bedford-Stuyvesant community in Brooklyn. Time and time again she watched neglected trees die. At last she decided to do something about it. She began by talking to her neighbors about fixing up their block.

"Everyone seemed to think we ought to have a block association," Mrs. Carthan recalls. However, at that time, the idea never crystallized. So she sent out fifty or sixty postcards to all the houses on the block, calling for a meeting. On the day of the meeting about seven people showed up and voted to call themselves the *T* and *T* (for Tompkins and Throop streets) Vernon Avenue Block Association.

They started small that first year, with a back-to-school party for the children. The kids had a good time, and people were brought together. But it didn't bring them any closer to improving the appearance of the block. Their first fund-raising event was held the following summer. It was a successful barbecue and fried-chicken dinner, and they made about $200.

What would be the best way to spend all that money? Mrs. Carthan remembered how lovely the block had looked when she was young. She suggested buying and planting trees. "They almost threw me out of the association," she laughs. "They argued, 'Trees make leaves, and we'll only have to sweep them up. We don't have to buy trees. The city is supposed to give us trees.' Well, in the end, we bought four trees.

"By next year's block party, we didn't have the hassle about what to do with any money we raised. We would plant more trees. I sat down and wrote a letter to the mayor, telling him what we were doing and why. And I invited him to the party. Well," says Mrs. Carthan triumphantly, "he came! And that sort of put us on the map, because he arranged for our block association and three others to meet with the Parks Department. Out of

that meeting was born the tree-matching program in Bedford-Stuyvesant." The Bedford-Stuyvesant Beautification
Committee was formed to administer the program.

This was when Mrs. Carthan's new career began to
blossom. "We planted trees on four blocks that year. By the
next year, twenty-one blocks joined up and were planted
with trees. Of course," she explains, "people tended to think
that they didn't have to do anything more about the trees.

They thought they would just grow. Well, we thought we'd better do a further educational job there."

The Neighborhood Tree Corps was set up. "After school, the children were trained to sweep the garbage, pull the weeds, till the soil, and water the trees. They were paid three to five dollars a week, depending on age. And," she smiles, "we really worked them. The children had to bring their pails to the blocks — we didn't want to use hoses. We wanted them to ring doorbells and explain to the adults what they were doing and why."

The children, who are from nine to fifteen years old, are members of the Neighborhood Tree Corps. They take care of the trees in the neighborhood and learn about other plants and the environment. For Mrs. Carthan, mixing education and beautification is the way to rebuild. "The whole community is beginning to be beautiful again. And you know those people who left?" she says, with a smile. "Why, some of them are coming back now."

Understanding What You've Read

1. Why did Hattie Carthan start the *T* and *T* Vernon Avenue Block Association?
2. What successes has Hattie Carthan had since she began her block beautification project?
3. Why is it important to bring young people into the Neighborhood Tree Corps?

Applying the Skills Lesson

1. What facts from the selection would you include in notes for each of the following topics?
   a. fund raising
   b. education
   c. planting and care of trees
2. If you were interested in what young people can do to help the community, what points from the selection would you include in your notes?

Suppose you were interested in Lee Trevino's trials and successes before he reached the pro golf circuit. As you read this selection, look for the kinds of information you would jot down in your notes.

The great outdoors is nature's custom-made recreation area. It provides us with ski slopes, baseball and football fields, campsites, and golf courses for people like . . .

El Viejo's Grandson

by Jerry Izenberg

He was called *El Viejo.* When Lee Trevino looks back on the years during which the old man shaped him, it is never grandfather. It is always El Viejo—"The Old Man." That is the way Lee Trevino remembers him.

El Viejo was the man who held the small family together. He worked six days a week for a dollar a day. In the morning, before the dawn broke, Lee Trevino would hear the sounds of El Viejo making coffee and the quiet way in which he closed the door and slipped off into the dew-fresh grass outside to begin the long working day. After dark, he would return.

Lee Trevino is a Mexican American, and he takes his heritage as a thing of pride. Once he was sitting in a Miami hotel room the day before the Doral Open Golf Tournament. He was speaking about the days of deep struggle and the Mexican American kids who still have too much of that left to face.

"I want," he said, "to be someone they can look up to. We don't have enough heroes for them now. In Dallas, there are successful Mexican American businesspeople. But kids don't understand business, and so they can't appreciate what these people have done. I'm no superman, but I want them to see that there's a way up for everyone."

Lee Trevino's way up was long and hard and lonely. But he never quit, and he is there now. He plays in the biggest golf tournaments of them all, and he wins a lot of them. He has twice been the U.S. Open Champion. He makes television commercials and has his own syndicated golf show.

But he still recalls the years of hunger. He remembers the fact that, unlike so many of the top professional golfers in the game today, his road to success was, in reality, "the road of the streets."

Two places in Dallas shaped his career. The first was a driving range and pitch-and-putt course called Hardy's. The second was a municipal golf course called Tennyson Park.

At Hardy's, Trevino served as the entire grounds crew. He retrieved the balls that lay scattered on the driving range. He sold the buckets of balls and cleaned and repaired the clubs.

But the professional golf tour was always uppermost in Trevino's mind. He couldn't afford to play at a plush country club, so he took up a kind of semipermanent residence at Tennyson Park. The more he played, the better he became. After a while, a job opened up in El Paso, Texas, at a place called the Horizon Golf Club. It didn't pay much, but Trevino took the job anyway. And it should be noted that before he would leave Horizon, he would be a part owner in the club.

It was, then, from Horizon and the city of El Paso that Lee Trevino burst upon the national golf scene. He decided in 1967 to try to qualify for competition in the U.S. Open, to be played later that year at the Baltusrol Golf Club in Springfield, New Jersey. He not only qualified, he also won the qualifying competition. The few extra dollars that winning provided him with paid for his plane ticket to New Jersey.

When Trevino got to New Jersey, nobody knew his name. Nobody took him seriously. He lived in a small motel, and each night, even though he was among the leaders in the tournament, he would walk down the highway to get himself the cheapest meal he could find.

Baltusrol was a place of high excitement that year. The big names dominated the course. Trevino was lost in the shuffle. On the last day, as thunder and lightning rumbled overhead, Trevino was a late finisher. But he played exceptional golf and finished in the top ten. People began to wonder who the guy from El Paso was.

The following year, the Open moved to Rochester, New York. This time Trevino was no stranger. Now he had a following. As he played his way through the last practice round, a sizable gallery began to assemble to follow the short, muscular guy who always took time off during practice to banter back and forth with the spectators. Still, nobody thought he would win.

Nobody except Lee.

Perhaps it was because the hunger was great within him. Perhaps it was the need to prove himself after all those years of nothing. Whatever it was, Trevino played magnificently. When the tournament ended, Trevino had shot a seventy-two-hole total of 275, four strokes better than Jack Nicklaus, the favorite. Trevino was the U.S. Open Champion.

In the big press tent afterward, Trevino clowned, grinned, and told stories about his youth. Then he invited everyone to come to the best Mexican restaurant in town as his guest that night.

Afterward, I wondered how he could tie up such a large place on such short notice.

"It wasn't short notice," he laughed. "I rented it yesterday."

"But yesterday," I said, "you could have no way of knowing. . . . I mean yesterday . . . well, suppose you had lost today?"

"Then," Lee Trevino grinned, "I would have had a problem. I would have had an empty hall and no money and a large bill. I guess you might say I won this one for the rental of the hall."

And so it went with Lee Trevino. He moved on to England to play in the British Open. The British golf fans —among the most knowledgeable in the world—loved him.

The grandson of El Viejo had become a superhero on both sides of the Atlantic.

Of course, the achievements do not end there. In 1971, Trevino again won the Open, and again it was Nicklaus whom he had to beat. They had to go an extra day through an eighteen-hole playoff to decide it, but Trevino won it by three strokes.

Now he is older. His name is accepted along the golf tour as a true superstar, right beside Jack Nicklaus, Arnold Palmer, and all the rest. And his role in terms of what he means to other Mexican Americans has grown in stature.

What Lee Trevino has accomplished is no small thing. But then you could expect nothing less. It is the legacy of El Viejo.

Understanding What You've Read

1. Who was El Viejo?
2. According to the author, in what ways did Hardy's and Tennyson Park shape Trevino's career?
3. How did Trevino earn the fare for his plane ticket to Springfield, New Jersey, for the U.S. Open?
4. After the U.S. Open in Rochester, Trevino said, "I won this one for the rental of the hall." What did he mean?

Applying the Skills Lesson

1. Suppose you were going to take notes on the topic *Lee Trevino's feelings about his heritage.* What information from the selection would you include in your notes?
2. Prepare to take brief notes on the selection you just read by answering the following questions.
   a. *Who* is the selection about?
   b. *What* are this person's achievements?
   c. *When* did he achieve these things?
   d. *Where* did he achieve these things?

   Remember, it is not necessary to write complete sentences when taking notes.

TEXTBOOK STUDY

Taking Notes

When you take notes on textbook material, try to answer the five questions, *Who? What? When? Where?* and *Why?* The answers usually will be the most important information in the selection. As you read the following textbook excerpt, refer to the sidenotes. They will point out some of the important information you should include in your notes.

Taking Notes in Science

Your notes should include information on these topics.

You may want to look up the definition of this word and include it in your notes.

What facts will you include in your notes for the topic *white blood cells*?

Why isn't it necessary to include this information in your notes?

Particles in the Blood. In the photograph here, the red clump in the spun blood is composed of red blood cells, white blood cells, and platelets; however, most of the material is red blood cells. A single drop of blood contains several million red blood cells. Millions of these cells are produced every minute in the marrow of your long bones, such as your arm and leg bones. There are about 600 times as many red blood cells as white blood cells.

White cells are able to change their shape. In this way, they can pass through tiny openings in the walls of the capillaries, directly into the tissues. There the white cells protect the body by "eating" bacteria and allowing damaged tissue to repair itself. If you visit the doctor and complain about feeling badly, the doctor may decide to take a blood sample. The doctor will compare the number of white cells to the number of red cells in your sample. If there are more white blood cells than normal, this is evidence that your body is producing extra white blood cells to fight an infection.

Blood platelets are much smaller than red or white blood cells. Whenever a capillary is cut, platelets in that place break up and release chemicals which cause proteins in the plasma to form a thread-like network. This network helps the blood clot and stops bleeding.

— Exploring Life Science
Allyn & Bacon

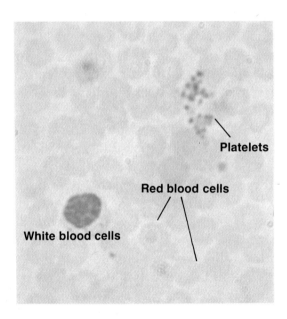

Platelets

Red blood cells

White blood cells

> **The photograph helps you see the relative sizes of the particles in the blood. You can include this information in your notes.**

Building Skills

Suppose you wanted to take notes on red blood cells, white blood cells, and platelets. Which of the following phrases would you include under each topic?
1. attack bacteria
2. made in bone marrow
3. control clotting
4. able to change shape
5. can pass through openings in capillaries
6. about same size as white blood cells

Taking Notes in Language Arts

This textbook excerpt is not accompanied by sidenotes. Read the selection, and look for the important points you would want to include in your notes. Then answer the questions that follow.

It's time for a short review before you write your story. The first thing to remember is that you are writing a story, not a novel. You want to focus on one incident and create a story about it. You aren't expected to do everything that's been discussed in this chapter. But you should establish the basic story elements — setting, point of view, characters, and dialogue.

As you begin your story, establish the setting as soon as possible so that your readers will know where and when the story is taking place. You can describe the setting very briefly or in great detail. The amount of space that you devote to description of the setting depends on two things — how important the setting is to the rest of the story and how familiar you think the setting will be to your readers. Also, keep in mind the mood of your story, and make sure that the setting doesn't clash with the mood. If the mood of the whole story is mysterious and eerie, the setting probably wouldn't be bright and sunny. If you want to establish a distinct mood in your readers' minds, the setting is the place to do it.

The point of view — who is telling the story — should be quite clear from the very beginning. Note this quotation, which is the beginning of a story by a high school student:

I'm a boy. I'm five years and one month old. My name is William Henry Hunson, III.

—Cassie German, "Willie's Confessions"

The words *I'm* and *my* show that this story is told from the first person point of view. Although you don't have to be this direct, your readers should have no trouble figuring out who is telling the story. If you want to show the thoughts and reactions of only one particular character, the first person point of view will be the best for your story. But if you want to show the thoughts of most or all of your characters, the third person point of view will give you the freedom you'll need. When a story is told from the third person point of view, the author uses the words *he* and *she* to refer to the characters.

—Growth in English
Laidlaw Brothers

Building Skills

1. On which of the following topics would you take notes?
   a. writing the novel
   b. story setting
   c. story mood
   d. details in the story
   e. a story's point of view
2. Using your answers to question 1, what important points made in the selection would you include in your notes for each topic?

Books About the Great Outdoors

Exploring the Insect World by Margaret J. Anderson. McGraw, 1974. *This book discusses various insects and explains how to do simple projects that test insect behavior.*

American Indian Tribes by Marion E. Gridley. Dodd, 1974. *Included are biographies of distinguished Native American leaders and information about the major tribes.*

Eight Black American Scientists by Robert C. Hayden. Addison-Wesley, 1970. *Over 200 years of American history are covered in these biographies. Included are Benjamin Banneker and George Wahington Carver.*

Wildlife in Danger by Alan C. Jenkins. St. Martin, 1974. *Animal extinction and effective conservation measures are the subjects of this book.*

Block by Block: Rebuilding City Neighborhoods by Martha Munzer. Knopf, 1973. *This is the true story of how the residents of three New York City neighborhoods worked together to rebuild their community.*

Famous Mexican Americans by Clarke Newlon. Dodd, 1972. *The biographies of many well-known Mexican Americans, such as Anthony Quinn, Henry Ramirez, and Pancho Gonzales, are included.*

Recycling Resources by Laurence Pringle. Macmillan, 1974. *This book has suggestions for finding practical recycling methods for waste products.*

Arms of the Sea: Our Vital Estuaries by Elizabeth Shepherd. Lothrop, 1973. *The author explains the formation of estuaries and their importance in helping to maintain the balance of nature.*

Wild Orphan Babies: Mammals and Birds by William J. Weber. Holt, Rinehart & Winston, 1975. *Weber has prepared a practical manual on how to care for orphaned or injured wildlife.*

CHANGES

SKILLS LESSON

Prove It! . . . Separating Fact from Opinion

Read the following statements. Which are facts? Which are opinions?

1. The Amazon is the longest river in the world.
2. Skiing is a difficult sport.
3. Early morning is the best time of day.
4. Galileo invented the thermometer in 1593.

The first and fourth statements are **facts.** Both have been proved and can be checked in a reference source such as *The World Almanac*. The second and third statements, however, are the writer's personal **opinions.** You can't prove that skiing is difficult for everyone. Some people may think it's easy to ski. You also can't prove that early morning is the best time of day. For some people, the evening may be the best time of day.

You're likely to find factual material in encyclopedias and textbooks. Sometimes the authors express their opinions, but the main purpose of such books is to give you information on a particular topic. Essays and letters to the editor, on the other hand, are two kinds of writing in which the authors express mostly opinions.

Facts help you to learn about the world around you. People's opinions are important because they can help you understand how others think and feel about things.

The Importance of Separating Facts and Opinions

Many kinds of reading selections blend facts and opinions. Newspaper and magazine articles, advertisements, and nonfiction books are some examples. As a critical reader, you should be able to tell the difference between statements of fact and statements of opinion. This will help you to recognize when a writer may be trying to persuade you into thinking a certain way by stating his or her opinion. Then, you may be getting only one side of the story—the writer's side. When you read a statement of fact, however, you can use that fact to form your own opinion.

Read the advertisement below and look for the facts.

FOR SALE: 10-speed bicycle.
Perfect condition. Hardly ever used.
Well-balanced wheels, comfortable seat.
$75.

How many facts about the bicycle are listed in the advertisement? There are two: (1) It has ten speeds; and (2) It costs seventy-five dollars. Everything else is the owner's opinion. Perhaps if you saw the bicycle, you might not think it is in perfect condition, or that the wheels are well balanced, or that the seat is comfortable. Also, you and the owner may have different opinions of what is meant by "hardly ever used." What facts might you need to form your own opinion about the bicycle?

Using Word Clues to Identify Opinions

Sometimes an opinion is easy to spot because one or more words identify the statement as an opinion. Read the sentences below. How do you know they are opinions?

Many sports experts believed that the sixteen-year-old was too young and inexperienced to win a medal in the Olympic games. However, they thought she would benefit from the chance to enter the competition.

In the first sentence, the word *believed* signals an opinion. What word in the second sentence alerts you to an opinion?

Other words and phrases that could signal opinions are *feel, according to the writer, consider, assume,* and *judge.*

Identifying Opinions Without Clues

Very often, selections you come across will not contain word clues to signal statements of opinion. Because of the way it is presented, an opinion may seem to be a fact. As you look for opinions, ask yourself, "Is this statement a fact that can be checked in a reference source, or is it a reflection of the writer's feelings?"

Read the following paragraph and look for the facts and the opinions.

The title "Empress of the Blues" was given to the greatest of all blues singers, Bessie Smith. Born in 1897, Bessie Smith was well known among blacks by the time she was in her late teens. For many years she worked to develop a blues style that no other singer has since been able to approach.

Since the paragraph mixes fact and opinion, let's look at the facts first. One piece of information you could check in a reference work is Bessie Smith's birth date. You might also be able to find out if she really was called "Empress of the Blues." But there isn't any reference book that can prove to you that Bessie Smith was the greatest blues singer. Nor can you prove to everyone's satisfaction that no other singer has been able to approach her blues style. These ideas are the author's opinion. You might share the opinion, but that doesn't make it a fact.

Opinions Based on Facts

Very often, an author will use proven facts to strengthen or support an opinion. Read the paragraph below. What is the author's opinion? What are the facts that support the opinion?

Americans are great inventors. World industry can thank them for the cash register, the adding machine, and the elevator. Appliances such as the electric razor, the lawn mower, the toaster, and the vacuum cleaner were developed in the United States. Americans also are responsible for such inventions as the zipper, the safety pin, and the ballpoint pen.

The author's opinion is stated in the first sentence: "Americans are great inventors." To support this opinion, the author lists several inventions that were developed by Americans. You, the reader, are able to judge the worth of the author's opinion based on the facts that are presented.

Sometimes, however, an author does not state enough facts to support his or her opinion. Read the following paragraph and find the author's opinion.

The Amazon is the most dangerous river in the world. It is the home of a small fish called the piranha. The mouth of the piranha is filled with razor-sharp teeth that can tear an animal to shreds in a few seconds.

What is the author's opinion? It is stated in the first sentence: "The Amazon is the most dangerous river in the world." To support this opinion, the author talks about the flesh-eating piranhas that live in the river. But is this enough information to show you that the Amazon is the most dangerous river *in the world?* What other kinds of facts could the author have given?

The more facts a writer states to support his or her opinion, the more worthwhile the opinion.

Try This

1. Explain why writers often state both facts and opinions in the same selection.
2. Which of the following statements are facts? Which are opinions?
   a. The country of Sri Lanka was formerly called Ceylon.
   b. Charcoal is the best material to use for sketching.
   c. The saxophone was named after its inventor, A. J. Sax.
   d. The Grand Canyon is the most breathtaking of all natural wonders.
   e. When an object moves at the speed of sound it is traveling at Mach 1.

VOCABULARY STUDY

Big Burst's Reply to Lester . . . Synonyms

Dear Mr. Zerb:

   You certainly do like to write letters, Mr. Zerb, but it is our opinion that you have sent us a <u>sufficient</u> amount. In fact, we have received enough mail from you to fill a station wagon. We <u>propose</u> that you stop complimenting us, and we also suggest that you spend your time chewing Big Burst Sugarless Bubble Gum instead. We certainly agree with you that our gum is <u>superb</u>. Our desire is to make an excellent product. But why <u>restrict</u> yourself to telling us about it? Why limit your praises to our ears?

   However, we do want you to be a satisfied customer for as long as possible. So we've decided to send you a gift: 60,000 cases of Big Burst Sugarless Bubble Gum. And you will be happy to know that you won't have to keep running out to check your mailbox for the package. Just listen for the sound of our helicopter.

                    Big Burst Sugarless Bubble Gum

Word Play

   Reread Big Burst's letter and find the synonyms for each of the underlined words.

393

N. Scott Momaday

N. Scott Momaday writers who have Prize. He is also, is one of the few won the Pulitzer so far, the only *Native American to have won this important award.*

Momaday, a Kiowa, resides in San Francisco and is a professor of English at Stanford University in California. He is proud of his Native American heritage and of his accomplishments as a writer and teacher. He likes to collect Native American baskets, blankets, and jewelry. Among his hobbies are bicycling, hiking, photography, and watching football on television.

Momaday feels it is important to preserve Native American folktales and legends. "Stories are handed down from one generation to another as they are remembered," he explains. "Not one was ever written, and they will be lost forever if not collected now."

Momaday also believes that Native American culture is important for all Americans. "The Kiowa tell wonderful stories, full of beautiful and intricate plots, with great concern for human attitudes and their relation to nature." These concerns are reflected in Momaday's Pulitzer Prize-winning book, House Made of Dawn. *Another of his books,* The Way to Rainy Mountain, *traces the history of the Kiowa people.*

The father of three daughters, Momaday himself helps his children to understand and appreciate their heritage. In the selection that follows, he describes the yearly visit he and his children make to a Kiowa reservation. It is a time to celebrate their heritage as Kiowa and renew old friendships.

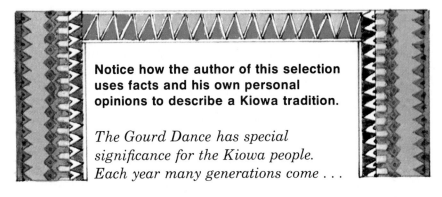

Notice how the author of this selection uses facts and his own personal opinions to describe a Kiowa tradition.

The Gourd Dance has special significance for the Kiowa people. Each year many generations come . . .

To the Singing, to the Drums

by N. Scott Momaday

The Taimpe [tīm′pā], or Gourd Dance, is an old tradition in the Kiowa tribe. It is performed on July 4 at Carnegie, Oklahoma. Each year the Kiowa gather in celebration. . . .

From the window of the plane I can see to the horizon. Even at 25,000 feet there is a sense of vastness in the landscape of the Great Plains. I wonder that it always takes me by surprise. It is a mood in the earth, I think suffered here only. It is a deep intelligence in the soil, deeper than the land patterns that I see below. It is as deep as the roots of a single tree or the blood of the buffalo.

At the Will Rogers World Airport at Oklahoma City, my father and my three daughters are waiting for me. Something now of the ritual proper has begun. Generations have come together. The blood has begun to flow toward the center of time.

My children have a sense of the occasion, not of what it is, but *that* it is. It is a formality that gives shape to their lives.

We drive westward on the freeway. The little girls chatter in the back seat. My father's hands are dark, laid lightly on the steering wheel of the rented car. I used to stand beside him when he painted, watching him touch the brush to the paper. I wondered how he could make such fine lines of color. I wondered how it was that his hand was so sure, so true to him.

It seems to me now that his granddaughters, too, must wonder at the same thing. Cael, the oldest, has gone to school at his easel. Certainly, she has seen that his hand is an instrument which turns the images in his mind's eye into pictures. She will be a writer and a painter, she tells me. She will illustrate her own books.

At Chickasha we are on the edge of the old world that I knew as a child. We leave the freeway and move on Oklahoma 9, a more familiar and friendly way. At Anadarko we stop at the Southern Plains Museum to look at the arts and crafts exhibit there. This, too, we do each year, and always at the same time of day. It is where I complain that we are late, that the dance has already begun.

My father begins to recognize the landmarks of his growing up, and this excites the girls and me. "My dad and I used to come this way in a surrey," he says, pointing out a grove. "There we used to stop, every time, and eat. We ate watermelons. My dad loved watermelons." The girls look hard into the grove, trying to see the man and the boy who stopped there in the other time.

Carnegie is a small town in the Southern Plains. In July, the wide, glass-and-metal-bordered streets reflect and seem to intensify the sun. The light is flat and hard just now in the early afternoon. The day is at white heat. Later the light will soften and colors will flow upon the scene. The town will melt into motion. But now it seems deserted. We drive through it.

The celebration is on the north side. We turn down into a large hollow among trees. It is full of camps and cars and people. Children run about, making festival noises. Firecrackers are snapping all around. We park and I make ready. The girls help me with my traditional clothing. I am already wearing white trousers and moccasins. Now I tie the black velvet sash around my waist, placing the beaded tassels at my right leg. The bandoleer of red beans, which was my grandfather's, goes over my left shoulder. I decide to carry the blanket over my arm until I join the dancers. We make our way through the camps. Old people are lying down on cots and benches in the shadows. We smell hamburgers and popcorn. Later there will be fried bread, boiled meat, Indian corn.

My father is a man of great presence, a certain figure in the world. He is tall and good-looking. There is a quality about him most often called charm. I believe it is good will. He simply enjoys society. There is a deep-seated, native vanity to him, an ethnic confidence, and it is attractive. It is good to see him here among our people.

Mamedaty was my grandfather's name. It means "sky walker, one who walks in the sky." In my mind's eye I see him in silhouette, walking in the plain against a copper sunset. He lives for me in his name.

We greet Taft Hainta [hīn'tə], the leader of the Taimpe society. He embraces us. Jill, my daughter, gives him a hundred-dollar bill. This, too, is traditional. Each year she makes the donation to the fund for the next year's celebration. It is good that she gives a gift on her birthday. Taft sees that the girls are seated comfortably in view of the dance ground. It is not easy to find a good seat. There is a large crowd, and the shade is thickly populated.

Each year it seems there are more and more young people. They come from far away, simply to be here, to be caught up in this returning. They come to enter into the presence of the old, original spirit that resides here.

For a time we stand on the edge of the crowd and watch, taking hold of the music and the motion. I pick out friends and relatives. Fred Tsoodle [tsoo'dəl] is always there. He saw to my initiation five years ago. He taught me how to take steps, how to wear the regalia, how to hold the gourd and the fan properly. My cousin Marland Aitson is across the circle. There is room next to him. I go there.

The sun descends upon the trees. There is a giveaway. People are standing in the circle, calling forth those to whom they will make gifts. I close my eyes, open them, close them again. There are so many points of color, like points of flame. The sun presses upon me. I feel the heat of it at my center. The heat is hypnotic. The scene is kaleidoscopic. It is as if I am asleep.

Then the drums break, the voices of the singers gather to the beat. The rattles shake all around—mine among them. I stand and move again, slowly, toward the center of the universe, in time, in time, more and more closely in time.

There have been times when I have wondered what the dance is, what it means, and what I am inside of it. And there have been times when I have known. Always, there comes a moment when the dance takes hold of me and becomes the most meaningful expression of my being. And always, afterward, there is rejoicing among us. Here and there the old people tell stories of Creation, of the good and bad things in the world, and especially of that which is beautiful. We have made our prayer, and we have made good our humanity in the process. There are lively feelings. There is much good talk and laughter. And there is much that goes without saying.

Understanding What You've Read

1. What significance does the Gourd Dance have for the author?
2. What are some of the traditions involved in the celebration of the Gourd Dance?
3. In the last paragraph of the selection, the author states, "And there is much that goes without saying." What do you think he means?

Applying the Skills Lesson

1. Which of the following statements made by the author of the selection are facts? Which are opinions?
   a. It is a mood in the earth, I think suffered here only.
   b. My children have a sense of the occasion.
   c. We drive westward on the freeway.
   d. At Anadarko we stop at the Southern Plains Museum to look at the arts and crafts exhibit there.
   e. The bandoleer of red beans, which was my grandfather's, goes over my left shoulder.
   f. Each year it seems there are more and more young people.
2. What are the author's opinions about his father? Explain your answer, giving examples from the selection.

TEXTBOOK STUDY

Separating Fact from Opinion

Writers of textbooks do more than list only facts. They sometimes include personal opinions as well. As you read the following selection, use the sidenotes to help you identify the facts and the author's opinions.

Separating Fact from Opinion in Language Arts

People use comparisons, then, because it is a natural thing to do, as natural as talking, and because it helps them describe their world more accurately. But why do people keep thinking up new comparisons? Why not just use the old ones over and over again? What is there about a fresh comparison that pleases?

This question asks for the reader's opinion.

To understand this appeal, you might compare some comparisons. Begin with one by Sydney Smith, an English writer of the nineteenth century:

This is a fact that can be proved. Where might you look to check this fact?

Daniel Webster struck me much like a steam engine in trousers.

Now Smith could have written something like this:

Daniel Webster struck me as a man of great vigor and emotional force.

Both of these sentences convey more or less similar meanings. But which gives you a sharper picture of Webster? Which is more vivid?

Here is another illustration of how comparison works to enliven description. This one's a little tricky. It was written by Ring Lardner, the American short-story writer. He is describing a young man staring at a girl:

Why is this statement an opinion? Whose opinion is it?

He gave her a look you could have poured on a waffle.

Lardner's comparison is good for two reasons. First, it's more vivid and original than a flat statement like, "He gave her a look that was soft and sweet." Second, he added an interesting twist by dropping part of the comparison. Stretched out to its full length, Lardner's comparison would read like this:

He gave her a look that was like a syrup you could have poured on a waffle.

By scrapping part of the comparison, Lardner surprises and delights you with the directness of his humor.

— Growth in English
Laidlaw Brothers

How does the writer support this opinion?

Building Skills

1. Which statements in the selection are the author's opinions? Which statements are facts?
2. How are the quotations used to support the author's opinions?
3. The quotation from Sydney Smith expresses an opinion. What is the opinion?

Separating Fact from Opinion in Social Studies

The following excerpt is not accompanied by sidenotes. See if you can separate the facts from the author's opinions. Then answer the questions that follow.

There are "great towers and temples . . . and buildings rising from the water." This is how one Spanish conqueror described the great Aztec capital in 1519. By using canals, dikes, and bridges, the Aztecs built a great urban center on islands in Lake Texcoco. People traveled by boat through the canals to great temples. They raised their food on artificial islands and sold it in the huge city market.

Modern Mexico City is built on the ruins of the old Aztec capital. It lies on land that was once the bottom of Lake Texcoco. As Mexico City grew, wells were drilled. Water was taken from below the surface of the lake bed. The soil is like a sponge full of water. As more and more water was taken out, the buildings sank in the soft soil. In some places the level has gone down 25 feet. Now, to save the buildings of Mexico City, no more wells can be drilled. And water must be brought in from other places.

Automobiles and factories are ruining the air of Mexico City. The cold air acts like a lid. It holds down the dirty air for days at a time. People from the countryside still go to the city in great numbers. There are now over 9 million people in Mexico City. The large population is creating problems the ancient Aztecs never had to face.

—*World Geography Today*
Holt, Rinehart & Winston

Building Skills

1. The author of the selection believes that Mexico City's large population is creating problems. What facts from the selection support this opinion?
2. What factual information about the ancient Aztecs is presented in the selection?

SKILLS LESSON

Is That a Fact? . . .
Separating Facts from Fictional Details

Many nonfiction books and articles have been written about events which took place hundreds or even thousands of years ago. Since the author could not have experienced the event, he or she usually begins by doing research. The facts that the author gathers are then used as the basis for the article. However, not every statement in the article is a fact. Some statements, and even entire scenes, may only be *based on facts*.

Read the paragraph below.

Winter, 30,000 B.C. — A howling wind blew the thick snow into great drifts. The hunters pulled the animal skins around their bare shoulders and headed back toward the cave. Their luck had not been good. Tor had been badly injured in the chase. Many spearheads were lost. The only prize was a small deer that somehow would have to feed three families.

The writer is describing an event that might have taken place 30,000 years ago. There are no photographs or written records of such an event. There are, however, cave paintings and fossils. These supply us with a few facts about life at that time. The writer used these facts to create the specific details in the paragraph. These **fictional details** make the facts more interesting.

Creating Fictional Dialogue

As in the previous paragraph, fictional details can describe a setting or event. Fictional details also can be used to re-create a discussion between two people. For example, the passage below is a discussion between Harry Houdini and his brother. (Houdini's real name was Ehrich Weiss.)

"Ehrich, what are you doing up at this hour?"

"I'm rehearsing a magic trick. I'll be famous someday."

"You won't be anything except sleepy," replied his brother. "Go to bed. All your rustling is keeping me awake."

"Not until I'm satisfied with this trick. And don't call me Ehrich any more. I'm changing my name to Harry. Harry Houdini."

"It's a stupid name," Houdini's brother mumbled.

Houdini was insulted. "It is *not* stupid! I think it has a nice, magical ring to it."

"Maybe," said his brother. "But nobody will ever remember it."

Do you think the conversation was exactly like that? It seems highly unlikely. After all, it could not have been tape-recorded, and probably neither Houdini nor his brother took notes. So you can assume the author imagined the conversation. However, the author based the conversation on certain facts:

- Houdini and his brother shared a bedroom when they were young.
- Houdini often practiced his magic tricks when everyone else was asleep.
- Houdini had decided to become a magician at an early age.

Checking Out the Facts

How can you tell the difference between the facts and fictional details in a selection? You might ask, "Which details can be checked in a reference source?" Sometimes the sources an author used are listed in the introduction or bibliography of the book. Historical facts can be checked in newspapers, encyclopedias, almanacs, and dictionaries. Even a photograph can be helpful.

The Importance of Separating Facts from Fictional Details

Critical readers don't accept everything they read as fact. Authors who use fictional details to describe a scene or re-create a conversation are probably not trying to mislead you. Their purpose is to make the factual information more interesting and colorful. However, you should always be aware that some details in a selection are not, and very often can not, be facts. Such details are only *based on* factual information.

Usually, an author is using fictional details when:

- The event being described took place before recorded history.
- The event being described was not witnessed by the author.
- It is unlikely that anyone was recording or taking notes during the particular conversation.

Sorting out factual information and fictional details isn't always easy. While you are reading, you should constantly ask yourself, "Is that true?" "Where can I check that?" Questions such as these will help you understand and enjoy what you read.

Try This

The details listed below are taken from the last paragraph on page 405. Which are statements of fact?
1. Early hunters wore animal skins as clothing.
2. One of the hunters was named Tor.
3. Early hunters used spears as weapons.
4. One of the hunters in the group was injured in the chase.

Quick Change, Inc. . . . Suffixes

"Welcome to Quick Change, Inc. State your name and problem, please."

"My name is *Curve*. That's just 'a bend' or 'a twist.' I want to be a word with class."

"No problem for QCI. We'll just chop off the *e*, add a *-ture*, and poof! *Curvature!* A word with class. It means 'the state of being curved,' as in the *curvature* of a circle. Happy? Good. Next customer!"

"I'm *Revolve*. That's too short. Don't get me wrong. I like my meaning, 'to go around in an orbit.' But, gosh, I want to be longer."

"That's very simple, Revolve. If we remove the *-ve* and hook on *-ution*, you become *Revolution*, 'the act of a body going around in an orbit.' Now you can appear in this famous sentence: *The earth's revolution is 365 1/4 days.* OK, who's next?"

"My name is *Delicate*. People call me 'dainty' and 'pleasing to the senses.' I don't like those definitions. I want some excitement in my life."

"Easy as pie. All we do is change your *-te* to *-cy* and you become *Delicacy,* 'something rare and pleasing to eat,' like snails or a fancy dessert. Say . . . that reminds me. Now that you're a *delicacy,* do you have any good suggestions for lunch?"

Word Play

QCI challenges you to use each of these word pairs in the same sentence: *delicate/delicacy, curve/curvature, revolve/revolution.*

As you read this selection, notice how the author uses fictional details to paint a picture of what might have occurred centuries ago.

Part of the beauty of the English language lies in the stories of . . .

How Words CHANGE

by Eloise Lambert

The story of a word begins with the story of its creation. Like a baby, however, a new word is only at the beginning of its life story. The rest of that story lies in how the word changes in appearance, where it has come from, where it goes in the world, and what it becomes.

For example, let us look at the life story of a word that every English-speaking person uses. As the story unfolds, suppose you see at what point in the word's development you recognize it as one of your own.

Many centuries ago, when Latin was spoken in what is now Italy, a merchant was sailing the seas in search of new goods to take to the Roman markets. The merchant stopped at a Persian port. There he found a delicious fruit and brought samples of it to Rome.

MY GOODNESS, CLOVIS! WHAT IS THIS FRUIT?

Now, the merchant spoke very little Persian and did not stop long enough to ask for the Persian name of the fruit. When he arrived in Rome, he

410

WHY, IT'S JUST A PERSICUM MALUM.

was asked by Roman buyers what the fruit was called. "Oh, it's just a Persian apple," he said, "a *persicum malum.*"

Later on, when the customers came back for more of the fruit, they dropped the *malum.* "That *persicum* was quite good," they said. "We'd like to order more." Soon the fruit became known all over the Empire as *persicum.* Finally the fruit and its name reached the Germanic lands to the north. But in German it became *persoc.* In this form it was carried to Britain by the early Anglo-Saxons.

Meanwhile, things were happening to the word *persicum* in the other lands to which it had traveled. In Italy, people speaking quickly often left out the *r* before the *s* (in much the same way that some English speakers say *hoss* instead of *horse*). *Persicum* became *pessicum.* Then the *i* was hurried over so fast that it, too, was eventually dropped. The Italians also changed the ending *-um* to *-a,* as they did in the case of a good many fruits. The result was *pesca,* which is what the Italians call the fruit to this day.

From Italy, this form moved to France. The French, however, turned the Latin *-ca* into *-che.* So now *persicum,* with its Latin, Italian, and French changes, had become *pesche.* Then it went to Britain, where it found itself face-to-face with its cousin *persoc,* used by the Saxons. The English people now had two words for the same fruit. So they tossed out the old *persoc* in favor of the new *pesche.* Another change turned it into *peach,* which is what we call it today.

The Nature of the Change

Our language is full of these life histories of words. They are important as well as interesting, because they show how a word, once it has been created, can move about in the world. As it moves, it undergoes changes in pronunciation and spelling.

It is easy to understand how a word can move from one country and language to another. Soldiers, tourists, and business people have carried words from one country to another throughout the ages and still do so today. But now we have added word-carriers, such as radio, TV, and the movies.

Many English words change in interesting ways upon entering foreign languages. *Bulldog* becomes *bouledogue* in French. *Pullover* turns into *pulova* in Italian. *Beisbol* is the Spanish-American form of *baseball*. So it is not puzzling that *persicum* became *peach* in English. The same forces at work in language cause all of these changes.

Words change in sound and spelling not only when they move from one country to another. They also change within their own home boundaries. Nowadays, with the wide use of dictionaries and spelling books, spellings do not change very often, but pronunciations still vary. One American may say *to-MAY-toe*; another, *to-MAH-tuh*; a third, *ter-MAY-ter*, or even *MAY-ter*. But if these people know how to spell, they will all write *tomato*.

There is still more to the story of a word than how it comes into being or changes in spelling and pronunciation. A word may also change in meaning.

At one time, a *villain* was a slave attached to the villa (house) of an overlord. In medieval plays there often appeared a character who stood for such a slave. At first this character took the part of a clown and was rather a funny fellow. Later the villain began to show up as the person who had done the dirty work in the plot. So the *villain* who was a slave became the *villain* who is a wicked plotter and comes to a bad end in the last act.

Many writers have said that every person on earth has a story worth telling. The same is also true of words. For every word in our language, there is a story. Our English dictionary, which is really a storybook of words, is filled with them. If you have the chance to look in one of the larger dictionaries, you will find that it tells more than a million stories of how words have changed.

Understanding What You've Read

1. In what three ways can a particular word change?
2. Name three factors that can bring about changes in words.
3. How has the word *villain* changed in meaning over the years?

Applying the Skills Lesson

1. What fictional details does the author supply in the third and fourth paragraphs of the selection? On what facts did she probably base her description?
2. What facts does the author present to the reader through the use of the fictional dialogue on page 411? What reason might the author have had for using this fictional dialogue?

As you read, look for the facts that the author tells you through his use of fictional dialogue.

Changes in medicine occur at a fantastic pace. One of the most far-reaching changes was brought about by . . .

ALICE HAMILTON: DOCTOR IN INDUSTRY

by David K. Boynick

In one important way, Dr. Alice Hamilton was different from other first women in medicine. She was the leader in the development of industrial hygiene and the prevention of occupational diseases.

In an earlier industrial age, many workers absorbed poisonous chemicals and fumes. They breathed them into their lungs and ate them with the food from their lunch boxes. Occupational diseases caused suffering, crippling, and death.

Now, in a thousand industries, workers do their tasks in greater safety. This is because Dr. Hamilton was able to name the diseases connected with certain industrial jobs. She traced their causes and worked for their prevention.

Alice Hamilton was born in New York in 1869. Quite early in her life, she became concerned with poverty, hunger, and sickness. In her was a need to serve.

Alice made up her mind to become a doctor. She studied medicine at the University of Michigan and later in New England.

When Northwestern University offered her a job teaching pathology, she accepted. It was a chance to work in the field for which she had trained. She taught classes during the day on weekdays. Evenings, weekends, and summers, however, were spent at Hull House. Hull House was a social settlement house in a Chicago slum area. Dr. Hamilton worked on a number of medical projects there to help the poor.

With Julia Lathrop, another Hull House resident, she went to visit a large Illinois hospital. The women were shocked by the bleak wards and the hundreds of patients in rags. Together, they proposed a list of improvements for the hospital. Many of their ideas were accepted and carried out. Alice then began a clinic for children at Hull House.

Branching Out

Hull House's activities grew in size and number. Alice Hamilton's spare-time services grew, too. She worked in adult educa-

tion courses. She helped many people find jobs. She looked into the causes of a dangerous outbreak of typhoid.

Her medical work also moved ahead. While teaching at Northwestern, she spent two days a week doing research. Although she liked research, something was missing. At Hull House, Alice had a sense of service to people. In her laboratory work, people were far away. She thought it would be wonderful to do something in which she could use all her training and experience.

Julia Lathrop

In 1909, the Governor of Illinois decided that a study should be made of industrial sickness in the state. He appointed an Occupational Disease Commission.

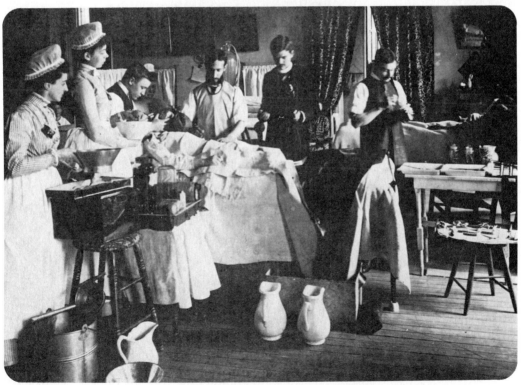

(top) *A Glasgow, Scotland, hospital in the late 1800's;* (bottom)
An operation at Bellevue Hospital, New York, in the late 1800's

Before the commission could get started, however, they needed an expert to take charge of the work. Nowhere in America was there an expert in occupational diseases. There was no such thing as industrial medicine. There was virtually nothing in the medical books about occupational diseases.

When the commission asked Dr. Hamilton to become director of the study, she agreed.

The commission studied the problem of carbon monoxide in steel mills. Besides directing that program, Dr. Hamilton made herself responsible for an investigation of lead poisoning.

Except for carbon monoxide, lead is the oldest of the industrial poisons. It may cause palsy, paralysis, coma, mental breakdown, convulsions, and death. Dr. Hamilton's group read hospital records, talked with union officials and workers, and interviewed doctors and pharmacists. The group's aim was to find out how many deaths had been caused by lead poisoning.

The findings of the Occupational Disease Commission were fruitful. Among other things, they dealt with lead and brass poisoning in the steel mills, boilermakers' deafness, and an eye disease of coal miners. In the report, Dr. Hamilton named several trades that had never before been thought dangerous. She also stated that lead poisoning came from breathing lead dust and fumes. The air, she said, must be kept clean.

Out of the commission's reports came a law which said that workers who became ill or injured as a result of their jobs could receive certain benefits. It was the first such law in America.

The Problem of Lead Poisoning

Dr. Hamilton then undertook almost a one-woman fight against industrial diseases in America.

In one study she reported that the air in several lead-producing plants was thick with dust and fumes from piles of lead and from roasting furnaces. When Edward Cornish, president of the National

Lead Company, came to visit one of his plants, Dr. Hamilton went there to see him. She was sure, she told him, that his workers were being poisoned.

Cornish was angry. At first he didn't believe her. "We have never had reports of lead poisoning," he said. "But I'll give you a chance to prove you're right. You come back with proof that my workers are being poisoned, and I'll make any changes you think are necessary."

The next time Cornish came to Illinois, Dr. Hamilton showed him the medical records of twenty-two of his employees sick with lead poisoning. Cornish made good his earlier promise. He put engineers to work to come up with ways of controlling dust and fumes. Dr. Hamilton suggested that the

workers have a medical examination once a week. Cornish established a medical department in each of his company's plants. Industrial medicine was growing.

After two or three years, Alice Hamilton knew that with industrial medicine she had found her life's work. "It had the challenge and excitement of exploration," she said. "Moreover, much of what I discovered was useful to human well-being."

Danger! Acid!

Once, in a little railroad station in a small town, Dr. Hamilton got a clue to another industrial danger. The eyes of a dozen people waiting for a train were all on two men. At first, Dr. Hamilton thought the two were circus clowns. Their clothing was spotted yellow. Their hair was streaked with yellow. Yellow color had stained their faces.

No, these men were not clowns. But what were they? One of the two men told her, "We're canaries, lady."

She was puzzled. "You mean you work in a dyeing plant?"

He grinned. "No, lady, we work in the Canary Islands." Then he pointed to some factories in the distance. "That's what we call them. We make picric acid."

She asked, "Is it dangerous?"

The workman sadly nodded.

Workers in an iron foundry in 1873

"That's why we're leaving. When they're making the acid, sometimes there's an explosion. An orange smoke comes out. You breathe it. It doesn't burn much. You don't think too much about it. But a little later, you're dead."

Dr. Hamilton spent many days in the area studying plants producing acids. She saw nitric acid, a dangerous caustic, being made in tightly covered mixing vats. In one day she saw eight vats burst into pieces.

Doctors then knew little about the dangers of certain acid fumes. In most plants, engineers were working toward finding safeguards. Until they succeeded, however, there would be many deaths. Dr. Hamilton studied the cases of people who had become sick and even died from the fumes.

In 1917, the United States went to war. The military chemicals industry grew. Dr. Hamilton's work became even more important. In Washington, the National Research Council set up a committee of experts to serve as Dr. Hamilton's consultants.

Dr. Hamilton's reports were the basis for many improvements. By the time of World War II, most of the dangers had been eliminated. By then, the United States Public Health Service had established a branch dealing only with industrial poisons. Industrial medicine and hygiene had arrived. Through the efforts of Dr. Alice Hamilton, factory health conditions were at last changing.

Manufacturing steel with the Bessemer process, 1875

Understanding What You've Read

1. How did Alice Hamilton first become involved with research on occupational diseases?
2. What was the purpose of the Illinois Occupational Disease Commission? What were Dr. Hamilton's findings as a result of her investigations?
3. What improvements were made in the National Lead Company's plants as a result of Dr. Hamilton's investigations?

Applying the Skills Lesson

1. The author of the selection used fictional details and dialogue to recreate the scene between Alice Hamilton and Edward Cornish (page 419). On what facts did the author probably base the scene?
2. What specific facts do you learn about conditions in acid factories of the early 1900's from the fictional dialogue on pages 419–420?

Separating Facts from Fictional Details

You have seen that authors may use facts and their own imagination to re-create a scene or a conversation. As you read the selection that follows, use the sidenotes to help you separate the facts from the fictional details.

Separating Facts from Fictional Details in Science

What words in this sentence tell you that the author will be using fictional details?

Picture a scene such as this. The time is some 200 million years ago, the Mesozoic era, the Triassic period. Suppose we could re-create this scene with living organisms. The ponds would be full of fish —lobe-finned fish and lungfish, cartilaginous fish and bony fish. These may have fed on each other. Certainly the fish had plenty of aquatic insects to serve as food.

At the edges of the ponds would be several large reptiles, looking somewhat like modern crocodiles. But the fossil evidence indicates they are only distantly related. Between the ponds you could find the descendants of the ancient forests of club mosses and horsetails—much smaller than their ancestors of the Coal Age forests. The environment had begun to dry out. The cycads, ancient conifers, and ginkgoes were becoming the dominant forms in the nearby forests.

The author has based the fictional details on facts that scientists have been able to learn from fossils.

Among the horsetails you might find some fast-moving, lizardlike reptiles with small, sharp teeth indicating adaptation to an insect diet. Slender dinosaurs (reptiles), not very large—about 1 to 2 meters (3 to 6 feet) long—might also be found scurrying, fleeing from a predator or pursuing their prey.

No one has ever seen living dinosaurs. How then is the author able to state their size?

—Life: A Biological Science
Harcourt Brace Jovanovich

Building Skills

1. The illustration on page 422 is a re-creation of a scene during the Mesozoic era. How do you think the artist was able to re-create such a scene?
2. Which of the following are facts that can be proved?
   a. the existence of dinosaurs
   b. the texture and color of a dinosaur's skin
   c. the existence of club mosses and horsetails
   d. the size of Mesozoic forests and ponds

More Than Meets the Eye . . .
Drawing Conclusions

Very often, an author suggests but does not actually state an idea. But, by considering the details that are given, you can *infer* the idea the author wants to get across. This is called making an **inference.**

Read the following sentences. What ideas can you infer from each one?

1. After the race, the breathless runner nearly collapsed into the arms of his coach.
2. Adrienne is reading *Cat Among the Pigeons* by Agatha Christie, and she can't put the book down.
3. Dark, gray clouds rolled in as lightning flashed in the distance.
4. Whenever Rosa plays the guitar at a party, everyone stops talking and gathers around her to listen.

424

What can you infer about the runner in the first sentence? The details tell you that he was breathless and about to collapse. Even though it is never stated, the details indicate that the runner was exhausted.

In the second sentence, you can infer that Adrienne is enjoying *Cat Among the Pigeons*. What detail suggests this idea?

What point is the writer making in the third sentence? Which details help you to see that a storm is brewing?

What can you infer about Rosa's guitar playing in the fourth sentence? What two details give you the idea that she plays well?

Now read the paragraph below. What can you infer about Lynn, the weather, and the time of day?

Lynn pulled her collar up and headed home. Most of the street-lamps were out, and she had trouble finding her way through the darkness. The wind howled, scattering dry leaves along the side-walk. Lynn shivered and forced her frozen hands into her pockets. Her ears were red, and they had begun to sting. Seven blocks seemed like an endless journey.

By paying attention to the details, you can infer a number of things. What do the howling wind and dry leaves tell you about the weather? It is a cold, windy day. What time of day is it? Based on the details in the second sentence, you can infer that it is night. Which details can you use to infer that Lynn is not wearing gloves or a hat?

Drawing Your Own Conclusions

Drawing conclusions is an inference skill you will find yourself using very often. When reading short stories, novels, and other kinds of fiction, you may draw conclusions about the characters, the settings, or the events that take place. In nonfiction articles, you may draw conclusions from the facts that the author gives you.

To draw a correct conclusion, you have to consider all the relevant or important information. You should also consider your own past experiences in arriving at a conclusion. Use your reasoning to decide how all this information is related.

Read the paragraph below. Which details help you draw a conclusion about Angela's choice of a birthday gift?

Angela bought a birthday present for her sister Dolores. At first, Angela couldn't decide whether to buy Dolores a tennis racket, an easel, or new ski poles. She knew that when Dolores was younger she did a lot of painting. In the past few years, however, Dolores had been more interested in athletics. Tennis and skiing were her favorite sports, but she already had all the ski equipment she needed. Angela thought for a while and finally chose what she believed was the perfect gift.

What did Angela buy? How did you come to the conclusion that Angela bought a tennis racket? You probably considered all the information about Dolores in the paragraph. Then you looked at the presents Angela was considering. Based on the information, you could eliminate everything except the tennis racket. Why didn't Angela buy the easel? Why didn't she buy the ski poles?

Unnecessary Information

You won't always have to consider all the information in a selection in order to draw a conclusion. Read the next paragraph and then answer the question that follows.

Alaska was the forty-ninth state to be admitted to the Union. It is over twice the size of Texas. Alaska is bounded on the north by the Beaufort Sea. The Bering Sea lies to the west, and the Pacific Ocean lies to the south. Canada borders Alaska on the east.

From the facts above, which of the following can you conclude about Alaska?

    a. Alaska is an island.
    b. Alaska is a peninsula.
    c. Alaska is landlocked.

The facts in the paragraph tell you that Alaska is bordered on three sides by water. From your experience, you know that a peninsula is a body of land surrounded on three sides by water. You can therefore conclude *b,* "Alaska is a peninsula."

Which facts in the paragraph are *not* important in helping you draw this conclusion?

Try This

Read the paragraph below and then answer the question that follows.

Three hundred eighty people live in Lugnut, Kansas. In 1977, Lugnut suffered an outbreak of Bogus flu. One hundred cases were reported. Immediately, a team of doctors began working on a vaccine. The following year, 200 people in Lugnut volunteered to receive the flu vaccine. Of the 200 volunteers, three people got Bogus flu. Of the people who did not receive the vaccine, fifty cases of flu were reported.

Which of the following can you conclude?
1. The people of Lugnut are not as healthy as the rest of the population.
2. The Bogus flu vaccine was generally effective.
3. Every doctor in Lugnut worked on the Bogus flu vaccine.

The First Wooden Cave . . . Meanings from Context

CARPENTER BUILDS FIRST

It was reported yesterday that Ernest T. Pennyweight, 52, has built the world's first wooden cave. According to Mr. Pennyweight, "Rock is a thing of the past. It does not deserve the *reputation* that it has. Its fame and good name as a building material for caves are a big mistake. *Eventually,* the public will wise up. Yes indeed, soon people will realize that trees are our best source of caves."

Mr. Pennyweight now *resides* in his wooden cave, located near a mountain one kilometer east of Highway 52. A pet raccoon named Stanley also lives with him.

428

WORLD'S WOODEN CAVE

"Wood doesn't get cold in the winter like rock does," says Mr. Pennyweight. "And I can paint a much smoother *image* of an animal on the walls. When you try to draw an exact likeness of a zebra on rock, it comes out bumpy.

"Only problem is," he adds, "I've got to be on the lookout for splinters."

Word Play

Match the words in Column A with their definitions in Column B.

A	B
reputation	lives in or at
eventually	a true likeness of something
resides	a good name
image	in the course of time

Nature surprises and delights us with its many changes. Some of the most fascinating changes occur in those . . .

Animals That Hide, Imitate, and Bluff
by Lilo Hess

You are walking through the woods. A small moth flutters by. Its bright red wings shine in the sunlight. Then suddenly it disappears. It takes patience, a trained eye, and a little luck to discover it again. But the moth looks different now. Its beautiful red hind wings are folded and hidden by gray-brown fore wings that look just like the bark on which it has settled. Only a small shadow betrays its whereabouts.

You come across a nest of baby rabbits hidden in the soil. Their gray-brown coloring blends with the background. When they sense an enemy is near, they lie very still until the danger has passed. Unless they move, the enemy cannot see them.

The baby rabbits and the moth are safe because they are protectively colored, or *camouflaged.* The word *camouflage* comes from the French *camoufler,* which means "to conceal by disguising."

There are several kinds of camouflage in nature. Some animals blend with the background. Others resemble objects. Still others look like more dangerous animals. Camouflage also refers to the ability of some animals to bluff in order to escape an enemy.

Blending In

When a fawn is born, it is very helpless. Since it cannot escape its enemies quickly enough, it has other ways to survive. Its fur is speckled with white. When it lies or stands motionless, it blends with the sunlight and grasses and is almost impossible to see.

Ground-nesting birds and their eggs are spotted to match their background. The grouse, a popular game bird, survives because it is protectively colored and has the ability to *freeze* — to stand or crouch motionless. Some grasshoppers look like blades of grass when seen head on. Caterpillars, moths, and butterflies are often beautifully marked. Against the surrounding weeds, however, they seem to disappear.

In one experiment, ten colorful moths were released in a large cage containing branches with leaves of different colors. When the moths came to rest, it seemed as if they had vanished, and it was hard to find them again.

Now You See It . . .

Several animals can change their body color to match dozens of backgrounds. The most well known is the chameleon. This lizard's skin color changes due to differences in emotions, light, and temperature. But since its body color is mostly green or brown, it is also camouflaged well in its surroundings.

The varying hare, or snowshoe rabbit, changes the color of its fur with the seasons. During the summer its gray-brown color matches the soil and leaves. Late in the fall, white fur grows and replaces the hare's brown coat. This allows the hare to blend with the light snow dotting the autumn landscape. By the time the snow lies thick on the ground, the hare is all white except for its ears and a small spot on its nose. In the spring the color change is reversed. The hare is brown again by the time the snow has melted. Since the varying hare is active in both the winter and the summer, these color changes are necessary to its survival.

Many fish can change color to match their surroundings. Young flounders or sole do this by concentrating or dispersing red, yellow, and black pigments in their skin.

You can run a little test at home to show this kind of camouflage. Young flounders or sole are often sold in tropical fish stores. They can live for a few months in fresh water, but must then be placed in salt-water tanks. To see the color changes, put a fish in a shallow glass dish filled with water from its tank. Spread backgrounds of different colors and textures (such as sand or pebbles) underneath the glass dish. The fish will try to camouflage itself by matching the general pattern or color of the background. Of course, there is a limit to the fish's ability to change colors. It most easily produces light pink, pale yellow, green, different shades of brown, white, gray, and sand colors. It also imitates small or large spots or patches. A color change sometimes takes several hours or even days.

Disruptive Coloration

Sometimes military equipment is painted with zigzag lines to distract the eye from the natural outline of the objects. This type of camouflage is called *disruptive coloration.* It often occurs in the animal kingdom.

The tiger, with its red-brown color and black stripes, stands out when seen in an empty cage at a zoo. But in the tall grasses of its native jungle, it blends right into the landscape. The black and white stripes of the zebra and the spots and patches of the leopard and giraffe blend with trees, bushes, grass, and shadows.

Look-Alikes

Insects' lives are very short, and they have many enemies. So the more noninsectlike they look, the better their chance of survival. The trick is to imitate plants or objects that hold no interest for their enemies.

The stick caterpillar is very well named. It looks almost exactly like a brown or green twig. This caterpillar is also called a measuring worm or inchworm. It walks by arching its body, stretching out and grasping the twig with its front feet, and then looping its body again to bring the hind feet forward. When danger is near, the stick caterpillar stretches its body away from the branch and remains perfectly still, like a twig, until the danger has passed.

In the Amazon River in South America lives a small fish that is shaped and marked like a waterlogged leaf. This leaf fish is flat. Its back has ridges that resemble the edges of many leaves. The fish further imitates a leaf by floating on its side or standing very still with its head down. It can also change colors from tan to dark brown or gray. In addition, the patterns on its skin fade or darken until they match the surroundings. Thus, the leaf fish is quite safe from enemies that do not like the taste of "waterlogged leaves."

The Bolder, the Better

Some animals find protection by matching the colors or shapes of their background. Others do just the opposite. Many harmless insects show bright, bold colors. Their enemies are tricked into thinking that they are poisonous or bad tasting. Still other insects copy the frightening faces of some dangerous animals to scare their enemies away.

When a hungry bird is about to pick up a swallowtail caterpillar for its lunch, it is probably scared away by the sudden appearance of large, snakelike eyes. These false eyes are just markings behind the caterpillar's head, where the real eyes are.

The caligo butterfly of South America has markings under its wings. These markings look like the large, staring eyes of an owl. The lantern fly of Brazil has a large, peanut-shaped, hollow head. The head is decorated with what look like the large eyes, nostrils, and teeth of an alligator.

Appearance as well as behavior helps an animal survive. Some creatures, therefore, have developed more than one kind of camouflage for protection. The little screech owl flies and hunts at night. During the day, however, its soft, uneven markings blend with the bark of the trees in which it sleeps. If the owl is disturbed, it tries to make itself as thin as possible. If the danger persists, the owl clicks its bill, pops its eyes, and fluffs out its feathers to look large, fearsome, and too big to eat.

The porcupine fish can puff itself up with water if an enemy tries to catch it in the water. If the fish is caught on the surface, it puffs itself up with air. Its spines, usually pressed close to its body, become stiff and stand out and can tear the mouth of an attacker.

Wearing Masks

Masking is another trick some animals use to fool their enemies. One measuring worm camouflages itself by masking. Its brown color and straight shape would easily be seen on a white flower or a green leaf. But the worm tricks its enemies by first cutting tiny pieces of leaves from the plant. It then ties them to its body with silk threads which it spins from special glands. When the worm has finished decorating itself, it looks just like its surroundings. If the decorations are pulled off, the worm quickly goes to work to replace them.

Every meadow, field, prairie, beach, and backyard is home to creatures that escape their enemies by changing the color or shape of their bodies. Finding and studying them can give us new knowledge about the wonders and mysteries of living things.

Understanding What You've Read

1. How does the snowshoe rabbit make use of camouflage to protect itself?
2. What is *disruptive coloration*? Briefly describe the way a particular animal uses disruptive coloration.
3. What is *masking*? How does one measuring worm use masking to protect itself?

Applying the Skills Lesson

1. Think about the animals mentioned in the selection that use camouflage for protection. Which of the following conclusions can you draw about the kinds of animals that use camouflage?
   a. Birds do not use camouflage to escape enemies.
   b. Most animals that use camouflage for survival would be helpless without it.
   c. Insects are the only creatures that use camouflage.
2. An experiment with moths is described in the third paragraph on page 432. What conclusion can you draw about the moths?

The Victorian Age was a time of great change, ushered in by one of England's most honored queens, . . .

VICTORIA

by Lydia Farmer

The word *Victorian,* named for Queen Victoria, describes an age when far-reaching changes and reforms were taking place in England. The *Victorian Age* covers the longest rule of any monarch in English history—sixty-three years.

Alexandrina Victoria was born in Kensington Palace in London, on May 24, 1819. Her father was Edward, Duke of Kent, brother of the king of England. Edward died when Victoria was still a baby. Her mother, the Duchess of Kent, was also named Victoria.

In the family, Victoria was called Drina, a shortened form of her first name. Drina was seven when she paid her first visit to her uncle, King George IV. At the time, Victoria did not know she would one day be queen. When she was twelve, however, her tutor traced for her the genealogy of English royalty. As they reached the end, Victoria cried with surprise, "Why, I cannot see who is to come next, unless it is myself!" When told that this was true, she said simply, "I will be good."

When Victoria was seventeen, her mother's brother Leopold decided that the time had come to choose her future husband. He sent six of his German nephews, two at a time, to visit her at Kensington Palace. Her cousin Albert proved to be her favorite. He was her own age, fond of music, a gifted pianist, and spoke English well. Victoria liked him, but she was not yet interested in marriage.

439

A New Role

The coming of age of Princess Victoria was celebrated by a state ball. For her eighteenth birthday present, King William IV (who had succeeded George IV) gave her a grand piano and an allowance of 10,000 pounds a year. Now she could be independent.

A month later, the king, who had been very ill, grew suddenly worse. Early in the morning of June 20, 1837, he died. However, he had been comforted by the knowledge that his niece would become queen.

In one night Victoria's life changed completely. The first thing she did was write a letter to her uncle Leopold in Belgium. In her journal she wrote, "I am very young and inexperienced, but I am sure that very few have more real good will and more real desire to do what is fit and right than I have."

By the time she had spent two years in her new role, Victoria had learned a great deal. She enjoyed both her responsibilities and her new independence. Albert returned to England in 1839. Soon after, Victoria's ideas about marriage changed. The wedding took place the following year.

As the years passed, Victoria continued the wise policies she had begun during her early years as queen. She followed the actions of her ministers closely, arguing strongly when she did not agree. However, she never tried to change a policy once it had been set by them.

Victoria gave birth to her first child, a daughter, and in November 1841, the prince of Wales was born. As the family grew, Victoria and Albert felt more and more the need of a retreat from London and Windsor Castle. Albert built a castle, Balmoral, far off in the Scottish Highlands. Here the family enjoyed picnics, walks, and hunting. Victoria was to spend her happiest days at Balmoral.

But England and Victoria were to experience an unhappy time from 1853 to 1856. The Crimean War took a heavy toll in both lives and money.

Until 1861, when both her mother and her husband died, Victoria had known little real sorrow. Now she was overcome with grief. For years, she was able to do no more than the most important duties of state.

Despite this, England continued to prosper. Victoria's dominion extended to India, Egypt, South Africa, Australia, Canada, and scores of islands, large and small. The saying "The sun never sets on the British Empire" became literally true.

British Royalty Since 1714

George I = Sophia Dorothea
(1714-27)

George II = Caroline of Anspach
(1727-60)

Augusta of Saxe-Coburg-Gotha = Frederick   William

Augusta = William   **George III** = Charlotte
(1760-1820)

Caroline = **George IV**   Frederick   **William IV**   Edward = Victoria Mary   Ernest
(1820-30)   (1830-37)   Louisa

Victoria = Albert of Saxe-Coburg-Gotha
(1837-1901)

Edward VII = Alexandra of Denmark
(1901-10)

George V = Victoria Mary of Teck
(1910-36)

Edward VIII   **George VI** = Elizabeth   Mary   Henry   George
(1936)   (1936-52)   Duke of Gloucester   Duke of Kent

Philip = **Elizabeth II** Margaret   William   Richard   Edward   Alexandra   Michael
         (1952-)

Charles   Anne   Andrew   Edward

George III
(1760-1820)

George IV
(1820-30)

Edward VII
(1901-10)

George VI
(1936-52)

Elizabeth II
(1952-)

Note: Kings and Queens are shown in boldface type

The Industrial Age in England

The Industrial Revolution, which began in the early 1800's, was a major force for change during the Victorian Age. The steam engine brought a web of railways throughout England and Scotland. The use of steam power to run ships allowed greater trade with the rest of the world. The penny post, with its first adhesive stamp, made communication easier. The telegraph brought Great Britain and the places that made up its empire closer together.

The greatest change, however, was to an economy based on machines instead of farming. During Victoria's rule, law after law was passed for improving the conditions of workers. For the first time, they had a voice in management and began wielding power.

There were laws passed to improve conditions in factories, mines, prisons, housing, schools, and hospitals. One of the greatest advances was the extension of voting rights to all men. Before 1884, voting was based on income or savings. Afterward, even the poorest man could cast his vote.

The Victorian Age also produced some of England's greatest literature. Tennyson, Browning, Dickens, George Eliot, and the Brontë sisters number among the writers of the time.

Toward the end of the nineteenth century, the population of England had greatly increased. The country was richer through the growth of its industry and trade. The British Empire was at the height of its glory. Victoria had become the symbol of the English monarchy. She was a much-loved queen in a time of great change.

Understanding What You've Read

1. How did eighteen-year-old Victoria feel about assuming the duties of queen? Support your answer with examples from the selection.
2. Why were the years 1853 to 1856 an unhappy period for England and Queen Victoria?
3. Explain four major changes that occurred in England during the Victorian Age.

Applying the Skills Lesson

1. What conclusion can you draw about England's strength as a nation during the Victorian Age? State three facts from the selection to support your conclusion.
2. Based on the chart on page 441, what conclusion can you draw regarding the kings and queens of England?

TEXTBOOK STUDY

Drawing Conclusions

As you read textbooks, look for more than just what the words and pictures actually say. By drawing conclusions based on the facts that are presented, you can increase your understanding of the material. Read the following textbook excerpt and refer to the sidenotes. They will help you to draw conclusions.

Drawing Conclusions in Social Studies

In the 1500's and 1600's, caravans of camels moved across the desert of northwestern China. Numerous canals and rivers carried boatloads of goods to and from coastal provinces. The few Europeans who were allowed into China at that time marveled at the large amount of goods that were exchanged. They thought that China carried on more trade within its boundaries than all the European nations did together.

Because there were many ways to distribute resources and goods to different parts of the nation, many areas of China began to specialize in certain products.

What can you conclude about the kind of climate necessary for the growth of cotton?

Areas with a damp climate, such as those near the coastal cities of Shanghai and Hangchow, became centers for cotton spinning. Later they supplied cotton cloth to much of Europe. Another area, in southeast China, became famous for its fine pottery. Europeans, who bought it eagerly, began to call it "china."

It may seem that China—the greatest empire on earth at that time—was ready for the industrial revolution even before it occurred in England. However, China did not begin to develop its economy beyond a traditional agricultural basis until the early 1900's. Why had this large empire existed for centuries without discovering technology and mass production?

The answer lies in several important Chinese values that lasted for generations. Many Chinese, including most government leaders, followed the teachings of a philosopher named K'ung Tzu, or Confucius, who had lived about 500 B.C. Confucianism, as his teaching was called, taught the people to respect the past and to look to traditions for guidance. Nothing was considered valuable unless it compared favorably with standards taught by the learned men of the past. How do you think the Chinese regarded new ideas in economics and industrial technology?

Based on this statement, what can you conclude about the quality of the products produced by the Chinese?

— Sources of Identity
Harcourt Brace Jovanovich

Building Skills

1. Based on the second paragraph, what can you conclude about the area of China that became famous for its fine pottery?
2. Based on the information in the selection, how would you answer the question asked by the author in the last sentence?

Drawing Conclusions in Science

This textbook excerpt is not accompanied by sidenotes. As you read, look for the kinds of information you need to draw conclusions about the experiments. Then answer the questions that follow.

Regulating Your Body

Think back over the last few school days. What has been your routine? When did you go to bed? At what times did you have something to eat? Make a chart such as the one shown here. Continue keeping a chart like this one during the next few days.

Time	Eating	Sleep	Temp.
_____ Date			
6 AM		awake	
7	Breakfast		
8			
9			
10			
11			
12	Lunch		
1 PM			
2			
3	Snack		
4			
5			
6	Supper		
7			
8			
9		to bed	
10			
11			
12			

Your Body Clock. Now measure a more subtle change that your body goes through each day, over which you have no control. Take your own body temperature hourly throughout one entire day. Try also to take your temperature several times at night. Be sure you use the same technique each time you take your temperature. Compare your chart with those of your classmates. Do you notice any regularly recurring events? If so, what are they?

Now try varying your routine to see what effects it will have. Go to bed one hour earlier than usual, and set your alarm clock for one hour earlier than usual. Continue to eat your meals at the same times as you did before. What do you think this change in routine will do?

No doubt our bodies have timing devices that tell us when to go to sleep, when to eat, and when to wake up. What are some other events which occur with regularity in your body?

— Exploring Life Sciences
Allyn & Bacon

Building Skills

1. How will taking your temperature every hour help you to draw a correct conclusion about regular changes in your body temperature?
2. Suppose you took your temperature only once a day for a week. Could you draw a conclusion about your regular body temperature from this information? Why?

Use Your Judgment . . . Finding and Judging the Author's Conclusions

"For goodness sake, Doris. This is not the time to take a photograph."

After studying the details of the situation, the woman in the cartoon drew a **conclusion.** In other words, she considered all the facts and how they related to one another. They seemed to "add up" to one idea: "This is not the time to take a photograph." This idea is her conclusion.

Finding the Author's Conclusions

After stating a number of facts, authors very often draw a conclusion based on those facts. Read the paragraph below. Which sentence is a conclusion based on the information given in the other sentences?

All milk products have protein. Cheese is a milk product. Therefore, cheese has protein.

The sentence "Therefore, cheese has protein" is a conclusion. It is based on the facts stated in the first two sentences. These facts are the evidence that the author uses to support the conclusion. Read the paragraph that follows. Look for the conclusion.

Scientists have measured the speed of a number of different animals. All were animals that travel on land. It was found that the cheetah can reach speeds as high as 112 kilometers an hour. Every other animal was clocked at slower rates. The cheetah is the fastest land animal.

The author's conclusion is stated in the last sentence: "The cheetah is the fastest land animal." What facts in the paragraph support this conclusion?

Recognizing a Faulty Conclusion

Read the sentences below. What is wrong with the conclusion?

All professional athletes do exercises. Lila's brother does exercises. Lila's brother must be a professional athlete.

Just because Lila's brother does exercises doesn't mean he is a professional athlete. Maybe he just enjoys doing exercises. Maybe he is exercising because he plans to try out for a team. Maybe he is an amateur athlete. In this case there is not enough information to draw a conclusion about whether or not Lila's brother is a professional athlete. So the conclusion that has been drawn is faulty based on the information given.

Now read the paragraph below. Find the conclusion.

Early in the morning the sun is low in the eastern sky. A few hours later, it is directly overhead. By evening, the sun is in the west. It is clear, therefore, that the sun revolves around the earth.

The conclusion states that the sun revolves around the earth. We know, of course, that this is not true. How, then, did the writer arrive at this conclusion? The facts state three different daily positions of the sun. *But that is all the facts tell you.* The writer assumed that if the sun starts out in the east and ends up in the west, it is moving around the earth. However, there are no facts given about the movement of the earth. The writer arrived at a faulty conclusion because he or she did not have all the facts.

Try This

Read the paragraph below and then answer the question that follows.

The eighty-eight constellations turn in the nighttime sky in sparkling star patterns. But to find them, you have to know what to look for. Leo, the lion, looks like a bright question mark. Ursa Major is probably the most well-known constellation. Its English name is the Great Bear, yet it seems more like a water dipper. Sagittarius, the archer, is shaped like a teapot. Corvus, the raven, is a lopsided square. Draco, the dragon, however, looks like a dragon. Just scan the sky for its head and long, snakelike body.

Read the following conclusions. Which are valid?
1. All the constellations are named for animals.
2. The names of the constellations do not always describe their shapes.
3. All the constellations are easy to find.
4. The constellations have names.
5. The North Star is in the handle of the Little Dipper.

VOCABULARY STUDY

The 16-Kilometer Journey . . . Prefixes and Suffixes

Balloon, Rail, Nation, and Case went traveling together to search for prefixes and suffixes.

1. After 2 kilometers, Balloon saw a sign for the suffix *-ist*.

2. *-ist:* one who performs an action

11. At 13, 14, 15, and 16 kilometers, the four travelers found four sentences.

10. *en-:* within, into

9. Case saw a sign for the prefix *en-* at 10 kilometers.

12. Which word belongs in which sentence?

13. The seven countries signed the _____ agreement.
14. As we lifted off, the _____ explained how to land and steer the huge balloon.
15. We rode through the city on the _____.
16. To become a butterfly, the caterpillar must _____ itself in a cocoon.

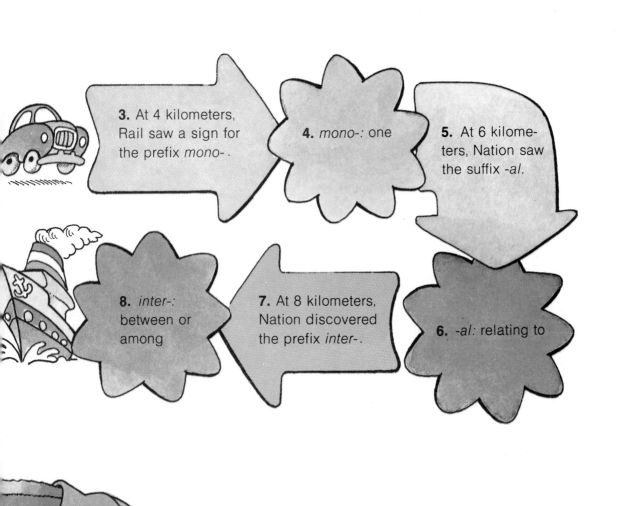

3. At 4 kilometers, Rail saw a sign for the prefix *mono-*.

4. *mono-:* one

5. At 6 kilometers, Nation saw the suffix *-al.*

8. *inter-:* between or among

7. At 8 kilometers, Nation discovered the prefix *inter-*.

6. *-al:* relating to

Word Play

Use the definitions for the prefixes and suffixes above to figure out what each of these words means: *cartoonist, monosyllable, entrap, intercontinental.*

In the middle of her career, she completely changed her artistic style. Today, our museums are richer for the determination and talents of...

MARY CASSATT

by Winthrop Neilson *and* Frances Neilson

"The Boating Party" by Mary Cassatt

As you read this selection about Mary Cassatt, look for the conclusions the authors draw.

Mary Cassatt was born in 1844 in Allegheny City, Pennsylvania. She was fifth in a family of seven children. Her mother loved Europe and managed to take the family abroad for a long stay while Mary was still young.

After some years in Europe, the Cassatts returned to the United States, where Mary received her education. Her family moved from Philadelphia to the suburbs, and from one house to another. Somewhere along the way, Mary became interested in painting.

At that time, the Pennsylvania Academy of the Fine Arts maintained a school in Philadelphia for painters. Mary entered the academy as a student and began her studies by copying the works of the masters. She was a student at the Pennsylvania Academy for four years.

Much later in life, Cassatt told a French interviewer: "At the academy one drew so much better after classic copies. There was no teaching there. I think that painting is not taught, and that one does not need to follow the lessons of a teacher. The teaching of museums is sufficient."

Mary decided to make painting her career in 1868. She was twenty-four. This was a good four years after she completed her academy studies.

(right) "Salvatore Mundi" by Correggio
(below) "The Lamp" by Mary Cassatt

With her decision, she announced to her family her plans of going to Italy, alone. Her father had doubts about his daughter traveling by herself to Europe. However, he allowed her to go, though sometime later he and his wife moved to Paris with their younger children to follow their serious-minded daughter.

Success in Europe

Mary first traveled to Parma, in northern Italy. There she found the works of Correggio [kə·rej′ō], the late Renaissance painter who lived in the early 1500's. "What a master!" she exclaimed. She studied his works for eight months. She then traveled to Spain, where she saw the masterpieces of Peter Paul Rubens, a Belgian artist, in Madrid's Prado

456

"At the Milliner's" by Edgar Degas

Museum. She moved on to Antwerp, in Belgium, where she could absorb all the knowledge and technique of Rubens as if he were a living teacher.

Throughout these months of self-directed study, she continued with her painting. Mary Cassatt's reputation as an artist began to grow. She sent a painting to the annual Salon of Paris and it was accepted—a great honor for a young painter. (At that time, Mary was twenty-eight.)

The following year, her entry to the Salon was again accepted. This painting showed a young girl handing refreshment to a brightly costumed toreador. Its subject reflected Mary's stay in Spain.

Mary was living in the clouds. She moved to Paris. Then, in the following year, her bubble burst. The Salon rejected a portrait of her sister Lydia. It was a bitter disappointment, enough to make anyone but a dedicated artist give up. But every artist knows rejection, and Mary was not about to give up. She simply had not yet found herself.

Degas and the Impressionists

One day, a friend brought Impressionist painter Edgar Degas to Mary's studio. His visit changed her life. He saw her work and liked it. They became immediate friends. From then on, Degas's criticism of her paintings brought out her true ability. He asked her to join the Impressionist movement. Joyfully, she accepted.

"A Cup of Tea" by Mary Cassatt

Edgar never married. Probably Mary's was the closest friendship he ever had with a woman. When Edgar had trouble finding the right model for his paintings, Mary posed for him. Mary never married either. Her art was her life. The two were friends for forty years, though not without difficulty. Both had strong personalities, and they very often clashed. When they did, six months or more might go by without their seeing each other. But something always brought them back together again.

Mary Cassatt's real introduction into the world of great art came with her representation in an Impressionist show in 1879 in Paris. She exhibited a painting called "La Loge." It showed a girl in a box at the opera, smiling and holding a fan. The work was superb. The feeling and composition were of the highest quality. But the new Impressionist movement was strange and laughable in most people's eyes. The Paris critics blasted the show. They did, however, compliment the works of Mary Cassatt and Edgar Degas.

At the next Impressionist show, artist Paul Gauguin remarked, "Mademoiselle Cassatt has much charm, but she has more force."

"At the Opera" by Mary Cassatt

(top left) "The Fitting" by Mary Cassatt (top right) "The Letter" by Mary Cassatt (bottom) "Woman Dressing Girl for Sanboro Dance" by Utamaro

The Oriental Influence

The next factor in Mary's development, and a major influence on many French painters, was an 1890 exhibition in Paris of Japanese prints. Most artists had some familiarity with the art of Japan, though it was new to Paris. Degas was one of the first to see the simplicity of Japanese line, the composition of form and color, and the Oriental feeling. When the 1890 exhibition of prints came to Paris, a whole new wave of inspiration swept over the French artists.

460

From then on, Mary's print making was influenced by the Japanese style. She had no fear of adopting changes in her work. She continued to grow as an artist.

In 1891, Mary had her first single-artist show. Though she was nervous, the show came off well.

She was gaining recognition.

Perhaps the highest point of Mary's career was a series of ten prints done early in the 1890's to match the style of the Japanese. They were superb. These prints, and the ones that followed, have been known and respected from that time until today.

Mary Cassatt had become one of America's great artists. Her oil paintings, pastels, and prints are in leading museums and private collections throughout the world. Her work has left a profound stamp on the history of art.

Understanding What You've Read

1. What formal art training did Mary Cassatt have?
2. Who was Edgar Degas?
3. What factors affected Mary Cassatt's development as a major American painter?

Applying the Skills Lesson

1. In the third paragraph on this page, the authors conclude that Cassatt "was gaining recognition." On what facts from the selection do the authors base this conclusion? Do you think it is valid? Why or why not?
2. Read the following facts. Which ones can be used to support the conclusion that Mary Cassatt's paintings are masterpieces?
   a. Cassatt's paintings sell for a great deal of money.
   b. Cassatt's paintings hang in several leading museums throughout the world.
   c. One third-grade class in a Pennsylvania elementary school enjoyed looking at Cassatt's paintings.
   d. Many art critics have praised Cassatt's work.
   e. Cassatt's paintings are very colorful.
   f. Cassatt's style is studied in many art schools.

Use the diagrams that accompany this selection to help you judge the validity of the author's conclusions.

The patterns of the eighty-eight sky constellations seem to be fixed and constant. Yet, thousands of years will reveal . . .

The Constellations' Changing Faces

by Henry J. Phillips

The discovery that stars move would have come as quite a shock to the scientists of the Middle Ages. To these people, the stars were fixed. The sun and planets changed their positions in the sky, but the stars did not. A popular idea of the time was that stars were encased in a crystal sphere. They were all believed to be the same distance from the earth.

But facts gathered during the Renaissance changed this picture of the universe. The discovery that stars move was the turning point.

Edmund Halley's Discovery

In 1718, British astronomer Edmund Halley was studying some very old calendars and star charts. Among these was the famous *Almagest* of Ptolemy, written in the second century A.D. Halley found that some of the brighter stars had different positions in the sky in 1718 than those listed by Ptolemy. Earlier, anyone's reaction to this discovery would have been that Ptolemy had incorrectly recorded the stars' positions. But Halley and others no longer believed that such differences were due to earlier mistakes.

Halley noted that most of the other recorded stars were still in their recorded places. He thought that a careful scientist like Ptolemy would not have misplaced such important stars. Halley reached the only possible conclusion: The stars had really moved.

By 1718, many astronomers knew that stars are suns like our own. They only look like points of light because they are so far away. Halley said that all these suns were moving through space and were not fixed in their positions at all. When he published his discoveries, his ideas were almost instantly accepted. The "fixed stars" were gone forever.

It's easy to understand why no one had spotted this movement before. The stars are so far away that even the speediest present no change in position to the naked eye over a person's lifetime.

We can now figure out the stars' positions in the sky for thousands of years in the future. We can also

Edmund Halley at his telescope

figure their positions in the distant past. With new equipment, scientists can measure the movement of a star in a single year. It is easy, then, to know the changes our constellations will undergo—and, in fact, are undergoing right now.

Then and Now

A well-known picture found in many astronomy books shows how Ursa Major, the Big Dipper, looks today and how it will look 100,000 years from now.

Five of the Big Dipper's seven stars are part of a large group of stars moving through space in the same direction and at the same speed. Two of the dipper's stars, however, are not part of this group. They are moving in different directions. Thus, our Big Dipper is losing its shape little by little.

Ursa Minor, the Little Dipper, is also changing. Only one star is moving very fast. However, since it is the faintest, its motion may not be easy to see. But the Little Dipper is slowly losing its shape, too. Polaris, the last star in the dipper's handle, will someday no longer be the most northern star in the sky.

Cassiopeia, the queen, is an example of a constellation in which all the stars are quickly flying apart from each other. By A.D. 101,976 Cassiopeia's W shape will become a triangle.

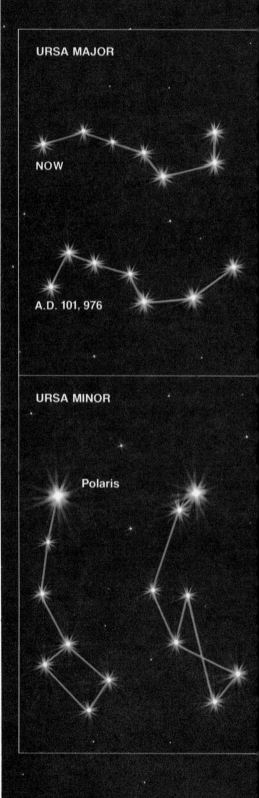

URSA MAJOR

NOW

A.D. 101, 976

URSA MINOR

Polaris

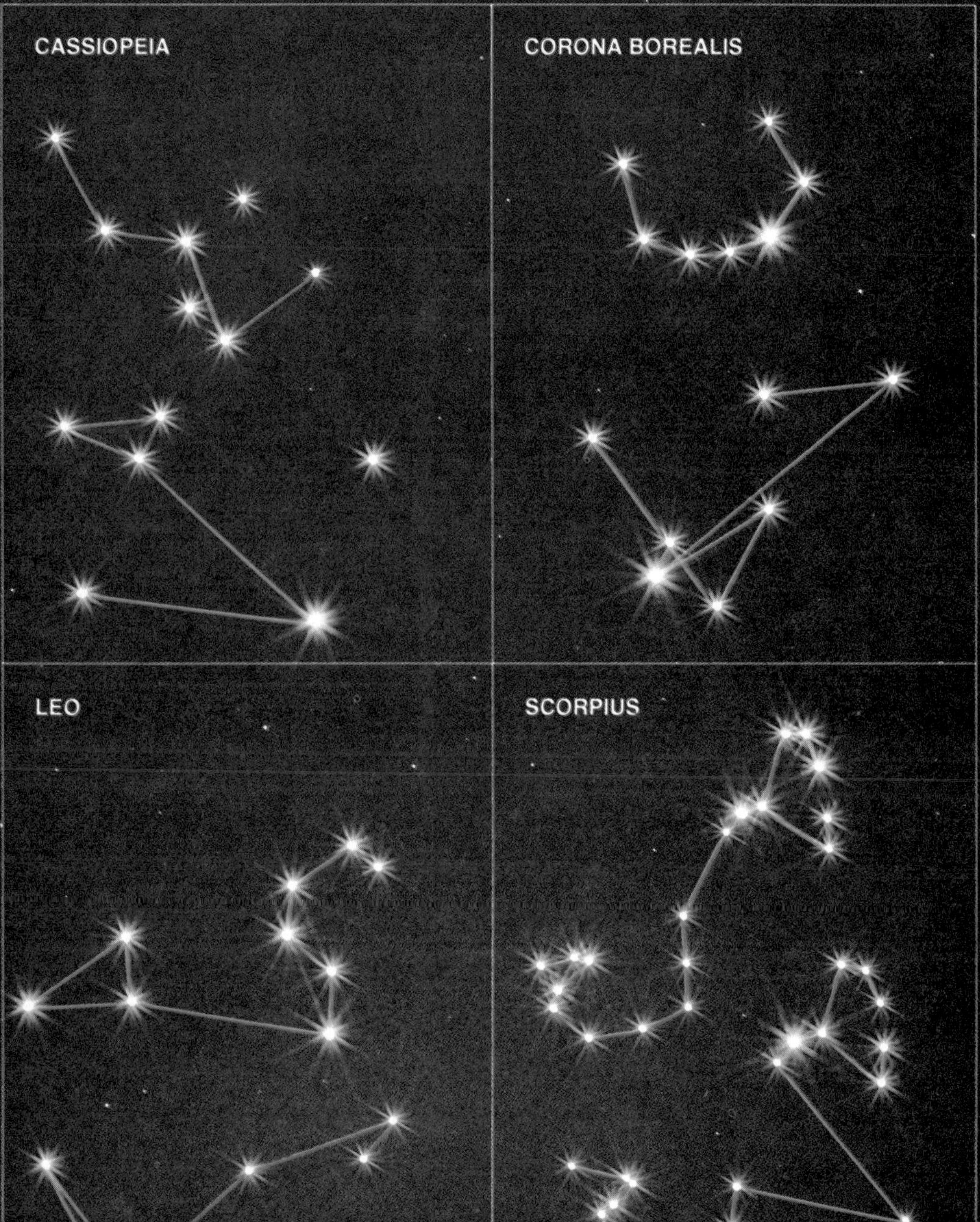

CASSIOPEIA

CORONA BOREALIS

LEO

SCORPIUS

Corona Borealis, the Northern Crown, is another constellation that is being changed by the movement of its stars. In the future, it will bear no likeness to the crown it appears to be today.

Several stars in Leo, the lion, are moving very quickly. The sickle is getting wider and the triangle is getting narrower and longer. We can only wonder what new name might be given to this constellation in the future.

Scorpius, the scorpion, will not go to pieces as completely as some other constellations. A great many of its stars are part of a separate group, just as those in the Big Dipper. These stars are all heading in the same direction. Only two do not belong to the group, and if the connecting lines to these two stars are not drawn, Scorpius's shape will be as good as ever.

The great square of Pegasus, the winged horse, will not always be as square-shaped as it is now, but it will remain a landmark in the sky. Orion, the hunter, is another constellation that will be fairly stable through the years.

Other changes besides those noted here are possible. Some faint stars may brighten as they come close to the sun. Others may dim as they move away.

We have learned that the sky above us is a place of great change. Planets and stars are ever on the move. How beautiful our constellations seem to us now. . . . How beautiful they still will seem in the future!

Understanding What You've Read

1. Why are the patterns of the constellations changing?
2. Who was Edmund Halley? How did he come to notice that the stars were moving?
3. How do you think the names of the constellations were chosen?

Applying the Skills Lesson

1. What conclusion does the author draw in the second paragraph under the heading "Then and Now"?
2. On what facts is this conclusion based?
3. Is the conclusion valid? Explain your answer.

TEXTBOOK STUDY

Finding and Judging the Author's Conclusions

Authors sometimes present a number of facts and then draw one or more conclusions. An important critical reading skill is being able to recognize an author's conclusions and judge their validity. As you read the following textbook excerpt, refer to the sidenotes. They will guide you in drawing conclusions about the information presented.

Finding and Judging the Author's Conclusions in Social Studies

Motives for Food

This sentence states the purpose for the experiment. What do the other sentences do?

In a well-known experiment, psychologists investigated some of the reasons why people eat different foods. In this experiment, three babies were allowed for many months to choose their meals from a wide variety of things to eat. Each baby had certain periods in which he or she showed a preference for one kind of food—eggs or cereal, perhaps.

What is the main idea of this paragraph?

When the experiment began, one baby had a disease called rickets, which is caused by a lack of vitamin D. For a while, he chose large quantities of cod liver oil, which happens to be rich in vitamin D. When his disease was cured, he stopped taking the cod liver oil.

The results of this experiment showed that all three babies were as healthy and grew as normally as babies whose feeding was supervised by adults. They chose to eat exactly the same foods an expert would have chosen for them—a balanced diet. Their needs for certain kinds of food at certain times motivated them to make the right choices.

This is the author's conclusion. On what facts was the conclusion based?

— Sources of Identity
Harcourt Brace Jovanovich

Building Skills

1. Suppose the baby with rickets did not choose foods containing vitamin D. Which of the following conclusions would be valid?
   a. All babies choose foods to meet their needs.
   b. Babies do not need vitamin D.
   c. Further experimentation should be done.
2. Suppose the author only used the information in the second paragraph to draw his or her conclusion. Would the conclusion still be valid? Explain your answer.

SKILLS LESSON

All Things Considered . . . Generalizing

"So that's what earthlings look like."

In an earlier skills lesson, you saw how the information in an article can lead you to draw a conclusion. **Generalizing,** which is like drawing a conclusion, is another kind of inference skill. When you make a generalization, you consider the facts and details and make a broad statement based on them.

Read the next paragraph. Answer the question that follows it.

Thousands of years ago, an underwater volcano erupted in the Pacific Ocean. Lava spilled from the mouth of the volcano. As the lava cooled, it formed the long chain of islands we know today as Hawaii. When the volcano on Krakatoa erupted, it formed the island of Anok Krakatan. Many of the islands in the Mediterranean also are the result of volcanic activity under the sea.

From this information, which of the following generalizations can you make?

a. All islands are formed from volcanic explosions.
b. Volcanic explosions always form islands.
c. Many islands have been formed from the explosions of underwater volcanoes.

Your answer to the question above should be *c*: "Many islands have been formed from the explosions of underwater volcanoes." You were able to make this generalization based on the three examples given in the paragraph.

You should note that there are exceptions to the statement. The Bermuda Islands, for instance, are coral formations. Which word in sentence *c* tells you that there are exceptions to the generalization?

When you make a generalization, you should consider all the available information and the knowledge you have from your own experiences. If you are certain there are no exceptions to your generalization, you may use words such as *all, everybody, always,* and *never.* If there probably are some exceptions, be sure to use qualifying words such as *some, many, often,* and *most.*

Finding the Author's Generalization

Sometimes authors will state a generalization based on a number of facts. Read the paragraph below. Look for the generalization.

Most living things on earth need air and water to survive. The air we breathe is 21 percent oxygen, a gas that is necessary for cell growth. Our bodies are almost 70 percent water. Since we lose water daily, we must take in water to maintain the very strict balance. The desert camel is one of the animal kingdom's greatest water savers. Yet the camel's outside limit without water is thirty-four days.

The first sentence states a generalization: "Most living things on earth need air and water to survive." Notice that it is a broad statement about living things *in general*. The author supports this generalization with the information in the paragraph. What does this information tell you? Through examples, it illustrates the need for food and water. Are there any exceptions to this generalization? Yes, but very few. Some kinds of bacteria can live without air and water. Since these are the only exceptions, the generalization is valid.

False Generalizations

Sometimes a writer may make a generalization that has many exceptions to it. If the writer has based his or her generalization on very few examples, the generalization can be false. Read the paragraph below. Look for the false generalization.

My sister Annette shouts at me for the least little thing. If I borrow one of her books, and she later decides she wants to read it, she becomes very upset. She yells and carries on even after I've returned the book to her. Annette has shocking red hair. I guess that explains her behavior. Most redheads have bad tempers.

The writer has made a false generalization in the last sentence: "Most redheads have bad tempers." He or she has based this generalization on only one example, Annette. Perhaps Annette does have a bad temper. But that doesn't mean *most* redheaded people have bad tempers. In fact, a person's temper has nothing to do with hair color.

Another example of a false generalization would be: "All gold-medal winners in the Olympics break world's records." There are several Olympic gold medalists who did not break records.

Try This

1. Which of the following statements are generalizations?
   a. Most office buildings are equipped with typewriters, telephones, and copying machines.
   b. The earth has only one moon.
   c. Many Americans know the words to the "Star-Spangled Banner."
   d. The capital of Norway is Oslo.
   e. Many artists' children have artistic talent.
2. Which of the following generalizations are probably false?
   a. It always snows in the winter.
   b. Most musicians can read music.
   c. People born in the winter are healthier than people born in the spring.
   d. All libraries contain reference books.
   e. Many fruits grow on trees.

VOCABULARY STUDY

The Wanted Poster . . . Antonyms

"Here's the wanted poster you asked for, Sheriff. It says: '$500.00 REWARD for the capture of Wally Wooly. You'll recognize him by the *intricate* designs on his hat. He stays in *bleak* hotels, and his clothing shows he is a man of great *poverty*. He has been known to *retreat* whenever he is faced with danger.' How's that?"

The sheriff's eyes nearly popped from his head. "What nonsense!" he shouted. "The poster is all wrong! Wally Wooly's hat doesn't have *intricate*

designs. It's a simple, baby blue ten-gallon hat. He won't ever be found in *bleak* hotels, either. Wooly likes colorful, bright hotels.

"A man of great *poverty?*" continued the sheriff. "Ha! Wally Wooly's loaded with money!

"And another thing. This rotten, no-good rascal doesn't *retreat* from danger. With his six guns blazing, he rushes forward to meet it. Now change the poster or we'll never capture him!"

"Yes, sir," said the deputy. "Right away!"

"Incidently, Mortimer," said the sheriff, "where'd you get all this wrong information?"

"Oh, from some rich stranger passing through town," said Mortimer, "wearing a baby blue ten-gallon hat. . ."

Word Play

Match the words in Column A with their definitions in Column B.

A	B
intricate	to turn back or away
bleak	lack of money
poverty	having many parts or designs
retreat	colorless

475

Centimeters, kilometers, kilograms. They never change. Or do they?
To become the standards they are today, there had to be a . . .

MEASURE FOR MEASURE

by Roy A. Gallant

As you read this selection, you can use the facts the author presents to draw a number of generalizations.

Many units of measure were invented by the Egyptians several thousand years ago. They were based on different parts of the human body. It seems that people liked to "size up" nature by relating it to themselves.

The *foot* unit was the length of an adult human foot. Three grains of barley placed end-to-end made one finger, or *digit*. Four digits equaled one *hand*. We still use this unit to measure the height of horses. We say that a horse is seventeen hands high, for example.

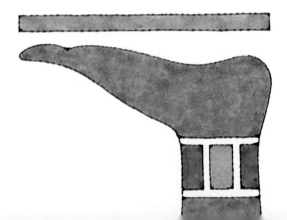

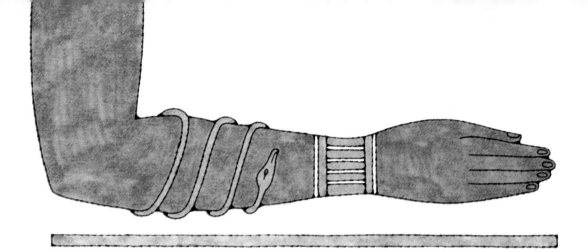

The distance from the tip of the middle finger to the elbow was one *cubit*. Two cubits equaled one *arm*, and one arm, measured from the fingertips to the chin, was one *yard*.

Those units worked well enough for short distances, but not for longer ones, such as the distance between two villages. The Egyptians used a larger unit called the *pace* for such measurements. It was equal to two regular steps and was measured from the heel of one foot to the toe of the same foot on touching the ground again. The pace was also equal to the length of the outstretched arms. One hundred paces therefore equaled 200 yards (or 200 arm lengths), which the Egyptians called a *stade*.

Later, the ancient Greeks took over the stade, calling it a *stadion*, as an official unit of distance for the Olympic foot races. That is why the place where the foot races were held came to be called a *stadium*. The Romans adopted the stade from the Greeks. Ten stadia in Roman times became one *mile*.

Egyptian units of measure based on parts of the body seem to have been spread by traders of the eastern Mediterranean Sea—to the Greek cities, later to Rome, then into Europe of the Middle Ages, and through England to the United States.

Measuring Volume

The Egyptians hit on a very simple and useful way of measuring large and small amounts of things. They either doubled a unit or took half of it to make a new unit. Then they doubled or halved the new unit to make more new units. For example, when the Egyptians wanted to measure out small amounts of liquids or grain, they used a unit called the ro. A ro of something was equal to a mouthful! With the ro as a base unit of volume, other units were made to measure larger and larger volumes.

UNITS OF VOLUME

two ros (mouthfuls)	=	one handful (jigger)
two handfuls	=	one jack (jackpot)
two jacks	=	one jill
two jills	=	one cup
two cups	=	one pint (mugg or jug)
two pints	=	one quart
two quarts	=	one pottle
two pottles	=	one gallon
two gallons	=	one pail
two pails	=	one peck
two pecks	=	one bushel
two bushels	=	one strike
two strikes	=	one coomb
two coombs	=	one cask
two casks	=	one barrel
two barrels	=	one hogshead
two hogsheads	=	one pipe
two pipes	=	one tun

The Need for a Standard . . . Any Standard

It's easy to see what's wrong with using feet, arms, hands, and fingers as units of measure. Let's say you wanted to buy a field 200 paces long on each side. By using such a measuring system you might get more or less land, depending on whether the person who paced off the field had long or short legs. If there are only a few people and plenty of land, the difference of a few feet or a few yards might not be very important. But in a town or city, where there are a lot of people all wanting enough space in which to live, a difference of a few feet can become very important.

The ancient Egyptians knew the importance of agreeing on a standard length of a pace, and on standard units of volume and weight. But whose arm, hand, or foot would be the standard? It was simple: The parts of the body of the king or queen then in power would become the official standard. Unfortunately, the standard would have to be changed each time a new king or queen came to power! The new ruler surely would have a longer or shorter foot than the last king or queen. And so it went for centuries.

The English finally agreed to a standard length for the yard unit by using the length of the arm of Queen Elizabeth I. In fact, by the year 1592, most of the English units of measurement had been given standards that everyone agreed to use.

But before that time there had been many problems. For one, a pint in one English county might be larger or smaller than a pint in another county. Another problem was that the king or queen could change the standard measuring units when it seemed a good idea to do so. What happened as a result may seem funny to us today. It was not very funny several centuries ago, especially to the people who were poor.

In England of old, the poor could not afford to buy their food in large amounts. They were forced to buy a few pennies' worth at a time. They usually ordered only a jackpot or two of cereal, milk, honey, or wine.

King Charles I, who lived in the 1600's, was a reckless spender and soon drained the royal treasury. In order to raise more money, he decided to put a sales tax on the jackpot. As if that weren't bad enough, he also made the size of the jackpot smaller! Not only did the poor people have to pay more than they did before when they bought a jackpot of cereal, but they were now getting less cereal!

Before long, the jackpot—and the jill along with it—went out of use as units of measure. The people could not express their anger openly over the trick tax move. But they did make their feelings known by making up a rhyming joke: "Jack and Jill went up the hill to fetch a pail of water; Jack fell down and broke his crown, and Jill came tumbling after." The "crown" in the rhyme refers, of course, to the king, and "Jack" and "Jill" are the "fallen" (in value) units of measure.

As with the yard, many other English units changed from place to place and time to time before the government eventually standardized

all units. The English mile at one time was 6,000 feet. At another time it was 5,000 feet. In addition, a mile of 5,000 feet often was longer or shorter in one county than it was in another. Once again, the people expressed their annoyance over such a lack of order with the following verse.

There was a crooked man,
And he walked a crooked mile,
*   He found a crooked sixpence*
Against a crooked stile;
*   He bought a crooked cat,*
Which caught a crooked mouse,
*   And they all lived together*
In a little crooked house.

Probably there are many other Mother Goose rhymes and innocent nursery songs that were written for the same reason these were.

The outcry from the public came because it was so easy for people to be cheated by sly merchants. When a person bought something, he or she wanted a "full measure." But a full measure in one shop was not the same full measure used in another shop down the street.

By 1592, many of the differences over what a "full measure" should be had been cleared up. But others still remained, and they remained for more than 200 years. A traveler through the British Isles could find at least four different quantities for the unit of measure called the *peck*. A trader who bought a peck of potatoes in Ireland, where the peck was long (larger), and then sold it in Scotland, where the peck was short, would make a profit. Knowing where to buy long and sell short was an art that any successful trader soon learned. Still, the British were trying to develop standard units of measure, but the change was a slow one.

The French, too, were giving their units of measure a standard, but in a much better way than the English were going about it. While the English kept to their old units based on parts of the body, the French invented new units. Their basic unit of length was called the *meter*. The meter was also used as a base to work out units of volume and mass (or weight).

In the 1700's, the French measured the curvature of the earth's surface at different places and figured out the distance from the North Pole to the equator. They agreed to call one ten-millionth of that distance one meter (which is equal to 39.37 inches). Later, they made a master meter stick by marking that distance on a bar of metal made of platinum and iridium. The bar is kept at the same temperature day and night so that it will not stretch or shrink.

In the early 1900's, the distance from the poles to the equator was measured more accurately than it had been two centuries earlier. It was found that the distance marked on the master meter stick was not exactly one ten-millionth of the pole–equator distance. There was no need to change the length of the meter unit, though, because it does not really matter whether it is exactly one ten-millionth of the pole–equator distance or not. What does matter is that everyone agrees that the length of a meter is exactly the same as the distance marked on the platinum–iridium bar. And that is what a *standard* is—something to which everyone agrees.

Once the length of the meter was agreed upon, other units of length could be based on it. The units were 10 times (decameter), 100 times (hectometer), 1,000 times (kilometer), and so on, longer than the meter. Or the units were 1/10 (decimeter), 1/100 (centimeter), 1/1,000 (millimeter), and so on, smaller.

This system of measuring, called the *metric system*, is now used through most of the world. Once you are familiar with it, it is much easier to use than the clumsy English system. Until recently, the United States was the only major nation using a system of measurement based on the length of Queen Elizabeth's arm.

An International Language

As soon as the metric system was introduced, scientists all over the world saw what an excellent system it was. It would serve as an international "language" of measurement. This would make it easy for scientists, engineers, and traders in one country to exchange information with their colleagues in other countries. Today, all scientists use the metric system.

Thomas Jefferson, President of the United States from 1801 to 1809, was a scientist. He knew of the French development of the metric system and saw its advantages over the English system. Being President at the time the metric system was still new, he was also in a good posi-tion to encourage its use in the United States. But for some reason he did not.

Soon Congress came to see the advantages of changing over to the metric system. In 1866, an act was passed that made the metric system legal for use in the United States. It took more than a hundred years, however, to become official.

Understanding What You've Read

1. What was the greatest problem with measuring units based on parts of the body?
2. Where does the word *stadium* come from?
3. How was the length of the meter determined?

Applying the Skills Lesson

1. What generalization can you make regarding the measurements invented by the early Egyptians? What details from the selection could you use to support your generalization?
2. Based on the information in the selection, what generalization can you make regarding nursery rhymes? What information leads you to make this generalization?

Try to make some generalizations as you read this selection.

For hundreds of years they lived in a rain forest, isolated from other human beings. It was not until the 1970's that the world finally met . . .

THE TASADAY:
Cave People of the Philippines

by Rebecca B. Marcus

On June 7, 1971, a helicopter landed in the rain forest of Mindanao in the Philippines. Out stepped one man, Manuel Elizalde, who had come to make contact with the Tasaday. These people, he had heard, lived in caves on a wild, almost unexplored part of the island. From the Tasaday, Elizalde hoped to learn how the early Stone Age people lived.

As soon as the helicopter touched down, one frightened member of the Tasaday tribe stepped out of the forest to greet Elizalde. Little by little, Elizalde was able to gain the man's confidence. Soon, more Tasaday appeared, curious to see the stranger who had dropped from the sky. During Elizalde's visits to the forest they told him much about their way of living. Yet it was eight months before they invited him to their settlement.

The Cave People

In the Filippino language, the name *Tasaday* means "People of the Caves." And this is indeed what Elizalde saw. Twenty-seven people were living in a few limestone caves in a cliff overlooking a rushing stream.

Thick forest growth hides the Tasaday settlement so well that it cannot be seen from the air. Sometimes it is impossible to spot from just a few yards away. There are no roads in this part of the forest. Except by helicopter, there is no way to reach the settlement from the outside. The Tasaday have been living apart from other groups in the forest caves for possibly a thousand years.

No one knows how the Tasaday first came to this forest. They are, however, native Filippinos. They are of slight build, have brown skin, high cheekbones, and dark, curly hair.

The Tasaday have no need of a chief or leader. They share their food and few, simple tools. These gentle people live in peace and harmony with each other. There are no words in their language for anger, war, or weapons.

A family is made up of a husband and wife and their children. Sometimes there are three generations living together. Each family collects its own firewood and does its own cooking. But children are free to wander over to another family and eat with them if they are hungry and their own meal is not ready.

There is plenty of food to be found in the forest, so there is no need to store or grow any. The Tasaday dig up wild yams—their main food—and find bananas, palm-leaf buds, ginger, berries, and other forest plants. Crabs, tadpoles, frogs, and small fish are special delicacies. The ones that are not eaten as soon as they are caught are wrapped in a leaf, twisted into a cone, and brought back to the family.

The Tasaday use very simple tools. A hammer is a rock from the river, bound with a vine to a piece of wood. A scraper, used for sharpening bamboo strips into knives, is made from a piece of stone ground to a sharp edge. Leaves or lengths of hollowed bamboo are used as dishes and pots.

The Changes Begin

In the 1960's, a chance meeting with a man from another tribe brought about a few important changes in the lives of the Tasaday. The man's name was Dafal. He was a trapper from the Blit tribe, which lives a little more than a day's foot-journey away. The Blit people are more advanced than the Tasaday because they have sought contact with the outside world. They use iron tools, live in thatched huts, raise cattle, and plant some crops.

One day, Dafal went deeper into the rain forest than usual to set his traps. Suddenly he came across two men who, frightened by the stranger dressed in clothing they had never seen, started to flee. Dafal called out not to be afraid. He promised he would not harm them. The men seemed to understand. Slowly they came toward him. Dafal and the Tasaday were able to talk with each other since their languages are very much alike.

After a while the Tasaday became curious about Dafal's iron knife, his animal traps, and his clothing. Dafal, in turn, was curious about people who had never seen such things before. At his suggestion, Dafal returned with the Tasaday to their settlement.

After seeing where the Tasaday lived, Dafal understood why no one had known about them. They never had to go more than a mile along the riverbank for food. They did not hunt, made no paths in the forest, and never sought contact with others.

Dafal quickly set about introducing the People of the Caves to different kinds of food. He taught them to set animal traps. He also gave them some bows and arrows, a few iron-tipped spears, some simple tools, bits of cloth, and three knives.

Dafal showed the Tasaday how to prepare a new food called *natek*. With the knives he had given them, they cut down palm trees and split them. Then they scooped out the center and actually made the food. Until that time, the Tasaday had eaten only what they could pick or catch without traps, hooks, or nets. After they learned to make natek, they did not have to depend on the wild yam as their chief food. They found the natek nourishing and tasty. As they themselves say, "We have become fatter."

For the most part, the Tasaday have given up the bows and arrows and spears that Dafal brought. They do not seem to want to learn the skills needed to use them. So far, they have not become good trappers either, and they do not set traps often. They have, however, developed a liking for meat. When they do set traps, they catch wild chickens, monkeys, wild pigs, and, once in a while, a deer.

Although the Tasaday occasionally enjoy meat, their diet is predominantly vegetarian.

PANAMIN

For several years, Dafal was almost the only outside person who had ever seen a Tasaday. In time, however, a few people from other tribes also got to know the Tasaday and were able to learn a little of their language. In 1971, Dafal took a bold step. He had learned that the Philippine Association for National Minorities — PANAMIN—was searching for hidden tribes. Dafal sent word that he knew of such a tribe. The chief of PANAMIN, Manuel Elizalde, was excited by this information and made plans to seek out the Tasaday.

Since Elizalde first met the Ta-

saday he has become their trusted friend. When they hear the sound of his helicopter, "the big bird," they leave whatever they are doing and head for the clearing where it is to land. Elizalde brings medicine and iron tools. He has also taught the Tasaday to count, something they enjoy doing very much.

But more important, PANAMIN has gotten the Philippine government to set aside 55,000 acres of the forest for a national reserve. All logging has been stopped in this part of the forest. Very few outsiders are allowed to enter the reserve. Those who do may not bring in tools or presents unless approved by PANAMIN. The government believes the Tasaday should not be pushed into a way of life they may not want.

The Tasaday are bright and alert. They have learned much from the anthropologists who come to study them and to learn how early Stone Age people lived. When they see ways of making their lives more comfortable, they are quick to adopt them.

At one time, their caves were completely bare, and the floors were dusty and sooty from their fires. Now the Tasaday build low platforms spread with bamboo and split bark, just as they have seen the anthropologists do in their tents.

It is too soon to know how much their lives will be changed after having seen "great wonders" such as helicopters, cameras, and transistor radios. PANAMIN hopes the Tasaday tribe stays very much as it is, safe in its own territory. But what will happen as the children grow up? Will they be content living in caves? As yet, no one can tell.

Understanding What You've Read

1. How did Dafal discover the Tasaday?
2. How did the Tasaday's way of life change after their encounter with Dafal?
3. What steps are being taken by PANAMIN to preserve the Tasaday's way of life?

Applying the Skills Lesson

Based on the information presented in the selection, which of the following generalizations are valid? Explain why you think so.
1. Tribes of people can exist completely isolated from the world for hundreds of years.
2. Primitive people can never adapt to a modern society.
3. People can survive on foods found in the forest.
4. All primitive people are peaceful.
5. Even primitive societies have a counting system.
6. People can communicate with each other even though they speak different languages.

TEXTBOOK STUDY

Generalizing

As you read your textbooks, you will come across generalizations. Critical reading means being able to recognize the authors' generalizations and judge their validity. As you read the following textbook excerpt, refer to the sidenotes. They will help you identify the generalizations.

Generalizing in Language Arts

What about interests, ideas, abilities?

Stop and think about yourself and the people you know. You'll probably find that your ideas and interests vary from theirs a good deal. You may be interested in going out for sports, while your closest friend prefers playing in the band. You're studying math and science, while he or she considers English and history far more interesting.

The author is making a generalization about people. Can you think of any exceptions?

Your father may be a lifelong Democrat and your uncle, a staunch Republican, while your aunt is an "independent" voter who believes it's the person and not the party that counts.

What generalization does the author make in this last paragraph? How does the author support the generalization?

People differ widely in their talents and abilities, too. Some individuals are highly talented in music or art, while others can't play a note or draw a straight line. Some are very skilled in public speaking; others can't give the briefest speech without getting acute stage fright. One person may be handy with tools, while another can't drive a nail straight. Some of your friends can read dozens of books and clearly remember the important dates and events and ideas in each.

492

Others have trouble remembering what they read but can easily recall things they hear.

—*Patterns of Language*
American Book Company

Building Skills

1. How does the author support the generalization in the second paragraph? Is the generalization valid or faulty? Why?
2. Which of the following facts could the author have used to support the generalization stated in the fourth paragraph, "People differ widely in their talents and abilities"?
   a. Two people filled out questionnaires. The results showed that they had different abilities.
   b. One thousand people filled out questionnaires. The results showed that they had different abilities.
   c. The author noticed that the members of one family played different musical instruments.

Generalizing in Science

The following textbook excerpt is not accompanied by sidenotes. As you read, look for the generalizations. Then answer the questions that follow.

Relating the Concepts

Schleiden and Schwann developed the cell theory more than a hundred years ago in 1839. They stated that the cell is the unit of structure and function for all living things. They based their work on the investigations of many scientists of many nations—Leeuwenhoek, Hooke, Dutrochet, Malpighi.

Today, the cell theory is still true (except for such organisms as the viruses). But it has been extended greatly.

Through the study of living things, you come to know the beauty of the organization of living things. Their organization seems so simple, so economical in design. Yet there is unity. The unit of organization of the multicellular organism is the cell. The cell is also the unit of function.

— Life: A Biological Science
Harcourt Brace Jovanovich

Building Skills

1. a. What generalization is stated in the first paragraph?
   b. What is the exception to this generalization?
   c. Is the generalization valid? Why or why not?
2. Which of the following statements are generalizations?
   a. Schleiden and Schwann developed the cell theory more than a hundred years ago in 1839.
   b. Through the study of living things, you come to know the beauty of the organization of living things.
   c. Living things' organization seems so simple, so economical in design.
   d. The unit of organization of the multicellular organism is the cell.

SKILLS LESSON

A Different Way to Look at It . . .
Recognizing Slanted Writing

Why do you think the man in the cartoon prefers to have people think of his clothes as *lively*? What kind of picture forms in your mind when you hear the word? Is it different from the picture you get when someone uses the word *loud* to describe clothes?

The man in the cartoon is using **slanted language.** He wants to get people to think of his manner of dress in a certain way. He probably considers the word *lively* more flattering than the word *loud.*

Authors also use slanted language in order to get you to agree with their opinions. Many times, only one word is enough to influence your way of looking at something.

For example, read the two columns of statements below.

A	B
Joanne paid $1,000 for that car.	Joanne paid $1,000 for that lemon!
Luis's party was quiet.	Luis's party was boring.

Notice that the two sentences in each column give you totally different pictures of the car and the party. After reading the first sentence in column A, you might believe that Joanne got a good deal on the car. The first sentence in column B, however, substitutes the word *lemon* for the word *car.* Now what is your impression of the deal that Joanne made? What does the word *quiet* suggest about Luis's party? What does the word *boring* suggest? Since the words do not mean the same thing, they create two different pictures in your mind about the party.

Objective Writing and Slanted Writing

When authors give you all the important information and expect you to draw conclusions from it, they are writing **objectively.** Encyclopedias and most of your textbooks are written objectively. So are many books and newspapers and magazine articles. The following paragraph presents information objectively.

The word *bowdlerize,* which means "to censor beyond reason," comes from the actions of Dr. Thomas Bowdler. Bowdler said that some writers, such as Shakespeare, were not fit to be read. He published his own versions of books and plays in which he had cut large portions of the original material.

This paragraph was written objectively because the author presented only the facts about Bowdler. The author was careful not to make any statements that could not be proved. Moreover, the author did not offer his or her own opinions about Bowdler. The author is leaving it up to you to draw your own conclusions.

Suppose, however, that the author wanted to convince you that Bowdler was foolish. He or she might have written the paragraph differently, using slanted language along with the facts.

Dr. Thomas Bowdler was a quack who couldn't stand sickness or the sight of blood. He left his practice in London and traveled in Europe, calling himself "the Reverend Doctor." This humorless buffoon felt that Shakespeare and other great writers were "objectionable" and "not fit to be put into the hands of children." So Bowdler cut out the most important parts of these authors' works. For example, he made the evil Macbeth appear to be an angel. With insane vanity, Bowdler claimed that, because of his bowdlerizing, "no man ever did better service to Shakespeare."

The information in this paragraph is not presented objectively. Some examples of the slanted language used are:

- quack
- humorless buffoon
- insane vanity

In addition to these phrases, the author presents facts that make Bowdler look ridiculous. The reader, therefore, is led to believe that Bowdler was a fool.

Information That Is Omitted

Sometimes a writer presents only one side of the story by leaving out or ignoring several key facts. Read the advertisement below. What does the writer lead you to believe about the house?

HOUSE FOR SALE
Two-story hillside home located on large wooded lot.
Very private. Wood-burning fireplace. Front yard. Terrain suitable
for cross-country skiing.   Sterling Rawel Agency   731-4556

When you compare the picture of the house to the information given in the advertisement, you can see that the writer did not state anything that wasn't true. The house does indeed have two stories, and it certainly is located on a large wooded lot. No one can argue that it isn't private. However, many facts have been left out. For example, you are not told that the large wooded lot is 1,500 hectares of untouched forest! You also are not told that the single wood-burning fireplace is the only source of heat for the entire house. Although the house has two stories, the second is nothing more than a loft you reach by ladder. The advertisement, therefore, is slanted, because the writer has omitted several key details that would probably influence your decision about the house. What other details would you want to know before seriously considering buying the property?

498

Try This

Which sentence in each pair below is an example of slanted writing?

1. a. Hugo Wallaby, who plays for the Grover City baseball team, can't hit the broadside of a barn.

   b. Hugo Wallaby, who plays for the Grover City baseball team, has a batting average of .143.

2. a. The thirty-three children in Mrs. Sims's fourth-grade class visited the Museum of Science and Industry.

   b. The Museum of Science and Industry was invaded by the thirty-three screaming monsters in Mrs. Sims's fourth-grade class.

3. a. Two hundred people were cured with the experimental vaccine.

   b. Of the 8,000 people who were given the experimental vaccine, 200 people were cured.

The Problem . . . Multiple Meanings

"We're sick of all this confusion, Mr. Property," said the definitions. "One Word, One Definition! That's our motto. Take *digit*, for example. It can either mean 'a finger or toe' or 'a number.'"

"Look here," shouted one definition of *flounder*. "As 'a food fish,' I refuse to share the same word with 'to move clumsily'!"

"But those are the two definitions of *flounder*," said Mr. Property. "Please, everyone. Try to be reasonable."

"Reasonable!" cried one definition of *reflect*. "I am 'to change the direction of light.' The other meaning of *reflect*, 'to think or

500

consider,' is always getting my phone calls."

"But that's how our language works," said Mr. Property. "Just think of yourselves as having two different personalities. Of course, I don't have your problem."

"Oh, really?" cried the definitions. "Then suppose you tell us why sometimes you can mean 'a quality or trait,' and other times you're 'a piece of real estate.'"

Mr. Property smiled weakly. "Know something?" he said. "Suddenly I'm beginning to understand your problem."

Word Play

Which word above and which definition describe:

1. something found in a pair of gloves
2. something that can be eaten
3. something to build a house on
4. what a mirror does

As you read this selection, watch for examples of slanted writing.

With our feet firmly on the ground, we turn our eyes skyward and murmur . . .

IF I HAD WINGS

by Harvey S. Firestone, Jr.

From the earliest days, people looked at the birds and wished they could fly.

According to a Greek myth, a man named Daedalus made wings of feathers, wax, and thread for himself and his son Icarus. In vain, Daedalus warned the boy not to fly too close to the sun. Excited over gaining the power of flight, Icarus sailed higher and higher. Soon the sun began to heat the wax in his new wings. They melted, and the boy fell into the sea. Daedalus alone reached safety.

Another myth tells us that Kai Kawaus [kī kä·wä′əs], a Persian king, had a carriage built with cornerposts made of spears. Pieces of meat were placed on the spears, just out of reach of four young eagles that were hitched to the frame. As the eagles beat upward trying to get at the meat, the carriage rose after them into the sky.

Yet these stories long remained only stories. People still could not fly.

A Few Rough Landings

Science began to consider flying in the thirteenth century. An Englishman named Roger Bacon proposed filling a large globe of thin copper with hot air. This was to be launched from some high place, like the top of a mountain. According to Bacon, it would "float like a vessel on water."

It was the sixteenth century before anyone is known to have tried to fly. In January of 1503, Giovanni Battista Danti carried a glider of some sort up the tower of a church in Perugia. It was his idea to fly off the ramparts. The machine caught on the building, however, and crashed. Danti suffered a broken leg.

Next came Leonardo da Vinci. Leonardo spent hours just watching birds. He believed that people could learn to fly in the same way that birds do. He designed wing-flapping machines, as well as a helicopter, parachute, and a lifejacket for a flier downed in water. By 1505 or 1506, he was ready to try his hand at flying. He settled on a wing-flapping machine for the trip. He chose a mountain for the launching place.

That was all, though. Leonardo never quite "got off the ground."

Flap Those Wings!

For nearly three more centuries, most of the people who dreamed about flying and tried to figure out how to do it used or copied birds. Flapping wings were the rage. The flier either went into space carried by a flock of well-trained birds, flapped his or her own wings, or rode in a machine that used flapping wings.

Some scientists were on the right track. Giovanni Alfonso Borelli pointed out in 1680 that human beings couldn't lift their own weight by just flapping their arms.

But people kept building wings and trying to fly with them. As late as 1742, the Marquis de Bacqueville [mär·kē' də bäk·(ə·)vēl'] jumped from a riverside Paris building, hoping to fly across the Seine River. Instead, he fell in a heap on a washerwoman's barge.

Two French brothers straightened out the world's thinking and got it flying. Joseph and Etienne Montgolfier [ā·tyen' môn·gôl·fyā'] were papermakers, but they were more interested in studying the nature of air.

One November day in 1782, Joseph had an idea. He asked his landlady for a scrap of silk, cut it, and sewed it into an oblong bag. He then held the bag mouth down over his fireplace to catch the smoke. The bag began to swell. When it looked full, he took it away from the fire and let go of it. It shot to the ceiling, startling his landlady and exciting him.

"Get a supply of taffeta and ropes," he shouted. "You will see one of the most astonishing things in the world!" He instantly wrote to his brother.

The Montgolfiers were careful, scientific workers. They were hot on the trail of a discovery that they were sure would make them world famous. Yet they took their time. Their first outdoor experiment, made secretly, was a success. A balloon rose seventy feet before it settled to earth. But they made two more private tests anyway, with bigger balloons and thicker smoke. They seem to have felt that the thicker the smoke in the bag, the better its lifting properties. On June 4, 1783, the people of Annonay saw a great linen-and-paper bag rise 6,000 feet after it had been filled with smoke.

Startled, the Academy of Sciences invited the Montgolfiers to exhibit their balloon in Paris. Their show was so successful that the brothers decided to try something extra. They attached a basket to their balloon and loaded it with a rooster, a duck, and a sheep. After a one-and-a-half-mile flight, the three animals landed dizzy but safe.

Into the Air, Sort Of

Less than one year after the Montgolfiers' balloons, a young French doctor named Jean-François Pilâtre de Rozier [zhäN'fräN·swä' pē·lä'trə də rō·zyā'] became the first person in history to fly. Pilâtre de Rozier made two ascents in a Montgolfier-type hot-air balloon that was held to the ground by ropes. On November 21, 1783, with the Marquis d'Arlandes [mär·kē' där·länd'], he made the first balloon flight.

The balloon they used was seventy feet high and forty-six feet in diameter. It had gold designs all over it and carried its own smoke-making source. Pilâtre de Rozier and the Marquis d'Arlandes took off in it from gardens outside Paris. And what a flight they had!

Early in the flight, the marquis discovered that sparks from the fire were burning holes in the ropes that held the balloon. Worse still, the sparks were burning the balloon itself! Quickly, the marquis splashed the bottom of the balloon and the ropes with water.

After a five-mile ride the balloonists headed for a landing. The age of flight had been born.

Europe became balloon wild. Everyone thought, talked, and dreamed balloons. They were woven into tablecloths, painted on fans, and used as clock designs. And everyone who could went up in a balloon. A Madame Thimble was the first woman to fly in France, in June 1784. In 1785, Mrs. L. A. Sage became the first woman to fly in England.

The balloonists were ready to try anything. About a year after the marquis's flight, the English Channel was crossed in a balloon by a Frenchman, Jean-Pierre François Blanchard, and Dr. John Jeffries, his English sponsor. They had a hair-raising trip from Dover, England, to France. They had to throw almost everything they had overboard to lighten the load, but they landed safely in a clearing near Calais.

One Englishman, Charles Green, made over 500 flights and took up thousands of people without any trouble. In 1836, he made the first long cross-country (and cross-water) flight, from London to Germany, in a beautiful red-and-white-striped balloon. The trip took eighteen hours.

505

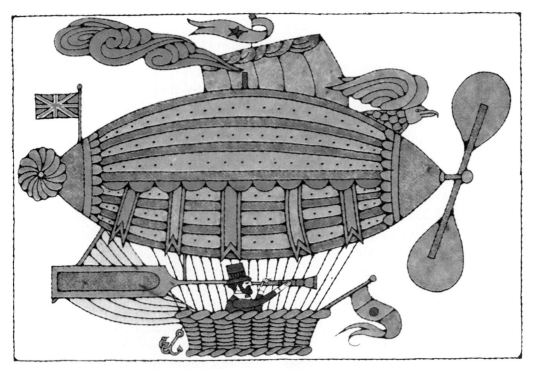

Two other Englishmen, Henry Coxwell and James Glaisher, got up 37,000 feet in a balloon.

Controlling the balloon was a problem for the aeronauts from the very first. Some people suggested that balloons be made with oars, paddlewheels, trained eagles, and sails. It soon became clear that the two things needed to give the flier control over the balloon were a more easily directed shape and a mechanical source of power.

The shape was easy. A Frenchman, M. J. Brisson, built a cigar-shaped balloon in 1784.

The main problem was the source of power. All known types were tested. In 1852, the famous French balloonist, Henri Giffard, built a 132-foot, cigar-shaped balloon. A three-horsepower steam engine beneath it turned a propeller. If the winds were not too bad, it could do six miles an hour. But the steam engine was too heavy for practical use.

By now, some deep thinking on heavier-than-air flights was going on, and the outcome was to cause quite a few changes.

An Englishman named Sir George Cayley built the first truly steerable glider in 1804. During the next half-century he built many more. One was so big that it carried a ten-year-old boy off the ground for several yards. He built one in 1854 that was as large as a World War II fighter craft. He talked his coachman into going up for a flight in it.

"Please, Sir George," the frightened servant said after he'd flown across a little valley. "I wish to give notice. I was hired to drive and not to fly."

At about the same time, William Samuel Henson was working out an idea of his for a powered, fixed-wing airplane. With the help of a mechanic, Henson built a twenty-foot model of it.

Also at that time, Jean-Marie Le Bris built a glider with graceful, down-curved wings that measured fifty feet tip to tip. When he was ready to test his craft in 1855, it was placed on a farm cart hauled by a horse. Le Bris gave the go-ahead. The driver urged the horse forward into the wind. As the cart picked up speed, Le Bris twisted the wings of the glider to catch the air, and the glider rose to a height of 300 feet.

After he had flown about 200 yards, Le Bris saw that the driver of the cart had become tangled in a rope trailing from the glider. He was swinging, terrified, beneath him. Very carefully, Le Bris descended until the man was once again on the ground. Then he safely landed his glider.

Octave Chanute of the United States was best known for his experiments with devices to make gliders more stable. A kindly, warm-hearted man, Chanute was the person to whom newcomers to the field turned for advice. In May 1900, Chanute received a letter from a fellow in Ohio. The letter read:

For some years I have been afflicted with the belief that flight is possible. . . .

The letter was signed Wilbur Wright.

Success at Last

It was December 1903. Wilbur and Orville Wright headed for Kitty Hawk, North Carolina. They had a big new biplane that they hoped to fly under power.

They moved the airship out to the top of a sixty-foot monorail track that had been laid to guide the plane down a sand dune.

The plane had two pairs of forty-foot fabric-covered wings, one above the other. The pilot had to lie flat on the lower wing. In front of him was the front rudder, with which he could control the rising and falling of the machine. Behind him were two rudders to steer right or left. On either side of his feet were the propellers.

They flipped a coin, and Wilbur won first try.

It was only a fair day for flying. The wind was light and not coming from quite the right direction. However, Wilbur was later to blame his failure to fly that day not on the weather, but on his poor judgment in trying to get the plane into the air too quickly. It stalled and crashed.

By December 17, the Wright brothers were ready to try again. This time it was Orville's turn. The wind was blowing at more than twenty miles an hour from the north. The monorail track had been laid on flat land. The sole onlookers were five men from a nearby lifesaving station.

Just after ten-thirty in the morning, the plane began to move along the track into the wind. Wilbur ran beside it, steadying the right wing. One of the lifesaving men snapped what was to become a very famous picture: the first controlled, powered plane to fly, with its wings five feet off the ground.

This, at last, was true flight, and it produced one of history's greatest changes. Human beings were off the ground and in the air.

Understanding What You've Read

1. In what ways did people copy birds in an attempt to fly?
2. What major contribution did the Montgolfier brothers make to the world of flight? Why can their work be considered a "turning point"?
3. How does this selection illustrate the inventiveness and determination of human beings? Use examples from the selection to support your answer.

Applying the Skills Lesson

The first sentence in each of the following pairs appears in the selection you just read. The second sentence is another way of saying the same thing. Which sentence in each pair is an example of slanted writing?

1. a. Europe became balloon wild.
   b. Europeans became interested in ballooning.
2. a. The balloonists were ready to try anything.
   b. Many balloonists were very courageous.
3. a. He [Sir George Cayley] talked his coachman into going up for a flight in it [the glider].
   b. Sir George Cayley used a servant as a guinea-pig passenger in his makeshift glider.

TEXTBOOK STUDY

Recognizing Slanted Writing

Most textbooks authors try to be objective when presenting information. Sometimes, however, you will come across slanted writing. As you read the following textbook selection, the sidenotes will help you recognize the slanted writing.

Recognizing Positive Slanted Writing in Social Studies

A Cosmopolitan City

New York has long been considered the gateway to the United States. The Statue of Liberty, standing at the entrance to New York Harbor, has welcomed millions of immigrants to this country. A steady flow of tourists and travelers come to dine at its famous restaurants and to visit the city's concert halls, theaters, museums, and art galleries.

What does this word mean?

Thousands of students attend New York's many colleges and universities. It is the home of the United Nations. This makes New York a diplomatic center.

Nearly all of the people who visit New York admire the famous skyline and take a trip to the top of the Empire State Building.

The author talks about many places in the city in a positive way. What kinds of places has the author left out?

Natives of New York City, on the other hand, look upon the few blocks which surround their apartment house or building as their "hometown." For them, this is the most important part of the city.

What kind of picture do you have of this city after reading the selection? Why?

—*World Geography Today*
Holt, Rinehart & Winston

509

Building Skills

1. Each of the phrases below appears in the selection you just read. Do these phrases create positive or negative images about the city?
   a. the gateway to the United States
   b. has welcomed millions
   c. its famous restaurants
   d. many colleges and universities
   e. a diplomatic center
   f. admire the famous skyline
2. What impression does the author want the reader to have about the city?

Recognizing Negative Slanted Writing in Social Studies

There are no sidenotes accompanying this textbook selection. As you read, compare this picture of a city to the one described in the previous selection. Look for the ways the author uses negative slanted language. Then answer the questions that follow.

Security Versus Change

Often, newcomers find it hard to accept life in the cities. Emigrants from rural areas face many unknowns when they go to live in a large city. Many of them choose to move to the biggest cities in the United States. Once they are there, they must learn many new ways. They must learn them very quickly if they are to stay because they have no choice about going back until they earn enough money to do so.

Many aspects of city life may be quite different and even unpleasant to new-comers. Riding buses and trains may prove very unsettling at first. The city's sanitation system may seem very elaborate and expensive, yet it does not keep the city as clean as their former home was, where there were fewer people.

Many people come to the city with money, or with jobs waiting for them, only to find that they need much more money to live in the city than they expected. The higher costs of renting shelter and buying food and clothes may be a complete surprise.

Many others do not have jobs when they arrive in the city. They come looking for better work than they had back home. However, they may not be skilled for the jobs that are available. How do you think the unemployed and unskilled people survive in the cities?

— Sources of Identity
Harcourt Brace Jovanovich

Building Skills

1. Each of the following phrases appears in the selection you just read. Do the phrases create positive or negative images about the city?
   a. newcomers find it hard
   b. emigrants from rural areas face many unknowns
   c. they must learn many new ways
   d. they have no choice about going back
   e. riding buses and trains may prove very unsettling
   f. the higher costs of renting shelter
2. What impression does the author want the reader to have about the city?

Books About Changes

Words from History by Isaac Asimov. Houghton Mifflin, 1968. *The author traces the interesting and often humorous histories of many English words.*

Victoria, Queen and Empress by Neil Grant. Watts, 1970. *This is the interesting biography of Queen Victoria, whose reign was the longest in the history of Great Britain.*

The Elusive Zebra by D. C. Ipsen. Addison-Wesley, 1971. *Here Ipsen explains the usefulness of the zebra's stripes and the way colors and patterns serve as protection for a number of animals.*

Wonders of Measurement by Owen S. Lieberg. Dodd, 1972. *This concise book includes information about systems of measurement, as well as instructions for measuring various things.*

The World of Mary Cassatt by Robin McKown. T. Y. Crowell, 1972. *The life and times and artistic accomplishments of Mary Cassatt are detailed in this engrossing biography.*

Guideposts to the Stars by Leslie Peltier. Macmillan, 1972. *This is a clear, easy-to-understand introduction to stargazing. The author explains how to locate many of the constellations by using fifteen of the brightest stars as guides.*

Indians of the Southern Plains by William K. Powers. Putnam, 1971. *The Cheyenne, Iowa, Pawnee, Kiowa, and Osage are a few of the many tribes discussed in this informative book.*

Historic Plane Models: Their Stories and How to Make Them by Frank Ross, Jr. Lothrop, 1973. *This book provides simple instructions for building models of famous aircraft, such as the Spirit of Saint Louis.*

People in Twilight: Vanishing and Changing Cultures by Adrien Stoutenburg. Doubleday, 1971. *Included are descriptions of the Eskimos, the Australian aborigines, the Pygmies, and other cultures that are being affected by our technological society.*

512

Glossary

This glossary is a little dictionary. It contains the difficult words found in this book. The pronunciation, which tells you how to say the word, is given next to each word. That is followed by the word's meaning or meanings. Sometimes, a different form of the word follows the definition. It appears in boldface type.

The special symbols used to show the pronunciation are explained in the key that follows.

PRONUNCIATION KEY*

a	add, map	m	move, seem	u	up, done
ā	ace, rate	n	nice, tin	û(r)	urn, term
â(r)	care, air	ng	ring, song	yōo	use, few
ä	palm, father	o	odd, hot	v	vain, eve
b	bat, rub	ō	open, so	w	win, away
ch	check, catch	ô	order, jaw	y	yet, yearn
d	dog, rod	oi	oil, boy	z	zest, muse
e	end, pet	ou	out, now	zh	vision, pleasure
ē	even, tree	ōō	pool, food	ə	the schwa,
f	fit, half	ŏŏ	took, full		an unstressed
g	go, log	p	pit, stop		vowel representing
h	hope, hate	r	run, poor		the sound spelled
i	it, give	s	see, pass		a in above
ī	ice, write	sh	sure, rush		e in sicken
j	joy, ledge	t	talk, sit		i in possible
k	cook, take	th	thin, both		o in melon
l	look, rule	th	this, bathe		u in circus

Foreign: *N* is used following a nasal vowel sound:
French *Jean* [zhäN]

In the pronunciations an accent mark (′) is used to show which syllable of a word receives the most stress. The word *bandage* [ban′dij], for example, is stressed on the first syllable. Sometimes there is also a lighter accent mark (′) that shows where there is a lighter stress, as in the word *combination* [kom′bə·nā′shən].

The following abbreviations are used throughout the glossary: *n.,* noun; *pron.,* pronoun; *v.,* verb; *adj.,* adjective; *adv.,* adverb; *prep.,* preposition; *conj.,* conjunction; *interj.,* interjection; *pl.,* plural; *sing.,* singular.

---

*The Pronunciation Key and the short form of the key that appears on the following right-hand pages are reprinted from *The HBJ School Dictionary,* copyright © 1977, 1972, 1968 by Harcourt Brace Jovanovich, Inc.

A

a·bid·ing [ə·bī′ding] *adj.* Continuing without changing or growing less; lasting.

a·bol·ish [ə·bol′ish] *v.* To do away with; put an end to.

a·bom·in·a·ble [ə·bom′in·ə·bəl] *adj.* Horrible.

a·bun·dance [ə·bun′dəns] *n.* A full or plentiful supply.

ac·com·plished [ə·kom′plisht] *adj.* Skillful, as in an art or in social graces; well-trained.

ac·quaint [ə·kwānt′] *v.* To introduce; make known to: *acquaint* someone with the law.

a·cre·age [ā′kər·ij] *n.* The number of acres in an area.

a·cute [ə·kyōot′] *adj.* **1** Sharp; intense: *acute* pain. **2** Coming to a sharp point.

ad·min·is·ter [ad·min′is·tər] *v.* To be in charge of; manage.

aer·i·al [âr′ē·əl] *adj.* Of or in the air.

aer·o·naut [âr′ə·nôt] *n.* A person who flies an aircraft, especially a balloon.

af·flict·ed [ə·flik′tid] *v.* Given pain or trouble.

ag·gres·sive [ə·gres′iv] *adj.* Quick to attack or start a fight.

ag·o·niz·ing [ag′ən·īz·ing] *adj.* Very, very painful. — **ag·o·nize,** *v.*

al·gae [al′jē] *n., pl.* A group of simple plants that grow in water and damp places. Algae do not have true roots, stems, or leaves.

al·ge·bra [al′jə·brə] *n.* A branch of mathematics that deals with the relations between numbers and uses letters or other symbols to stand for numbers.

Al·gon·qui·an [al·gong′kwē·ən *or* al·gong′kē·ən] **1** *adj.* Related to the family of languages spoken by many tribes of Native Americans. **2** *n.* A family of languages spoken by many Native American tribes.

al·ly [ə·lī′ *or* al′ī] **1** *n.* A close friend or helper. **2** *v.* To unite for a particular purpose. **3** *n.* A person or country joined with another for a particular purpose. — **al·lies,** *pl.*

al·ma·nac [ôl′mə·nak] *n.* A yearly calendar giving facts about the movements of the sun and moon and predictions about the weather.

al·ter·na·tive [ôl·tûr′nə·tiv] *n.* A choice between two or more things.

am·bled [am′bəld] *v.* Moved at an easy pace.

am·phib·i·an [am·fib′ē·ən] *n.* Any animal, such as the frog, that can live both on land and in water.

am·pu·tee [am′pyōo·tē′] *n.* A person who has had a part of the body (leg, arm, hand, etc.) cut off.

an·thro·pol·o·gist [an′thrə·pol′ə·jist] *n.* A person who studies the ways humans have developed through history, including their customs and beliefs.

ap·praise [ə·prāz′] *v.* To judge the worth of; set a price on.

aq·ua·naut [ak′wə·nôt] *n.* A person who explores deep in the ocean for an extended period of time.

a·quat·ic [ə·kwat′ik] *adj.* Living or growing in or near water.

arc [ärk] *n.* A part of a curve, especially of a circle.

ar·chae·ol·o·gist [är′kē·ol′ə·jist] *n.* A specialist in the study of past times and cultures.

ar·dor [är′dər] *n.* Strong feeling: He loved his puppy with *ardor.*

ar·ti·fact [är′tə·fakt] *n.* Anything made by human work or art.

as·so·ci·a·tion [ə·sō′s(h)ē·ā′shən] *n.* **1** An organization of persons with a common purpose. **2** The act of seeing or making a connection between things.

as·sur·ance [ə·shōor′əns] *n.* A positive statement intended to give confidence.

as·tound·ed [ə·stoun′did] *adj.* Completely surprised; amazed; dumbfounded. — **as·tound,** *v.*

as·tro·naut [as′trə·nôt] *n.* A person who travels in space.

as·tron·o·mer [ə·stron′ə·mər] *n.* A person who studies the stars, planets, and other heavenly bodies.

a·tom·ic clock [ə·tom′ik klok′] *n.* A clock controlled by the radiation of certain atoms or molecules. Such clocks keep very accurate time.

at·trib·ute [ə·trib′yōot] *v.* To consider something as belonging to or caused by something else: Many stories *attribute* slyness to foxes.

a·vi·a·tion [ā′vē·ā′shən] *n.* The science or techniques of building and flying aircraft.

B

bal·loon·ist [bə·lōōn′ist] *n.* A person who rides in or operates a balloon.

ban·do·leer [ban′də·lir′] *n.* A broad belt worn over one shoulder and across the chest. Often a bandoleer has pockets for carrying ammunition or is worn as part of an official or ceremonial costume.

bank·ing [bang′king] *v.* **1** Hitting (a ball) in such a way that it bounces off the rim or edge; a term in billiards. **2** Heaping dirt or snow into a pile.

ban·ter [ban′tər] **1** *v.* To tease or joke playfully. **2** *n.* Playful teasing; joking.

ba·rom·e·ter [bə·rom′ə·tər] *n.* An instrument for measuring air pressure, used in forecasting the weather.

beau·ti·fi·ca·tion [byōō′tə·fə·kā′shən] *n.* The act of making beautiful.

Be·tel·geuse [bēt′(ə)l·jōōz] *n.* A reddish, giant star in the constellation Orion.

bil·liards [bil′yərdz] *n., pl. (takes sing. v.)* A game in which hard balls are hit by long rods called cues, played on an oblong, cloth-covered table with cushioned edges.

bi·plane [bī′plān′] *n.* A type of airplane having two sets of wings, one above the other.

bleak [blēk] *adj.* **1** Gloomy; dismal. **2** Exposed to wind and weather; bare: *bleak* hills.

bog [bog] *n.* Wet and spongy ground, such as a marsh or swamp.

brack·et [brak′it] **1** *n.* A shelf held up by a wooden or metal support. **2** *n.* The support itself. **3** *n.* Part of a group or series: six-to-nine age *bracket.* **4** *n.* Either of two marks, [ ], used to surround and separate inserted words or figures. **5** *v.* To group together.

brake shoe [brāk′ shōō′] *n.* One of two metal pieces that press on a brake drum to slow or stop it.

bra·va·do [brə·vä′dō] *n.* A show of bravery without much real courage or confidence.

brows·ing [brou′zing] *v.* **1** Glancing at a book, reading a little at a time. **2** Feeding on or nibbling at grass, leaves, etc.

buf·foon [bə·fōōn′] *n.* A clown.

bu·reau [byōōr′ō] *n.* **1** A government department. **2** A chest of drawers, usually with a mirror.

C

cam·ou·flage [kam′ə·fläzh] **1** *n.* Any disguise that hides or protects. **2** *n.* The act or technique of using paint, leaves, etc., to change the appearance of military equipment and troops to hide them. **3** *v.* To change the appearance of, so as to hide.

can·o·py [kan′ə·pē] *n.* Any covering overhead. — **can·o·pies,** *pl.*

ca·pa·bil·i·ty [kā′pə·bil′ə·tē] *n.* Ability or skill. — **ca·pa·bil·i·ties,** *pl.*

cap·il·lar·ies [kap′ə·ler′ēz] *n., pl.* Narrow, threadlike blood vessels that connect the arteries with the veins. — **cap·il·lar·y,** *sing.*

car·bon mon·ox·ide [kär′bən mə·nok′sīd] *n.* A colorless, odorless, very poisonous gas given off when fuel is burned.

car·di·nal point [kär′də·nəl point′] *n.* Any of the four main points of the compass: north, east, south, west.

car·ti·lag·i·nous [kär′təl·aj′ə·nis] *adj.* Of or like cartilage, a tough, elastic tissue that connects some bones.

car·toon·ist [kär·tōōn′ist] *n.* A person who draws humorous pictures or comic strips.

caus·tic [kôs′tik] *n.* A substance capable of eating or burning away living tissues.

cel·lu·lose [sel′yə·lōs] *n.* A substance forming the main part of the cell walls of plants.

chlo·ro·plast [klôr′ə·plast] *n.* A part of a plant cell where chlorophyll is found.

cho·re·og·ra·pher [kôr′ē·og′rə·fər] *n.* One who plans the movements for a dance.

chro·nol·o·gy [krə·nol′ə·jē] *n.* A list of events in the order they happened.

cir·cuit [sûr′kit] *n.* **1** A periodic trip through a set of places, usually connected with one's work. **2** A route or path that turns back to where it began.

---

add, āce, câre, pälm; end, ēqual; it, īce; odd, ōpen, ôrder; tŏŏk, pōōl; up, bûrn;
ə = a in *above,* e in *sicken,* i in *possible,* o in *melon,* u in *circus;* yōō = u in *fuse;* oil; pout;
check; ring; thin; this; zh in *vision.*

cir·cum·stance [sûr′kəm·stans] *n.* Something connected with an act, event, etc.: the *circumstances* of a crime.

civ·il ser·vant [siv′əl sûr′vənt] *n.* A person who works for a government.

clas·si·cal [klas′i·kəl] *adj.* 1 Following a strict, established form. 2 Of or characteristic of the culture of ancient Greece or Rome.

clock·work [klok′wûrk′] *n.* A machine driven by a spring, used to run a clock, mechanical toy, etc. —**like clock·work** In a regular, precise, orderly way.

clot [klot] *n.* A mass resulting from the thickening of a liquid, such as blood.

clus·ter [klus′tər] 1 *v.* To group together. 2 *n.* A group of things of the same kind.

cock·pit [kok′pit′] *n.* 1 A low part in the back of the decked area of a small boat from which the boat is steered. 2 The section of some airplanes where the pilot sits.

col·league [kol′ēg] *n.* A fellow worker in a profession or organization; associate.

col·o·ny [kol′ə·nē] *n.* 1 A group of animals or plants of the same kind that live together. 2 A group of people who live in a land separate from, but under the control of, the country from which the group came.

com·mer·cial [kə·mûr′shəl] *adj.* Having to do with financial profit.

com·mis·sion [kə·mish′ən] *n.* 1 A group of people chosen to do certain things: a *commission* to study cable TV. 2 A written paper giving certain powers, rights, and duties.

com·mit·ted [kə·mit′id] *v.* 1 Pledged (oneself); made known one's views: He *committed* himself to support the bill. 2 Done; performed.

com·pact·ed [kəm·pak′tid] *v.* Packed or pressed firmly together.

com·pli·cat·ed [kom′plə·kā′tid] *adj.* Tricky; involved; not simple.

com·po·si·tion [kom′pə·zish′ən] *n.* The organization of the parts of something, as a work of art.

com·rade·ship [kom′rad·ship] *n.* A feeling of close companionship or friendship.

con·ceive [kən·sēv′] *v.* 1 To understand: I can't *conceive* why he would leave. 2 To form an idea.

con·cept [kon′sept] *n.* A general idea.

con·coc·tion [kon·kok′shən *or* kən·kok′shən] *n.* Something, such as food, made by mixing ingredients.

con·firmed [kən·fûrmd′] *v.* Made certain of; verified.

Con·gres·sion·al Dis·trict [kən·gresh′ən·əl dis′trikt] *n.* The designated region from which a member of Congress is elected.

con·i·fer [kon′ə·fər *or* kō′nə·fər] *n.* Any tree or shrub that bears cones, such as the pine, fir, or spruce.

con·ning tow·er [kon′ing tou′ər] *n.* The observation tower of a submarine.

con·stel·la·tion [kon′stə·lā′shən] *n.* A group of stars to which a definite name has been given, such as Orion or the Big Dipper.

con·sum·er [kən·sōō′mər] *n.* A person who uses goods or services.

con·ti·nen·tal shelf [kon′tə·nen′təl shelf′] *n.* A shallow plain under the ocean, forming a border of a continent.

con·tro·ver·sy [kon′trə·vûr′sē] *n.* An argument or debate on a matter about which opinions differ.

con·ven·ient [kən·vēn′yənt] *adj.* Handy.

con·ven·tion·al [kən·ven′shən·əl] *adj.* Usual or ordinary.

con·vey [kən·vā′] *v.* 1 To make known; communicate: *convey* ideas. 2 To carry from one place to another; transport.

coot [kōōt] *n.* A web-footed water bird having short wings.

Cop·tic [kop′tik] *n.* An ancient Egyptian language.

cor·o·nar·y ar·ter·y [kôr′ə·ner′ē är′tər·ē] *n.* Either of the two main blood vessels that supply blood to the heart.

cor·rec·tion [kə·rek′shən] *n.* The act of changing in order to improve.

cor·rec·tive [kə·rek′tiv] 1 *adj.* That corrects or tends to correct: *corrective* measures. 2 *n.* Something that corrects.

cos·mo·naut [koz′mə·nôt] *n.* An astronaut.

cos·mo·pol·i·tan [koz′mə·pol′ə·tən] *adj.* Common to all the world; not local or limited.

cot·y·le·don [kot′ə·lēd′(ə)n] *n.* The first leaf, or either one of the first pair of leaves, sprouting from a seed.

coun·ter·march [koun′tər·märch′] *n.* A march back.

cow·pea [kou′pē′] *n.* **1** A bushlike plant related to the bean, widely grown in the southern United States. **2** The seed of this plant, which can be cooked and eaten as a vegetable. Also called *black-eyed pea.*

crank [krangk] *n.* **1** *informal* A person with strong and unreasonable feelings about something. **2** A part or handle that is used to turn something.

cre·ole [krē′ōl] **1** *adj.* Cooked with tomatoes, peppers, spices, etc.: shrimp *creole.* **2** *n.* (*written* **Creole**) A descendant of the original French settlers in Louisiana.

crit·i·cal [krit′i·kəl] *adj.* **1** Involving judgment as to the truth or value of something. **2** Likely to find fault; disapproving.

crock·er·y [krok′ər·ē] **1** *adj.* Made of baked clay, such as dishes. **2** *n.* Dishes or earthenware so made.

cross sec·tion [krôs′ sek′shən] *n.* A slice, real or imaginary, cut straight across something.

cru·sade [krōō·sād′] *n.* A struggle against evil or for a cause.

cru·sad·er [krōō·sā′dər] *n.* A person who fights in favor of a cause.

crys·tal·lize [kris′tə·līz] *v.* **1** To form or cause to form into crystals. **2** To become clearer and more definite: When did your plans *crystallize?*

cul·ti·vat·ing [kul′tə·vā·ting] *v.* **1** Planting and caring for. **2** Preparing land for the growing of plants.

cu·ri·ous [kyōōr′ē·əs] *adj.* **1** Odd; interesting. **2** Eager to know or learn more.

cur·rent [kûr′ənt] *n.* The part of any body of water or air that flows more or less in the same direction.

cur·va·ture [kûr′və·chər] *n.* A curve or curved condition.

cy·cad [sī′kad] *n.* A kind of tropical plant, usually having a thick trunk with a crown of large, leathery leaves.

cy·to·plasm [sī′tə·plaz′əm] *n.* The basic living matter of a cell outside the nucleus.

D

de·fen·sive [di·fen′siv] *adj.* Protecting.

de·fer [di·fûr′] *v.* To yield to the opinions, wishes, or decisions of another out of respect.

de·fi·ance [di·fī′əns] *n.* Bold opposition to power or authority; refusal to submit or obey.

de·fi·cien·cy [di·fish′ən·sē] *n.* A condition of being lacking or not complete. — **de·fi·cien·cies,** *pl.*

de·gree [di·grē′] *n.* **1** A unit — 1/360 of a circle — used for measuring parts of curves and thus for mapping the earth and locating places on it. **2** A unit for measuring temperature. The symbol for degree is °. **3** A step in a series or a stage in a process.

de·hy·drat·ed [dē·hī′drā·tid] *adj.* Lacking water or moisture; dried. — **de·hy·drate,** *v.*

de·ject·ed [di·jek′tid] *adj.* Unhappy.

del·i·ca·cy [del′ə·kə·sē] *n.* **1** Choice food. **2** Fineness of structure, design, etc.: the *delicacy* of a butterfly wing. — **del·i·ca·cies,** *pl.*

del·ta [del′tə] *n.* A piece of low land shaped like a fan, formed at the mouth of a river by deposits of soil or sand.

de·pressed [di·prest′] *adj.* Gloomy or sad.

de·pres·sion [di·presh′ən] *n.* **1** A low place in a surface; hole. **2** Low spirits; gloom or sadness. **3** (*written* **the De·pres·sion**) A period during the 1930's when business was sharply reduced and a great many people were out of work all over the world.

de·scen·dant [di·sen′dənt] *n.* Someone's child, grandchild, great-grandchild, etc.

de·scend·ed [di·sen′did] *v.* **1** Came or derived by birth from a certain source: *descended* from a duke. **2** Moved from a higher to a lower point.

de·tri·tus [di·trī′təs] *n.* **1** Small bits of crumbly material. **2** Loose particles of rock separated from masses of rock.

---

add, āce, câre, pälm;   end, ēqual;   it, īce;   odd, ōpen, ôrder;   tŏŏk, pōōl;   up, bûrn;
ə = a in *above*, e in *sicken*, i in *possible*, o in *melon*, u in *circus*;   yōō = u in *fuse*;   oil;   pout;
                        check;   ring;   thin;   this;   zh in *vision.*

dig·it [dij′it] *n.* **1** A finger or toe. **2** Any of the numerals from 0 through 9.

dip·lo·mat·ic [dip′lə·mat′ik] *adj.* Of or having to do with the handling of relations between nations.

dis·a·bil·i·ty pen·sion [dis′ə·bil′ə·tē pen′shən] *n.* An allowance regularly paid to a person who has retired from work because of injury.

dis·crim·i·nat·ed [dis·krim′ə·nā·tid] *v.* **1** Showed prejudice or partiality; excluded a person or group unjustly. **2** Recognized a difference between.

dis·in·te·grat·ing [dis·in′tə·grā·ting] *v.* Falling apart.

dis·pers·ing [dis·pûr′sing] *v.* Scattering or spreading in many directions.

dis·tant [dis′tənt] *adj.* Far off in space or time.

dis·tinct [dis·tingkt′] *adj.* **1** Easy to see or understand; sharp and clear. **2** Not alike; clearly different or separate.

dis·tinc·tive [dis·ting′tiv] *adj.* Serving to mark out as different or special: a *distinctive* writing style.

dis·tort·ing [dis·tôr′ting] *v.* **1** Twisting or bending out of the normal shape. **2** Changing (something) to create a false impression.

dis·tor·tion [dis·tôr′shən] *n.* **1** The act of twisting or bending out of the normal shape. **2** Something which has been changed to create a false impression.

di·vert·ed [di·vûr′tid] *v.* Turned aside.

dom·i·nant [dom′ə·nənt] *adj.* Most powerful, influential, or important.

dom·i·nate [dom′ə·nāt] *v.* To control.

do·min·ion [də·min′yən] *n.* Supreme power or authority; rule.

do·ry [dôr′ē] *n.* A flat-bottomed rowboat having high sides and well adapted to rough weather, used for fishing.

dras·tic [dras′tik] *adj.* Serious or severe.

dubbed [dubd] *v.* **1** Gave a name or nickname to. **2** Made someone a knight by tapping his shoulder with a sword. — **dub,** *v.*

dune bug·gies [d(y)ōōn′ bug′ēz] *n., pl.* Jeeps for driving on sand. — **dune bug·gy,** *sing.*

du·ra·ble [d(y)ōōr′ə·bəl] *adj.* Lasting a long time without wearing out.

dusk [dusk] *n.* The darkest part of twilight, just before night falls.

E

---

e·col·o·gist [i·kol′ə·jist *or* ē·kol′ə·jist] *n.* A person who studies the relationships between living things and their surroundings.

ec·o·nom·i·cal [ek′ə·nom′i·kəl *or* ē′kə·nom′i·kəl] *adj.* Not wasteful; thrifty.

ee·rie [ir′ē] *adj.* Causing or arousing fear; weird; strange.

e·lat·ed [i·lā′tid] *adj.* Joyful; delighted; very, very glad. — **e·late,** *v.*

e·la·tion [i·lā′shən] *n.* A feeling of joy or triumph.

e·lec·tron·ics [i·lek′tron′iks] *n.* The branch of engineering dealing with planning and making radios, televisions, computers, etc.

el·i·gi·ble [el′ə·jə·bəl] *adj.* Capable of or legally qualified for something.

e·lu·sive [i·lōō′siv] *adj.* Escaping or avoiding capture.

El Vie·jo [el vyā′hō] *Spanish* The Old Man.

em·broiled [em·broild′] *v.* Involved in disagreement or conflict.

em·bry·o [em′brē·ō] **1** *n.* An animal or plant in its earliest stages. **2** *adj.* Of such an animal or plant.

em·i·grant [em′ə·grənt] *n.* A person who leaves a country to settle in another.

e·mo·tion·al [i·mō′shən·əl] *adj.* **1** Expressing or arousing emotion, or strong feeling. **2** Of or related to the emotions — love, anger, etc.

em·phat·ic [em·fat′ik] *adj.* Forceful.

en·cased [in·kāst′] *v.* Enclosed in or as if in a case.

en·chant·ed [in·chan′tid] *adj.* Charmed; interested; delighted. — **en·chant,** *v.*

en·li·ven [in·lī′vən] *v.* To make lively, cheerful, or more spirited.

en·sign [en′sīn *or* en′sən] *n.* A flag.

en·trap [in·trap′] *v.* To catch in or as if in a trap.

en·vi·ron·ment [in·vī′rən·mənt] *n.* The conditions and surroundings that have an effect on the development of a living thing.

e·quiv·a·lent [i·kwiv′ə·lənt] *n.* Something that is equal in worth, force, amount, etc.

e·ro·sion [i·rō′zhən] *n.* The wearing away or gradual destruction of something by the action of water, wind, or acid.

es·tab·lished [ə·stab′lisht] *v.* Set up or founded on a firm or lasting basis.

es·tu·ar·y [es′chŏŏ·er′ē] *n.* The broad meeting place of a river and sea, where the tide flows in. — **es·tu·ar·ies,** *pl.*

eth·nic [eth′nik] *adj.* Of, having to do with, or belonging to a specific group whose members share the same culture, language, or customs.

e·ven·tu·al·ly [i·ven′chŏŏ·əl·lē] *adv.* In the course of time; in the end.

ev·o·lu·tion [ev′ə·lŏŏ′shən] *n.* The changes that take place in the slow development of something.

ex·e·cute [ek′sə·kyŏŏt] *v.* **1** To carry out; do: *The acrobat will* execute *a daring stunt.* **2** To put to death by a legal order.

ex·pe·di·tion [ek′spə·dish′ən] *n.* A trip, march, or voyage made for a definite purpose.

ex·tinc·tion [ik·stingk′shən] *n.* The condition of no longer existing.

ex·tract [ik·strakt′] *v.* To draw out, as by pulling, etc.

ex·trac·tion [ik·strak′shən] *n.* The act of drawing out, as by pulling, etc.

F

---

fa·cil·i·ties [fə·sil′ə·tēz] *n. pl.* Things that make some action or work possible or easier: *good library* facilities. — **fa·cil·i·ty,** *sing.*

fac·tor [fak′tər] *n.* One of the elements or causes that help to produce a result: *Practice was a* factor *in our victory.*

fate [fāt] *n.* **1** Final outcome; end: *The jury will decide his* fate. **2** A power supposed to fix what happens in advance; destiny.

flab·ber·gast·ed [flab′ər·gas·tid] *v. informal* Amazed greatly; astounded.

flail·ing [flāl′ing] *v.* Swinging the arms about wildly.

flick·er [flik′ər] *v.* **1** To flutter or make a trembling motion; wave to and fro. **2** To gleam or burn with an unsteady light.

flit·ting [flit′ing] *v.* Moving or flying quickly and in short bursts; darting.

floe [flō] *n.* A large, almost flat field of floating ice.

floun·der [floun′dər] **1** *v.* To struggle clumsily; move awkwardly. **2** *n.* A flatfish used as food. — **floun·der** or **floun·ders,** *pl.*

flour·ished [flûr′isht] *v.* Grew or fared well; thrived.

fluke [flŏŏk] *n.* **1** *informal* Any piece of good luck. **2** Another name for a flatfish, or flounder. **3** A barb on the head of an arrowhead or harpoon. **4** Either of the two parts of a whale's tail.

flushed [flusht] *v.* Became red in the face.

fore [fôr] **1** *adj.* At or toward the front or beginning. **2.** *adv.* In or toward the bow of a boat.

for·mal·i·ty [fôr·mal′ə·tē] *n.* **1** A customary act or ceremony. **2** Strict, organized character or quality. — **for·mal·i·ties,** *pl.*

for·mat [fôr′mat] *n.* The form, size, arrangement, and style of something.

found·ry [foun′drē] *n.* A place where molten metal is shaped in molds.

frag·ment·ed [frag·men′tid] *adj.* Broken up in pieces. — **frag·ment,** *v.*

frig·id [frij′id] *adj.* Very, very cold.

frol·icked [frol′ikt] *v.* Played in a frisky way.

G

---

gal·ler·y [gal′ər·ē] *n.* **1** The spectators at a tennis or golf match. **2** A long corridor or hallway, sometimes with one open side. — **gal·ler·ies,** *pl.*

gal·lows [gal′ōz] *n., pl. (takes sing. or pl. v.)* A wooden framework used for hanging criminals.

gar·fish [gär′fish] *n.* A freshwater fish with a long body and snout and sharp teeth.

gath·er·er [gath′ər·ər] *n.* A person who lives by gathering the food that grows wild in a particular area.

---

add, āce, câre, pälm;   end, ēqual;   it, īce;   odd, ōpen, ôrder;   tŏŏk, pōōl;   up, bûrn;
ə = a in *above*, e in *sicken*, i in *possible*, o in *melon*, u in *circus*;   yŏŏ = u in *fuse*;   oil;   pout;
check;   ring;   thin;   this;   zh in *vision*.

ge·ne·al·o·gy [jē′nē·al′ə·jē *or* jē′nē·ol′ə·jē] *n.* A record of the ancestors and descent of a person or family. — **ge·ne·al·o·gies,** *pl.*

gen·er·a·tion [jen′ə·rā′shən] *n.* **1** One step or stage in the history of a family. **2** The average time between any two such successive steps, about thirty years. **3** The act of producing or causing to be.

ge·o·me·tric [jē′ə·met′rik] *adj.* **1** Having points, lines, angles, and surfaces. **2** Of or according to the principles of geometry. See *geometry.*

ge·o·me·try [jē·om′ə·trē] *n.* The branch of mathematics that studies the relationships among points, lines, angles, surfaces, and solids.

gey·ser [gī′zər] *n.* A natural spring which, from time to time, sends up a fountain of hot water, steam, or mud.

gink·go [ging′kō *or* jing′kō] *n.* A large tree with fan-shaped leaves native to China and grown in the U.S. — **gink·goes,** *pl.*

gourd [gôrd *or* gŏŏrd] *n.* **1** A kind of squash with a hard shell. **2** A container or rattle made from the dried shell of a gourd.

gra·cious·ly [grā′shəs·lē] *adv.* With grace, kindness, or politeness.

grit [grit] *n.* **1** Small, hard particles of sand, stone, etc. **2** Courage.

Gulf Stream [gulf strēm] The warm ocean current that flows out of the Gulf of Mexico, northward along the east coast of the U.S., then northeasterly toward Europe.

H

ha·lo [hā′lō] *n.* A ring of light.

has·sle [has′(ə)l] *n. slang* An argument; fight.

hear·ing [hir′ing] *n.* **1** An official examination, as by a court. **2** The ability to hear.

hec·tare [hek′târ] *n.* A unit of surface measure in the metric system, equal to 10,000 square meters, or about two-and-a-half acres.

her·ald [her′əld] *n.* A person or thing that announces something to come; messenger.

her·ba·ceous [(h)ûr·bā′shəs] *adj.* **1** Not woody. **2** Of, like, or having to do with an herb or herbs, plants used for medicine, seasoning, etc.

her·i·tage [her′ə·tij] *n.* A tradition, belief, attitude, etc., handed down from the past.

he·ro·ic [hi·rō′ik] *adj.* Of or like a hero; brave.

hi·er·o·glyph·ic [hī′ər·ə·glif′ik *or* hī′rə·glif′ik] *adj.* Using a picture or symbol to represent an object, idea, or sound. — **hi·er·o·glyph·ics** *n., pl.* A system of writing using such pictures or symbols.

ho·gan [hō′gən] *n.* A Navajo dwelling made of sticks and branches covered with earth.

horse·tail [hôrs′tāl′] *n.* **1** A flowerless plant with hollow, jointed stems. **2** The tail of a horse.

hu·man·i·tar·i·an [(h)yōō·man′ə·târ′ē·ən] **1** *n.* A person concerned with or working for the human good. **2** *adj.* Concerning the furthering of human good.

hu·mil·i·ty [(h)yōō·mil′ə·tē] *n.* The condition of being or feeling humble; modesty.

hu·mus [(h)yōō′məs] *n.* Rich, dark soil containing decayed plant and animal matter.

hyp·not·ic [hip·not′ik] *adj.* Causing or having to do with hypnosis, a sleeplike condition in which a person is responsive to suggestions or instructions.

I

i·con·o·scope [ī·kon′ə·skōp] *n.* In photography, a kind of viewfinder.

ig·nit·ed [ig·nī′tid] *v.* Set on fire; sparked.

il·log·i·cal [i·loj′i·kəl] *adj.* Lacking in sound reasoning.

im·age [im′ij] *n.* **1** A mental picture. **2** A statue or other likeness of a person or thing.

im·mense [i·mens′] *adj.* Very large; huge.

Im·pres·sion·ist [im·presh′ən·ist] *n.* A member of a school of painting (**Impressionism**), popular in the late nineteenth century, which emphasized a visual impression of the subject rather than exact details.

im·pru·dent [im·prōōd′(ə)nt] *adj.* Not having good judgment; unwise.

in·cor·rect [in′kə·rekt′] *adj.* Not correct, proper, true, etc.

in·cred·i·ble [in·kred′ə·bəl] *adj.* Beyond belief.

in·ex·pen·sive [in′ik·spen′siv] *adj.* Costing little.

in·fe·ri·or [in·fir′ē·ər] *adj.* Not as good in quality, worth, etc.

in·flu·en·tial [in′floo·en′shəl] *adj.* Having an important effect on others.

in·her·ent [in·hir′ənt *or* in·her′ənt] *adj.* Being in something as a built-in quality or part.

in·i·ti·a·tion [in·ish′ē·ā′shən] *n.* **1** The steps in making someone a member of a group, usually through ceremonies or tests. **2** The starting or setting up of something: the *initiation* of changes.

in·sol·u·ble [in·sol′yə·bəl] *adj.* **1** Incapable of being dissolved. **2** Incapable of being solved.

in·te·grate [in′tə·grāt] *v.* To bring together; unite.

in·tense [in·tens′] *adj.* Very strong, great, or deep.

in·ter·con·ti·nen·tal [in′tər·kon′tə·nen′təl] *adj.* Between or able to travel between continents.

in·ter·na·tion·al [in′tər·nash′ən·əl] *adj.* Between or among nations.

in·ter·pre·ta·tion [in·tûr′prə·tā′shən] *n.* **1** The act of giving one's understanding of something. **2** The act of explaining or making clear.

in·tri·cate [in′tri·kit] *adj.* Complicated or very involved.

i·rid·i·um [i·rid′ē·əm] *n.* A metallic element similar to platinum.

ir·reg·u·lar·ly [i·reg′yə·lər·lē] *adv.* In a way that follows no rules, laws, or patterns.

i·so·lat·ed [ī′sə·lā·tid] *adj.* Placed apart or alone; separated from others. —**i·so·late,** *v.*

J

ja·ve·li·na [hä·və·lē′nə] *n.* A wild pig.

jeop·ard·ize [jep′ər·dīz] *v.* To put in danger.

K

ka·lei·do·scop·ic [kə·lī′də·skop′ik] *adj.* Always changing, such as in views, pattern, etc.

kin·ship [kin′ship] *n.* Relationship, especially by blood.

L

lair [lâr] *n.* The den of a wild animal.

land·scape [land′skāp] *n.* **1** A stretch of natural scenery on land as seen from a single point. **2** A painting of such scenery.

lan·o·lin [lan′ə·lin] *n.* A fatty substance obtained from sheep wool and used as a base for ointments, cosmetics, etc.

launch [lônch] **1** *n.* Take-off. **2** *v.* To move or push (a boat, etc.) into the water. **3** *v.* To hurl; fling: *launch* a rocket.

lead [lēd] **1** *n.* A long, narrow passage of water in an ice field. **2** *v.* To guide or conduct.

leaf mold [lēf′ mōld′] *n.* A rich soil consisting mostly of decayed leaves.

Leeu·wen·hoek [lā′vən·hook], **An·ton van,** 1632–1723, Dutch naturalist and one of the first scientists to use a microscope.

leg·a·cy [leg′ə·sē] *n.* **1** Something inherited, as a trait: his *legacy* of good cheer. **2** Money, property, etc., that is left to one by a will.

lime·stone [līm′stōn′] *n.* A type of rock, such as marble, that contains mainly calcium carbonate.

lim·i·ta·tion [lim′ə·tā′shən] *n.* Something that limits, especially a shortcoming.

lit·er·al·ly [lit′ər·əl·lē] *adv.* **1** Actually; without exaggeration. **2** Word for word.

lobe [lōb] *n.* A curved or rounded part that sticks out, such as an ear *lobe.*

log·a·rithm [lôg′ə·rith·əm *or* log′ə·rith·əm] *n.* The exponent that must be applied to a number, usually 10, in order to make some other number: Since $10^2 = 100$, the *logarithm* of 100 to base 10 is 2.

log·i·cal [loj′ə·kəl] *adj.* **1** Following reasonably: It seemed the *logical* thing to do. **2** Making use of formal reason.

loi·ter [loi′tər] *v.* To linger or dawdle; hang around.

lore [lôr] *n.* Facts or stories about a subject.

---

add, āce, câre, pälm;   end, ēqual;   it, īce;   odd, ōpen, ôrder;   took, pool;   up, bûrn;
ə = a in *above,* e in *sicken,* i in *possible,* o in *melon,* u in *circus;*   yoo = u in *fuse;*   oil;   pout;
check;   ring;   thin;   this;   zh in *vision.*

lux·u·ri·ant [lug·zhŏŏr′ē·ənt] *adj.* Growing thickly and abundantly.

M

---

ma·gen·ta [mə·jen′tə] *adj.* Purplish rose or purplish red.

main·tained [mān·tānd′] *v.* **1** Supplied with means of support; provided for: We *maintained* an animal shelter. **2** Carried on or continued: The car *maintained* its speed.

man·a·cle [man′ə·kəl] *n.* A handcuff.

man·grove [mang′grōv] *n.* An evergreen tree or shrub of warm, marshy regions.

ma·nia [mā′nē·ə or mān′yə] *n.* **1** An exaggerated interest, desire, or enthusiasm. **2** A mental disorder.

ma·nip·u·late [mə·nip′yə·lāt] *v.* To operate or work with the hands; handle.

mar·row [mar′ō] *n.* A soft, spongy substance found in the hollow centers of many bones.

mast [mast] *n.* A long pole set upright in a sailing ship to hold up the sails.

maze [māz] *n.* A confusing network of paths in which it is hard to find one's way.

me·di·e·val [mē′dē·ē′vəl, med′ē·ē′vəl, *or* mē·dē′vəl] *adj.* Of or relating to the Middle Ages, the period in European history from about A.D. 450 to 1450.

mem·brane [mem′brān] *n.* A thin, flexible layer of tissue that covers or lines certain organs or parts of plants and animals.

mem·o·ra·ble [mem′ər·ə·bəl] *adj.* Worth remembering; hard to forget.

me·thod·i·cal·ly [mə·thod′i·k(ə)lē] *adv.* In a strict, orderly way.

mi·crobe [mī′krōb] *n.* An organism too tiny to be seen except with a microscope, especially one of the bacteria that cause disease; a germ.

mi·cro·cli·mate [mī′krō·klī′mit] *n.* The kind of weather in a small area, such as a forest or city, or within a confined space, such as a greenhouse, cave, or building.

min·i·mal [min′ə·məl] *adj.* Smallest or least possible.

min·i·mum [min′ə·məm] *n.* The smallest or least possible amount. — **min·i·mums** or **min·i·ma**, *pl.*

min·is·ter [min′is·tər] *n.* **1** The head of a department of a government. **2** A member of the clergy, especially one who is the pastor of a Protestant church.

mi·nor·i·ties [mə·nôr′ə·tēz] *n., pl.* Groups of people different in some way from the larger groups of which they are a part. — **mi·nor·i·ty,** *sing.*

min·ute [min′ət] *n.* **1** The sixtieth part of an hour; sixty seconds. **2** A unit of measure for mapping the earth and for locating places on it; one-sixtieth of a degree. See *degree.* **3** *(pl.)* An official record of the events of a meeting.

mock [mok] **1** *adj.* Not real, but made to look real. **2** *v.* To make fun of, often by mimicking.

mold·er [mōl′dər] **1** *n.* A person who shapes something, usually materials such as wax, clay, or metals. **2** *v.* To decay gradually.

mo·men·tum [mō·men′təm] *n.* Force or speed, usually growing in strength: The rolling stone gathered *momentum.*

mon·arch [mon′ərk] *n.* A ruler, as a king, queen, etc.

mon·o·rail [mon′ō·rāl′] **1** *adj.* Having a single track or rail. **2** *n.* A railway whose cars run on or hang from a single track or rail.

mon·o·syl·la·ble [mon′ə·sil′ə·bəl] *n.* A word of one syllable.

mo·not·o·nous [mə·not′ə·nəs] *adj.* Not changing in pitch or tone.

mo·tive [mō′tiv] *n.* A reason or cause that makes a person act.

mu·ci·lage [myōō′sə·lij] *n.* A sticky substance used to glue things together.

mul·ti·cel·lu·lar [mul′ti·sel′yə·lər] *adj.* Made up of many different cells.

mu·nic·i·pal [myōō·nis′·ə·pəl] *adj.* Having to do with a town or city.

myth [mith] *n.* **1** A traditional story, usually about gods, heroes, etc. **2** Any made-up story, person, event, etc.

N

---

na·sal·i·ty [nā·zal′ə·tē] *n.* The quality or an instance of using sounds that are made through the nose.

nat·u·ral·ist [nach′ər·əl·ist] *n.* A person trained in the study of nature, especially as related to the earth and living things.

nau·ti·cal [nô′ti·kəl] *adj.* Having to do with ships, sailors, or sailing.

Near East [nir ēst] The region, mainly in southwestern Asia, surrounding the eastern Mediterranean Sea and including Egypt, Iran, Iraq, Israel, Jordan, Lebanon, and Saudi Arabia.

neg·lect·ed [ni·glek′tid] *adj.* Uncared for. — **neg·lect,** *v.*

no·mad·ic [nō·mad′ik] *adj.* Of or having to do with nomads, people who move regularly from place to place to find food and water.

nom·i·nat·ed [nom′ə·nā·tid] *v.* Named a candidate for an elective office.

nov·el [nov′əl] **1** *n.* A long fictional story. **2** *adj.* New or different; unusual.

nu·cle·us [n(y)ōō′klē·əs] *n.* The small central mass in most plant and animal cells that contains material necessary for the cell's growth, reproduction, etc. — **nu·cle·i** *or* **nu·cle·us·es,** *pl.*

nu·tri·ent [n(y)ōō′trē·ənt] **1** *n.* Food. **2** *adj.* Giving nourishment; nourishing.

O

ob·ses·sion [əb·sesh′ən] *n.* A thought, feeling, or idea that fills the mind and cannot be driven out.

oc·cu·pa·tion·al [ok′yə pā′shən·əl] *adj.* Having to do with work or business.

of·fen·sive [ə·fen′siv] *adj.* **1** Attacking. **2** Unpleasant or disagreeable.

op·ti·cal il·lu·sion [op′ti·kəl i·lōō′zhən] *n.* Something that gives a false impression to the eye.

op·ti·mism [op′tə·miz′əm] *n.* The tendency to see the bright side of things.

or·gan·elle [ôr′gən·el′] *n.* A distinct structure within a cell, having its own specialized functions.

or·gan·ism [ôr′gən·iz′əm] *n.* An animal or plant considered as a structure with parts that depend on each other.

or·i·gin [ôr′ə·jin] *n.* The beginning of the existence of anything.

o·ver·view [ō′vər·vyōō′] *n.* The general picture; view which includes everything.

ox·i·dize [ok′sə·dīz] *v.* To undergo the process of combining with oxygen: When iron *oxidizes*, rust results.

P

pa·lo ver·de [pä′lō vûr′dā] *n.* A small tree found in the southwestern U.S., with smooth green bark and yellow flowers.

pal·sy [pôl′zē] *n.* A form of paralysis resulting in weak muscles and trembling limbs.

Pa·pa·go [pä′pä·gō′] *n.* A Native American tribe of Arizona.

par·al·lel [par′ə·lel] **1** *n.* One of the imaginary numbered circles around the earth that go in the same direction as the equator, used to indicate location. **2** *adj.* Never having a point in common: *parallel* lines.

par·a·ple·gic [par′ə·plē′jik] **1** *n.* A person who is paralyzed from the waist down. **2** *adj.* Paralyzed from the waist down.

par·a·site [par′ə·sīt] *n.* A plant or animal that lives in or on another and gets its food and often its shelter from the other.

Par·lia·ment [pär′lə·mont] *n.* **1** The chief lawmaking body of Great Britain or of the independent Commonwealth countries. **2** (*written* **par·lia·ment**) An assembly which makes the laws of a country.

pass·a·ble [pas′ə·bəl] *adj.* Capable of being passed.

pas·tel [pas·tel′] *n.* **1** A chalklike colored crayon. **2** A drawing made with such crayons. **3** Any delicate, soft, pale color.

pa·thol·o·gy [pə·thol′ə·jē] *n.* The branch of medicine concerned with the origin, nature, causes, and development of disease.

---

add, āce, câre, pälm;   end, ēqual;   it, īce;   odd, ōpen, ôrder;   tŏŏk, pōōl;   up, bûrn;
ə = a in *above*, e in *sicken*, i in *possible*, o in *melon*, u in *circus;*   yōō = u in *fuse;*   oil;   pout;
check;   ring;   thin;   this;   zh in *vision.*

pel·la·gra [pə·lā′grə *or* pə·lag′rə] *n.* A disease resulting from a lack of niacin in the diet.

phe·nom·e·na [fi·nom′ə·nə] *n., pl.* Events or conditions that can be observed and described scientifically. — **phe·nom·e·non,** *sing.*

pho·net·ic [fə·net′ik] *adj.* Representing sounds as they are actually spoken.

phys·i·cist [fiz′ə·sist] *n.* A person who studies matter, energy, motion, and the ways they relate.

pic·ric ac·id [pik′rik as′id] *n.* A poisonous, yellow, bitter acid.

pic·to·graph [pik′tə·graf] *n.* A picture used to represent an idea.

pig·ment [pig′mənt] *n.* **1** A natural substance that colors living cells or tissue. **2** Coloring matter that can be mixed with a liquid, used to make paint, etc.

pi·le·at·ed [pī′lē·ā·tid] *adj.* Crested. — **pileate,** *v.*

pi·o·neer [pī′ə·nir′] **1** *adj.* Leading the way, as in the development of a new field, etc. **2** *n.* One of the first explorers or settlers of a new place.

plas·ma [plaz′mə] *n.* The liquid part of blood, without the red and white blood cells.

pla·teau [pla·tō′] *n.* A wide stretch of high, flat land.

plate·let [plāt′lit] *n.* One of the tiny round or oval bodies found in blood and necessary for the clotting of blood.

plat·i·num [plat′ə·nəm] *n.* A heavy, gray, metallic element that does not tarnish, is very resistant to chemicals, and can be easily worked into many shapes.

plot·ter [plot′ər] *n.* A person who secretly plans something, usually something evil.

plush [plush] *adj.* Suggesting wealth or ease.

pol·i·cy [pol′ə·sē] *n.* A plan or method of action or conduct. — **pol·i·cies,** *pl.*

poll [pōl] **1** *n.* A collection of votes or opinions, as in an election or survey. **2** *n.* (*often pl.*) The place where votes are cast. **3** *v.* To record the votes or opinions of: *poll* the voters. **4** *v.* To cut off or trim the hair, horns, etc., especially of an animal.

po·ten·tial [pə·ten′chəl] **1** *n.* What someone is capable of: fulfill your *potential.* **2** *adj.* Possible: *potential* dangers.

pov·er·ty [pov′ər·tē] *n.* The condition of being very poor.

pray·ing man·tis [prā′ing man′tis] *n.* An insect, something like a large grasshopper, that folds its forelegs as if in prayer.

pred·a·tor [pred′i·tər] *n.* A person or animal that lives by preying on others.

pre·dict [pri·dikt′] *v.* To state beforehand; foretell.

pre·dict·a·ble [pri·dikt′ə·bəl] *adj.* Capable of being stated beforehand.

pref·er·ence [pref′ər·əns] *n.* **1** A favoring of one person or thing over another. **2** A person or thing favored over another.

pre·his·tor·ic [prē′his·tor′ik] *adj.* Of or belonging to the period before the start of written history.

pre·oc·cu·pied [prē·ok′yə·pīd] *adj.* Fully interested in or concerned with something. — **pre·oc·cu·py,** *v.*

pre·serve [pri·zûrv′] **1** *v.* To keep from danger or harm; protect. **2** *n.* (*usually pl.*) Fruit that has been cooked, usually with sugar.

pre·tense [pri·tens′ *or* prē′tens] *n.* Something pretended; a false act, appearance, etc.

pre·test [*v.* prē·test′, *n.* prē′test] **1** *v.* To test before, in order to find out what part of the tested topic needs work. **2** *n.* A test given before a topic is studied.

prey [prā] *n.* Any animal seized by another for food.

pri·ma·ry [prī′mer·ē] **1** *n.* A preliminary election in which each political party chooses those candidates it wishes to run for public office. **2** *adj.* First in time or importance.

pri·mate [prī′māt] *n.* Any of a group of advanced mammals, including apes, monkeys, and humans.

prim·i·tive [prim′ə·tiv] *adj.* Coming from or belonging to the earliest times.

pro·found [prə·found′] *adj.* **1** Intensely felt: *profound* appreciation. **2** Showing deep intellect or knowledge.

prompt·ly [prompt′lē] *adv.* Quickly; without any delay.

pro·pelled [prə·peld′] *v.* Caused (something) to move forward.

prop·er [prop′ər] *adj.* **1** Meant in the strict sense: We live in the city *proper,* not in the suburbs. **2** Suitable; fitting.

prop·er·ties [prop′ər·tēz] *n., pl.* **1** Special qualities or characteristics that belong to something: Liquids and solids have different *properties.* **2** Things that are owned, such as real estate, stocks, etc.; possessions. — **prop·er·ty,** *sing.*

pro·pose [prə·pōz′] *v.* To put forward for acceptance or consideration; suggest: *propose* a plan.

pros·pect [pros′pekt] **1** *n.* An outlook. **2** *n.* (*often pl.*) Something with a chance for future success. **3** *n.* The scene spread out before one's eyes. **4** *n.* A likely buyer or candidate. **5** *v.* To explore or search, as for oil, gold, etc.

pro·spec·tive [prə·spek′tiv] *adj.* Being still in the future; expected.

pros·pec·tor [pros′pek·tər] *n.* A person who explores a place for gold, oil, etc.

pros·per·i·ty [pros·per′ə·tē] *n.* A successful or thriving condition; wealth, success, etc.

pro·vi·sion [prə·vizh′ən] *n.* **1** A requirement or condition. **2** The act of providing or supplying.

pru·dent [prōō′dənt] *adj.* Having good judgment; careful.

psy·chol·o·gist [sī·kol′ə·jist] *n.* A person who studies the mind and the way it works.

pub·lic·i·ty [pub·lis′ə·tē] *n.* **1** The attention or interest of the public. **2** Any information intended to bring public notice to a person or thing.

Q

quack [kwak] *n.* A person who pretends to have great knowledge, especially of medicine.

quad·ri·ple·gic [kwod′rə·plē′jik] **1** *n.* A person who is paralyzed from the neck down. **2** *adj.* Paralyzed from the neck down.

quar·ry [kwôr′ē] **1** *n.* A place in the ground from which stone is taken. **2** *v.* To dig stone out of such a place.

R

ram·part [ram′pärt] *n.* A bank of earth, often with a low wall on top, surrounding a fort, castle, etc., as a defense.

range [rānj] **1** *n.* The extent or set of limits within which something can move, vary, or be found: the *range* of a voice. **2** *n.* An open area over which animals roam and feed. **3** *n.* A row, line, or series, as of mountains. **4** *n.* A cooking stove. **5** *v.* To vary or be found within certain limits: Their ages *range* from six to twelve.

re·ac·tion [rē·ak′shən] *n.* An action in response to an event, etc.

re·al·i·ty [rē·al′ə·tē] *n.* The state of being real; actual existence.

re·ap·praise [rē′ə·prāz′] *v.* To make another judgment of something or someone.

re·as·sur·ing [rē′ə·shōōr′ing] *adj.* Building confidence; comforting. — **re·as·sure,** *v.*

re·clined [ri·klīnd′] *v.* Lay down, lay back, or leaned back.

rec·og·ni·tion [rek′əg·nish′ən] *n.* **1** Fame; great praise. **2** The act of recognizing or knowing again.

re·cur·ring [ri·kûr′ing] *v.* Happening over and over, usually at regular intervals.

re·flect [ri·flekt′] *v.* **1** To show or express: The books he reads *reflect* his interests. **2** To throw or send back heat, sound, light, etc. **3** To think; consider.

re·form [ri·fôrm′] **1** *n.* A change for the better, as by the correction of wrongs, etc. **2** *v.* To make better by correcting wrongs, etc.

ref·uge [ref′yōōj] *n.* Shelter; protection.

re·ga·li·a [ri·gā′lē·ə *or* ri·gāl′yə] *n., pl.* The symbols and emblems of any society, order, etc.

re·gard·ed [ri·gär′did] *v.* **1** Looked on or thought of in a certain way: He *regarded* his hero with awe. **2** Looked at closely or with great attention.

re·ject·ed [ri·jek′tid] *v.* Refused to take, accept, recognize, etc.

---

add, āce, câre, pälm;   end, ēqual;   it, īce;   odd, ōpen, ôrder;   tŏŏk, pōōl;   up, bûrn;
ə = a in *above,* e in *sicken,* i in *possible,* o in *melon,* u in *circus;*   yōō = u in *fuse;*   oil;   pout;
check;   ring;   thin;   this;   zh in *vision.*

rel·a·tive·ly [rel′ə·tiv·lē] *adv.* As compared with something else or with a standard; comparatively: *relatively* easy question.

rel·e·vant [rel′ə·vənt] *adj.* Connected with or having to do with the point, matter at hand, etc.

rel·ic [rel′ik] *n.* Something remaining from what has disappeared or been destroyed: a *relic* of ancient Greece.

re·match [rē′mach] *n.* A contest held again between the same contestants.

re·mote [ri·mōt′] *adj.* Very far away.

Ren·ais·sance [ren′ə·säns′] *n.* The great revival of art, literature, and learning that marked the fourteenth through sixteenth century in Europe.

ren·dered [ren′dərd] *v.* **1** Melted down. **2** Gave or presented: *rendered* a bill for payment.

re·nowned [ri·nound′] *adj.* Famous.

re·place [ri·plās′] *v.* **1** To put back in place. **2** To take the place of.

rep·re·sen·ta·tion [rep′ri·zen·tā′shən] *n.* Anything that symbolizes or stands for something else: The model airplane was a good *representation.*

re·pub·lic [ri·pub′lik] *n.* A government in which officials are elected by and represent the citizens.

rep·u·ta·tion [rep′yə·tā′shən] *n.* The general estimation in which a person or thing is held by others.

re·serve [ri·zûrv′] **1** *n.* Government land kept for a special purpose. **2** *v.* To hold back or set aside for special or future use. **3** *n.* Something reserved.

re·side [ri·zīd′] *v.* To make one's home; live.

re·source [ri·sôrs′ *or* rē′sôrs] *n. (often pl.)* A supply of something that can be used or drawn on: natural *resources.*

re·spell [rē·spel′] *v.* To spell again, sometimes using a different spelling system.

re·stored [ri·stôrd′] *adj.* Brought back to an original or former condition. — **re·store,** *v.*

re·strict [ri·strikt′] *v.* To hold or keep within limits; confine.

re·test [*v.* rē·test′, *n.* rē′test] **1** *v.* To test again. **2** *n.* A test being given for the second time.

re·treat [ri·trēt′] **1** *n.* A quiet, safe place; refuge. **2** *v.* To withdraw; go back. **3** *n.* The act of retreating.

re·trieved [ri·trēvd′] *v.* Got back; regained.

re·vi·val [ri·vī′vəl] *n.* A restoring or coming back to life or vigor.

re·vived [ri·vīvd′] *v.* **1** Gave new strength or vigor. **2** Brought or came back to life or consciousness.

rev·o·lu·tion [rev′ə·lōō′shən] *n.* **1** Movement in a circle or other closed curve. **2** The overthrow of a government by those once under its control. **3** Any great change.

Reyk·ja·vik [rā′k(y)ə·vik′ *or* rā′k(y)ə·vēk′] *n.* The capital of Iceland.

rind [rīnd] *n.* A skin or outer coating that may be peeled or removed, as of bacon, fruit, etc.

rit·u·al [rich′ōō·əl] **1** *n.* A body of rites and ceremonies. **2** *adj.* Having to do with a ritual.

root·ed [rōō′tid] *v.* Turned up or dug with the snout, as pigs do.

ro·se·ate spoon·bill [rō′zē·it *or* rō′zē·āt spōōn′bil′] *n.* A reddish wading bird with a broad, flat bill, spoon-shaped at the tip.

rout [rout] **1** *n.* Total defeat. **2** *v.* To defeat totally.

Rwan·da [rōō·än′də] *n.* A country in central Africa.

S

sa·gua·ro [sə·gwä′rō *or* sə·wä′rō] *n.* A large desert cactus of the southwest U.S.

sa·lon [sə·lon′] *n.* **1** A gallery for showing works of art. **2** A rather elaborate and formal room for entertaining guests.

salt pan [sôlt′ pan′] *n.* A wide hole in a desert that collects water during a rainfall.

scale [skāl] *n.* A fixed proportion between one thing — as an area of land — and another thing — as a map of that area.

scal·lop [skol′əp *or* skal′əp] *n.* **1** A small sea animal with fan-shaped, ribbed shells. **2** One of several half circles used as a design or border.

scant·y [skan′tē] *adj.* Barely enough.

schol·ar [skol′ər] *n.* A person who has learned a great deal through study.

scoff [skof *or* skôf] *v.* To jeer or show scorn.

scope [skōp] *n.* **1** An instrument, as on a rifle, that lets one see a target better. **2** The area covered; range: the *scope* of a lesson.

script [skript] *n.* A way of writing.

sea·far·er [sē'fâr'ər] *n.* A sailor.

sea·son·al [sē'zən·əl] *adj.* Having to do with or happening at a certain season or seasons.

seat [sēt] *n.* **1** Membership in a legislature, stock exchange, etc.: a Congressional *seat.* **2** Something on which one sits.

seep·age [sē'pij] *n.* The act or process of soaking through or oozing.

set·tle·ment house [set'(ə)l·mənt hous'] *n.* An institution offering advice, entertainment, etc., for the people of a poor neighborhood.

sex·tant [seks'tənt] *n.* An instrument for measuring angular distance, as of a star, the sun, etc., above the horizon.

sheer [shir] *adj.* Complete; absolute.

shim·mer [shim'ər] *v.* To shine with an unsteady, glimmering light.

shotput [shot'pŏŏt'] *n.* A sport in which a heavy metal ball is thrown for distance.

shrew [shrŏŏ] *n.* Any of various small mouselike mammals that have long snouts.

shroud·ed [shrou'did] *adj.* Covered by or as if with a shroud, a cloth for wrapping the dead.

sil·hou·ette [sil'ŏŏ·et'] *n.* The outline of a person or object seen against a light or a light background.

sim·plic·i·ty [sim·plis'ə·tē] *n.* **1** An absence of decoration; plainness. **2** The condition of being free from difficulty.

skep·tic [skep'tik] *n.* A person who doubts what many people accept as fact or truth.

sledge [slej] *n.* A kind of sled mounted on low runners, used for moving loads.

sledge ham·mer [slej' ham'ər] *n.* A large, heavy hammer.

sleek [slēk] *adj.* Smooth and glossy.

slight [slīt] *adj.* **1** Slender or frail. **2** Small in amount or importance; not great or serious.

slough [slou *or* slŏŏ] *n.* A place of deep mud or still water, such as a swamp.

sni·per [snī'pər] *n.* A person who shoots at people from some hiding place.

snuffed out [snuft' out'] *adj.* Put out; extinguished. **– snuff out,** *v.*

sole [sōl] **1** *n.* A flatfish related to the flounder. **2** *adj.* Only: the *sole* person on the island.

so·nar [sō'när] *n.* A device that finds things under water by using sound waves.

Song·hai [song'hī'] *n.* An ancient African kingdom.

so·phis·ti·cat·ed [sə·fis'tə·kā'tid] *adj.* **1** Highly developed. **2** Cultured and worldly.

source [sôrs] *n.* **1** A person or thing from which something starts or comes. **2** The beginning of a stream or river.

span [span] **1** *n.* The greatest distance that the tips of the thumb and little finger can spread. **2** *n.* A period or distance. **3** *v.* To stretch across.

spe·cies [spē'shēz *or* spē'sēz] *n.* **1** A group of living things that are more or less alike. **2** A distinct sort or kind.

spec·i·men [spes'ə·mən] *n.* A small amount taken as a sample of a whole.

spell·bound [spel'bound'] *adj.* Still and quiet, as if bound by a magic spell.

sphere [sfir] *n.* Any round body or object having the surface the same distance from the center at all points; a ball.

spike [spīk] *n.* **1** A sharp or pointed metal piece, as on the sole of some shoes worn in sports. **2** A very large nail. **3** A young mackerel.

spi·ral [spī'rəl] *n.* A cone-shaped coil.

spliced [splīst] *v.* Joined by twisting together, overlapping, etc.

spon·sor [spon'sər] *n.* A person who takes responsibility for another person or thing.

spon·ta·ne·ous gen·er·a·tion [spon·tā'nē·əs jen'ə·rā'shən] *n.* The theory that living things can arise from nonliving matter.

squelch [skwelch] *v. informal* To subdue or make silent.

sta·ble [stā'bəl] *adj.* **1** Not likely to change; long-lasting. **2** Not easily moved or shaken.

stalk [stôk] **1** *n.* A stem of a plant or any supporting or connecting part. **2** *v.* To approach (game, prey, etc.) secretly.

stand [stand] **1** *n.* A group of plants or trees. **2** *n.* An opinion, attitude, or position. **3** *v.* To take or keep an upright position.

stan·dard·ized [stan'dər·dīzd] *v.* Made to conform to a standard, or established measure.

---

add, āce, câre, pälm;   end, ēqual;   it, īce;   odd, ōpen, ôrder;   tŏŏk, pōōl;   up, bûrn;

ə = a in *above*, e in *sicken*, i in *possible*, o in *melon*, u in *circus;*   yŏŏ = u in *fuse;*   oil;   pout;

check;   ring;   thin;   this;   zh in *vision.*

stat·ic [stat'ik] *adj.* Not active, moving, or changing; at rest.

stat·ure [stach'ər] *n.* **1** Status gained by growth or achievement: moral *stature.* **2** Natural height, as of a person.

staunch [stônch *or* stänch] *adj.* Firm and dependable; loyal.

stile [stīl] *n.* A step or series of steps on each side of a barrier to aid in getting over it.

strain [strān] *v.* **1** To pour or squeeze through a strainer, sieve, etc. **2** To injure by overuse. **3** To make a great effort.

strand·ed [stran'did] *adj.* Left behind; abandoned; cut off. — **strand,** *v.*

strat·e·gy [strat'ə·jē] *n.* A plan.

strik·ing [strī'king] *adj.* Appealing strongly to the eye or to the imagination; impressive.

stroke [strōk] *n.* **1** A single movement, as of the hand, the arm, or a tool: a tennis *stroke.* **2** The act of striking: a *stroke* with a hammer.

strut [strut] *v.* To walk in a vain way.

stunned [stund] *v.* **1** Surprised; shocked. **2** Paralyzed; made unable to act.

sub·hu·man [sub'(h)yōo'mən] *adj.* Less than human; animal.

sub·merged [səb·mûrjd'] *adj.* Underwater. — **sub·merge,** *v.*

sub·tle [sut'(ə)l] *adj.* **1** Not direct or obvious; hard to see or understand. **2** Able to see fine distinctions.

suc·ces·sion [sək·sesh'ən] *n.* A group of persons, things, or events that follow one after another.

suf·fi·cient [sə·fish'ənt] *adj.* Equal to what is needed; enough; adequate.

su·perb [sŏo·pûrb'] *adj.* **1** Excellent; outstandingly good. **2** Grand; majestic.

su·per·vised [sōo'pər·vīzd] *v.* Directed and managed (employees, a process, etc.).

sur·rey [sûr'ē] *n.* A light, two-seated carriage.

sur·vey·or [sər·vā'ər] *n.* A person who measures and maps land.

swag·ger [swag'ər] *v.* To walk in a proud or insolent way; strut.

swell [swel] **1** *n.* The long, continuous body of a rolling wave. **2** *v.* To increase or cause to increase in size, amount, etc.

syn·di·cat·ed [sin'də·kā·tid] *adj.* Sold to many newspapers, magazines, television, or radio stations. — **syn·di·cate,** *v.*

syn·thet·ic [sin·thet'ik] **1** *adj.* Of, having to do with, or using synthesis, the combining of separate parts into a whole. **2** *adj.* In chemistry, made artificially by synthesis rather than occurring naturally. **3** *n.* Something synthetic, as some kinds of fabrics.

T

ta·co [tä'kō] *n.* A Mexican sandwich consisting of a filling rolled in a tortilla [tôr·tē'(y)ə], a thin, flat cornmeal cake.

taf·fe·ta [taf'ə·tə] *n.* A fine, stiff, shiny fabric.

tan·ta·liz·ing [tan'tə·lī·zing] *adj.* Teasing or tormenting, as when something that one desires is kept just out of reach. — **tan·ta·lize,** *v.*

tech·ni·cian [tek·nish'ən] *n.* A person skilled in the use of the instruments, machinery, or details of an art or science.

tech·no·log·i·cal [tek'nə·loj'i·kəl] *adj.* Having to do with technology, the application of science in industry.

tem·per·ate [tem'pər·it] *adj.* **1** Moderate in temperature; mild. **2** Showing self-control in one's actions.

ten·sion [ten'shən] *n.* The act of stretching.

tern [tûrn] *n.* A small, gull-like bird.

ter·race [ter'is] *n.* A raised, level space, as for crop-growing, dug out on the side of a hill.

tex·tile [teks'til *or* teks'tīl] **1** *adj.* Related to weaving or woven fabrics. **2** *n.* A woven fabric.

the·o·ry [thē'ə·rē *or* thir'ē] *n.* A suggested explanation. — **the·o·ries,** *pl.*

ther·a·py [ther'ə·pē] *n.* Treatment for a disease or handicap. — **ther·a·pies,** *pl.*

thrashed [thrasht] *v.* Made violent swinging or twisting movements.

tid·al [tīd'(ə)l] *adj.* Of, having to do with, or caused by the tides.

tol·er·ance [tol'ər·əns] *n.* **1** The ability to withstand the bad effects of something that might be harmful. **2** A fair attitude toward others, regardless of differences in beliefs, customs, race, etc.

to·pog·ra·phy [tə·pog'rə·fē] *n.* The physical parts of a region, such as mountains, rivers, lakes, etc. — **to·pog·ra·phies,** *pl.*

tra·di·tion·al [trə·dish′ən·əl] *adj.* Of or related to tradition, the customs, tales, etc., passed down from one generation to the next.

trans·par·ent [trans·pâr′ənt] *adj.* So clear as to be easily seen through.

trav·erse [trav′ərs *or* trə·vûrs′] *v.* To pass or travel over, across, or through.

trawl·er [trô′lər] *n.* A fishing boat that uses a trawl, a great fishing net towed along the bottom of the sea.

tro·phy [trō′fē] *n.* An object that represents a victory or success. — **tro·phies,** *pl.*

tu·ber·cu·lo·sis [t(y)ōō·bûr′kyə·lō′sis] *n.* A disease chiefly affecting the lungs.

Tuc·son [tōō·son′ *or* tōō′son] *n.* A city in southeast Arizona.

tur·gor pres·sure [tûr′gər presh′ər] *n.* The pressure against the cell membrane from within by the cell contents.

U

u·nan·i·mous·ly [yōō·nan′ə·məs·lē] *adv.* With or in total agreement.

un·du·lat·ing [un′d(y)ə·lā·ting] *adj.* Moving like a wave. — **un·du·late,** *v.*

u·ni·ty [yōō′nə·tē] *n.* The quality of being one or the power of acting as one; oneness.

up·start [up′stärt′] *n.* A person who has suddenly become wealthy or important, especially one who is conceited.

V

va·lid·i·ty [və·lid′ə·tē] *n.* The condition or quality of being truthful or reasonable.

van·i·ty [van′ə·tē] *n.* Too much pride in oneself or one's appearance.

vast·ness [vast′nis] *n.* Very great expanse; great distance or size in all directions.

veg·e·ta·tion [vej′ə·tā′shən] *n.* Plantlife.

ver·i·fy·ing [ver′ə·fī·ing] *v.* Proving to be true or accurate; confirming.

ver·sa·tile [vûr′sə·təl *or* vûr′sə·tīl] *adj.* **1** Having many uses. **2** Able to do many things well.

ves·sel [ves′(ə)l] *n.* **1** A hollow container, such as a bowl. **2** A large boat. **3** A tube or canal for carrying a body fluid: blood *vessel.*

vic·to·ri·ous [vik·tôr′ē·əs] *adj.* Having won.

vir·tu·al·ly [vûr′chōō·əl·ē] *adv.* Practically; in effect, though not in fact.

vol·ume [vol′yəm *or* vol′yōōm] *n.* **1** The measure of space inside a closed figure of three dimensions. **2** A book.

W

wake [wāk] **1** *n.* The trail of rough water left by a moving vessel. **2** *v.* To stop or cause to stop sleeping.

wa·ter clock [wô′tər *or* wot′ər klok′] *n.* A device for measuring time by a regulated flow of water.

whim·si·cal [(h)wim′zi·kəl] *adj.* Odd, quaint, or fanciful, usually in an amusing way.

white·out [(h)wīt′out′] *n.* A stormy condition at sea in which breaking waves make it impossible to see.

whole·sale [hōl′sāl′] **1** *n.* The selling of goods in large quantities, usually at lower prices. **2** *adj.* Having to do with this method of selling.

woe·ful·ly [wō′fəl·lē] *adv.* Sadly.

Y

yam [yam] *n.* **1** A kind of sweet potato. **2** The edible root of any of several vines growing mostly in warmer places.

Z

zon·ing [zō′ning] *adj.* Related to an area set apart by law for a certain use. — **zone,** *v.*

---

add, āce, câre, pälm;   end, ēqual;   it, īce;   odd, ōpen, ôrder;   tŏŏk, pōōl;   up, bûrn;
ə = a in *above,* e in *sicken,* i in *possible,* o in *melon,* u in *circus;*   yōō = u in *fuse;*   oil;   pout;
check;   ring;   thin;   this;   zh in *vision.*

Index of Titles and Authors

Alice Hamilton: Doctor in Industry, 414
And Then There Were None, 334
Animals That Hide, Imitate, and Bluff, 430
Annie Dodge Wauneka,
   Navajo Crusader, 230
Arthur Mitchell, Dancer, 206
At the Pole, 156
Atwater, James, 194
Balchan, Andrea, 114
Bearden, Romare, 246
Boynick, David K., 414
Briggs, Charlie, 312
Brown, Dee, 94
Brownmiller, Susan, 222
Buchwald, Art, 356
Callahan, Celeste, 142
Case of the UFO's, The, 114
Champion's Spirit, A, 142
Clark, Dr. Eugenie, 38
Collett, Rosemary K., 312
Congresswoman from Brooklyn, The, 222
Constellations' Changing Faces, The, 462
Creature Called Bigfoot, The, 120
El Viejo's Grandson, 374
Farmer, Lydia, 438
Fiore, Mary, 76
Firestone, Harvey S., Jr., 502
Fossey, Dian, 138
Fresh Air Will Kill You, 356
Gallant, Roy A., 476
George Washington Carver,
   Pioneer Ecologist, 290
Giants of Easter Island, The, 12
Graham, Shirley, 290
Gridley, Marion E., 230
Henderson, Harry, 246
Hess, Lilo, 430
Horace Pippin's Struggle to Create, 246
How Words Change, 410
If I Had Wings, 502
Into the Lairs of "Sleeping" Sharks, 38
Izenberg, Jerry, 374
Key to the Unknown:
   The Rosetta Stone, 56

Korn, Benita, 370
Lambert, Eloise, 410
Lauber, Patricia, 268
Lipscomb, George D., 290
Lover of Nature, A, 354
Making Friends with Mountain Gorillas, 138
Marcus, Rebecca B., 484
Mary Cassatt, 454
McIntyre, Loren, 22
Measure for Measure, 476
Miles, Betty, 350
Miller, Floyd, 156
Momaday, N. Scott, 394
Mystery of the Ancient Nazca Lines, The, 22
Neilson, Frances, 454
Neilson, Winthrop, 454
Norman, James, 56
Orphan of the Wild, An, 312
Park of Life, A, 268
Payne, Leslie, 274
Pease, Nicholas, 206
Pettit, Ted S., 336
Phillips, Henry J., 462
Pringle, Laurence, 318
Ridgway, Captain John, 194
Rivera, Geraldo, 176
Rowing the Atlantic, 194
Saguaro, Forest of Unreality, 274
Search for Nessie, The, 76
Special Kind of Courage, A, 176
Standing Bear, Chief Luther, 354
Stout, Carrol Alice, 12
Taking Action — The Story
   of Mount Trashmore, 350
Tasaday: Cave People of the Philippines,
   The, 484
To the Singing, to the Drums, 394
Tree Lady, The, 370
Victoria, 438
Warrior Ants, The, 94
Wexler, Mark, 334
Where Rivers Meet the Sea, 318
Wise, William, 120
World in a Jar, A, 336

1
2
3
4
E 5
F 6
G H 7
I 8
J